# RICHARD DUKE OF YORK, FATHER OF KINGS

# RICHARD DUKE OF YORK, FATHER OF KINGS

## THE ORIGINS OF TUDOR ENGLAND

PAUL L. DAWSON

FRONTLINE
BOOKS

RICHARD DUKE OF YORK, FATHER OF KINGS
The Origins of Tudor England

First published in Great Britain in 2025 by
Frontline Books
An imprint of Pen & Sword Books Ltd
Yorkshire – Philadelphia

ISBN 978 1 03612 611 7

Typeset by Lapiz Digital
Printed and bound in the UK by CPI Group (UK) Ltd, Croydon, CR0 4YY.

The Publisher's authorised representative in the EU for product safety is Authorised Rep Compliance Ltd., Ground Floor, 71 Lower Baggot Street, Dublin D02 P593, Ireland.
www.arccompliance.com

For a complete list of Pen & Sword titles please contact

PEN & SWORD BOOKS LIMITED
47 Church Street, Barnsley, South Yorkshire, S70 2AS, England
E-mail: enquiries@pen-and-sword.co.uk
Website: www.pen-and-sword.co.uk
or
PEN AND SWORD BOOKS
1950 Lawrence Road, Havertown, PA 19083, USA
E-mail: uspen-and-sword@casematepublishers.com
Website: www.penandswordbooks.com

*To Jane Dawson (1953–2008)*
*My mother sought to explore the life of the duke and the*
*politics leading to his death in her MRes thesis, to be completed*
*at the Institute of Medieval Studies in Leeds. A cancer diagnosis in*
*2000 robbed her of the opportunity to commence her study expanding*
*her undergraduate thesis. A devoted Ricardian, she sought to rehabilitate*
*the duke of York and the Battle of Wakefield from obscurity.*

*I hope in completing her work, it is a fitting tribute*
*to her life and passion for history.*

# CONTENTS

# LIST OF PLATES

# ACKNOWLEDGEMENTS

If the City of Wakefield in West Yorkshire is known for any event, it is the battle that took place on 30 December 1460. A man who would be king, rightfully named as such by Parliament, was killed: an event that shaped European history. Not since the sibling rivalry between Henry and William Rufus, and later between Robert Curthose and his Plantagenet family, had the nation at large been shaped by such a death. The death of the duke of York changed the history of the nation in the same way that the more famous Battle of Bosworth did. He was the father of two kings, Edward IV and Richard III, great-grandfather to Henry VIII. This book seeks tell the story of the duke's tumultuous life and his tragic death.

In completing this research, I must thank a friend of some 40 summers, Dr P. Judkins for his support (moral and financial) to be able to 'pick up' where my mother left off. I must also thank Sally Fairweather for her forbearance in accompanying me on research trips to Paris and elsewhere to track down obscure references to the duke, Wakefield and the events of 1460 across England and Europe. Professor Michael Hicks, Professor John Watts, Dr Simon Payling and Dr Livia Visser-Fuchs must be thanked for their comments on my thinking. Dr Christopher Watson is to be singled out for his generous help in transcribing the Manor of Wakefield material: without his help this book would be lacking perhaps its most important contribution to the study of the Battle of Wakefield. Helen Cox, the most recent writer on the Battle of Wakefield, needs recognition for her own study of the events of December 1460 and keeping the battle in popular imagination through local talks and activities. Dr Tim Sutherland also needs recognition: his pioneering work on Towton has been an inspiration for my own on Wakefield.

In particular, Dr David Grummitt is also to be thanked for his friendship, help transcribing original documents and his critical comment on my thinking. Your friendship and support is greatly and humbly appreciated.

Of the archives and libraries I have accessed in the quest to find the duke of York, Marie-Dominique Pineau of the Archives Cote d'Or needs to be thanked for assistance with accessing material relating to the Battle of St Albans. The staff at Archives Communales at Mantes la Jolie again deserve praise and thanks for their generous assistance, so too their colleagues at the Bibliothèque Nationales de France, those at the Archives Département du Nord at Lille. Giuseppina Bertoni must be thanked for her assistance with accessing archives in Milan. Her generous time in helping with translating transcripts is gratefully acknowledged. I must thank the staff at the Staatsbibliothek zu Berlin in assisting in my research as well as The National Archives at Kew and the British Library, as well as the West Yorkshire History Centre, especially Helen Walker. Richard Knowles FSA, a noted scholar on the Wars of the Roses and the Battle of Wakefield in particular, is also to be thanked. Unless noted translations are my own, and I accept full liability for errors.

Paul L. Dawson, Wakefield, 30 December 2024

# INTRODUCTION

Like no king before or since, Richard III is either loved or loathed. He was the last medieval king: his death in battle marked the birth of the Tudor age. Richard has been in the headlines since he was reburied in Leicester Cathedral in 2015, with his champions the Richard III Society seeking to exonerate him as a usurper and murderer. Yet what of his father? The duke has received little serious scholarship.

Richard Plantagenet, 3rd duke of York has been the subject of much less academic scrutiny than his more illustrious, or infamous, sons, depending on one's bias. Just two biographies have been written about the duke in the last century of scholarship on the Wars of the Roses.

The first, by P.A. Johnson published in 1988, draws heavily on archive sources from various repositories across the United Kingdom and Europe, as well as chronicles and other material. It is an excellent – if dry – academic study of the duke.[1] More recently Mathew Lewis – we note secretary of the Richard III Society – has produced a popular biography of the duke. The book has two substantial omissions: it has no footnotes or references of any sort, and compounding this defect has no bibliography. Therefore, the diligent reader has to take it on trust that what is said is correct, nor can one refer to the bibliography as a 'jumping-on point' to broaden one's own reading.[2] In both cases, the biographers paint the duke as the wronged party, with legitimate grievances against the crown – which he did have to some extent – and shows him to be the only man to save the crown from the ineptitude of Henry VI. Yorkist propaganda is left unchallenged. Both writers shy away from the duke's death. Nor is any exploration made of the sources used, and their bias, particularly Warwick's 'Apology', which forms part of the work of Wavrin. Neither writer examines in depth the duke's last 18 months, and both fail to discuss the immediate political situation that led to the duke's death, and the reasons why the Battle of Wakefield was fought. Perhaps this is understandable.

One of the fascinations of Richard, duke of York, and his sons, is the loss of potential. As with the death of JFK, Ricardians mourn the loss of what could have been: a golden moment that was never allowed to be. The same is true of his son Richard: a hero, the greatest king England ever had, destroyed by the Tudors, is a common theme in populist narratives of Richard III, with social media becoming an echo-chamber repeating the same idealistic notions about their hero. Declinist nostalgia which says everything was better in the past, coupled with this grief for a golden moment that never happened, aligned with the love of lost causes (Richard III was never going to reign for a long time, like Napoleon in 1815: both were fated to lose due to their own actions. Richard, when failing to answer charges levied by Charles VIII of France that he had murdered his nephews, caused many Yorkists to back Henry Tudor. Even if Richard did not kill the boys, the charges which he never refuted, lost him vital support) results in populist histories which tell the stories the fans want to hear.

The history surrounding the events arouses much strong emotion in a veritable replay of the Wars of the Roses. On one side are the 'Ricardians', those who passionately believe in the Yorkist cause, and on the other those who back Henry VI and the Tudors, claiming that Edward IV was a war criminal, murderer, usurper and thief by taking Edward's actions in his first two years as king out of context of the time in which he lived.[3] Much of the debate and argument on the events of 1460 in particular and the epoch in general, is written often from the biased perspective of chroniclers who provide hearsay evidence and not facts. The bias of the chronicles and antagonism between two groups of people who would seem to be at least superficially to be perfectly normal, sane human beings, in accusing 'the other side' of war criminality and their chosen man to be a 'saint', rather gets in the way of critical and evaluative history. Social media has elevated this clash of polarised identity politics over men and women dead some 500 summers ago into a trite contest of 'Top Trumps' that bears no real resemblance to the study of history. Populism, anti-intellectualism and declinist nostalgia all feed into this: Richard III and his father both died before their time, it can be argued, and their deaths left their ambition unfilled and a 'longed-for golden age' never occurred. Into this vacuum of 'what if's' populist histories 'fill in the blanks', bemoan the Tudors and any historian who criticises their beloved hero. Richard III is elevated to a position beyond criticism.

## Notes on the sources

How do we know about events in the past? Because someone wrote it down. Archaeology shows us the material culture of the past – the pots, the pans, the houses – but cannot say what happened and when.

History can do that. Yet history is not some single monolithic entity that is rigid, inflexible and unchanging. So often we hear 'you're changing history!', often as an insult. Yet this is exactly what historians do. We take what evidence there is and come to a conclusion. History constantly changes as more sources – points of data – come available.

In the story of the duke of York which follows, I seek to look beyond the story the victors wrote: the Yorkists and their modern-day popular propagandists. It is easy to write history with hindsight, it is much harder to be objective and be even-handed when we know the outcome. In re-telling the story of the duke of York, I seek to get 'to the truth' by stepping back from mythos and propaganda, and to treat all participants in our story as even-handily as possible. This approach will raise the ire and wrath of many; but as historians we must challenge our sources and ask were the Yorkists telling the truth. Many of the key witnesses to the events 1455 to 1460 were far from bias free, many writing to suit their own agendas. Warwick, writing in spring 1461, was writing to make sure history was what he said it was, as Dr Livia Visser-Fuchs has shown. We must always question the sources, look for the bias and seek corroboration. Often, the claims the Yorkists made in contemporary sources do not stand up to scrutiny. If this opens the way for a charge of Lancastrian bias, so be it.[4]

As critical and evaluative historians, we must always ask questions, challenge the narrative, ask how we know X Y Z. We must use our faculties for reasoning to come to our own conclusions, not from reading others' opinions, but from our own study of sources created at the time these events took place. Usefully, contemporaries to English chroniclers in France and Milan compiled a history of the events as they unfolded, wrote them up within a few months, and were not affected by the Yorkist or Tudor propaganda that infects English recollections. Yet these external witnesses to English history are seldom used: English history is largely written from accounts written by and for English readers. In this way, history has become an 'echo-chamber' and the events divorced from broader context, and a broader range of sources of information. This is largely through a lack of language skills, biases, an unawareness of European archive and library holdings or even an inability to process the realisation that our European neighbours wrote about the history of the Wars of the Roses, and what they say may be more reliable than Anglocentric studies.

I must also stress that there is no such thing as contemporary history; the sources are not written down as the events actually happened. These documents are written by contemporaries – by people who lived at the time, and in some cases lived through the experiences and events they document – and primarily comprise letters and legal documents. Some of these contemporaries produced long narratives – we call them chronicles – and were in essence proto-historians. Many such 'historians' wrote later than the events they retold. In either case history is created when the real-time events are recorded on the written page, whether in hours, months, years or decades: all history is written after the fact. The chief narratives of the Wars of the Roses were written after the accession of Edward IV: they have their own particular 'spin' on the events. As Professor Pollard acknowledges:

> The chronicle and narrative sources which shaped the traditional interpretation have been revealed to be inadequately informed, frequently inaccurate and often partisan, not only in their accounts of battles, but also in their general political commentary.[5]

The world in which York lived was literate: this study is based primarily on archive documents that seldom see the light of day: legal documents, manorial accounts and court rolls, all written in a mix of Old English and Latin, found in The National Archives at Kew or the British Library. Difficult to read, it is understandable why reliance is placed on 'user-friendly sources'. By this I mean published translated transcripts, which reflect a selection of the material that exists and more over are UK based. These accounts and legal documents for manorial administration – not necessarily the court cases per se – are more objective and more reliable than chronicles because they are dated, in many cases written by the immediate circle of the Yorkist network within weeks of the events happening: they offer a 'snapshot' and are immediate, unlike chronicles. It does not mean, though, they are true, as the letters themselves are biased towards the aims and objectives of the writer.

As we hinted at about non-UK sources, a vast wealth of material for the Wars of the Roses exists outside of UK archives. Why? The Wars of the Roses were just one small aspect of a broader European conflict. In this conflict alliances were made and had to maintained. In the realpolitik of the era, Maragret, York and Warwick were sending letters to European allies to seek military and financial aid. It also meant that allies of either contesting faction wrote about each other and corresponded with allies in England. This material has largely been ignored in the construction of narratives of the Wars of the Roses. These letters, nearly all of them being dated, offers a direct snapshot of the events as they were understood to have occurred. Many are reporting 'gossip' – i.e. what people think knew what happened – whilst others reported first-hand accounts of battles and events within days of them occurring and provide a biased, but fixed, chronology which is not provided by the chronicles and proto-historians.

Indeed, French proto-historians, like their English counterparts, creating histories of a particular king, e.g. Charles VIII, reported news from England and elsewhere in a manner that was useful to the king: the events in England showed the perils of a weak monarchy as a lesson for all 'princes' to learn. However, the French and Burgundian sources have their own bias, being either pro York or Henry VI, but provide a discourse of these events seen from across the Channel, distilled by both official channels of information and gossip.

These sources, as Paul Fussell has established, occupy a place between fiction and autobiography.[6] Neuroscientist John Coates conducted research into memory between 2004 and 2012 found that what is recalled from memory is what the mind believes happened rather than what actually happened. This effect is often referred to as 'false memory'.[7]

False memory is created by the writer in two ways. Firstly, having read material since the event described took place, which has overwritten their own memories, they then write down and recall what they have read since the event rather than what they witnessed happen. Secondly, false memory can be created by the mind recording memories of what it thinks ought to have happened.

Therefore, the historian's primary aim is decoding the language of the source used, to understand the ideological intentions of the author, and to locate it within the general cultural context to which the source material belongs.[8]

Chapter 1

# BEGINNINGS

The Wars of the Roses has left an indelible mark on our collective memory and imagination; perhaps because of its perceived unprecedented frenzy of violence that came to a head in the blood-soaked massacre at Towton on 29 March 1461. The prelude to the events that tore the nation apart was the removal from the throne of Richard II (1367–1400) and his replacement by Henry Bolingbroke (1367–1413): neither side was prepared to compromise, resulting in the Battle of Shrewsbury in 1403. Henry IV was succeeded by his son Henry V (1386–1422), who used the opportunity of war with France to unite the elite behind him: he narrowly escaped a coup in 1415. Henry V won a victory at Agincourt, but his early death in 1422 and succession by his son Henry VI (1421–71) sparked a crisis resulting in decades marked by acts of extreme violence. This was not a civil war, but a conflict between magnates. It did not come to totally consume the nation state on the scale of the Wars of Religion in France or the English Civil War did. During the two decades known as the Wars of the Roses, the fighting in the first two lasted in total no more than six months at most. Hardly an age of unrest. Yet the blame for the civil unrest when it came, lies beyond just Henry VI.

Firstly, economically Europe was in a deep recession that lasted most of the fifteenth century. The trade in wool was the bedrock of the nation's economy, much as it was in later decades. During the first part of the century the structure of the English economy transitioned from a supplier of raw materials – fleece, thread etc – to finished goods. London became the epicentre of the trade in goods such as woollen broadcloth to Europe. Cloth exports averaged 55,000 lengths per year c.1440 compared to about 9,000 sacks of fleece. From 1450 the flow of finished cloth dropped to about 40,000 lengths, falling to 30,000 lengths from 1455. Wool exports dropped to under 8,000 sacks.

Political instability destabilised the economy and international trade. It meant much lower tax revenues. It was not only the wool trade that collapsed. The export of tin dropped by over half between 1415 and 1465. Imports of luxury goods, for example wine, also slumped. By the end of the 1440s, political instability and a credit crunch prompted a protracted recession known to historians as the 'Great Slump'.[1] This was not just an English problem: all of Europe felt the same credit crunch. A silver bullion crisis never dissipated. On one level, Henry VI was simply the victim of the 'Great Slump', but there is no doubt that through his advisors, Henry made things worse. Trade wars are never a good idea, especially with your closest neighbours, in this case Burgundy.[2]

With a depressed economy and trade at a standstill, many blamed the crown, even though the king had almost no economic influence. He could levy taxes, start trade wars and impose fines, but in any real modern sense of economics, the government had an almost imperceptible effect on 'balancing the books'. Parliament chose increasingly not to levy taxes: therefore reduced royal income meant reduced spending on defence and offence. With depressed living standards, the king's extravagant building projects at King's College Cambridge and Eton were seen as symptomatic of royal excess which made the poor poorer. As ever, foreigners were blamed by many in England, resulting in riots in London and elsewhere.

It can be argued that the economic difficulties in the middle decades of the fifteenth century – the mid-century crisis – were exacerbated by the political instability surrounding the king. Henry suffered from mental health concerns. Mental illnesses are health conditions involving significant changes in thinking, emotion, or behaviour (or a combination of these). Mental illnesses are associated with distress and/or problems functioning in social, work, or family activities. Henry's mental collapse in 1453 was a crisis point in a long-term illness, impacting his mental capacity from an early age. He may have suffered with a degree of learning difficulties. Mental health is the foundation for thinking, communication, learning, resilience, and self-esteem, and moreover the key to personal well-being, relationships, and the ability to contribute to community or society. While mental illness can occur at any age, three-fourths begins by age 24: the first recorded major symptoms of Henry's illness become apparent before he reaches 20. I believe that Henry was mentally incapable of being monarch, and therefore others ruled in his place. How far these men conducted day-to-day business is impossible to say: the conclusion of Watts and Carpenter, I believe, best fits the evidence of Henry's diminished responsibility. Mental illness involves multiple factors, including biology and neurochemistry, as well as both physical and psychological trauma. It has taken me years to be comfortable to talk about my own brain trauma and its resulting changes to my neuropathy, and years in psychiatric care in consequence with a diagnosis of acute C-PTSD. My own illness is like Henry VIII, who like me suffered a severe traumatic brain injury. Henry VI's illness is altogether different, resulting from neurochemistry and biology. Henry's illness was not the fault of the person, the family, or anyone else. Yet it left him incapable of strong, decisive, effective, consistent leadership.

As John Watts has argued persuasively, although Henry matured into adulthood, he was never capable of acting as king, and his personal rule was almost non-existent. Henry lacked the independence of will to make authoritative decisions, during what would be 40 years of minority governance. Henry's lack of real grip on power and affairs of state – as well as on sanity – allowed powerful noble families to jockey for power and prestige: ego, greed and avarice saw many leading advisors abuse their position for personal gain.[3] Supporting this conclusion, Christine Carpenter believes that Henry cannot be held accountable for any part of his rule that occurred in his name: the 'nothingness' of the king resulted in a concerted effort by the nobility to create a semblance of monarchy.[4]

Into the vacuum of governance came leading men: Cardinal Beaufort (1375–1447), William de la Pole (1396–1450) 1st duke of Suffolk, and Cardinal Kemp (1380–1454). These men, in an impossible situation of a nothing king, did the best they could: that they steadied the ship of state and kept it afloat financially speaks much about them. Kemp's death meant there was, by and large, no impartial figure around which both governance and monarchy could be improvised. The absence of such a figure, able to control feuding magnates, meant that the sham monarchy of the 1440s based on consensus broke down into total disunity; with Kemp's death (if not before since the loss of Normandy and Cade's Rebellion of 1450), there was no pretending anymore that Henry was an active agent in government. Into this void York and Edmund Beaufort (1406–55) jostled for power.[5] This conflict was framed largely over royal competency to manage the state's finances, internal administration and also to manage the war with France.[6]

Henry's nullity, economic uncertainties and factionalism about who controlled the king were the primary interplaying factors that pulled the nation to pieces. Factionalism was not just limited to those around Henry. With real-time revenue from trade declining, it meant incomes from rents – mostly from land – became of increasingly importance.

Status and prestige were linked to land holdings, and it comes as no surprise that we see control of land – therefore income!! – as the cause of intra-familial disputes growing in this period when we look at the archives of the Court of King's Bench.[7] A need to retain and control land for rental incomes, making leading families more disposed to use violence to protect their living standards, was a factor that led to war. Popular support for leaders who offered to 'solve' endemic structural economic issues also became another contributing factor.[8] War was not initially inevitable, but it became so. The great nobles owned huge swathes of land, and drew their local supporters into a succession of confrontations, repressions, scandals and murders, disrupting the country's equilibrium in unprecedented ways. Personal and familial feuds were fought out in pitched battles in an ever-changing sea of shifting loyalties, 'double games' and terror. These themes recur throughout our narrative as it unfolds.

But it was not just elite tensions that led ultimately to war. Another important factor was the relationship between the ruler and the ruled. The Peasants' Revolt of 1381 marked a significant change in the relationship between the mass of the population, the commonweal – the *communitas* – and the monarchy, which framed the nature of York's discord with Henry and Edmund Beaufort from 1450 to his death. Vital principals concerning the commonweal and matters of constitutional propriety were at stake, central to the functioning of the political state. That some form of coherent government was possible is reflected in the fact war did not break out until the king's prolonged inability to provide a satisfactory focus for monarchy became clear and, moreover, the desperately-sought consensus collapsed. The die was cast for a brutal clash of clans in a real-life 'Game of Thrones' that would go onto define the age.

The conflict has been given the name 'the Wars of the Roses': but a better and more fitting name would be 'the Hatred of the Clans'.[9] What it was not was a civil war.[10] Naming the era the 'War of the Roses' has, I believe, totally distorted our understanding of what happened, and in the popular imagination it has become seen as an era of total war in the image of the Second World War. Differing factions used localised grievances as an excuse for violent acts of retribution. Even then, extreme acts of violence resulting in death was a discrete, minority activity, as we shall explore. Membership of the factions was fluid, and loyalty was not always to the leader of the faction, but to the clan or family leader.

This 'clash of clans' was played out on the European stage: Brittany, Burgundy, France, Milan and the Papacy all sought to benefit from internal disorder in England. Dukes, kings, princes and the Pope all supported one clan against another for their own benefit. Between 1450 and 1500, despite party pressure and foreign interference, the Royal State attempted to keep the peace, with different factions claiming the crown and then losing it. It was a turning point in national history; perhaps the most serious crisis suffered until Parliament went to war with the King at the end of the 1630s.

Chapter 2

# RICHARD DUKE OF YORK: THE MAN WHO WOULD BE KING

I have known of the duke of York all my life: his death at the Battle of Wakefield is 'drummed into' most schoolchildren, and the battle is one of the few internationally important points of history from my home city. Yet, despite his death, little was said about the man behind the title in those long-ago school lessons. So, who was he?

Richard, duke of York was the great-grandson of a king. His grandfather Edmund, duke of York (1341–1402), was the fourth surviving son of Edward III (1312–77) and progenitor of the Yorkist line. He was the first family member to engage in what was clearly treasonable behaviour. All three of his children – Edward, duke of York (1373–1415), Constance, Lady Despenser (1375–1416), and Richard, earl of Cambridge (1385–1415) – would go on to participate in treasonous behaviour as well. Edmund was regent of England in 1399 while Richard II and Edmund's son Edward were in Ireland, and he was therefore de facto head of the government when Henry Bolingbroke (1367–1413) landed at Ravenspur. Whether Edmund's hand was forced or not in 1399, his choice in supporting Bolingbroke was a turning point in history, and heralded what would be a century-long ordeal over who ruled England. Bolingbroke was the son of John of Gaunt (1340–99), Edward III's fourth son (third surviving son). York's claim was senior. Edmund, duke of York died on 1 August 1402.

Richard of York was born on 21 September 1411 to Richard of Conisbrough (1375–1415), the 4th earl of Cambridge, and his wife Anne Mortimer (1388–1411), the daughter of Roger Mortimer (1374–98), the 4th earl of March. She belonged to a house that had an

6

arguably better right to the English throne than the current king. Anne Mortimer was connected to Edward's third son (second surviving son), Lionel of Antwerp, the duke of Clarence (1338–68). It was through his mother's side that York would later make his bid for the throne.

Richard was only four years old when he was left an orphan by his father's execution for treason in August 1415, and then turned into a duke and landholder by the death of his uncle Edward, duke of York, at Agincourt in October later that same year. It was the discovery and swift execution of Cambridge, Thomas Grey of Northumberland (1384–1415) and Henry Scrope of Masham (1373–1415), as T.B. Pugh adroitly states, which ensured 'that dangerous malcontents and dissidents among the English baronage had already been eliminated' who could have gone on and disrupted the minority of Henry VI. The conflict over who ruled was pushed forward a generation.[1]

As York was an orphan, his property was managed by royal officials. He himself was placed under the guardianship of Robert Waterton (1360–1425), a landowner at Methley, local to Wakefield, and also constable of Pontefract Castle. This was unusual: it was common that most wards of noble birth were taken into the royal household or their wardships sold to other great noble families. Waterton was a long-trusted Lancastrian retainer, who had traditionally used to deal with problematic royal 'guests' by Henry IV and Henry V. Indeed, Waterton had been in charge of Richard II's confinement at Pontefract Castle in 1399 shortly before his death. Following Agincourt, he was responsible for the care of numerous noble prisoners who included the Marshal of France Jean le Maingre, Charles of Artois, duke of Orleans, and Arthur de Richemont (1393–1458), the future duke of Brittany and Constable of France who appears later in our story. From the forgoing, it could be concluded that the young Richard was a political prisoner, especially as he was kept away from public gaze during the reign of Henry V in a politically unimportant West Yorkshire backwater.[2] We cannot say if it WAS considered as such.

York was also the heir of his uncles Edward, duke of York, who died at Agincourt, and Edmund Mortimer (1375–1425), earl of March in 1425 through whom he received the lands and titles of the Mortimer family. The young Richard became ward of Ralph Neville, 1st earl of Westmorland (1364–1425), in 1423. The following year he was betrothed to his daughter Cecily Neville (1415–95), and they were married by October 1429. Cecily Neville was the youngest of twenty-two children, in this case born to Mortimer's second wife Joan Beaufort (1377–1440), daughter of John of Gaunt. Joan's brothers were Cardinal Beaufort and John Beaufort, earl of Somerset (1373–1410), father of

John Beaufort (1404–44), 3rd earl of Somerset. Officially the Beaufort claim to the throne had been disallowed by Henry IV. The children of Richard and Cecily could claim descent from Edward III, and in theory unified the Lancaster and York lines into a single family, allowing for the Salic law, much as Tudor (Beaufort i.e. Lancaster) and York were united in 1486. The 'realpolitik' of the marriage meant that Richard was now related to much of the English upper aristocracy, many of whose members had themselves married into the Neville family. His key political ally was his brother-in-law the earl of Salisbury. Salisbury and his eldest son the earl of Warwick would shape the destiny of York and his family. Richard Neville, 5th earl of Salisbury (1400–60) led the cadet branch of the Neville family. Born in 1400, he was the third son (and tenth child) of Ralph de Neville, 1st earl of Westmorland, by his second wife, Joan Beaufort, mentioned earlier. Based on Middleham in North Yorkshire, he controlled vast swathes of Yorkshire. Richard married Alice Montagu (1407–62), daughter and heiress of Thomas Montagu (1388–1428), 4th earl of Salisbury. The date of Richard and Alice's marriage is not known, but it must have been before February 1421, when as a married couple they appeared at the coronation of Queen Catherine of Valois. Of their sons, Richard (1428–71), 16th earl of Warwick, and George (1432–76) dominated politics and the Church, the latter being Bishop of Exeter, Chancellor of England and Archbishop of York. Salisbury's brother William (1405–63), Lord Fauconberg, served alongside the duke of York in France. Also serving was Salisbury's illegitimate nephew 'the bastard of Salisbury', Sir John Montagu, illegitimate son of Thomas Montagu, who headed the lists of bannerets and knights of the duke's forces in 1441.[3] He was possibly killed at Towton in 1461. Fauconberg, Warwick and Salisbury will figure largely in our story.

In October 1425, when Ralph Neville died, he bequeathed the wardship of York to his widow, Joan Beaufort. In spite of his father's plot against the king, along with his provocative ancestry – one which had been used in the past as a rallying point by enemies of the House of Lancaster – Richard was allowed to inherit his family estates without any legal constraints, which seems all the more remarkable. Henry VI would have known that York would become the mightiest subject in the land, especially as the duchy of Lancaster and its ducal office were retained by the crown. We wonder, if a duke of Lancaster as an equal to York had existed, would the mid-century crisis have developed as it did? It has been argued that attempts were made to recreate the duchy in the late 1450s to buttress Henry's weak position, but it is doubtful if Henry ever had full control of the gentry in the duchy, and that attempts were needed to add the duchy to the oldest royal lands, in an openly partisan policy shows the weakness of Henry VI as a usurper. Previous kings like Edward I were given power over their subjects with willingness, they did not have to bargain for it. Perhaps the need to rely on duchy revenues to fund the royal household, and the need to centralise power in Henry explains why there was no duke of Lancaster, merely Henry as de facto duke, a subject of the crown, a private citizen as it were, sitting on the throne. Leaving York without a rival was storing up problems.

York was knighted on 19 May 1426, and was present at the coronation of Henry VI on 6 November 1429 at Westminster. He was constable of England from 20 January 1430, and was present at the coronation of Henry as King of France in Paris in 1431. On 12 May 1432, he came into his full inheritance, and on 22 April 1433 York was made a Knight of the Garter.[4]

## Rouen

As York reached his majority, events were unfolding in France concerning Henry V's legacy. In the spring of 1434, York attended a meeting of the Great Council at Westminster which attempted to conciliate the king's uncles, the dukes of Bedford and Gloucester (heads of the regency government), over disagreements regarding the conduct of the war in France. Two options existed: either England had to conquer more territory to ensure permanent French subordination, or territory had to be conceded to obtain a negotiated settlement. During Henry VI's minority, his Council took advantage of French weakness and the alliance with Burgundy to increase England's possessions, but following the Treaty of Arras of 1435, Burgundy ceased to recognise the English king's claim to the French throne. Whilst Henry VI's uncles John, duke of Bedford (1389–1435), and Humphrey, duke of Gloucester (1390–1447) were alive, the French possessions would never be given up. Bedford's death on 14 September 1435 (aged 46) changed all of that. His widow (they had married in 1433), Jacquetta of Luxembourg (1415–72) married Richard Wydeville (1405–69), 1st earl Rivers, and were the parents of Elizabeth Woodville (1437–92), wife of Edward IV. That marriage lay in the future.

In May 1436, nine months after the duke of Bedford's death, York was appointed to succeed him as commander of the English forces in France. Rather than receiving the same powers Bedford had enjoyed as 'regent', York was forced to settle for a lesser role as 'lieutenant-general and governor', under which terms he was not allowed to appoint major financial and military officials. The fall of Paris (his original destination) led to his army being redirected to Rouen. The duke met with some successes in recapturing French-held fortresses in the Pays de Caux, although no attempt was made at this stage to retake Harfleur or Dieppe, which had recently been taken back by the French. York's limited success all came to a juddering halt as he had not been paid by the exchequer in England. By the time the money ran out, it was already known by Henry and his councillors that York did not want to extend his period of service; he was thanked for his services and was asked to stay in France until Richard Beauchamp (1382–1439), 13th earl of Warwick, arrived to take over in November 1437.[5]

Warwick was a sick man, but during his tenure the English military position was maintained and in fact witnessed some small gains with the recovery of parts of the Pays de Caux. However, Harfleur and Dieppe remained in French hands. The earl, due to illness we suppose, never seems to have left Rouen, and he died there on 30 April 1439.

During York and Warwick's tenure, active command was given to John Talbot (1387–1453), 1st earl of Shrewsbury. Edmund Beaufort (1406–55) was given command of the province of Maine and the captaincy of Alençon, one of the primary garrisons of Normandy and an essential base for operations in Maine, in March 1438.

John Beaufort (1404–44), earl of Somerset, was named as replacement in May 1439: he was to lead an expedition to last six months to safeguard English possessions in France.[6] He had only been released after 17 years' captivity in France in the summer of 1438 when he was appointed. It helped the brothers' uncle was Cardinal Beaufort, who in effect bankrolled the crown. Indeed, it was primarily through the cardinal's loans that war had been financed between 1437 and 1439. We note John Beaufort took over a number of important captaincies – Cherbourg, from his uncle the cardinal, and Avranches, Tombelaine and Regneville from William de la Pole, duke of Suffolk.[7]

By 1439 the English presence in the Île de France was limited to three important strongholds, at Pontoise, Creil and Meaux. Meaux was the target of a major French attack which began on 20 July. Taken by surprise, John Beaufort raised a relief force in August.[8] Somerset's ad hoc contingent united with one led by Sir Richard Harrington, bailiff of Caen, at Argentan on 2 August. This small army picked up carts and other ordnance when it had reached Pont-Audemer, before crossing the Seine.[9] Somerset hoped to link up with retinues being sent from England under Sir Richard Wydeville, Sir William Peyto and Sir William Chamberlain, a total of 900 men. Striking before the relief force could arrive, the French attacked Meaux on 12 August, and took the town. Pontoise was threatened. The fortification at Marche, to which the garrison at Meaux had fallen back, fell on 15 September, by which time Somerset had left for England. It was brother Edmund who sent news from Rouen to the cardinal and the English party at Calais that Marche had fallen. Military operations continued under John Talbot and Edmund Beaufort. Any hopes for a new offensive were thwarted when news of a large French force being assembled reached Rouen in late October 1439. Somerset was re-appointed lieutenant of Normandy in December.[10] He pledged to Henry to supply 100 lances and 2,000 archers.[11] He left with an army numbering just over 2,000 men in early January from Poole.[12] He was in Rouen on 28 January.[13] Under Somerset, French attacks were held at bay, but it was clear that without reinforcements, and money, the English in Normandy faced considerable difficulties in maintaining their possessions.

With Warwick's death, Henry VI's government cast around for a replacement: Somerset was retained till a permanent replacement was found. Humphrey, duke of Gloucester was duly appointed, yet Henry V's brother would not take command, York going in his place. If Somerset felt aggrieved when York and not himself was appointed Lieutenant of France – supreme commander – on 2 July 1440 we cannot say. The sense of grievance between these two men has been 'backdated' from the 1450s, and sensationalised by Yorkist accounts and chronicles – the Pastons were amongst the duke's most apologetic propagandists – to justify the events of 1455 and later. We have to see behind this façade of Yorkist spin to look objectively at the events of the time. Somerset took the field with his army in February 1440, operating in conjunction with Talbot and Fauconberg. During August 1440 Talbot besieged Harfleur, which had been in French hands for five months. King Charles VII of France sent a large army under Richemont, but failed to relieve the siege. The town fell to Talbot and Somerset by 28 October, and Somerset received the surrender of Montivilliers on 2 November. Taking Harfleur was a major success, which raised the possibility of further English gains, notably retaking Dieppe. Edmund Beaufort had shown himself to be a highly skilled and capable field commander as well as directing sieges. His military reputation was superior to York, who like Warwick before him had delegated command to Talbot. Edmund Beaufort was a skilled administrator and commander. Elder brother John's appointment was only temporary, and he knew this when he took the post, until a permanent replacement could be found.[14]

Untested and untried, York was a gamble. Edmund Beaufort was the best man for the job. York had a lot to prove. Did he feel this sense of testing? Did Somerset feel the loss of prestige? Edmund remained as governor and count of Maine and Anjou: this separation of governance and power had precedent, and probably owed a great deal to the ambitions of the Beaufort family. It placed York and Beaufort as rivals in France, and gave York command of a far smaller territorial area than Bedford had commanded, or York had previously. It was understandable that Edmund Beaufort, ennobled as marquis of Dorset, was given a degree of reward and recognition for service, but undeniably it created a division of interest in the war effort, when unity was needed. Somerset and Fauconberg's successful siege of Harfleur led Henry VI to make both men Knights of the Garter. Somerset had acquitted himself very well indeed, having secured a treaty with Jean, duke of Brittany not to aid England's enemies.

York was named captain of Rouen sometime in November 1440 and had the same powers that the Bedford had earlier been granted.[15] In February 1441, with rumours of a major French force gathering to attack Normandy, York was sent to France with a large army. This took time to assemble. His retinue included the earls of Oxford, Ormonde, lords Bourchier and Clinton, as well as Sir Richard Wydeville, six baronets, thirty knights who included Sir William Oldhall, 900 men-at-arms and 2,700 archers, and landed in June.[16]

The duke arrived in France as Charles VII (1403–61) was preparing an army to evict the English from the Île de France. Pontoise was the last stronghold in the Île: capturing the town would secure both the Île and Paris. For the campaign of 1441, Charles assembled an army of 5,000 men, led by himself and Constable Arthur de Richemont, and accompanied by a powerful train of heavy artillery under Jean Bureau. The town and castle of Creil was besieged on 8 May, the walls being breached by the French siege guns. Charles had invested heavily in gunpowder technology, and his artillery train was the largest and most technologically advanced of the period. Unable to withstand the French bombardment, the English garrison led by William Peyto surrendered on 25 May. Charles' attention switched to Pontoise, investing the town on 6 June.

The English garrison of roughly 1,500 was supported by John Talbot with approximately 3,000 men. Since May, the French garrison at Louviers had been building a defended encampment on the Seine to restrict the flow of men, food and munitions from Rouen to Pontoise along the river. Charles made Maubuisson Abbey his headquarters. With the English controlling one bank of the Oise River and the French the other, in order to gain a foothold to assault the town directly, Prigent de Coëtivy threw a pontoon bridge across the river and captured the Abbey of Saint-Martin outside the town walls. With a bridgehead created, Bureau's guns pounded the barbican at the end of the town bridge for 15 days and the position was subsequently taken. The situation for the English by the first week of July was precarious at best.

On landing, the duke quickly moved his forces down the Seine towards Pontoise. The duke joined Talbot on or sometime around 15 July.[17] He had with him two earls, six knights banneret, 30 knights, 657 men-at-arms, and 2,100 archers.[18] On York's arrival, the garrison at Pontoise was replaced. He did not stay in the town, however, but lodged at Ennery, a little over a mile due north. Conversely his army camped at Hérouville, a couple of miles north-east of Ennery, and like Pontoise itself on the right bank of the Oise which runs almost north-south through Pontoise. Charles VII gambled on the English not being able to withstand the siege due to lack of food and munitions, and would not be drawn into a direct confrontation.

Sometime on 18 or 19 July, York decided to move his men north along the right bank of the Oise: ostensibly he was looking for an opportunity to cross and attack the French main army from the rear. Troops under Talbot feigned a diversionary crossing at Beaumont, which drew away the troops led by Charles d'Artois, count of Eu, from Charles' main army. Under cover of darkness, York used a pontoon bridge to cross the river Oise during the early hours of 20 July near the abbey of Royaumont, approximately six miles upstream.[19] The duke then came into action against a column led by Guillaume de Chastel. Chastel was killed, and lies buried in the Abbey of Saint Denis in Paris. Charles, warned of the duke's approach, panicked and retreated to Poissy, close to Paris. With the English in a far stronger position, the duke must have felt that Pontoise was safe, at least for the time being. The campaign was over by 27 July, or at least York's participation in it.[20] He was back at Rouen by 5 August, or sooner, leaving Talbot in command.[21] The audacious crossing of the Oise and the flight of the king of France are remembered as part of the duke of York's epitaph 35 years later: the significance of this is that he must surely have considered that he had done all he could to secure Pontoise.

With York back in Rouen, the estates general of Normandy was summoned: York knew that with food and other provisions desperately low at Pontoise, he needed financial aid to continue the fight. Simultaneously, York began negotiating a truce with Jean, duke of Brittany: he did not need a war on two fronts. For the French, not everything was proceeded as planned. Charles VII faced his own problems. Since York's daring attack, many of his senior field commanders felt the siege was lost but, unwilling to raise the siege, Charles persisted in his ambitions, resuming his bombardment on 16 August which lasted for a month. A force under the sires de Lohéac and de Bueil stormed through a breach in the town wall on 16 September and captured the church of Notre Dame, killing twenty-four out of thirty English defenders. Three days later, Charles ordered an all-out attack. Breaking into the town, the French cut down 400–500 of the English garrison and hundreds more were captured, including the garrison's commander Lord Clinton, in return for minimal French casualties. Despite the brilliance of the short campaign, Pontoise fell on 19 September 1441.[22]

York's efforts thereafter were centred firmly on holding Normandy: to this end he signed a treaty with Isabelle duchess of Burgundy, at Dijon on 23 April 1443, which created an indefinite truce between England and Burgundy. Despite the solitary victory, there was precious little success to show for all the military expenditure since the previous Parliament closed. With the English ejected from the Île de France, the theatre of operations shifted to the Pays de Caux, and, as in the 1430s, York delegated the command to Talbot. It was Talbot who brought further reinforcements over from England in the summer of 1442, and began the investment of Dieppe.[23]

Optimism that Dieppe, Evreux, Louviers and other places lost to the French could be re-taken was deeply misplaced. Rather than a successful re-occupation, it seemed by summer 1443 it was inevitable that consolidation rather than further offensive warfare was the only course of action. Stepping back to early 1443, during February the English Council had debated in Henry VI's presence the need to send an army to Normandy, to reinforce Gascony against Charles VII, or to do both. With fears of attacks into Normandy, it was prudent to give the duke of York reinforcements. Yet, as documents at The National Archives at Kew, London show, Henry and the Council chose an altogether different solution.

## John Beaufort

Sometime during 1442 Cardinal Beaufort had begun planning a large-scale attack on France. Rather than defending Gascony and Normandy, the cardinal believed the best form of defence was attack. John Beaufort was named commander by his uncle and given 600 marks worth of land, and the king's rights to any percentage of any profits resulting from the campaign were waived: the sole purpose was to restore John Beaufort's finances. The cardinal ensured his nephew was made a duke, to give him parity with York. As the financier of the government, it was almost impossible to object to the cardinal's plans.[24]

Somerset's appointment deliberately undermined York's authority as lieutenant general, his new army had priority over York's command, and perhaps shows Henry's displeasure at the duke's handling of the military situation: Henry had written to the duke expressing his displeasure at York's failure to bring Charles to battle in the Seine and Oise campaign of 1441. Somerset's appointment also undermined his own brother. Somerset was to launch an offensive against towns and castles and lands at present occupied by the French between Normandy and Gascony. The aspiration of both the cardinal and his nephews was to carve out a Beaufort patrimony from conquests in Anjou and Maine. To do so, Somerset was to strike deep into French-held territory and to try, if possible, to engage the forces of Charles VII.[25] Friction between York and Somerset aided neither party. York had to contribute to the upkeep of Somerset's army as it marched through his territory, raising a myriad number of complaints.[26] Dieppe was relieved on 14 August. Somerset marched through Maine and Anjou, laying waste to the countryside as far as Angers, and defeated a French army under Richemont, intent on relieving the siege of Pouancé which Somerset had unwisely invested without siege artillery. Unable to take the town, he headed to La Guerche, held by the duke of Brittany, a 'soft' target as its walls were in poor condition and the castle was undefendable. Somerset justified his attack on the town because the truce had lapsed and the new Duke Francis was in concert with Charles VII. Indeed, it was held by the French duke of Alençon, and had been the base of operations for French raids on Avranches the year earlier. It was a legitimate target, but almost provoked all-out war between Britanny and England, which could be ill afforded.[27] Somerset's lack of aggression in bringing about a major battle with Charles VII, failure at Pouancé and the debacle at La Guerche, was symptomatic of the situation, as Christine Carpenter notes 'because there was nobody with the authority to formulate and force through a clearly thought-out policy'.[28] The humiliating withdrawal resulted in accusations of incompetence and corruption: a lot of money and resources that could be ill-afforded had been squandered whilst Normandy was in desperate need of reinforcements. Insistence on his own area of command and lack of co-operation with York were ill-advised hubris by the over-confident Somerset. When his six-month term of office was up, his position was not renewed. He left France in disgrace. The failure exposed divisions between Cardinal Beaufort and Suffolk. The lack of direction and a single vision for France lay with Henry VI and those around him: the failure was symptomatic of monarchy by committee, seeking consensus and swayed by powerful personal interests. That the monarchy did not break down in 1443 is testament to those around the king, endeavouring to make 'the system' work with a void at its heart. This weakness in the monarchy was to have fatal consequences, as we shall see. John Beaufort, earl of Somerset died on 30 May 1444.

If a gulf between York and Suffolk existed over policy concerning France, no trace can be found in contemporary records. Suffolk was, supposedly, York's enemy till his death in 1450. If anything, York and Suffolk were allies against the blundering of the Beauforts. York agreed with every step of foreign policy and negotiations with France, which he later retracted. Suffolk was in the ascendant, having undoubted mastery of the king. The sole isolated voice against Suffolk was Humphrey, duke of Gloucester.[29]

## Peace and plenty?

Realising that winning an offensive war in France was not possible, unless vast sums of money were invested which the exchequer simply did not possess, English policy in the hands of Suffolk now turned to a negotiated peace (or at least a truce) with France. Peace relieved much of the fiscal burden on the exchequer, and governance could be proactive rather than reactive crisis management.

Reflecting this change in policy, the remainder of York's time in France was spent in routine administration and domestic matters. Thoughts also turned to broader alliances. With a childless king, York was heir to the throne – unless Parliament voted to allow the Beaufort claim – and he ought to increase his own prestige and influence. In this 'game of thrones' York was bargaining with European monarchs for influence. York turned to his children to further this. His eldest, Edward (1442–83), had been born on 28 April 1442 at Rouen in Normandy. His low-key baptism has been suggested as evidence of his bastardy: but as his birth is more or less nine months after the duke's return from the 1441 campaign, sometime after 27 July, and before 4 August 1441, Edward was the legitimate son of the duke and duchess. Judging by archive documents held in the Bibliothèque Nationales de France Richard was not at Pontoise on 6 August and later. The reality is that York himself was in Rouen negotiating a truce with Jean, duke of Brittany. He left Talbot and Fauconberg to continue with the siege, whilst he concentrated on administrative affairs and arranging the victualling of the army. Talbot and Fauconberg were present on 11 August; if York had been, he would have been mentioned.[30] Therefore, beyond any shadow of a doubt, Edward was the legal and legitimate son and heir of Duke Richard and his wife, Cecily Neville. Suggestions contrary to this in the popular media fronted by Tony Robinson, based on research published by Dr Michael Jones, are incorrect. Despite not being true, the theory that Edward was illegitimate has gained popular credence, and is almost impossible to overturn. The low-key baptism may have been necessitated by a sickly child, not expected to live, perhaps because he was premature as Dr Laynesmith adroitly comments.[31] There was no terrible family secret about Edward being the bastard son of an archer, that forced his brother to take the throne in 1483. It is time this rumour was quashed for what it is: a pack of lies.

Brother Edmund (1443–60) was baptised at Rouen Cathedral: Edmund was considered as heir to his father's French lands, as Edward was to his English and Irish lands, which may also again explain the variance in ceremony. Edward as heir to his father's lands, and moreover to the crown of the England – at least potentially as Henry had no son – meant he was a useful pawn in his father's ambition. Duchess Cecily had a key role to play in her husband's ambition. She now had two sons and a daughter Anne (1439–76) to arrange the upbringing of. By now she was a toddler, having been born on 10 August 1439. The couple's first son, Henry, had been born on 10 February 1441. Evidently a sickly child, he seems to have died and been buried at Fotheringhay, we assume before the family embarked for Rouen that summer. The loss of Pontoise meant that the duchess had to show the wealth and status of the duke, and Henry VI, through displays of conspicuous consumption. She borrowed ornaments and vestments from Rouen cathedral to decorate the castle chapel at the feast of All Saints in 1442.[32] Conspicuous displays of wealth and luxury were an important facet of diplomacy. This helps explains the grand baptism of Edmund at Rouen cathedral using the reputed font of Viking chieftain Rollo in an unmistaken show of his own primacy in the duchy: it was a carefully stage-managed and choreographed event designed to impress both York's allies and enemies. It was a political necessity.[33] Indeed, *The Chronicle from Rollo to Edward IV* was designed to show this lineage.[34] In an era of disputed lineage and rightful kingship this document and the baptism were designed to reinforce the Yorkist claim to the throne of England, despite being 18 years apart. The chronicle was written sometime after March 1461, around the time of Edward's accession, to be circulated we suppose to rally support for his claim. That Edward was not baptised in Rollo's font was perhaps of no importance, but the connection to Rollo remained significant. So too the union of England and Normandy

Peace and consolidation was Suffolk's policy and a marriage alliance, it was hoped, would cement a lasting peace – or at least a truce long enough to gain breathing space – and retention of much of Henry V's gains. Suffolk held considerable influence over the king's household – any letters or instructions given in Henry's name would be have been vetted, if not written, by Suffolk.[35]

Through Suffolk's agency, in April 1444 Henry VI was arranged to be married to Margaret of Anjou (1430–82), second daughter of 'Good King Rene', king of Naples and duke of Anjou, and of Issabella, Duchess of Lorraine. Margaret's family included several prominent women exercising power in politics. The marriage brought a comparatively small monetary dowry, but importantly a 23-month truce with France with the cessation of Maine. It was genuine effort at peace. Her marriage to Henry VI had been negotiated by William de la Pole who arrived at Harfleur on 15 March 1444, and lodged with the duke and duchess of York on his way to visit Charles VII and Rene, duke of Anjou. Shortly after Suffolk had left Rouen, the pair departed on the 27th in the company of the bishop of Bayeaux, in something close to a royal progress to administer justice and to oversee administration of the Duchy. The were housed in the castle at Caen. The need for ostentatious displays of power and wealth may explain Cecily spending £376 buying 325 pearls, perhaps for this progress, and the duke spent £54 on a single cup.[36]

Suffolk agreed the truce on 28 May 1444 with Charles VII, who had married Margaret by proxy four days earlier. The new 15-year-old queen remained in France whilst Suffolk headed back to England and Henry, via Rouen. York had become a father for a fourth time when daughter Elizabeth (1444–1503) was born on 22 September 1444.[37] Suffolk returned to Rouen to collect the queen in March 1445. The duke of York had hosted the new queen when she had reached Pontoise on 1 April, and remained her guardian till she sailed for England from Calais, having lodged in Rouen until 11 April.[38] In order to impress the queen, and show the duke's pre-eminence, the pair spent lavishly on clothes and jewels: over £215 was spent on a single set of clothes for Cecily.[39] Margaret arrived in England on 19 April 1445. On 23 April 1445, she married King Henry VI at Titchfield Abbey in Hampshire. She was then crowned queen of England on 30 May 1445 at Westminster Abbey by John Stafford, Archbishop of Canterbury.[40]

In the wake of the marriage, with Henry's blessing, York sought to strengthen the new Anglo-French truce by arranging a royal marriage of his own. In February, with the duke of Suffolk's blessing, York began negotiations of his own with Charles VII. He wrote to the king in April that the:

> earl of Suffolk, has reported to me by mouth, I have learned that you are pleased to take the said marriage into consideration; and that when I should please to send my ambassadors to you to . . . the said matter, they would be welcome there.
>
> Concerning the which thing, most high, most excellent, and most powerful prince, and most redoubted lord, I am much comforted and joyful, in consequence of the singular and true desire which I have to acquire your friendship and society; and with all my affection I thank you for it most humbly.
>
> Your said letters by me received, I was immediately inclined to send my ambassadors to your highness, for the business; a thing which I could not do and accomplish so speedily as I could well have wished, in consequence of the arrival, on this side, of my lady the queen, whom, after that she was brought to and had arrived at the town of Pontoise, I have accompanied, as reason was, until she had embarked on the sea to go into England to the king, your nephew, and my sovereign lord. So I entreat you, most humbly, that of the delay of the mission of my said embassy to you, you would be pleased to have and hold me excused.
>
> In order to declare more fully to you the causes of this said excuse, and other things touching the said matter under consideration, I send, at this present time, to you my well-beloved messires Richard Merbury, knight, and Jehan Ernoys, esquire, to whom, as concerns what they shall say and show to you at this time on my part upon the said matter, may it please you to yield full faith and credence, and to say or cause to say, and declare to them, the district in which you are, or shall be disposed to be, about the time of the fifteenth day of the month of May next following, at which time I am determined and entirely disposed to send my said embassy to your said highness, in order to treat, discuss, and conclude the business of the said marriage.[41]

Whilst in Rouen in July 1445, Charles VII offered a dynastic marriage between Edward and his daughter Magdalene (1443–95), about which York replied:

> Most high, most excellent, and most powerful prince, and most dread lord, I recommend myself to you very humbly . . . I have understood the good disposition in the which you are to further the conclusion of the marriage of one of my three most honourable ladies, your daughters, and my eldest son Edouart of York, with which I am perfectly rejoiced and consoled, and thank you therein; for I am well aware that my said

eldest son could not be placed in and appointed to a more lofty position and connexion.

In your said letters Magdalene is named; but considering her very tender age, and that naturally and as speedily as age will permit, I desire that issue should proceed of my said eldest son, seeing by the report of the said Merbury and Harnoiz that this my eldest son is of an age better adapted to and suitable for madam Jehanne de France, one of your said daughters, I have settled and fixed upon her, if it be the good pleasure of your highness to give heed thereunto.[42]

Questioning Charles VII may not have been a 'clever thing to do' as we shall see. Simultaneously, Richard and Cecily were also planning the marriage of their daughter Anne to Henry Holland (1430–75). He was heir to John Holland (1395–1447), duke of Exeter, and would bind the family to the royal line and its administrative workings. They were married on 30 January 1446. Upon assumption of his title, Exeter proved to be loyal to Henry VI, and held command at Ludford Bridge in 1459 where his father-in-law was defeated and fled the country. But all that lay in the future, which in 1445 no one could have predicted.

The duke was at Honnefleu in September 1445, and agreed to the marriage with the younger princess: if a marriage was to take place, York had to do as he was told by Charles:

the said marriage already discussed as having reference to the most noble person of my lady Magdalene of France, of which I am most joyful and pleased; and in order to treat of and conclude the said marriage, I was disposed to send once more to you, at the beginning of this present month of September, as I have written to messire Pierre de Brezé, your councillor and chamberlain. But, most high, most excellent, and most powerful prince, the king, your nephew and my sovereign lord, has written to me and intimated that it is his good pleasure that I should come to him, to be present and assist in his general Parliament which shall presently be assembled and held, and at which he wishes to have the assistance of his princes and lords. In obedience to which royal commandment . . . I must necessarily be occupied in many and different affairs; for the which cause to accomplish my desire in this respect. Nevertheless, when I have reached my said sovereign lord and spoken with him, I am [illegible] to send to your said highness, in order to proceed to the accomplishment of the treaty of the said marriage.[43]

York and his family left the town on 10 October at the end of his five-year appointment in France.[44] To recompense York for the loss of revenue as lieutenant of France, a new *apanage* was created for him from the comtes of Evreux and Beaumont-le-Roger as well as the vicomtes of Orbec and Breteuil.[45]

York returned to England in sufficient time to attend the opening of the third session of Parliament on 20 October 1445. Due to the vagaries of history, there is no evidence of the specific business with which the session dealt. York told Charles that he had been recalled to discuss matters arising from the truce. The duke must have had reasonable expectations of reappointment to France.[46]

The planned marriage alliance was still under discussion. York wrote to Charles on 23 December 1445:

> In regard to the overtures made touching the treaty of marriage between madame Magdalene your daughter and my eldest son, in truth, most high, excellent, and powerful prince and very dread lord, I am always in the same will, desiring that (by the mediation of the grace of God) the affair may arrive at a good and effectual conclusion. So I intreat you that it would please you to hold me excused in that, upon this matter, I have not sent to you so speedily as I thought to have done; for my lord the king, as I have already written to you, has sent to me to come to him with all diligence, in order to assist at his Parliament in England assembled in this city of London, where I have recently arrived, as your said councillors know. But this occupation past, in the shortest time that I well can, I will send to you some of my people, in order to shew you and give you to understand at considerable length my desire and my intention in the matter aforesaid. And I pray you that you will not in anywise take the said delay in displeasure.[47]

Nothing ultimately came of this marriage alliance, but York was clearly moving to take his place on the European political stage. The dynastic marriage would have bound the house of Valois to York, and reflected Henry's own recent marriage. However, Henry had not married the daughter of a king. Any marriage between Edward, earl of March and a French princess would increase York's standing, and importantly claims to the crown. Such a marriage would have placed him as the premier noble in England, son-in-law of the King of France, and in theory any offspring of the marriage would have had French and English royal blood. The duke was clearly 'future proofing' his own position and legacy. Why the marriage failed to happen has been lost to history.

In Parliament's absence, Henry VI, but far more likely to be on Suffolk's agency, agreed to surrender Maine to France. Only Henry and his innermost circle were aware of this when Parliament opened on 24 January 1446. On 9 April, the last day of the Parliament, an important statement concerning future policy towards France was read by the Chancellor. The king had agreed to meet Charles VII in the following October to negotiate a lasting peace.[48] Suffolk's plan was a serious blow to the Beauforts, who sought to carve out a French demesne: how soon a rift emerged between the two is hard to say. Clearly Suffolk was not prepared to let the Beaufort interest stand in the way of his plans: the truce guaranteed the security of Normandy. York, thanks to Suffolk. prospered at the expense of the Beauforts and was the greatest landowner in England.[49] His position and importance to Suffolk's regime is reflect by the fact that York was appointed as lieutenant general once more on 13 April 1446; the duke was to administer Normandy and oversee the withdrawal from Maine.[50] The duke confirmed his position in a letter received at Mantes on 22 April 1446, stating that the government of France and Normandy had been entrusted to him.[51]

Shortly after his appointment, York became a father once more on 3 May 1446. This time a daughter, baptised Margaret (1446–1503). York himself was busy building a brick town house at Hunsdon, nine miles away from where Cecily gave birth at Waltham Abbey.[52]

The government was all too well aware that it did not have sufficient financial resources to restart the war. Those acting in Henry VI's place had no option at the turn of 1446–7 other than maintain the policy of appeasement: this meant continuing to reassure Charles VII that Maine would be surrendered to his hands. This did not mean, however, that further English lands were to be ceded. Henry was to travel to France to meet Charles, presumably accompanied by York and the troops agreed by the king's Council in July 1446 who were to reinforce the garrison of Normandy.[53]

The duke of York had spent the summer of 1446 expanding his land holdings, or at least interests, in Ireland.[54] York was in London by 30 November 1446, and attended Council on 7 December. He attended Council at Sheen on the 9th and 14th of the same month, the latter meeting agreeing to the recall of Parliament to be held in Cambridge, changed to Winchester and finally Bury St Edmunds by 10 February 1447.[55]

Privy Seal Adam Moleyns (?–1450), bishop of Chichester, was in France from July to November 1446, and was back in Council on 14 December along with Cardinal Kemp, the latter being to a large degree 'the power behind the throne'. Others in attendance were Suffolk, John Sutton (1400–87) baron Dudley, who from 1428–30 had served as Lord Lieutenant of Ireland, Reginald Boulers (?–1459), the abbot of Gloucester, Cardinal Beaufort, Edmund Beaufort and York himself.[56] The meeting that followed became heated.

Before the Council met, Moleyns raised concerns about the duke's conduct in Normandy. Part of Moleyns' reasoning for his visit to France was to audit spending. This was perfectly reasonable: an investigation was ongoing into John Beaufort's handling of the 1443 expedition. It was not, as many historians have claimed, a direct attack on York in favour of Edmund Beaufort. The expedition in 1443 had used up almost the entirety of exchequer funds for that year.[57] Questions had to be asked about where the money had gone.

Indeed, exchequer proceedings against John Beaufort began shortly after his death: writs were issued on 12 June 1444 to make investigations into his goods and chattels, and his executors were ordered to render the accounts of the expedition by 24 June 1444, which included payments for wages and ordnance.[58] The English exchequer seized Somerset's lands in Cottingham, Yorkshire to pay off some of his substantial outstanding debts.[59] The treasury in Normandy was investigated and measurers taken on 13 December 1445.[60] Local officials in Normandy were instructed to investigate and report all the levies made by Somerset.[61] In such an atmosphere, York was not being singled out or targeted for retribution by Edmund Beaufort nor anyone else. The government/crown – call it what you will – was investigating the perceived misappropriation of funds by Somerset: it made common sense to check York's accounts at the same time, especially at a period when officials in Normandy were instructed to seize all the property and goods of the late duke of Somerset for the satisfaction of his debts.[62]

As John Watts notes, Moleyns was a man of influence, and it is not impossible that short cuts in administrative practice could have been interpreted as embezzlement, especially in the light of the investigation into Somerset's affairs. Moleyns made much of the fact that York had paid Lord Scales, Sir William Oldhall (1390–1460) and Sir Andrew Ogarde between his leaving for London in October 1445 and until summer 1446, but not the soldiers in garrison. Since his term of office had expired, York had *no obligation* to pay the garrisons.[63] Until he was officially re-appointed, York had no recourse to pay wages: thus, between October 1445 and 13 April 1446, garrisons had gone unpaid due to a failure of government. This was not York's doing. The duke no doubt felt it his duty to pay Oldhall et al, as they would have been expected to have been paid, regardless of by whom. York petitioned the king to clear his name against Moleyns' alleged slander: it seems he could not face being questioned about his governance of Normandy. He 'blew out of all proportion' a reasonable investigation into his governance contiguously to that of the dead Somerset, as an attack on himself and his reputation. Acutely aware of the execution of his own father as a traitor, York used the situation to demonstrate his loyalty to the crown and castigate Moleyns. York seems to have understood being held to account as persecution: this personality defect would have important considerations in future years. It was a trait shared with the earl of Salisbury's eldest son, Richard. As a prince of the royal blood, York perceived any questioning of his actions as a slight to his personal honour: he felt himself to be above suspicion and reproach, with a highly developed sense of self, superiority and nobility. York understood Moleyns, despite being a bishop, to be 'no one', who had no right to question him. We see this same elitist sentiment metered out against Earl Rivers in spring 1460 by Salisbury and his son Richard. In consequence of York's attack, Moleyns was undeniably on the defensive according to Bertram Wolffe, and told the duke he was a consistent supporter of the duke and the policy of a vigorous defence of Normandy.[64]

The investigation into York was not out of spite to remove him from office as is frequently claimed. It was part of a broader investigation into public finances as we noted earlier: context is everything. York's response to Moleyns can be seen as a carefully orchestrated way of seeking public endorsement for his return to Normandy. York seems to have been saying his conduct was above reproach, and appealed to the commonweal for support.

The fact that this all became public was representative of the chaotic nature of government: it was not the first showdown between York and Henry, or York and the Beauforts. It represented something much deeper. Henry's actions showed how little real authority he carried. York had petitioned the king concerning Moleyns, and Henry reasonably enough passed the issue to the lords. Under earlier monarchs the peers would certainly have been expected to participate in any hearing of Moleyns' charges and York's answer, and they would then advise the king, and it was for the king to give his final arbitration in a binding judgement. This did not happen either now, or at any time later. Had it ever? It is undeniable that the 'standard operating procedures' of government such as changing ministers or conducting audits for payment had become cloaked in rumour and suspicion. Why? The king's word was insecure and almost meaningless, even when given in Council or judgement. Government instead was carried on much as it had done before during the minority: the Council and other ministers derived their backing and power to act not from the king but from the lords. The king had not authorised their actions: this gave birth to York's charge of treason against those whose policies had failed. Henry lacked the intelligence or willpower to govern: this meant the power which was traditionally vested in one man was fragmented amongst leading magnates, clerks and gentlemen of the household. The York-Moleyns affair was the first glimmering of the weakness of this arrangement. Without a single, strong voice of control, 'the ship of state' was steered by conflicting opinions over foreign policy, which led to the emergence of factionalism and ultimately the Yorkist revolution of 1460.[65]

Chapter 3

# CHAOS AND CONFUSION

Despite York's appeal to the commonweal to support his bid to return to France, he learned from the Council that he was not travel there as lieutenant general: Edmund Beaufort was to be sent in his place. Until then however, York seems to have maintained a degree of administration over Normandy.

It is impossible to say what impact Moleyns' censure had had on this decision, if any. The decision not to send York was not a slight against him, or to be seen as any form of censure as later Yorkist apologists claim, but a change in foreign policy. It is undeniable that if Maine was to be surrendered, the obvious candidate to succeed the duke of York was Edmund Beaufort. Why? He was the then governor of Maine. He was the right man in the right place to manage the withdrawal from Maine.[1] The marquis was to commence his tenure from 1 March 1447, with his appointment being dated Christmas Eve 1446. He was to cross to France with 300 lances and 900 archers.[2] York had been missing from the Council meeting at Sheen on 24 December which agreed Beaufort's position in France.[3] It is all too easy to read into this fact that the Council deliberately excluded York from its decision-making: yet we have no evidence of such suggestion of 'foul play'. All of the evidence concerning York's dealings with the court in the 1440s, when not blinkered by hindsight and Yorkist propaganda, do not show him to have been a hated outsider.[4]

Did Richard feel he had been cheated? It is hard to say, and it is undeniable that for many writers on the Wars of the Roses, this marked the beginning of the duke's feud with Edmund Beaufort, leading to the latter's death in 1455 and the inevitability of Richard's usurpation in 1460. Yet if we step back from pro-Yorkist chroniclers, like Gregory or the Abbot of St Albans who are writing after the fact, often by decades, and creating a narrative that fitted their political ends, the evidence of

26

this feud and dissatisfaction with Henry VI does not exist. It is myth making on the chronicler's part, blindly followed ever since.

As we have already noted, Parliament was recalled in early 1447. Some historians claim it was called to arrest Humphrey, duke of Gloucester, for an attempted coup.[5] No evidence existed for the supposed murder of Henry V's brother, but it is undeniable, however, that once the duke was dead on 23 February 1447, the official line put out by the crown was that there had been a plot to kill the king at Bury St Edmunds, even if the duke himself was not specifically named as being involved in it. This was emphasized by the fact that, in July 1447, some members of Gloucester's household were found guilty of intending to kill the king and to rescue the duchess from her imprisonment on charges of witchcraft.[6] One of the beneficiaries of Gloucester's death was the duke of York.[7]

Rather than seeking to arrest Gloucester, as claimed by historians like Johnson,[8] Parliament was called to consider two issues: taxes and foreign policy. Sitting with the peers was York, as well as Dorset, Suffolk, Northumberland and Salisbury, amongst others. In order for Suffolk to govern from the centre, Gloucester needed to be 'out of the way'; his death, likely from a heart attack triggered by the charges against him, solved a lot of Henry's immediate problems.

It is undeniable that Gloucester had been critical of Henry VI's foreign policy as betraying his brother, and was thus hardly likely to approve of plans to give up English rights in France, and in particular to the surrender of Maine. Yet what could he actually do? He had a claim to the throne this is true, but he had been in disgrace since 1441 and the trial of his second wife, Eleanor Cobham. As Carpenter correctly comments, he had been opposed to peace with France since 1439, and stood opposite Suffolk and Cardinal Beaufort. The trial ensured 'Gloucester was gagged'.[9] He had little influence remaining to him, and moreover, the surrender of Maine had already been agreed in December 1445, and France was to have taken over the territory by 30 April 1446. That this had not happened owed much to the chaotic nature of policy towards France, and the surrender date was pushed back by a year. Henry pledged to go France to meet his uncle Charles VII and to personally begin negotiations over Maine. Charles for his part was reluctant to extend the truce, which was due to expire, and refused to enter into further negotiations until Maine was in his hands.[10] Gloucester, had he lived, would no doubt have been the victim of factionalism within the power vacuum around Henry, as conflicting views over foreign policy were played out. As it was, he died of natural causes, perhaps from the shock of being arrested. York later claimed that those who murdered Gloucester had wanted to kill him: this is York the propagandist, claiming that Gloucester was killed for opposing Henry's foreign policy and he too had been banished to Ireland for doing so, after escaping a plot against his life.[11] York is writing his own history in a revisionary manner to exonerate his own treason. York's propaganda has shaped and still shapes – as he intended it to do – our understanding of the Wars of the Roses: we must look behind at the public image he created to understand the reality of events. York was objectively bending the truth to suit his own ends; he knew what happened and what the agenda of Parliament was in 1447.

Turning back to France, the English crown could ill afford to lose territory in France: rental incomes, tolls and other fees provided some degree of income to the crown. Despite Henry's promises, he did not travel to France, and negotiations dragged on into October.[12]

Symptomatic of this failure of government varying between Cardinal Beaufort and Suffolk as principal voice, Edmund Beaufort's tenure as lieutenant general of Normandy lasted just six weeks, and he never crossed the Channel. His indenture lapsed on 1 February 1447.[13] Yet no immediate successor was named. Was it York, or was it Beaufort? Edmund Beaufort, further ennobled as 2nd duke of Somerset, as count of Maine had almost regal powers, with his centre of government at Le Mans. His position, agreed in 1439, was for life, with a land grant dated July 1442, and allowed him to conclude his own alliances, separate from the primary English war effort.[14] Somerset had entered into private treaties with the dukes of Alençon and Anjou.[15] He was operating, perfectly legally, outside the direct control of the crown.[16] Re-appointing York in February, or least allowing Somerset's appointment to lapse and the position by default devolve back on York, was a common-sense policy decision by Suffolk: otherwise Somerset would have had almost total control of French possessions. It would have created an 'overmighty subject' and prevented any secession of Maine. Somerset was opposed to ceding his power, prestige, income and land without massive compensation. Having been seen as the man to deal with the withdrawal, different voices in government agreed that York was the man for the job. This changing policy represented fluctuations in influence over Henry and his inner circle. Somerset refused to relinquish control and accept York's appointment. Indeed, an eyewitness, Thomas Basin (1412–91), archbishop of Lisieux and personally known to the duke of York, recalled a period of confusion in Rouen in spring 1447, with proclamations being made for Somerset and then a different proclamation made by York. Both parties were backed by their own factions in the English council in Normandy, and at Council in England and around Henry VI. It seems Somerset refused to accede to the king's wishes.[17]

Henry's policy towards Normandy and France was confused, conflicting and chaotic: in this regard it reflected the differing viewpoints of those who held fragments of power, as Henry was unable, or willing to exercise royal power, and courting public opinion was 'the only judge of good faith' between the executive and commonweal. Henry, or at least those closest to him acting in his name, was unable to maintain a consistent line on policy as it vacillated between the then current sway of opinion. The corporate interest in maintaining the credibility of royal authority, sadly meant already fragmented power became more fractious as the body corporate could not agree a single line of action. The problem was one of royal authority: Henry's inability to govern 'set up a contest of authorities' between those around the king due to the lack of a single, strong voice at the centre of government. This, as John Watts elegantly explains, was a precondition to conflict.[18]

The vacillation of who was to be, or not to be, lieutenant in France was symptomatic of the problems at the heart of government. Suffolk's policy of appeasement with France still had vocal support from Cardinal Beaufort: his death on 11 April completed Suffolk's rise to pre-eminence.[19] The period of uncertainty ended when Henry formally announced on 13 April 1447 that York was to continue in office and not Somerset.[20] York was back in office. His acceptance showed his acceptance of the peace policy with France and support for Suffolk.[21] York and Suffolk were not yet on opposing sides, nor were York and Somerset. In May, York commissioned Lucas Le Jeune, lieutenant of the bailiff of Evreux, and Jean Rabasse, controller of the salt granary of Bernay, to receive the watches and magazines of the men-at-arms serving in Lisieux, Orbec, Conches, Beaumont and Bernay.[22] In July, York was described in a letter to the Chancellor of England as 'my lord the lieutenant and governor'.[23]

Amidst this tussle for power, Richard and Cecily rejoiced at the birth of a son, William, born on 7 July 1447, but he was buried at Fotheringhay shortly later. Quite how the duke reacted to the death is hard to say. He had already buried two sons, and would bury a third, John, in November 1448.[24]

As well as the lucrative officer of lieutenant in France, York found himself appointed lieutenant of Ireland on 30 July 1447, for a period of ten years. We can interpret this appointment in a number of ways. Given York's land holdings in Ireland, he was possibly the only candidate to deal with increasingly fractious Irish affairs. It had 'no malevolent design'.[25] The appointment made no stipulation York was to travel to Ireland, and he could govern via proxy.[26] More importantly, the post came with a substantial salary of 4,000 marks for the first year and £2,000 per annum thereafter, commencing on 29 September 1447.[27] We know the duke was in financial difficulties: he was owed the majority of his fee from Normandy and had had recourse to using his own funds to pay men like Oldhall.[28] The appointment was by means of compensation for the failure of the English exchequer to pay its bills. It is undeniable that the income from the Irish lieutenancy would have helped his financial position enormously and he had governance of a far larger tract of land than Normandy. He was re-appointed in 1450, and despite a brief break in office during 1453, held the post till 1459. If this was banishment, it was not understood as that at the time by the duke. He held two lucrative and powerful positions with the crown, and, after the king, was the most powerful noble in England.

Yet ever since 1447, based largely on the evidence of chroniclers like Gregory, the posting to Ireland was seen as a banishment and punishment for misdeeds in France. These seems very unlikely, and we cannot remove the suspicion that York himself pushed for the Irish position given (a) his land holdings there, (b) his desire for power, and (c) that no evidence exists that York was distanced from the regime of Henry and moreover, he was acting as part of government and attended the Council. He had been present at Council three days prior to his own appointment.

Evidencing the banishment theory, Johnson implies the date of appointment may have been significant: the duke opposed the surrender of Maine and was 'sent to Coventry', to use the popular vulgate for his position. Yes, the duke's appointment to Ireland was seen by contemporaries, such as the writer of Gregory's chronicle, as banishment, but significantly they are writing very much after the fact.[29] As I commented earlier, I do not believe this to have been the case. As the duke could govern Ireland by proxy, and indeed appointed Richard Talbot, archbishop of Dublin, to do so: he was not compelled to actually be in Ireland. Able to draw on all surplus revenues from the Irish exchequer, in addition to his fee, the appointment was beyond reasonable doubt in compensation for the impending loss of land in Normandy. If he had been exiled from the king's presence, the duke's continued presence there contradicts this somewhat.

Moreover, it is undeniable that Suffolk was promoting York over the Beauforts. Henry VI had no heir, and Suffolk was well aware that Henry was 'not fit for purpose'. If the Beauforts had prospered under their uncle's influence with the carving-out of a Beaufort hegemony in Maine and Anjou, why should not York be so honoured, especially as he had extensive lands in Ireland. The emergence of Beaufort and York as heirs apparent, with their own supporters, in the turbulent politics of the 1440s showed the weakness of Henry began soon after his majority in 1437. Whoever controlled the king, controlled the government. Beaufort and his family believed in their claim to power and authority to be from royal blood; opposing them was Suffolk and York, whose claim was also founded in royal blood. War was not inevitable in this 'clash of clans', but as early as 1446 the 'clock was ticking' slowly towards armed confrontation. York and Somerset should have been natural allies; both stood to lose land, prestige and income if the French lands were lost. The fact that negotiations over the surrender of Maine dragged on for years, shows the reluctance of Henry's peers to simply 'give away' Henry V's conquest – how in control was Suffolk in reality? Yet, the winner in all of this was York. York held two lucrative officers of state in Ireland and Normandy. Somerset, on the other hand, apart from his compensation for the loss of Maine, received no new titles, grants or land between 1434 and 1451. It was only when Somerset obtained full control of government with Suffolk and Moleyns' deaths in 1450 and 1451 that he was awarded lucrative grants.[30] Contrary to prevailing opinion, York was not ostracised and outside of court and governance as Johnson and Lewis argue: he was part of the inner workings of government. If anyone was 'on the outside looking in', it was Somerset.

Chapter 4

# SOMERSET'S FAILURE?

York's political career had peaked – for the time being at least – in summer 1447. He was richest and greatest noble in the kingdom and holder of two important offices of state, ruling Ireland and Normandy in the name of Henry VI. Ruling York's vast estates would have taxed the ability of the most competent of men: that he managed Ireland and Normandy speaks well of his ability to administer and delegate. Yet not being in Ireland or Normandy meant he did not see for himself the problems on the ground as they really were, relying instead on second-hand information.

By the time that York was appointed to Ireland, relations between France and England in early summer 1447 were at a very low ebb. Despite having agreed to surrender Maine, the English crown still had not done so. Coming under pressure from his uncle, on 22 July 1447 Henry VI, in the presence of York, Kemp, Somerset, Suffolk and other leading peers, pledged a solemn undertaking to effect the surrender by 1 November 1447.

A few days later on the 27th, in the presence of the French ambassadors, as well as York, Kemp and Suffolk, Somerset was promised substantial compensation for the loss of Maine. It was this meeting of the Council that appointed York lieutenant in Ireland. York continued as lieutenant of France.[1] The last recorded payment for York's duties as lieutenant in Normandy came at the end of November 1447.[2]

In the wake of the agreement, orders went to the captains in the area to implement it, but they refused to do so, perhaps on Somerset's orders.[3] Somerset had a lot to lose, and perhaps keenly felt his lack of reward compared to York, yet his intransigence in surrendering Maine resulted in a reprimand from Henry himself on 23 October. The duke of York was present to witness this harsh criticism. Henry – more likely Cardinal Kemp acting on his behalf, or Suffolk himself – informed

Somerset that his actions were jeopardising the handover; maybe this was exactly Somerset's intention.[4] Somerset refused any surrender of Maine unless he was paid a huge sum in compensation.

Tensions were eased on 13 November when Somerset's compensatory agreement was discussed. He was to receive 10,000 *livres tournois* a year drawn from the tax on wine, cider and other beverages in Normandy. This income had traditionally been paid to the Norman coffers, and such a substantial diversion of funds into private hands was both unprecedented and reduced the money available to finance defence. Yet, York as lieutenant agreed, the decision being further ratified by Humphrey Stafford (1402–60) duke of Buckingham, Suffolk, Ralph Cromwell (1403–55) baron Cromwell, Henry Scrope (1418–59) baron Scrope, Cardinal Kemp, Adam Moleyns and chancellor John Stafford (?–1452), archbishop of Canterbury.[5] To ensure he received the money, Somerset appointed his own receiver, John Kyriell, to see that the tax was levied.[6] The agreement was far more than the tax could actually raise: in 1433 it had only raised 1,200 *livres tournois* a year: it meant that the vast majority of tax income in Normandy was directed into Somerset's personal treasury, which the duke of York was to point out three years later.[7] York 'conveniently forgot' he agreed to the measure when writing in 1452. Perhaps more correctly, he was 'strong-armed' into agreement by Suffolk and Buckingham: perhaps York had no choice but to agree to the loss of revenue to the cash-strapped Duchy of Normandy. York's criticism of all of this occurred once Normandy had been lost, and his own views in 1452 may not have been those he held in 1447. If Maine was to be lost, the principal landowner, Somerset, had to be compensated. The English exchequer could not fund the compensatory payment as agreed, so the Norman exchequer became the source of the funds. Those present at the meeting all understood the need for restorative justice: only later was it realised that the act contributed to loss of Normandy. On 24 November 1447, Suffolk arranged for York to receive 7,500 *livres tournois* of his owed pay from this time in France.[8]

Henry VI wrote to Charles on 11 December, announcing Somerset's dispatch as the new lieutenant, who carried with him a payment of 4,000 marks for the defence and upkeep of the duchy.[9] Somerset had 1,000 archers with him.[10] Somerset replacing York had two reasons: Somerset may well have made the appointment part of his compensation for loss of prestige in governing Maine, and it prevented York from becoming 'an overmighty subject'.

What the duke felt about the loss of his post in France is not recorded. Whatever sense of grievance may have existed between York, Suffolk and Somerset, the three men clearly outwardly co-operated. York was also on sufficiently cordial terms with Somerset to hand to him rents in Normandy that had been paid to him, and were due to Somerset.[11] If both York and Somerset were 'mortal enemies' as mythos implies by this point, this magnanimous act by York rather contradicts this. These actions suggest that as 1448 dawned there was no public perception of irreconcilable differences between the three men. What York thought of Somerset in private is a different matter entirely, and is lost to history unless we backdate his claims from 1452 which is a dangerous supposition. The chronicle tradition that York was banished from the king's presence and he was affronted by Somerset is overly simplistic and retrospective. It is undeniable, however, that Henry VI – more reasonably those acting in his name – was prepared to allow a unique concentration of principal estates with one noble family. York's condemnation of Somerset was for his actions in 1449, not earlier. We also note that even though Somerset had taken the 'top job', York still held titles and offices in France and retained a considerable measure of authority there. He held full military authority in the strategically important apanage of Evreaux, Beaumont-le-Roger, Conches and Breteuil – granted in December 1444 – which generated the duke sufficient income to repair the castles at Conches and Beaumont-le-Roger during 1448.[12] York was at Fotheringhay in the first weeks of 1448.[13]

By February 1448, there was a real threat of war, as Charles VII drew his troops up to Le Mans, on the pretext that he would soon need to garrison the town and other castles as outlined under the prevailing treaty. Yet on arriving, Charles found no provisions had been made to hand over Le Mans or Maine. Fluctuating policy over France resulted in Henry reinforcing Somerset's army:

> And now it is come to our knowledge that a grete power and a mighty siege is laide before oure towne of Maunce and sharp werre dayly made to oure subgetts being thereinne ye which is no signe of peas but a likelyhode to ye werre. We therefore by the advice of oure Counsaill have ordeined that oure said cousin shall have with hym ijc speres and ijm bowes.[14]

In theory, this put Somerset's command on a wartime footing.

After an initial round of sabre-rattling from both sides, English policy switched back to diplomacy and peace. Unable to afford to fight France, diplomatic relations resumed, and on 11 March, the Treaty of Lavardin was signed, by which Maine would be handed back to France by 1 April 1450.[15]

The new treaty was merely a continuance of the existing truce, having been agreed on 15 October 1447 and to end on 1 January 1449. Under it, Henry was to travel to France to meet his uncle, but never crossed to France. In failing to travel, those around Henry were perhaps working to protect the mythos of Henry as an active monarch. If Henry met with Charles, the bluff that had been created to conceal the vacuum at the heart of government would be cruelly exposed. At the same time, the crown could ill afford war with France. Peace at any price was Suffolk's policy. The policy had worked well, and had every opportunity of lasting well into the next decade.

## Rouen

Somerset returned to Rouen in April 1448: he was no incompetent court favourite as later writers – those reliant on later Yorkist propaganda, and those directly impacted by William de la Pole, duke of Suffolk's governance such as the Pastons – claim. If anything, Somerset's war record, was superior to that of the duke of York. His defence of Calais under Bedford in 1436 resulted in Henry VI making him a Knight of the Garter as well as earl of Dorset. During his tenue as lieutenant in France, as we have seen, he commanded at two major English victories: the relief of Avranches and the capture of Harfleur. Avranches was one of the two garrisons in Normandy over which York had life captaincies, the other was Cotentin, exercised by York's lieutenant John Lamper. Somerset's victories may have irked York, but he could do little about it or he could have been thankful for the saving of both places. It is too easy to imagine bitterness between the two men. York, writing years later, imagined there was animosity but he was writing history as he wanted it recorded.

Resentment over the scope of York's administrative powers despite him no longer being lieutenant perhaps lay behind Somerset's course of action on arriving in the Duchy. It is undeniable that the duchy had a major cash-flow crisis, and Somerset sought to 'streamline' local governance, to root out corruption and to raise revenue. These reforms were sensible, but their practical application caused resentment both in Normandy and back in England. Perhaps resentment of York's continuing presence, albeit by proxy, underlay charges that his two garrisons had priority payment over other garrisons. Possibly seeking to undermine York, Somerset withheld payment from Avranches: York's lieutenant John Lamper had to arrest local officials operating under Somerset's jurisdiction and forcibly extract money to pay the garrison.[16] Here are, perhaps, the first glimmerings of a personal clash being played out in the open by the two men. A shortage of cash lay behind Somerset's actions in restructuring the administration of the duchy: he eliminated the office of local receiver and replaced them with inspectors appointed directly by him. Officials who refused to co-operate with Somerset were stripped of office.[17] York later claimed in 1452 this was a deliberate slight against men he had appointed, that Somerset had deliberately removed servants loyal to him from office with no compensation and in their place imposed men loyal to himself.[18] Equally provocative to York was the revival of the Échiquier of Normandy which had not operated since Bedford had died in 1435. This court, which provided a forum for criminal cases as well as domestic property disputes, was formally opened on 14 October 1448. Rather than 'starting from scratch' Somerset re-opened the court, and cases that had been in abeyance for over a decade or more were revived: a huge number of large fines were imposed and many were gaoled.[19] Perhaps the point was to raise money rather than administer justice, as York claimed in 1452.[20]

The confused nature of English policy – related as we said earlier to the factionalism around Henry himself – over France was responsible in precipitating the loss of Normandy. Having agreed to surrender Maine on 15 March 1448, the English 'dragged their feet' in leaving: to be fair, who could blame them? Leaving their homes and land, we can understand how these men came to resent Henry, Moleyns and Suffolk in equal measure. The men of the Maine garrisons, after the withdrawal commenced, rather than moving to reinforce the garrisons along the Norman border with France, moved to the west, to the Breton frontier, where some of them set about repairing the castle of Saint-James-de-Beuvron – an action which aroused protests, as the refortification of frontier castles was forbidden by the terms of the truce. The French reported major infractions of the truce committed by English soldiers evacuated from Maine.[21] The French herald reported on 2 August 1448:

> Since the arrival of Somberset, a person named Christoffe a Bealieu, Mudefort, Le Petit Trelot,[22] Seidre, Achetreton and many others of the party . . . who are under the charge and government of the said duke of Somb erset, have come to carry by assault the fortress of Saint James de Beuvron . . . and of places in dispute, claiming them to be in the jurisdiction of the king, and that the possession thereof ought to belong to him . . . the said occupation of Saint James is done in direct opposition to the tenor of the said truce.

The Herald of Valois further reported that Somerset refused to acknowledge the impingement of the truce. The Herald added that Somerset had told the French ambassadors that if they challenged his actions, he would have them arrested: Somerset was clearly 'sabre-rattling'. How much of this was Somerset's own doing, or policy? In acting in this way, Somerset had the backing of Adam de Moleyns as Privy Seal and Robert Roos (?–1448), who were also unwilling to negotiate with Charles. This appears to represent a rift in the consensus government around Henry. A new faction had opened up in the heart of government: Suffolk and York were at odds with Moleyns and Roos. York's public critique of Moleyns had drawn him to Somerset. If Henry had been a strong king, this rift amongst the nobility would not have occurred. It marked the beginning of factionalism around who controlled Henry. The Herald of Valois took pains to point out that Moleyns, Roos and Somerset's behaviour was 'in a style derogatory to the honour of the King, and different from what they had been used in time past by the duke of York'. How this must have stung Henry and Suffolk: Charles VII was openly criticising Henry's closest advisors, and comparing them unfavourably with York. The Herald of Valois furthermore told Henry in stark words that on Somerset's orders 'many murders and robberies have been perpetuated' adding that the unless Somerset obeyed the truce, war was the inevitable outcome.[23] When the thorny issue of Saint-James-de-Beuvron was discussed, Adam Moleyns, representing Henry – was this Suffolk's policy or Moleyns'? – replied that this could not be discussed, since Saint-James was on the frontier of Normandy with Brittany and not with France, 'and in the truce of the said King of England Brittany is included as of his obedience'. Moleyns further exacerbated the situation and declared that he had power only to negotiate with the French, 'not with the Bretons whose duke owed homage and fealty to Henry VI and not Charles king of the Francs'.[24] Moleyns was saying to Charles that if he had issues over the rebuilding of Saint-James-de-Beuvron in breach of the treaty, he had to take it up directly with Henry, as the castle bordered English and Breton lands. This was dangerous sabre-rattling: English policy was shifting towards a takeover of Britanny.

## International Relations

The defence of Normandy was part of a wider European conflict. At stake was the future of the French monarchy. France was indisputably the most populous and richest political entity of the period, reaching its zenith under Louis XIV 200 years later. This was not pre-destined. The conquests of Henry V and his allies in 1415–22 could have meant a strong French monarchy under the English crown; another option was the division of what we know as France into Breton, Burgundian, English and French control, i.e. long-term division between the Valois kings of France, and the house of Lancaster and its allies. Even after the French regained Paris, it was not inevitable that all English territories would be lost. French politics revolved around the great princes, the greatest being the Valois dukes of Burgundy, and secondly the dukes of Britanny. Burgundy controlled swathes of central France and the all-important Channel coast, Flanders, an area today divided into Belgium, Netherlands and parts of northern France. This mattered to England, as foreign policy aimed to prevent the French monarchy becoming too powerful: the duke of Burgundy, was perhaps the second richest and most powerful ruler after the king of France with territory overseen by France and the Holy Roman Empire. It was Burgundian territory along the Channel coast that the bulk of English wool was exported to, and from where an increasingly important trade in luxury goods and finished woollen cloth flowed to London. Antwerp was the entrepôt for English trade into Europe. England did not want France to occupy and control the Channel coast, and thus was a natural ally of Burgundy. A strong Burgundy meant a rival to France.

As we noted before, the second key ally in this anti-French coalition was Britanny. The dukes held it from the French crown, and had made themselves de facto independent of France, but owed fealty to the English crown. The French monarch could only appeal for Breton support through anti-English policy, hence Charles VII actively promoted civil strife in the ruling dynasty – as did Henry – as we commented before. The defence of Burgundy and Brittany was vital to English interest. Britanny was to hold Henry Tudor hostage from 1471. Whilst Britanny was an ally of England, then the threat from the Tudors was essentially neutralised. Richard III's diplomatic error in alienating Britanny meant Henry was allowed to slip into France, raise a Franco-Scottish army, with the support of key members of Richard's government, and depose him at Bosworth. As important to English interests was the defence the great French princes like the duc D'Alençon, Orleans, and Anjou, against the drive of Charles VII. Why? Charles's goal for his reign was the total conquest of France and the drive for great internal control over the geographical unit we consider as France. This meant rival illumination to ensure the effectiveness of the rule of the monarchy from Paris. Relations with foreign powers was part and parcel of the 'game of thrones' being played out across Europe.

A family dispute – sound familiar? – was the heart of who would govern Britanny, and to whom the duchy would look, France or

England. Gilles de Bretagne nephew of Charles VII, looked to Henry VI to support his campaign against French control of Brittany. His older brothers, Francis and Peter, were Francophiles. Their father Rochemont was Constable of France. Gilles had been arrested in 1446 after an abortive coup organised in London to place himself as in charge of the Duchy. The arrest of Henry's vassal was technically a breach of the existing truce, but it occurred during peace negotiations and when Henry's officials were seeking to appease Charles. English complicity in the failed coup had driven Gilles' brothers to support his father and Charles VII. In the battleground of Breton loyalty, if Henry could secure Gilles' release and restoration, it could lead some way at least to an effective Breton alliance, more so if Francis de Bretagne could be recruited to the English cause against France.[25] A strong Breton alliance would have given Henry an ally, and if Burgundy could be drawn into such an anti-French coalition, it might have been possible to reclaim Maine militarily, some may have thought.

With hindsight, this was all rather naïve and 'pie in the sky' thinking which lead to the total loss of Henry V's territorial gains. The English crown could not afford a war on two fronts, let alone full-scale war with France. If those who lay behind the plan thought that playing a 'double game' would be beneficial in the long term to the English presence in France, they were ignoring the facts of the matter. The lure was the wealth of Brittany, as Thomas Basin made clear.[26] England needed Breton gold to 'balance the books'. Such a plan is all reminiscent of Cardinal Beaufort's thinking from 1442, and may have originated with the cardinal himself,[27] Somerset, or others like Moleyns and Roos rather than Suffolk, who appears to have been sidelined at this point.[28] The blame for the fiasco lies with the group of advisors who were making determined efforts to find a solution for a non-operational king: however, collective responsibility was rather lacking as we shall see.[29]

Turning back to Somerset, if a rift existed between him and York at this stage, being compared directly with and unfavourably to York may well have been understood as a personal slight: yet we remember this was not York's action, but that of a third party who was criticising his behaviour. IF a rift existed between the two men in late summer 1448, this unfavourable comparison may be the first glimmerings of it being made public. In 1452, York made clear his own views – in hindsight and recorded by those who were biased against Suffolk's regime and also Somerset – that 'at the time of the delyverannce he would not agree thereto, unto tyme that he was recompensid' i.e. Somerset refused to hand over Maine till he had been paid in full that which was owed to him. If York resented losing his position in France, tellingly he made no mention at all of this in his 1452 articles. Nor did York level any charges of wrongdoing against Somerset in being appointed lieutenant in France. What York was concerned with was Somerset's appalling judgement and greed.[30] He was not the only one to note Somerset's greed. Thomas Basin tells us Somerset was a well-educated, sociable, handsome, courteous and kindly man. His defect, which compromised him totally, was avariciousness. Somerset, it could be said, was 'only obeying orders' concerning Saint-James-de-Beuvron, and the responsibility for that decision rested with those around Henry, who were aware that this broke the treaty if not legally, then in spirit. The problem was, when everything went wrong, those around Henry, acting in his name, refused to accept corporate responsibility for their actions: Henry was above censure, therefore many felt so were they, acting as they were in his proxy. Accountability, and the lack of it, undermined trust in the monarchy and the king in the eyes of the commonweal was governed by 'evil councillors'. That all lies in the future.

## The Auld Alliance

It was not only across the Channel that 'international relations' – a hugely misleading term – mattered. Scotland was still an independent nation. The Scottish crown looked to European allies against the English. The wardenship of the East and West Marches – dominated by two families, the Nevilles and the Percys – created a buffer zone with Scotland.

Influencing those around Henry and the events in France was the recent defeat by the Scots. Scotland, like England since 1437, was a country suffering from the rule of several relatively weak kings, who were unable to centralise royal power effectively. As a result, the realm had been ruled by several assemblies composed of noblemen from relatively few houses. It was into this context of feuding magnates, with enough power to challenge the crown, that James II became king at the age of six. During his minority, various large houses, predominantly the Black Douglas faction and the Livingston and Crichton families, jockeyed for control over James II and governance of the realm. The unrest in Scotland explains why resources were diverted to the border and not Normandy. Stretched thin, the English exchequer could not afford two wars no matter how hard it tried to balance the books. Scotland was the more pressing concern. The developing tussle for power, seems to have prompted Henry to exploit the situation in an escalating border conflict, and conflict between James II and his nobility.

The preamble to the failure was the sacking by Henry Percy (1421–61), the son of the earl of Northumberland (1393–1455), of the town of Dunbar in May 1448. In June, Richard Neville, earl of Salisbury and the warden of the West March, sacked and razed the castle and town at Dumfries. It was only natural that the Scottish Marcher lords would retaliate against English aggression which created a swirling maelstrom of competing ambitions. On both sides of the border extremely powerful magnates were in competition with each other, and moreover, were able to ignore the authority of, their respective Crown to suit their own desires. With both Henry VI and James II having a tenuous grip on power, it is not surprising that Henry VI saw the Scottish retaliatory raids into Northumberland as a direct assault on his kingship, and the Douglases saw the earlier English incursion not as an assault on Scotland, but on the power of their own house and positions as Wardens of the Marches. The Marcher earl of Douglas, with the earls of Angus, Orkney and Ormond, retaliated promptly and brutally, marching south and leaving a trail of destruction through Cumberland and northern Northumberland.[31] These raids then spurred Northumberland to retaliate with a major invasion, culminating in the Battle of Sark (my translation from the Latin, any errors are of my making):

> The duke of Warwick, Richard Neville gathered an army, and at the head of it he put Sir Thomas Harrington and lord Percy, son of the duke of Northumberland they were 15,000 men. They crossed the river Saionause. But Duke Douglas attacked with 6,000 Scotsmen and defeated almost all the English and turned them to flight; the foresaid commanders of the English were taken prisoner.
>
> When the earl of Salisbury, the father of the duke of Warwick, was informed of this, he prepared, it is estimated, 40,000 men, who again crossed the river; and again came the foresaid duke with his brother, the earl of Ormond. A terrible slaughter took place: a large part [of the English army], pursued by the Scots, was caught by the river and drowned, and the Scots ventured as much as miles across the river, as far as the port that is called Newcastle, destroying everything.[32]

The battle on 23 October 1448 was a decisive victory for the Scots, with many of Northumberland's force captured or killed, and apparently very few Scottish casualties in return. Retribution following the battle centred on personal strikes against the lands and holdings of Northumberland; Warkworth and Alnwick were sacked and burned, both situated deep in Percy lands. Neither side in this conflict could afford to show any hint of weakness, as their political and military power rested with their reputation as Wardens of the Marches. The victory of the Douglases raised their profile in the Scottish power struggles at the time, while simultaneously damaging the Earl of Northumberland's in England. For the earl of Northumberland, the humiliating defeat was damaging in several ways. His prestige and reputation as a warden of the March was certainly affected, he had to pay a ransom for his son and heir, who was languishing in captivity in Lochmaben Castle. Northumberland's ambition to regain the lands of his father and grandfather began to conflict with the ambitions of his northern neighbour, Richard Neville, the earl of Salisbury; the conflict of interests and ambitions between the two houses quickly turned into physical conflict between the hot-tempered scions of both houses. The battle dispelled the myth of English invincibility long before 1453. Henry had to seek a new truce with Scotland during 1449.[33] Recriminations between the Percys and Nevilles about who was to blame for the fiasco was formative in the destructive Percy-Neville feud which underplayed the politics of the next 12 years. The Battle of Sark and events leading to it, may have been influenced by the renewal of the treaty between France and Scotland in 1448. Soon after a new treaty was signed between England and Scotland, James II came into his majority. Faced with 'overmighty subjects' in the Douglases, James II precipitated a conflict to break their power and secure his position, culminating with the Battle of Arkinholm in 1455. It did not mark the end of the Douglas influence, however: Edward IV recruited them against Mary of Guelders in a battle for dominance in Scotland after coming to the throne.

## A cry for help

Moving back to the events of the second half of 1448, in response to Charles VII's accusations, Somerset through his spokespersons, likely to have been Thomas Hoo, Lord Hastings, chancellor of France, and Reginald Boulers, abbot of Gloucester, reported to Henry:

> The enemy daily fortify, repair, and reinforce all their garrisons on the frontiers of the king's obedience, moving about and riding within the said obedience, armed in large numbers, contrary to the tenor of the truces, committing innumerable murders and taking the king's subjects prisoners, just as if it was full war, along with other great and lamentable injuries, such as countless public robberies, oppressions and plunders; for which offences they have been summoned many times and required by my said lord of Somerset to cease from carrying out, and to make

remedy according to the tenor of the truces, but neither remedy nor reasonable answer has yet been made in any way; wherefore it may be supposed, by their perverse deeds and contrary disposition, that their intention is not to proceed effectively to any good conclusion of peace.[34]

Hard on the heels of defeat in Scotland, by early autumn 1448 war with France now seemed a possibility. Yet Henry VI left London and headed north. Leaving others to negotiate with Charles, he went to Beverley to the shrine of St John on pilgrimage. Moleyns or Suffolk wrote to Charles from Beverley, in the king's name, that the king had no intention of giving up Saint-James-de-Beuvron.[35] As John Watts notes 'mounds of documents, many of them bearing the royal signature, all of them bearing the royal signature . . . which declare the king himself was the author', yet these documents cannot be taken at face value; they are merely evidence of 'institutional and conceptual conditions of kingship' to make Henry VI formally responsible even if in reality he was not.[36] Henry lacked the inclination and capacity for government.[37] His pilgrimage at a time of national crisis is symptomatic of his inability to rule, and those around him being forced to make government work in spite of an ineffective nullity in the king.

Both French and English troops were infringing the truce. Both sides wanted war. France was prepared, England was not: the myth of Agincourt fatally lingered. Somerset wrote to Charles VII on 28 February 1449, stating that since August 1448 Robert de Floques and his garrison at Louviers had committed a number of outrages, attacking shipping on the Seine, seizing wine worth 800 *livres tournois*, about £46,667 in modern money, and raiding the village of Quévreville, near Pont-de-l'Arche. Somerset added that men from Mont-Saint-Michel and Granville were 'daily committing infinite crimes, murders, robberies, seizing labourers whom they seek out at night ten or twelve leagues away from their bases, putting them to ransom, as they still do, just as if it were war-time and open war at that'. Somerset added that 160 and 180 men from Dieppe, 'armed and armoured as if in time of war', had ridden into the parish of Torcy-le-Grand, ten miles south-west of Dieppe. Two men were killed.[38] Somerset wrote to Charles on 9 March 1449 that he agreed to demolish the new works at Saint-James-de-Beuvron and would send an embassy to meet the king to discuss the matter.[39] Somerset was endeavouring to step back from the brink of war.

Although the truce was technically in force until 1 April 1450, it was already clear that hostilities were likely to resume. The coming war was part of a large geopolitical 'game of chess' played out between France and her rivals, Britanny and Burgundy. Henry refused to abandon Giles de Bretagne against his pro-French brother, Duke Francis. French and English ambassadors met for the last time in mid-November 1448. War was coming it seemed, and money was needed. Henry recalled Parliament.

Any suggestion that Richard, duke of York was sidelined, in opposition to the King is simply not a sustainable hypothesis when tested against primary sources. Parliament met on 12 February 1449; York was one of four lay peers present. Taxation to pay for the war was amongst the first matters discussed, and a hoped-for revenue of £6,667 was to be used to garrison Calais. No English funds were ever earmarked for Normandy. Scotland in the wake of Salisbury catastrophic failure was more of a pressing concern. Indeed, the Norman exchequer was almost empty. As part of the Treaty of Lavardin, Henry had agreed to pay 24,000 *livres tournois* to landowners in Maine who were forced to hand their lands over to the French. As tax revenue was diverted elsewhere, the system of paying garrisons began to break down. If Normandy was to be held, it needed men to reinforce garrisons, and for that the duchy needed money. Yet what money there was, was being diverted into Somerset's purse, as was noted by both Norman chroniclers and York in 1452. Norman writers implied that Somerset reduced the garrisons to the bare minimum, and pocketed the pay of the men for his own gain. The Norman chronicler described York's governorship as a time of justice – a golden age as it were – as opposed to the nature of Somerset's own period in power, dominated by his greed.[40] York, after the events described how Somerset would not use the money he had personally received in compensation for Maine for the upkeep of the defence of Normandy and kept the money 'to his owne use and singular availe'.[41] In earlier years York had to spend his own funds to maintain garrisons: Somerset's lack of altruism and generosity, York believed, led to the loss of Normandy. In this view, another contemporary witness, Archbishop Thomas Basin noted that Somerset's greed overrode his positive characteristics.[42] York was well aware of this in 1448–9 as his chamberlain Sir William Oldhall complained that his rights to the income from the highly lucrative barony of Roncheville were contested by Somerset, who sought to take the revenue for himself. Oldhall failed in his complaint, and Somerset obtained the income, which cannot have endeared him to York's chamberlain.[43] Yet this did not lead to a breach between the two men: the two were in regular contract in new year 1449.[44] The two men were publicly at least on cordial terms. The tipping point was soon reached, however.

Contrary to assertions of historians like Ralph Griffiths, Suffolk did not lead a narrow and corrupt regime that silenced its critics, primarily

Humphrey, duke of Gloucester via assassination and exiling York to Ireland.[45] Such charges only came *after* the French policy failed, and fail it did, but not before 1449. Suffolk operated during an unprecedented constitutional crisis, and despite controlling Henry, he could not prevent others from presenting documents to Henry to sign unless he had the king under house arrest, which was impossible. It was thus inevitable that those around the king would seek to exploit the nullity of their monarch for their own ends. Both churchmen and nobles were able to exploit it, to use financial resources as well as grants and patronage on behalf of their own interests. It also meant that it was inevitable that those gathered around Henry would bicker and divide among themselves when there was no effective monarch to carry out his most essential job of kingship, that of wielding authority. It meant that Suffolk had as many allies and enemies who were willing to exploit the situation to their own advantage.[46] The absurdity of this mode of government is best demonstrated that both Thomas Courtenay, earl of Devon was granted stewardship of the Duchy of Cornwall which was also granted to Sir William Bonville: this was the immediate catalyst to the Courtenay-Bonville feud. A pattern of confrontation developed between the Percys and Nevilles, and between Baron Cromwell and the duke of Buckingham about who was the natural leader of the Duchy of Lancaster: with no duke as natural leader of the vast duchy, division and violence in Derbyshire and Staffordshire driven by political confusion was the outcome.[47]

Chapter 5

# DEFEAT

Despite reeling from the failure in Scotland, and well aware of the massive problems Somerset faced in defending Normandy, incredibly Henry's advisors were still pushing for war in France. Lack of money to finance offensive campaigns to defend the northern border as well as existing gains across the Channel directly influenced English 'foreign policy'. Failure on both counts was driven not by incompetence, but economic necessity. What was incompetent was to believe that a war could be won without adequate money, men and weapons.

Henry's policy in France was the best that could be hoped for in the economic reality that the state found itself in. Close to bankruptcy, a truce with France allowed reductions in military spending and garrisons. It meant that no new taxation was needed. Government could concentrate not on war, but on patronage; the great magnates and nobles were able to concentrate on the governance and organisation of their estates. The truce with France was due not to expire till 1450, and it could have been indefinitely prolonged into the 1460s.

In theory, the breathing space occasioned by the truce – *not* peace remember – should have been used to firmly establish the English in Normandy. Taxes had been voted for 1445–9 which generated a potential surplus, estimated to be about £30,000, to be spent on defence, if so chosen. The treasurer, Marmaduke Lumley, bishop of Carlisle, rather than spending on defence and consolidation, used the surplus to pay crown debts, owed since Beaufort's death and now due to be paid. It meant there was no surplus to pay for war when it came. Compounding this, Henry's household, by now over 800 men and costing over £27,000, was draining the revenue from the Duchy of Lancaster, whose costs since the royal marriage had almost tripled. So too was the £4,000 bill for Eton and King's College Cambridge. It meant new taxes were needed, which the taxpayers were increasingly reluctant to pay: when rebellion came in 1450, it was obvious 'to the man in the street' that taxes were not being used effectively. The garrison at Calais was owed £20,000 in wages: never a good idea not to pay your soldiers, if you want them to fight for you. Lack of leadership from those making a determined attempt to find a workable solution for a non-operational king – with which the nobility was complicit, including both York and Somerset – are at fault. Making matters worse, was the lack of urgency from both Somerset and York in consolidation of Normandy, and the lack of forward planning which hampered any military response to the crisis when it came.

## Fougères

In the wake of Northumberland and Salisbury's debacle at Sark, English military prestige had been lost. To regain both pride and 'to fill the coffers', a scheme that originated in late 1446 or early 1447 was incautiously put into operation. The reasoning was sound enough: in imitation of the Black Prince, a chevauchée would be launched against the border town of Fougères between Normandy and Brittany. One of the wealthiest trading centres, the loot would help pay crown debts and the Calais garrison. Secondly, the sacking would assert English military capabilities in France, and more importantly provide the stepping stone for further interference in the family feud between the dukes of Britanny. This was an internal conflict between England and its vassal, Gilles de Bretagne, and his family, the dukes of Britanny. The English position was emboldened during the renewal of the truce of Le Mans, where the mention of the subservience of the duke of Brittany to the king of England theoretically implied that the Valois could not intervene in Breton politics, even in the case of an English military expedition to the Armorican peninsula. Hence Moleyns and Somerset considered what was being planned as an internal affair and a punitive expedition against acts of Breton piracy. On paper at least, what was being planned, had nothing to do with the French, except of course the duke of Britanny, Francis was a Francophile, and his uncle Richemont – who was briefly duke himself 1457–8 – was constable of France. Incidentally, Richemont's third wife, Catherine of Luxembourg, was sister of Jacquetta, mother of Elizabeth Wydeville, later queen of England. In the heightened tensions of 1449, it was incredibly naïve to think that the duke of Britanny would not involve his ally Charles VII, and exploit the situation to evict the English from France. In trying to withdraw Brittany from its French allegiance, England incurred, naturally enough, the hostility of the Breton nobility who owed their position and pensions to Charles VII.

Brittany's allegiance to France was of paramount importance in the power-play between France and Burgundy. The fault for such naïve thinking that Charles VII would not be involved, lies with all those who governed in Henry's place: collaborative governance requires collective culpability. The launch pad of the chevauchée was to be the contested castle of Saint James de Beuvron which lay 14 miles north-west of Fougères.

On 11 March 1449, Somerset, against warnings from the Norman council not to proceed with the planned attack of Fougères, authorised the attack. Normandy was ill-prepared, lacked soldiers and weapons and moreover many of the castles needed repairs. The council clearly understood the chevauchée could precipitate a war that could not be won.[1] To override sensible and sound advice, Somerset must have been given definitive instructions to proceed by those closest to Henry. Those around Henry were not unanimous in their support either. John Talbot, earl of Shrewsbury, had initially been in full agreement with the plan, but once it had been put in execution, quickly realised the potential for total disaster: expressing deep misgivings, he advised Somerset to abandon his project.[2] It is impossible to know York's own thoughts: he must have been well aware of what was being planned. His failure to mention Fougères in his denunciation of Somerset, implies he, like Warwick and Salisbury, agreed with the plan. York of course later obfuscated the facts.

François de Surienne seized the town and castle of Fougères on 24 March 1449. Surienne took loot to the value of 2,000,000 *livres tournois* – hundreds of millions in 2024 – before establishing himself and his men in the castle.[3] Thomas Basin reports it was a raid motivated by greed.[4] According to Surienne's account of the whole affair, the town was to be used a bargaining chip in order to win the release the Anglophile Gilles de Bretagne from imprisonment by his Francophile brother.[5] Archbishop Thomas Basin noted that 'the audacity of this perpetration of crime' rested with Suffolk and Somerset 'who then were in the chief authority towards the king of the English'. Basin correctly noted, however, that it was those who gathered around Henry who made him give his 'consent and command. For it was feared, as it was discovered, that a total destruction of the truces might result from this . . . all the nobles of the English had praised the plan.'[6]

Basin was well are of the nothingness of Henry, and yet he still was surprised that Henry had agreed to the plan. Basin is quite correct that blame lay not with Suffolk, but with all those seeking to construct a king by proxy. Even despite the sacking, war was not yet inevitable. Greed made it so.

The duke of Brittany demanded Fougères's return and reparations, and when this was not forthcoming, appealed to Charles VII, who took up his cause with enthusiasm. To this end, Charles wrote to Beaufort demanding satisfaction for the seizure of Fougères and gave notice of retaliatory action if Somerset did not hand back the majority of the money and other goods looted from the town.[7] Surienne refused to hand over the city to the Breton authorities and the English, for their part, turned a deaf ear to the complaints of the Breton and French ambassadors, claiming that they were in no way responsible for Surienne's actions.

Furthermore, when pressed, Somerset showed no indication of handing back his loot: quite what happened to it is not clear. A large proportion was appropriated by the household, and a substantial amount found a home in Somerset's own treasury.[8] In retaliation, Robert de Floques, acting on Charles orders launched a raid to the gates of Mantes 30 miles away on 21 April. Floques, with the captain of the garrison of Louviers, Pierre de Brezé, set out with 500 men on the night of 8 May to take the important bridge at Pont-de-l'Arche. In the fighting which followed, on the following day William Neville, lord Fauconberg was captured along with 120 men. The town and its bridge, considered to be the gateway to lower Normandy, were in French hands. The way to Rouen was open. Charles VII outraged demanded from Henry an immediate answer to Somerset's 'outrage at Fougères' and other crimes. If Somerset paid reparations, war would be avoided, if not Charles had no choice but to declare war he warned Henry.[9] Somerset – acting on orders we suppose – refused to hand back the majority of the hard cash and other items he had looted.

Now facing war with France and Britanny, in desperation Somerset demanded aid from Parliament. Reginald Boulers, abbot of Gloucester makes clear that his presentation to Parliament was done so at the king's command, who may have been present. York certainly was:

> The king's uncle has commanded and made known throughout all his obedience that all nobles should prepare themselves to be ready, mounted, armed, and in all ways prepared as is fitting for men of arms, within fifteen days warning, upon pain of forfeiture of all their livelihood; the number of which men is great and inestimable. Also similarly the king's uncle has commanded that it to be proclaimed in every parish of his obedience, under the same penalty of forfeiture, that every 30 men shall provide a man with a horse and armed with a brigandine, and a leg harness, longbow or crossbow, and has expressly ordered that they do nothing other than exercise with their said bows and armour; the number

of such men so armed and arrayed, as is said by credible persons who have reason to know this, exceeds 60,000 men. This is the first part of our credence. The second part is to show that if war should occur, which God forbid, the country of Normandy is in no way sufficient in itself to offer resistance against the great might of the enemies, for many great reasons. First, there is no place in the king's obedience there which is provided for either in terms of repairs, equipment or any kind of artillery. Almost all places have fallen into such ruin that, even where they are full of men and materials, they are in so ruinous a condition that they cannot be defended and held. To make adequate provision for such repairs and equipment would incur inestimable expense.[10]

The abbot then explained why Somerset needed to communicate the position he was in, lest he open himself to criticism later by his silence. He was under no illusion that without money, Normandy would fall. Henry and his inner circle had known much of this since November 1448.[11] Somerset had done as well as he could to place Normandy in a defensible position given the lack of ready cash: he repaired a tower and parts of the castle at Bayeaux during September 1448.[12] He also ordered repairs of Avranches at the same time, which included the casting of a new bombard.[13] He had offered Mantes 200 *livres tournois* on 21 May to repair the defences.[14] But without additional funds to pay men, Somerset could do little.

Facing bankruptcy, all Henry could offer on 27 May, the last day of Parliament, was to revise Somerset's indenture as lieutenant general to reflect the possibility of open war. Hicks tells us when Parliament, which Warwick and his father Salisbury attended, met in mid-June, it approved what happened next, and effectively prevented Somerset from reaching a negotiated settlement.[15] Somerset was to be sent an additional 1,300 troops, due to muster for embarkation on 11 June.[16] For immediate needs, Sir William Peyto with 55 men-at-arms and 408 archers were dispatched at the end of July.[17] Parliament agreed to send a larger force to reinforce Somerset: 3,400 men under the veteran Sir Thomas Kyriell were to be sent to France. However, lacking the ability to quickly raise the necessary money to pay for men, weapons and equipment, the force was not ready to depart till 9 March 1450.[18] The late payment of the army was what probably prompted troops, on the verge of mutiny and who had had to resort to theft to feed themselves, to murder Adam Moleyns, the royal paymaster, in Portsmouth on 9 January 1450. These men were led by Cuthbert Colville, one of Kyriell's captains.[19] Perhaps significantly, Colville, who was charged by the Court of King's Bench as an accessory to murder, had formerly been in York's service in Normandy.[20] Colville left Portsmouth three weeks after the murder and headed to Winchester, raising a revolt at South Waltham against Suffolk.[21] Colville's own uprising was part of a swathe of discontent, known as Cade's Rebellion, which we come to shortly.

*\*\**

On the front line, Somerset's hands were tied by instructions from Parliament and men like the earl of Warwick, Moleyns and others. At the conference at Louviers held from 24 to 29 June 1449, the English ambassadors refused to deal with the French over the question of Fougères, claiming that the town belonged to a subject of Henry VI – Gilles de Bretagne – and in consequence the French ambassadors would therefore need a special mandate from the overlord, Henry VI, to negotiate. Somerset, more likely operating as he had been instructed to do, then made a fatal mistake: rather than returning the loot as asked by Charles VII, he requested that the English negotiators demanded reparations from the French for their abuses committed in Normandy, in particular those carried out against the town of Pont de l'Arche. Adding insult to injury, Somerset's men asked the French for the release of Gilles de Bretagne, knowing full well that Charles would not consent.[22] Unsurprisingly, the French ambassadors noted:

> Because also the people of the said Duke of Somerset have striven to make the duchy of Brittany contentious, which is one of the greatest matters and which most affects the king who can hardly have a future in this kingdom, by which many argue that whatever words of truce or peace that the said duke may have said, that he does not really want to come to the right conclusion.[23]

With hindsight, the right conclusion was to hand back the town and the loot and keep to the truce. Yet Parliament and those around Henry did not see it that way: it was not the capture of Fougères that triggered the resumption of the Hundred Years War but rather the dispute over the vassalage of Brittany, as Thomas Basin observed at the time.[24] War was now inevitable, despite the English being totally unprepared to fight. A contemporary noted:

> there is no doubt that the truces by them [the English] were broken, and even that, how much they were summoned, as said is, to repair and amend everything, of whom they did nothing, pretending to do nothing; . . . And it was lawful for you [Charles VII], for your people, for all good reasons, to wage war against them.[25]

On 16 July, Charles VII had made clear his intention to reopen the conflict if Fougères was not returned by the end of the month: Henry refused, and war was declared on 31 July.[26] Even before a formal declaration of war, Verneuil was attacked on 20 July: the garrison retreated to the citadel. Somerset despatched Talbot to lift the siege, and he arrived at Breteuil ten days later. Rather than attacking, his army swung north to Harcout, where he prepared to give battle on 2 August. But rather than give battle, he retreated to Rouen, where he arrived two days later. York's lieutenant, Thomas Kirkeby at Liseux had appealed for aid from Somerset on 13 August. Either unable to respond or unwilling, Somerset sent no aid. Kirkeby surrendered three days later. The agreement negotiated at Liseux by Archbishop Basin ended any resistance in the *vicomte* of Orbec.[27] The same situation was played out at Mantes: the town council appealed to Somerset in Rouen for help. With no reply from Somerset, the town council resolved on 20 August to surrender.[28] The town capitulated on 26 August.[29]

Somerset's failure to take an army into the field undermined the English position. He was prepared to see towns and castles fall, which had been left to their own defences, rather than risk Rouen. His strategy was naïve at best.[30] York in 1452 felt Somerset acted dishonourably and was, perhaps, a coward:

> the Duc of Somersett wold yeve noo counseile, aide ne helpe unto the capitains of diverse stronge places and garnisons which at that tyme, constreyned by nede, desired of hym provision and relief for abillement of werre to resiste the malice of their enemyes daily makyng fressh feetes of werre uppon theym; he gevyng theym noone aide nor help, but lete theym contynue in theire malice, howe be it that diverse places were lost before: and what tyme that the said places were beseged and sent for help and socour unto hym he wold graunte no maner of conforte, but suffred hem appoint and compounde with here enemyes as well as they myght for their ease and suretee, makyng no maner of provision for the kepyng of the places which remained.[31]

Somerset was vastly outnumbered and prepared Rouen for siege, but surrendered on 29 October.[32] York, as captain of Rouen, was highly critical of Somerset:

> insomuch that he made non ordinaunce nor provision for the town, castell, and places of Rouen, neither of men, stuffe ne vitaile, the knowlage that he had of youre enemyes comyng thereunto notwith stondyng, yevyng licence unto the Archiebisshopp, chanons and burgeys of the same toun for to goo or sende to compounde with youre enemyes for

the deliveraunce of the same . . . plainly ayeinst his promys, feith and liegeaunce that he of right oweth unto you, and ayeinst the tenure of the endentures made betwix youre highnes and hym of the charge of that londe, the which licence, and it had not ben don, the seid toun had abiden undre youre obeisaunce, the losse of whiche was a verray cause of the perdicion of Normandie.[33]

For York, it was treasonable that Somerset had surrendered Rouen without a siege: Somerset had gathered all available troops the town, and then failed to resist. York's charge 'never grained traction' against Somerset. Somerset had put up an albeit woeful bombardment of the French on 22 October, and then the following day began negotiations to surrender, perhaps a token gesture to fend off later criticism.[34] Important in this debacle, is who was captain of Rouen. If a town was surrendered with little or no fight, under codes of chivalry, the captain was dishonoured even if he was not present: the duke of York was captain of Rouen. By not putting up more than a 'token gesture' of defiance, Somerset had dishonoured York. It was extremely unlikely that Somerset surrendered to provoke and dishonour York. Upholding personal honour was of importance to York; his own father had been tried and executed on charges of treason in 1415. Somerset fell back to Caen. Normandy was lost, and with-it huge swathes of the duke of York's lands, and of those in his retinue.

Kyriell's army landed on 15 March 1450, much too little too late. In a pitched battle at Formigny, 5,000 English faced perhaps 4,000 French on 15 April. The outcome was a total disaster. Kyriell was captured and casualties amongst his armed in dead, wounded and prisoners amounted to more than 50 per cent. Vire fell soon after and Bayeaux on 16 May. Charles VII and his Breton allies invested Caen. Somerset again chose to negotiate, and Charles entered on 6 July. Somerset and what remained of his destitute and starving army arrived in London on 1 August.[35] He retained the full support of those acting in Henry's name: as a collective they had all agreed to the plan, each man was as guilty as the next.

## Ireland
What of York? Since Talbot (1387–1453), earl of Shrewsbury and of Waterford, had left Ireland in 1447, there had been no direct governance. York governed by proxy. Talbot had been in Ireland since October 1446 and again campaigned vigorously against intransigent Gaelic lords, and extracted several submissions. He returned to England in October 1447 after the truce with France broke down at the

end of the campaign. James Butler (c.1390–1452), 4th earl of Ormond, York's proxy, arrived in 1448 to settle the disputes that had arisen within his own lordship, which had the potential to engulf Ireland. The destabilising Talbot–Ormond feud, the origins of which dated back to 1414, ended with Butler's summons to England to face treason charges. These charges eventually led to a trial by combat between Butler and Thomas FitzGerald, prior of Kilmainham, although the matter was postponed several times. The issue dragged on for three years before Butler was acquitted in September 1447 by royal decree. Knowing, this, York chose to remain close to Henry and the centre of power.

York had sat in the sessions of Parliament, where he had listened to Somerset's report about the almost defenceless state of Normandy. Amidst the 'phoney war' that had existed since the sack and capture of Fougères, two of the king's sergeants-at-arms and others were commissioned on 16 April to organise ships to transport the duke and his entourage to Ireland.[36] This was roughly three weeks before Pont-de-l'Arche fell. Why? Had the duke realised that France was already all but lost and sought to distance himself from repercussions? Possibly. It is also possibly, that with rising tensions in Ireland York was ordered to Ireland: in the wake of the debacle at Sark, a third conflict zone in Ireland was the last thing those around Henry needed to be concerned with. Thus, it made sense to dispatch York to Ireland to 'knock heads together'. Parliament was prorogued on 30 May and was to meet again in Winchester on 16 June. Parliament ended on 16 July. If York attended, he can only have been present for the opening session, he sailed for Ireland from Beaumaris on 22 June.[37]

Whatever his own thoughts on the situation in France – and historians have ably filled the void with speculation – Richard was in Ireland by 6 July 1449 and was initially successful in winning support from both Irish and English magnates. During late July and into August, York led a small expedition into Leinster, an army of around 600 men raised and paid for by the crown. His main goal was to reassert the position of the earl of Ulster with respect to the Gaelic lords of Ulster, especially Eóghan Ó Néill at Drogheda 27 August 1449. York then led his forces to restore order in Kilkenny and Tipperary. A Great Council was assembled on 17 October for the purpose of binding new allies to the crown and planning a new campaign in spring 1450.[38]

On this evidence, it seems reasonable to suppose that York headed to Ireland to keep the peace rather than to avoid any repercussions from the fall of Normandy. Furthermore, there is no evidence that a major breach between York, Henry VI and Queen Margaret existed at this point. Indeed, as Dr Laynesmith notes, among the queen's expenses for 1449 was a gift of 66s 8d to Duchess Cecily's servants as a reward for taking a New Year gift to her. Similar sums were handed to the servants of the duchesses of Bedford, Buckingham and Exeter, Anne Montague. In 1448, it was Duke Richard's servants who had been so rewarded.[39] If any rift existed, it was not made public and the reported existence of such a rift, like the banishment theory, is reasonably, the application of Yorkist propaganda backwards in time to explain why armed confrontation came about. Because we know conflict did happen means it colours our reading of sources and understanding of events and the timeline to war. We have to judge the events of the period as they unfolded and try to ignore – or at least place to one side – the history of the period. In 1449 no one knew, or could have even guess, that the leading peers of the realm would be trying to exterminate one another within five years.

York became a father again on 21 October 1449, when Cecily gave birth to a son, George. He was baptised at Dublin's Dominican friary in the presence of James FitzGerald and James Butler, earl of Ormond as godfathers, to cement peace. Such optimism was short lived. Aware that he was desperately short of funds, York wrote to Henry VI in early May 1450. Henry responded on 17 May granting 4,700 marks, but not money was forthcoming. His agreement with the O'Neills had brought little advantage, but rather than being on the offensive, York was placed on the defensive.[40] In early summer 1450 York expressed his feelings to earl of Salisbury that he would rather be dead than blamed for the loss of Ireland. With no revenue, and no pay, governance of Ireland ground to a halt.[41]

Chapter 6

# INTO OPPOSITION

The fall of Rouen and Normandy triggered a wave of popular protest, known in part as Cade's Rebellion: this was one of the most serious uprisings since the peasants' revolts. The disasters in Scotland and France threatened to bring down the whole regime. Whilst Henry VI was internally insecure, foreign powers could and would exploit the situation. France had taken priority from 1440–7, and then Northumberland, in seeking to regain lost ancestral lands, had become drawn into a border conflict, and in doing so inherently destabilised the North and drew fiscal and military resources away from France. It can be argued, as Parliament did, that in the wake of Northumberland's failure, Scotland had to take priority over France in 1448, and led directly to failure of foreign policy in France. The great lords of the East and West March had failed. The lack of internal security would be exploited in coming years, and was not resolved until the coming of the Tudors.

Failure in the North had led to failure in France. Henry had no option but to recall Parliament: unable to defend Normandy, Parliament was needed to levy new taxes. It provided a platform for attacks on the government that were unprecedented since the 1380s. The gentry and nobles alike who had been paying taxes, voting and attending Parliament had a reasonable expectation of responsible government. Cade's Rebellion was the most serious uprising since 1381, and by April, it seemed that the government had lost control of London, and Parliament was called to reassemble in Leicester at the end of the month.[1]

For York, and the writers of Cade's manifestos, the blame for the ills affecting the country was obvious: the royal household and 'evil councillors'. Access to the king was controlled by the household; access to the king meant gaining access to the source of power in the kingdom, those ruling in Henry's place. This group included Adam Moleyns, bishop of Chichester, Bishop Aiscough of Salisbury, Ralph Boteler Baron Sudeley, the Lord Chamberlain and former Lord High Treasurer, John Beauchamp, 1st Baron Beauchamp of Powick, James Ffiennes Lord Say, John Beaumont,[2] and John Sutton. Suffolk had marred into the Beauforts, and was heir to their interest. Sudeley and Beauchamp were opposed to Suffolk's appeasement policy, Beaumont had been present at the arrest of the duke of Gloucester.[3] We note, that Richard Neville, earl of Salisbury had also participated in Gloucester's arrest: the house of Neville was allied with Suffolk and supported both his governance and policy decisions, ratified by others. York too had been that the 1447 Parliament at Bury St Edmunds in March. York and Salisbury were not outsiders looking in: they backed peace with France as the only pragmatic solution. They redacted their own personal history later to suit their own political ends: the victors write the history, and it is this biased Yorkist history which has come down to us. The Yorkist propaganda of being allies of 'good duke Humphrey' in the 1450s was just that.

It was culturally and politically impossible to lay the blame the loss of Normandy on Henry VI: he *must* have been given bad counsel by traitors. As Carpenter notes, those acting in Henry's name 'were confronted by the fact that they had made a series of decisions, or at least agreed to them, each one inexorably dictated by the last, that had led to total disaster in France, and that the nation was now calling for heads to roll'.[4] For the rebels it was obvious who was to blame and demanded that Henry 'take about him a noble person, the true blood of the realm, that is to say the high and mighty prince the duke of York, late exiled from our sovereign lord's presence by the false traitor Suffolk and his affinity'.[5]

For those who had been involved in government, they had found their scapegoat: Suffolk was not of the ancient nobility – almost no one around Henry since Gloucester's death was either – of whom York was the greatest, and it was Suffolk's lack of royal blood that had led to disaster. It was the perfect 'get-out clause'.

It was only princes of the royal blood who could save the situation, the commonweal demanded, which shows the power the concept of monarchy still held in setting persons apart and above others. An almost contemporary text the *Book of Fayttes of Armes and Chyvalrye* declares that 'Prynces soverayne . . . for none other thing were establysshed but for to doo right to everche of their sugettis that shold be oppressed for only extorcion and for to deffende and kepe them'. The writer adds 'ffor a kyng is a but a man sould . . . He may erre and mistake. . . Where-as good counsail may exclude [all] Wrong.'[6] One of the functions of the king was to impart virtuousness in rule and character on his council. That Henry was failed to do so – his evil councillors remained unchanged in their virtue in acting against the good of the commonweal and kingdom – showed his weakness in both character and personality. If Henry was ruling not for the common good, but moreover for the good of those closest to him, as Cade's manifesto hinted at and York stated, a new model concerning the conception of kingship was needed and from whence monarchy derived its authority.[7]

It was now that Suffolk's mode of governance, the only workable solution, showed its true weakness. Those gathered around Henry had pretensions to authority that was not theirs: their right to rule in the name of the king was a usurpation of the king's jurisdiction. In giving bad counsel, they had failed to be virtuous. The solution was the forceful assertion of rule to prevent the dominance of overmighty subjects. The argument went both ways. Factionalism became embedded in the body politic. In challenging Suffolk, York laid himself open to the same crime he accused Suffolk of. At this stage, the obvious solution, removing Henry, was not considered. That Henry was no way blamed in this, or became the target of public censure and opposition as Edward II and Richard II had become, recognises Henry's own weakness and that the leading subjects were well aware of Henry's limitations, and moreover that his personal authority was unconvincing. Governance was in his name, but not through his will. Henry was unable to convince the commonweal – and government critics – that his ministers were acting on his instructions. Clearly, with power dispersed among leading nobles and magnates, it was understandable that the commonweal looked for a champion and vented its anger against those it felt were responsible for the calamitous situation that had evolved since 1447.

Foreign policy had not been Suffolk's alone, and the fact that Suffolk had succeeded in 'keeping the show on the road', an almost impossible task, speaks well of his abilities, yet when Parliament opened on 6 November, he was accused of treason and collusion with the French. Those governing in Henry's place refused to accept collective responsibility. Suffolk faced his critics on 22 January 1450: he was placed in the Tower. On 29 January he was put on trial, but the king stopped the proceedings: Suffolk was to be exiled for five years. Suffolk became the sacrificial victim. He had won as many enemies as friends: his enemies were quick to blame him for all the ills the country faced. Found guilty by 'the man in the street' for the loss of Normandy, he was murdered trying leave the country on 2 May.[8] Shortly before his departure, Suffolk wrote to his son John de la Pole and entreated him to honour the de la Pole family's fealty to Henry VI:

> . . . above alle erthely thing . . . be trewe liege man in hert, in wille, in thought, in dede, unto the Kyng oure alder most high and dredde sovereygne Lord, to whom bothe ye and I been so moche bounde to; chargyng you, as fader can and may, rather to die than to be the contrarye, or to know any thyng that were ayenste the welfare of prosperite of his most riall person, but that as ferre as your body and lyf may stretche, ye lyve and die to defende it.[9]

Loyalty was a sense of obligation and not command, Pole told his son. John would marry a daughter of the duke of York in 1458.

With Suffolk dead and the new duke of Somerset tainted by association with his dishonoured brother and by his own actions, the man to fill the vacuum at the heart of government and to take up vacant royal authority of was the duke of York. With the king a nullity, the obvious solution to the vacuum in government was a new king: with no son, both Beaufort and York appeared as candidates. Recognising this tension, politics would shift uneasily from the preservation of unity under a sham king to utter disunity as two factions sought to fill the void of Henry.[10]

On 29 June, the mob murdered the bishop of Salisbury, William Aiscough, at Edington. Taken into consort with other attacks made against Henry's councillors, it led the suspicion that a broad-based conspiracy was being executed against the king's inner circle, linked to York.[11] The rebels were in London between 3 and 7 July. As we said earlier, the duke of York, then in Ireland, was seen as the panacea for all ills by rioters in East Anglia, London and the Midlands and the only man able to root out traitors who had badly advised the king.[12]

Yet York was in Ireland, and there was little he could actually do. Somerset was at hand, and stepped into the breach in government on Suffolk's fall. As John Watts succinctly notes, 'the duke's emergence as the king's chief minister within a few weeks of his return must have confirmed public impressions of a link between domestic corruption and defeat in France'.[13]

Henry's government, now headed by Somerset, responded in force: the nominal leader Cade was captured at Heathfield on 12 July and died of wounds soon after. With Henry and his council's attention focused on domestic affairs, Cherbourg, the last English possession, fell on 12 August 1450. Despite his culpability in the loss of Normandy, on returning to England Somerset found that his actions in propping

up the crown had assuaged him of any culpability in the fall of
Normandy: he quickly exploited the absence of York and the power
vacuum around Henry. He was appointed constable of England on 11
September and captain of Calais on 21 September.

## York's return

In Ireland, York had found a country on the brink of civil unrest, if
not outright war, but also one in economic distress, which meant the
duke was unable to meet any demands for troops in case insurrection.
In a letter which York sent from Dublin to his brother-in-law, the earl
of Salisbury, on 15 July 1450, he outlined his fears of insurrection in
Ireland and the lack of royal response to his request for aid: Henry
had no money to pay troops to send to Ireland. The duke was clearly
unaware that the Parliamentary session at Leicester had ended six
months earlier in November 1449 – he had not been called to the session
as he was in Ireland – as he wanted Salisbury to raise the matter at
Parliament. Hicks suggests, the duke 'wanted his letter to Salisbury
formally registered on the Parliament roll to exculpate himself from
any unfortunate consequences. He wished to avoid the sort of charges
being levied against those responsible for events leading up to the loss
of Lancastrian France.'[14] As the letter arrived too late to be registered,
it is possible that the duke returned to make his case in person, less
any slander or dishonour be attached to his name. Aware of the fate
of his father in 1415, York no doubt felt he needed to 'explain himself'
in person and demonstrate he had no links to Cade's Rebellion.
Supporting this hypothesis, contrary to the legends surrounding this
event, we note writs of summons for Parliament had had been issued
on 5 September before York's first bill of complaint was received by
Henry VI. Therefore, it seems extremely unlikely that the decision to
call a Parliament was specifically influenced by news of the duke's
impending return from Ireland: no one knew he was returning. Indeed,
it is more likely that York returned in full knowledge that a Parliament
would soon be called – and to which he was called – which would give
him the opportunity to present his concerns that he had expressed to
Salisbury over Ireland in person to Henry and to Parliament. York had
left Dublin soon after 28 August 1450, and landed in Wales around
7/8 September.[15] In the wake of Cade's Rebellion and Suffolk's death,
public interest in the Parliament was substantial, so much so that the
king and the lords anticipated the assembly to trigger further trouble.
York's return 'looked and smelled like trouble'.[16]

The problem York faced, having made up his mind to return and as
a prince of royal blood, and therefore the only natural arbitrator of the

nation's destiny, was that Somerset had already claimed that position using, by and large, the same argument. Somerset was the king's closest blood relative through the male line. Moreover, unlike York, Somerset was not the son of a traitor. Having lost Maine, Somerset had a vested interest in controlling Henry: he had no vast landed estates. The lost Beaufort inheritance in Maine gave him good reason to control the king to control grants, land and prestige. By not having to spend time on his estates tending to justice and administration like York, Somerset could afford to give Henry almost constant personal attention.[17]

York's exact agenda on his return and his motivation for embroiling himself in politics have been matters of much debate by historians. York knew from experience that Henry was a nonentity, and he donned the mantle offered to him by the rebellion. Had York planed this course of action before returning to Ireland? Possibly. He sought to exploit the demands made by Cade's rebels and also to find support from those who had 'raised an eyebrow' at Somerset taking over government in the wake of the disaster of France. York backed their call and adopted their campaign as his own. In doing so, he deliberately retrospectively allied himself with Humphrey, duke of Gloucester and distanced himself from his own agreement with, and co-operation with, Suffolk. Lacking a political following in England – his power base had been in France and Ireland – York was able to show himself as independent of the failed nobility, and rather than speaking for the nobility sought and articulated for the gentry and commonweal. It could be wrong to assume York was totally self-serving in his return: as a great landowner he needed a strong body politic to manage the ship of state to enable him to administer his lands effectively.

As York headed from Beaumaris, which he left about 28 August, his progress was slow as he was again intercepted by agents of Henry VI. He was at Denbigh by 7 September, found his journey obstructed when trying to pass through Chester and again at Shrewsbury on 12 September. York was almost excessively conscious of being seen to be loyal. His father's treason hung uneasily over his head like a sword of Damocles, as we noted earlier. In a letter drafted sometime before 12 September York publicly pledged his allegiance to Henry on his march from Wales. It may have been a formal supplication of loyalty. It is hard to say what his motives were, but from the duke's later statements, it was clear that he was both 'testing the waters' in sounding out government over the limits of its authority, and secondly, he needed to establish his loyalty to Henry. This latter point was important, as it meant York could shape his own narrative as offering advice at the side of the king and the commonweal against the 'traitors' who had given the king bad counsel that led to the loss of France.[18] In a second letter to Henry, he provided the king with additional details of the slanders and named the individuals who had attempted to arrest him at his landing at Beaumaris in north Wales. York alleges that he was to be arrested and gaoled in Conway Castle, and his chamberlain, Oldhall, was to be executed.[19]

The statement by York superficially correlates with two charges brought against Oldhall. The first charge related that on 16 March 1450, n the company of Sir William Ashton, John Framlingham and others at Bury St Edmunds, Oldhall plotted to murder Henry, the duke of Suffolk, the bishops of Salisbury and Chichester and other lords for the loss of Normandy and that York should seize the throne.[20] The second charge against Oldhall, was that he had precipitated Cade's Rebellion in concert with the duke of York.[21] Again, we note Sir William Ashton was charged on 12 April of raising the commons of Bury St Edmunds to support Cade.[22] Oldhall certainly had a grievance against Somerset, but how far he prompted Cade's Rebellion with York's blessing is unknown. Certainly, York was of the opinion by summer 1450 that attempts had been made – Somerset certainly laid these charges in 1452, but suggesting he orchestrated the charges two years earlier is stretching the limited evidence too far – to arrest him for treason. York, fairly reasonably, demanded the king examine the charges against him, Oldhall and others.

## York's bid for power

Before late November, it is extremely unlikely that Henry, or anyone else for that matter, anticipated that York would aim to assert his position against the king's 'favourites' and in particular against Somerset. Yet it is undeniable that some of those close to Henry considered York guilty of treason for his conduct in Ireland, and guilty of propagating Cade's Rebellion through Oldhall, and prevented him meeting the king, despite York's protestations of loyalty directly to Henry.[23]

The king, or more likely Cardinal Kemp, replied to York's grievances over the attempted arrest of Oldhall and himself and in doing so exposed the weakness of the regime. The king – Kemp – told the duke that because his name had been associated with the murder of Moleyns, and moreover as Cade's rebels had identified him as their de facto leader, many nobles and magnates had acted on their own initiative in the king's name – in essence being free to usurp royal jurisdiction – to arrest the duke and those they felt guilty of Moleyns' murder, and moreover inciting the rebellion. If Henry had been an active king, ruling with consent and partnership of the nobles and magnates, it is doubtful that this degree of factionalism or usurpation of royal authority would have arisen.

In the wake of this revelation, York, aware that government was not properly authorised by the king, in an opportunistic bid to continue the support from the commonweal, transformed his personal grievances into general criticism of the regime, in a bid for power. York, as a prince of the royal blood, felt he had a personal responsibility to restore government.[24]

In this, he was backed by John Mowbray, 3rd duke of Norfolk (1415–61). He, like York, had been named by Cade's Rebellion as one of the king's 'natural councillors necessary to reform the realm. Norfolk transformed his personal animosity with Suffolk and Somerset into a national cause.[25] It is hard to say 'who was in the driving seat': both men were seeking personal aggrandisement and to have a direct stake in how the country was governed. Norfolk had a proven track record of being a destabilising influence in his county and was little more than a 'disreputable thug'.[26] By stressing his loyalty, York embraced Cade's thesis and made it clear that the regime was discredited. In doing so York was able to weaponise Cade's Rebellion against Henry: it's very occurrence was proof of 'treason' at the heart of the regime. York, posing as the champion of the commonweal, and after months of rioting, understood he was the only man able to restore justice.[27] York's offer to act for the king and to root out the alleged 'traitors' was not acceptable to those who ruled through Henry. It was a veiled attempt to supplant Somerset. If York had succeeded, the men who had benefited from acting in the name of the king would be sidelined. This was unacceptable not only to Somerset but all those around Henry.[28]

To be fair to York, Suffolk's form of governance had failed; the nobility had failed. Change was needed. For those in power change had happened, and Somerset was the 'new broom'. Indeed, most of the nobles did not see York as a saviour – the Nevilles for example were happily linked to the court – on the contrary, whilst personal gain could be made, the status quo was to be maintained at all costs. Somerset had stepped into the power vacuum when the king had fled London in face of the rebels, and in doing so had won over the nobility and rid himself of any guilt for the loss of Normandy. York and Norfolk represented not the nobility, but the gentry, squirearchy and merchants, a more important grouping economically than the nobles. Moreover, in the shires, the immediate overlord – the lord of the manor – was owed more loyalty than the king. Local relationships and patronage were, it can be argued, more important than the patronage between nobles. We will come back to this later. York and Norfolk claiming to represent the commonweal was something that had not been tried since 1381, and were able to present themselves as representing a legitimate oppositional body. However, in adopting this position, both men had to be careful in case their support for the commonweal was seen as support for Cade's rebels, i.e. the mob. By September, both York and Somerset had backed themselves into opposite corners, from which neither could leave without considerable loss of face, or the destruction of the other.[29]

York arrived in London by 27 September and according to the Act of Attainder at Coventry in 1459 was backed by an army: contemporary chroniclers give the numbers as between 3,000 and 5,000 men.[30] Between his entry and 6 October, York submitted another bill to Henry. Unlike the earlier missives, York no longer dwelt on personal affronts, instead York noted heightened widespread concerns about the execution of justice, and urged the immediate arrest of those who were held to blame, offering his own services 'for to execute your comaundements in these premises of suche offenders and redresse of the seid mysrewlers'.[31] The presentation of the bill was bolstered by York's display of armed force and also public support. York demanded that the royal servants identified as traitors by Cade's Rebellion be punished for their misdeeds: York set out to purge the most unpopular members of the king's household and council, top of the list being Somerset.[32] The king, as sovereign, had freedom to appoint his own advisors; in demanding their dismissal and punishment York was directly challenging the king's authority.

The king answered some of the duke's requests. Henry – likely Kemp – reassured York as 'our trewe and faithful subiecte and as oure weel bilovid cosyn'. Henry also informed the duke that he would follow the duke's guidance on 'settyng up of iustice and spede punyschyng of certayn persons endited or noysed', and said that the king had decided to set up a 'sad and substantial consaile' of which York would be a member, but not leader. In his reply to York, Henry emphasised that action was to be taken against those accused of treason and misgovernance on collective advice of the chancellor and lords. In reinforcing a collective approach, rather than one led by York, Henry and his inner circle hoped to dissuade York from any ambition to lead a personal crusade against the alleged traitors.[33] Henry emphatically reaffirmed the authority of his government, and was ready to contemplate summoning the chancellor and the other lords to contemplate upon 'thise and other oure grete matieres'. Henry – Kemp more than likely – in acting in such an assertive manner, raised the possibility that the events leading up to the loss of Normandy and other policies in the 1440s had been his responsibility alone, and thus exonerated his ministers from being 'traitors'. The king was immune from allegations of treason. In raising this possibility, Kemp had passed collective responsibility to the king, and exonerated them of any wrongdoing. The result of this was that York was outmanoeuvred politically: despite his protests of loyalty, his actions had been seen as those of a troublemaker working against the best interest of the crown and regime. York's opportunism was barely concealed: York condemned Suffolk for narrow governance, and promptly suggested he replace Suffolk and act in a similar manner: his cognitive dissonance and ego left him wide open to being outmanoeuvred in exactly the manner we assume Kemp had done.[34] York left London for East Anglia on 9 October.

Having lost their first bid for power, York and Norfolk were prepared to escalate the situation. York's next bill made it clear that reform of government and punishment for abuses of power was insufficient retribution against those he held responsible for the loss of France. A reform of abuses did not go far enough: York was now determined to bring down the existing regime and remove its principal members from power. Somerset was now wanted by York. He was not named at this stage, but implicated along with the murdered Suffolk, Aiscough, and Moleyns.[35] York called upon the 'trewe lorids' to accept their responsibilities, and acknowledge that men around the king of low birth, had been responsible for the loss of France and the resulting rebellion. He demanded that justice was to be done as the sole remedy to pacify the angry commons. York made it clear that it was through the active or passive support of these 'low born' traitors – Somerset was a legitimised bastard we remember– by the lords, and sought to remove those from royal authority, those who he held responsible for usurpation of the king's authority. York was pressing the king and council to actually carry out its promise to remove the 'traitors' as he understood them to be, leaving the judgement of culpability to the judges and commissioners as the king may appoint. The judgement that Suffolk, Somerset and others were innocent because the king had been fully in control of government rang very hollow: York was well aware of the nothingness of Henry, but other than take up arms, he had been outmanouvred and 'had backed himself into a corner'.[36] York was now 'on the outside looking in' to government. For Somerset, Kemp and the nobility, York was tarred 'with the brush of traitorous incitement of the commons'.[37]

York's actions were his first attempt to show himself as *the* competent leader who alone was able to restore national finances and also national prestige. York sought to remove what he deemed to be the corrupt officers of state as both an appeal to Henry VI to show his loyalty, but moreover, to appeal to his fellow lords and the wider public. He had the backing of the commonweal, but failed to win leading magnates and lords to his cause. York and Norfolk had two options: accept defeat and the king's judgement or 'ramp up the pressure' on Henry. Never a man to compromise, the duke deliberately escalated the situation. York could have stepped back at this point in October 1450; he chose not to. Believing that he could 'do a better job' than the king and his circle, York's ego and self-belief drove him forward. No one knew better than he how to solve the problems facing the country: yet he had little basis for this other than hubris and a lust for power.

Chapter 7

# THE ROAD TO REBELLION

Having lost the first confrontation with Henry, for York to persevere with his line of attack and censure was to be marked as a traitor. He now sought to harness public anger to impugn the credibility of the regime: he sought to raise the commonweal like John Ball had done in 1381 to bring about concessions from the king.

York and his main ally, the duke of Norfolk, were at Bury St Edmunds on 15–16 October 1450. Writing from Framlingham on 22 October, Norfolk ordered John Paston to 'make you redy to awayte upon us at Yppiswich toward the parlement the vii day of Novembre in youre best array with as many clenly people as ye may gete for oure worship at this tyme'.[1] From here they proceeded to Fotheringhay, and on to Ludlow, arriving there on 5 November. During the progress, popular demonstrations against Somerset erupted, which were exceptionally likely to have had York's blessing. In Grantham, Lincolnshire, on 26 November, Somerset's house in the town was ransacked.[2] A few days later, some of Norfolk's men, identified as coming from Framlingham, attacked Somerset's property in Sidbury, Lincolnshire, removing silver plate and destroying worsted cloth.[3] At Corfe Castle in Dorset – Somerset's chief residence in the county – tenants of the duke of York attacked the castle and removed property, which Somerset alleged was worth 1,000 marks. He also levelled charges that York's men beat and maimed his servants during the attack.[4] One of York's key allies, Sir John Fastolf, drew up charges against Somerset for the loss of Normandy, which included premature surrender of Rouen, embezzlement of money from garrisons and the disappearance of the money from Fougères. He intimated that the money was in Somerset's own treasury. All three charges had the 'ring of truth' about them, and were impeachable offences, that Henry chose to overlook.[5] Indeed, Henry had ordered Somerset to ride into Kent to crush a further rebellion and restore order.[6] Somerset was at Council with Henry on 27 October, while York and Norfolk were missing.[7]

Parliament assembled on 6 November. York was absent, so too his ally Norfolk. In hindsight this was significant. The Commons chose as Speaker Sir William Oldhall, who had served under the duke in France in 1441, and who from 1444, if not earlier, had served as York's chamberlain and had been with him at least for some time in Ireland. Oldhall's appointment was significant in what happened next: York was planning a coup d'etat.

A contemporary writer observed (my translation from the German):

> And now on Monday shall begin Parliament, may God grant it to be good. London has fortified all the lanes with iron chains for the lords are not yet in agreement and the city is worried about a riot. They say here that the lord of York will come to London with more than 40,000 men and the duke of Norfolk will join him with more than 20,000 men, and the earl of Devon[8] will join them with more than 20,000 men. So will the prince of Exeter,[9] his grandmother was the sister of Henry IV, the king's grandfather, but he has [married] the prince of York's daughter; and also the old earl of Salisbury will come with great retinue, and the earl of Arundel[10] with great retinue, and the earl of Salisbury's son who has married the pious prince of Warwick's sister and is therefore earl of Warwick, and also the earl of Northumberland[11] will come with great retinue; they all favour the prince of York, and all the commons with them. On the other side are dukes of Buckingham and Somerset and others with the king.[12]

Violence was clearly anticipated: Norfolk, York and the earl of Devon were appointed to maintain law and order in the City of London for the duration of the Parliament by Oldhall.[13] That York planned a coup is implied by a merchant writing on 8 November, who confessed:

> I am worried, they are not yet agreed, there will be bloody heads yet . . . now that my lord of York has returned to England, I hope that now in this Parliament by the faithful prince of York the thistles may be pulled up from the good corn, for of the Council four princes have died in four years, namely my lord King's father's brother the prince of Gloucester, the pious prince of Somerset, the prince of Exeter, the young lord's father, and the faithful pious prince of Warwick, whom I hope God will avenge and has therefore plagued the land badly. Therefore, gracious lord your grace need not wonder that your fellow subjects and other travelling people come to harm here in England, if even such pious lords and even such as are of the King's blood die through such

false counsellors. And the King cannot be blamed, for he is a young and inexperienced lord, and he is kept sheltered like a Carthusian, I hope that in the negotiations everything shall be set right again, as it is I shall write to your grace.[14]

It seemingly was already common knowledge that the king was unable to act with full royal authority, and the merchant goes on to say on 15 November that York sought to use his position himself as an ally of Humphrey, duke of Gloucester in a daring attempt at realpolitik to woo a new power base:

Parliament began, in that also was entered a schedule by the Commons of England and the servants of the noble prince of York and also by servants and faithful of the noble prince of Gloucester desiring justice for the traitors who killed him so shamefully and were of counsel thereto. This has now been delayed until the noble prince of York comes with him of Norfolk and with Arundel and Northumberland and Devon; they have not arrived yet. When they come, may God give that they make all things well.[15]

As our writer alludes to, York entered London on 23 November with an army at his back, he himself bearing his sword upright in the manner of a king. His intent was obvious. Norfolk entered London on the following day, again accompanied by a large armed force.[16] According to Bale's Chronicle, York and his armed retinue went directly to Parliament and the king.[17] That York and Norfolk arrived in London with a substantial armed retinue at Dartford and Camberwell is referenced in that it consumed 999 sheep and 80 beef cattle over a period of ten days. That York had tight control on these men is evidenced that no recorded incidence of them looting for supplies was lodged: the duke was well aware that any hint of disorder would cost him popular and political support.[18]

York had tied his cause to that of Gloucester, happily perjuring himself for political gain. Our writer seems to be reporting 'the word on the street'. The Parliament Roll contains a common petition, the failure of which may have led to what happened next. The petitioners claimed that certain persons had been behaving improperly around the king's person, and requested that such people were to be removed from their offices by 1 December. Not only this, the demand was made that these persons were to be banned from the king's presence for life, and never to come closer than 12 miles unless summoned. The first name on the list was that of Edmund Beaufort, duke of Somerset, the second Alice de la Pole, dowager duchess of Suffolk. A further twenty-seven others were named, including Reginald Boulers, abbot of Gloucester. We can't help but suppose York and Norfolk, as well Exeter and others, were behind this.[19] The Parliament Roll records the king's reply to the petition. Henry stated he was not sufficiently appraised of any reason why such persons should be removed from his presence.[20] The Roll adds that if Henry took to the field against enemies and rebels, he was at liberty to call upon the service of any of his liegemen. He was right to be fearful.[21]

On 3 December 'a great shout was raised' against Somerset and other traitors.[22] The following day, according to the pro-Yorkist chronicler Benet:

> after noon, there suddenely rose against the duke of Somerset nearly a thousand men who intend to kill him. But, at the request of the Duke of York, the Earl of Devon quieted them and prudently took the Duke [of Somerset] secretly from the Friars on the Thames, and thence to the Tower of London.[23]

Hicks comments that York was most likely behind the attack simply because Somerset was the principal object in the way of his takeover of government. Hicks pithily says, 'I doubt if York was concerned that his rival should survive'.[24] Johnson reports that on the following day, there were attacks on the houses of Thomas, lord Hoo and Sir Thomas Tuddenham, erstwhile Keeper of the Great Wardrobe.[25] Rioting lasted for some 48 hours, but some semblance of peace was restored when the king rode through the city in the company of York and other lords on 5 January.[26] York's culpability for the violence is implied as Oldhall was charged for urging the 'men of Kent and others on 1 December 1450 to murder the king and his lords and destroy the courts and laws of the land'.[27]

Parliament met for a further 11 days before Christmas recess, re-assembling on 20 January 1451. When Parliament met again Henry was absent with a number of leading peers. Cade's Rebellion cast a long shadow and the fear of retribution influenced what happened. On 22 January, Stephen Christmas esq was reported as being engaged in rousing the men of Kent to fight the king, who he claimed intended to lay waste to the county with men levied in Cheshire and Lancashire. Christmas had been in York's household in Ireland, 1449–50. York, it seems, was destabilising the Parliament with the spectre of a new rebellion. Henry left London and rode with two nobles of Lancastrian lineage into Kent. Christmas was not brought to trial at Rochester till

17 February. The immediate response was the rejection of the broad-based council the king – or more likely Cardinal Kemp – had created months earlier, and York was to be directly excluded from this process. Henry and his inner circle were able to outmanoeuvre him and as Johnson notes 'the duke of York had lost the battle in Parliament'.[28]

If York was behind the revolt led by Christmas, he 'shot himself in the foot'. York thereafter was in abeyance. Somerset controlled Henry and inter alia government. York, unable to find legitimate grounds for opposition, and was forced to resort to means which emphasis the illegitimacy of his actions.[29]

## Succession politics

According to chronicler Benet, Thomas Young, MP for Bristol, asked Parliament to make it clear, for the sake of the security of the realm, that as the king had no issue who the heir was to be. In the annals ascribed to William Worcester he specifically states Young nominated the duke of York as heir. No original petition exists, but one for 1455 does. The chroniclers may have confused the two events. This event could be seen as an indication of York's ambitions regarding the throne; an alternative hypothesis is that, if York received official recognition as heir presumptive, it would greatly enhance his case to be head of the government. Rejection by Parliament shows two things: the strength of Somerset's position as he was able to discipline those who might have looked to York for leadership, both commons and gentry, but secondly, he was also occupying York's reformist position and hence his political support. The success of Somerset's first 18 months leading the consensus is best shown with Parliament's request for an Act of Resumption was granted in June. With it came a limited amount of banishment of non-noble household men: exactly what York had demanded. On the basis of the new financial prudence, Somerset to send an expedition to Gascony, but it was impossible to raise sufficient financial resources from either loans or taxation for this to be possible. Somerset was enforcing noble unity around the nullity of Henry. Like Suffolk, he knew if this mode of government was to work, it needed consensus. Somerset's success at this is exemplified by York's retreat from Westminster.[30] York was for the time at least nullified. Far more was at stake than culpability over the loss of Normandy, however: who the next king was to be was uppermost in York's mind.

Aware that until Henry had a son, or unless Parliament overturned legislation that forbade Edmund Beaufort from the line of inheritance to the crown, he was heir to the throne. Of royal blood, York believed he had the right to be at the centre of government and dictate royal policy, rather than the son of a legitimised bastard, Beaufort. York's belief in himself would trigger intermittent periods of civil strife to his own execution, and ultimately to the hated Beaufort family gaining the crown through Henry VII. The Beaufort claim to the crown had been legitimised by Richard II, but Henry IV had specifically excluded the family from the line of succession in 1407 by Letters Patent. Parliament of course could revoke, or replace them. Edmund, and his young aunt Margaret (1443–1509) heir of his brother John Beaufort (1404–44), could be named heirs apparent. Bastardy was a fluid concept: it was whatever Parliament said it was.

This placed York and Beaufort as rival claimants if Henry died before a child was born. Even if a child was born, and Henry died before the heir reached majority, the royal uncles could expect positions on a regency council or to rule as regent. York argued he was heir by right. In the short term, York only gained the support of Thomas Courtenay (1414–58), earl of Devon, and Edward Brock (1420–64) baron Cobham. Somerset had the support of almost all the other lords, who saw no need to cause a crisis. Henry had the divine right to appoint his advisors as he willed it: in simple economic terms, the government was beset by the Europe-wide recession, and regardless of the claims made by Cade's rebels, nothing really could be achieved. York, rather than merely desiring to part of government, wanted to control it. York had positioned himself as the popular leader, able to herald a new era of prosperity and expansionist foreign policy decisions. In this, he failed to understand the limits of kingship, and his own precarious position. John Watts succinctly notes, 'as the popular ferment of 1450 receded, York seems to have tried to regain his fading advantage by seeking public recognition as heir presumptive. The enterprise did not, could not, work.'[31] Henry publicly excluded the duke as first councillor, and retained Somerset. For York, it appeared that his political career was over for a third time.[32]

***

The fall of Bordeaux in July 1451 added a new edge to York's grievances with Somerset and inter alia the regime. Benet's chronicle alludes to the fact Richard Wydeville, lord Rivers, and 4,000 men had been assembled in Plymouth to land in France and to hinder the French re-conquest of Normandy. For whatever reason, Rivers never sailed.[33] Perhaps on the pretext of aiding the king's military expedition, York had raised a considerable armed retinue of 2,000: York used his force for 'peacekeeping' in a developing feud between the earl of Devon, Thomas

Courtenay, and Lord William Bonville (1392—1461) which broke out on 17 September.[34] This was not an isolated breakdown of unity amongst the great magnates. In Derbyshire, the duke of Buckingham was in open confrontation with a number of prominent landowners, the Blounts, Gesleys, Vernons and Longfords also involved. In the Midlands, Richard Neville, earl of Warwick was failing to recover the Beauchamp hegemony in the face of Somerset's interference with the Beauchamp inheritance. Indeed, an intractable wedge would develop between Warwick and Buckingham. Problems also flared in East Anglia. There, Henry Holland (1430–75) duke of Exeter, was in conflict with Ralph de Cromwell, 3rd baron Cromwell (c.1393–1456) over Ampthill Castle in Bedfordshire.[35] Despite Somerset's best efforts at consensus governance, by summer 1451, the nobility was fragmenting into two large, armed camps: one backing Somerset, the other looking to York.

In late summer, perhaps at York's instigation, these feuds took on a darker and more sinister connotation. William Oldhall was charged with plotting to the seize the king on 16 September.[36] If the charges levelled at the Court of King's Bench reflected reality, Oldhall planned to kidnap the king and put York on the throne.[37] Two days after the alleged kidnapping was to have taken place, rioting broke to in the West Country, instigated by, Sir Hugh Courtenay (1427–71) baron Cobham. The aim was to raise the people of Ilminster and Yeovil to support the duke of York in 'his false and traitorous purposes'.[38] The charges were dismissed in 1455.[39]

If the intention had been for York to muster an army and seize the king, this is not reflected in the almost rabidly pro-Yorkist chronicle by Benet, who tells us the duke sent 2,000 men to quell the rebellion.[40] The events in the West Country showed York that he was able to muster a large force of armed men. He had likely given the rebellion his blessing, and in acting as peacemaker, in terms of public perception, it showed York could succeed where Somerset could not in the county from whence he drew his title. In doing so York had usurped royal authority, cementing the belief amongst his political enemies that he was really a rebel, a traitor, no different the men of Kent. In reply, Somerset took the king, backed by an imposing gathering of nobles, to Coventry. Here Henry dealt with Bonville and other disturbers of the peace. Unlike York, Somerset was acting with the proper authority of the royal government.[41] York had failed again. Somerset was untouchable. Yet York had faced no repercussions for what he had done: it bolstered his egoistical belief that he could do what he like and face no consequences for it.

Chapter 8

# DARTFORD

By winter 1451, the duke of York was 'public enemy number 1', to use the vulgate: it is easy to see why. He had made three overt bids for power and lost. In doing so, he had made a lot of enemies. York's repeated failure made it clear that for most of the nobles, once they had got over the shocks of 1449–50, he was more a nuisance than the country's saviour. He could only draw to his side those who believed themselves to be excluded from power and reward. He found himself occupying the place Gloucester had occupied a decade earlier. His platform for opposition was created by the commonweal, which to the nobles made his position unappealing. In York's favour, the loss of France had broken the sense of unity amongst the nobles and magnates needed to make Suffolk's form of government around the nullity of Henry work in the long term.[1] Somerset, at the helm of the ship of state, had to silence dissent if government was to function: that meant clipping York and Norfolk's wings. In trying to silence York, or at least make him 'tow the party line', Somerset generated in York a sense of alienation and paranoia, that he would befall the fate of Gloucester. Aware that he was considered a disruptive personality, York protested his innocence in a letter to Henry:

> I Richard Duke of Yorke am informed, that the king my souveraigne Lord, is my heany Lord, greatly displeased with me and hath me in distruss by sinister information of mine enemies, adversaries and evill willers, where God knoweth, from whom nothing is hid, I have been and ever will be his true liege man . . . I have prayed the reverend father in God the Bishop of Hereford and my cosen the Earl of Shrewsbury to come hither, and heare my declaration . . . on the blessed sacrament and receive it, which I hope shall be my salvation.[2]

74

York, as ever, was protesting his loyalty, to ensure that whatever came next could not be construed as treason, and that he was a loyal subject seeking to help Henry.[3] Indeed, York made it evident in what followed that he was not challenging the king himself, only Somerset and those around him. In a letter to the City of Shrewsbury, no doubt for public consumption, on 3 February 1452, he argued that it ' . . . is not my will of my intention to displease my sovereign lord', adding: 'Seeing that the said Duke ever prevails and rules about the king's person, and that by this means the land is likely to be destroyed, I am fully decided to proceed in all haste against him, with the help of my liegemen and friends.'[4]

This speech was the equivalent of a declaration of war against Somerset and consequently would destabilise the next 30 years of English politics. Simultaneously, through open letters York once more began to explicitly accuse Somerset of culpability for the loss of Normandy and Guyenne. It is true that Somerset had personally profited from 10,000 *livres tournois* drawn from the tax revenues of Normandy: York argued that at the time 1447 to 1448 when funds were lacking for the defence of Rouen, Somerset could be understood to have contributed to the fall of Normandy through fiscal irregularity.[5]

Yet Somerset, as we made clear earlier, was not entirely at fault for the loss of France. With the truce with France, garrisons had been reduced to a peacetime footing: the English exchequer wobbled precariously close to bankruptcy and survived on loans. York knew this as well as Somerset. Somerset was not solely responsible for the Fougères attack, Warwick being as much as to blame as he was. York, in making reference to Somerset's poor administration of Normandy, flew in the face of facts. Somerset had endeavoured to regenerate the administration of the Duchy to make it more efficient at raising revenue: change always creates 'winners and losers'. It can be argued Somerset was more successful than York as lieutenant, his military record was equal to if not excelling York's. Refusal to negotiate after Fougères, was again not Somerset's fault, as he seems to have been given clear instructions by Henry VI how to proceed. Yes, he was an avaricious man, but when given the chance to make a lot of money, who would turn down that opportunity? Somerset was no evil councillor; he was simply human. The fault lay with those who governed in Henry's name. Parliament was also to blame: no one realised – it seems incredulous to us – that a war could not be won with a peacetime army that was chronically underfunded. The ghost of Henry V's English invincibility lingered until Rouen fell, thereafter the 'spell was broken'. Yet none of this was inevitable, as we have made clear. Those acting in Henry's name after Fougères, and his councillors and Parliament agreed. Could the duke of York have achieved more? He seemed to think so: but York undeniably had an overblown sense of self and his own capabilities. As heir apparent, he considered himself 'a cut above the rest'. Even if Henry had a child, as we noted earlier, York's own position was secure to some extent. As we noted earlier, if Henry died and the child was a minor, York stood a reasonable chance of being regent. If that child died before marriage – dying young was reasonably likely given that York had lost several of his own children as babes in arms or toddlers – and Henry had no further children, York was again 'in the frame' to be king. We must bear this in mind in what happened both in the next half decade and the options his son Richard faced. The duke of York, 'Uncle Richard', was happy to eliminate Edward Prince of Wales in 1460 politically: the failure to get rid of the prince there and then, came back to haunt York's son Edward. Whilst ever a claimant to the throne lived – Edmund Beaufort, Edmund and Owen Tudor, Edward Prince of Wales – York's position was not secure. Bastardy was fluid, as the legitimation of the Beaufort line showed only too well. Hence, when York had a chance, he exterminated his rivals. So Edward's elimination of Prince Edward, and his troublesome brother, secured his second tenure. Whilst ever a rival claimant was alive, no king was secure; the claimant had to be removed even if that meant the judicial murder of his siblings or nephews. Whilst ever a rival claimant lived, they were figure heads of a new faction. The politics of extermination, and 'an eye for an eye' destroyed the houses of York and Lancaster.

***

Returning to February 1452, in mustering Thomas Courtenay, earl of Devon, Cobham and others, York was building alliances and an army. Norfolk was given £200 and a gold cup to cement his loyalty. In his manifesto issued on 3 February, York raised the stakes further, proclaiming that Somerset was incapable of defending Calais, and suggested that Somerset was seeking to bring about his disinheritance, both of his lands and his status as heir apparent. Perhaps recklessly, York expressed his intention to remove the duke of Somerset, by force if necessary.[6]

The open letters and published manifesto made their way to the king and Somerset who had time to raise an army.[7] Henry appointed Buckingham and Bonville to command the Royal Army and they were sent to apprehend York on 16 February.

The denouement came at Dartford, where York met with the king on 1 March. The bishops of Ely and Westminster, and the earls of Salisbury and Warwick, were sent to meet with York to negotiate an armistice. The duke had hoped for a degree of popular support, particularly from London and Kent – hence his otherwise meaningless march to Dartford from Ludlow: it would have made more sense to advance straight to London if he had not expected to link with men who had risen in 1450 for Cade. This therefore opens a degree of speculation about the duke's involvement with Cade, and later charges against Sir William Oldhall as having the ring of truth about them. That the duke did not meet with substantial numbers from Kent is suggestive of the impact of Henry's oppressive measures taken against the rebels. Despite sending his petitions to Canterbury, Maidstone, Sandwich, Bristol, Winchester, Colchester, Oxford and other southern urban centres, they failed to rally to his cause.[8] York's failure to raise a mass rebellion in the manner of Cade, lost him credibility as representing national will. Outnumbered, York had no choice but to yield to royal authority as any further action was treason.[9]

Later Yorkist sources written to justify York's surrender imply that he did so on two provisos: that Somerset was removed from power, and he, the duke of York, was named heir. Henry we are told – and wholly unlikely – agreed to York's terms. On entering the king's tent, York discovered Somerset at liberty, apparently at the insistence of the queen.[10] This seems exceptionally unlikely as the queen was still a political nonentity at this stage, and would be till 1457. The supposed 'facts' about York's surrender are nothing more than retrospective justificative myth making. York had committed treason and was forced to make a public declaration to the king of his loyalty and future good behaviour. After his surrender, York was taken back to London, effectively a prisoner, under escort with the king. There he was made publicly to swear allegiance at St Paul's. This was followed by a commission to Kent, led by the earl of Shrewsbury, to deal with risings linked to the confrontation at Dartford, and a general pardon was issued in April. Its aim was to draw a line under all the events of 1450–2. The implication was that there would be a return to normality was emphasised by the confirmation of the announcement made earlier in the year that the king himself would lead an expedition to save Gascony.[11]

***

York had sailed exceptionally close to committing treason, for a fourth, perhaps fifth, time. Heads would have to roll on Somerset's orders. Acts passed at Parliament which assembled at Reading in spring 1453 made it clear that 'those assembled at the field of Dartford' were traitors 'unnaturally and against the duty and faith of your allegiance'. That York escaped attainder or imprisonment speaks openly of the special circumstances surrounding him as the king's cousin. He escaped from the episode almost totally unscathed. Yet York never accepted his lenient treatment, nor felt bound by the St Paul's oath, which he claimed was made under duress.[12] Further cementing his special place relationship with Henry – perhaps the king himself rather than Kemp – Henry agreed to listen to York's complaints about Somerset, and hoped private arbitration between the two men would investigate and impose a settlement, much as he attempted in 1458.[13]

York was confined to his estates: he was at Ludlow in July, and arrived at Fotheringhay by 11 August 1452. He lost his position as lieutenant of Ireland, which was handed to the earl of Wiltshire, further ennobled as the earl of Ormond.[14] York's humiliation was followed by a period of disgrace and eclipse for his allies. Bonville's dominance in the south-west grew rapidly, so it is not surprising that Courtenay was one of the first to endorse York's claim to be Protector.[15] The king was still childless, but his Tudor nephews, Edmund and Jasper, joined court in May. Jasper Tudor, ennobled as earl of Pembroke, benefited handsomely from the attainder of Sir William Oldhall. Brother Edmund was elevated as earl of Richmond. Were they to be the heirs? Somerset had made himself two new powerful allies.[16]

By late autumn, however, York had been rehabilitated and was busy dispensing the king's justice in the King's Forests south of the river Trent. Thus, York himself was not present when his son Richard (1452–85) – the future monarch – was born on 2 October 1452 at Fotheringhay. He sent his usual new year gifts to Henry and his queen on 1453. Margaret rewarded Duchess Cecily with a jewelled salt cellar worth £28. Somerset received 100 marks for his good counsel.[17]

# Chapter 9

# THE KING'S MADNESS

As 1453 dawned, York had been readmitted into public life. Somerset led an effective government. York had been unable to deprive Somerset of the position of being proxy for Henry, nor had he been able to find any legitimate grounds for opposition, and had been forced to resort to means that merely emphasised the illegitimacy of his whole position. York was behaving 'like a spoiled brat'. York knew only too well the need for noble consensus, and when the Council refused to listen to him, he rebelled in the name of the commonweal. In doing so, he argued, it was Henry and his regime who were rebellious in not listening to the will of the people. The continued endorsement of Somerset by the nobility, which included the Nevilles, Staffords and other leading families, merely reinforces the weakness of York's position.

Bolstering Somerset's position, an expedition had finally been despatched to Gascony under the earl of Shrewsbury in October 1452 which by early 1453 had had remarkable and unexpected success in recovering lost territory. The Parliament which met at Reading in March 1453, in addition to granting a large amount of taxation to pay for Shrewsbury's campaign, made its hostility to attacks on the royal household quite plain by attainting William Oldhall, who lost his estates although not his life. Once Parliament had been prorogued, the first half of 1453 was taken up with a royal judicial progress, centred primarily in the areas where York held lands, the Welsh border counties and eastern England. The object of the royal progress was simple, to clearly demonstrate the inviolability of the king's authority. Contrary to most popular histories, by late 1452 Somerset had managed to create government from the centre with a degree of authenticity. In learning lessons from Henry V in diverting factionalism into foreign policy, whilst ever it looked as if something could be salvaged from

Gascony, Somerset was able to bring the entire political nation together behind the king. Somerset's success made York's opposition untenable.

However laudable Somerset's aims, the resumption of feuding between nobles meant that consensus government was breaking down. In the North of England, relations between the Percys and the Nevilles, the two great families of the region, were deteriorating. In the Midlands, relations between the Nevilles and Somersets over the Despencer inheritance were leading inextricably to conflict. The developing breakdown in noble unity could have been resolved if Henry had been king in more than name. There was no impartial figure at the head of government, powerful enough to constrain the feuding magnates which slowly and inextricably meant there was no authority to hold back those who abused their proximity to the throne.[1] Factionalism, unchecked by the king, slowly but surely led to war. That Somerset had been able to contain these tensions speaks well of the man. His fall from power was not factionalism, but the total failure of Henry.

Always a liminal person, Henry's tenuous grasp on reality came to a sudden end in the summer of 1453. The English under Sir John Talbot were soundly defeated in battle at Castillon on 17 July 1453: the English presence in France was lost save Calais. This meant two things: once France was irretrievably lost, there was less incentive for the nobility to pull together in a unity government when crisis hit. Second, the loss of income and prestige from French lands made controlling rents and land all the more important in England, Scotland, Ireland and Wales.

It is possible that it was news of this disaster triggered King Henry's debilitating stupor. Henry was a 'poor coper', unable to function in a stressful environment; this was coupled with a marked degree of option paralysis – he was unable to make his mind up sufficiently for policy to remain consistent. Henry's judicial progresses over the previous year led to physical exertion which exacerbated his already limited mental capabilities and led to a total collapse. The exact date of its onset is not clear: early August seems as close as we can date the episode. He was physically and mentally unable to cope with the rigours of being a monarch. The king's pivotal position, at the meeting-point of the public and private spheres, was the basis of successful governance, which made Henry indispensable. With no king, the whole system of governance came to a juddering halt. Somerset was caught in a situation created by the incapacity of Henry: yes, he like Suffolk, Cardinal Beaufort and York were greedy and power hungry, and exploited the opportunities that the nullity of Henry created, but they were operating in an impossible situation. No one had been faced by the continued minority rule of a king before. All the main protagonists were as much victims as villains of Henry's incapacity. What Henry's illness actually was has been the subject of much debate. It is often said, the king was in a catatonic state:

> This is remarkably unlikely: in modern health care, a person in such a condition who is totally uncommunicative, has to be force fed with a tube, and catheterised in the worst-case scenarios. This was of course impossible in 1453. If Henry was in such a state, he would have died. Even with modern medicine, often the only cure for such a catatonic state is Electric Convulsive Therapy. Patients even in 2024 can die from such states which has historically been related to schizophrenia (catatonic schizophrenia). IF Henry was as unresponsive as has been claimed, he would have died within weeks of the onset of the catatonic condition. Henry, like his grandfather, suffered from some form of psychosis, potentially some form of schizophrenia, or perhaps depression with a degree of learning difficulty: he may have been autistic (in the 1940s autism and schizophrenia were considered to be the same thing) or had other special educational needs. From early age, Henry had been both paranoid and grandiose – he was the King and therefore exaggerated appropriate behaviour, yet was indecisive. Following this prolonged illness, Henry was apathetic with a hugely reduced capabilities, drive, interest and self-care, with hallucinations and religious delusions. In modern settings, we would bring him into a ward, observe his behaviour, conduct CT scans to look for a physical reason for his behaviour, blood and urine tests and have conversation with Henry. We cannot do this. We have to reconstruct his illness from little information that lacks sufficient detail to give a definite diagnosis. While mental illness can occur at any age, three-fourths of all mental illness begins by age 24. Henry was probably unwell since puberty or earlier. We all respond differently to stress and other external stimulants: a person's reaction, their standard 'coping mechanism', can and does have varied presentations. Herny was undoubtedly a "poor coper" with underlying issues.[2]

That this episode was part of an ongoing illness is implied by Somerset trying to 'carry on as normal'; moreover, none of the sources seems surprised and aghast that this illness had happened. No doubt Henry was ill on earlier occasions but not to the same severity. We see a marked degree of upshift in noble disunity from the early 1440s especially by 1445. Clearly Henry's illness was a constant issue, that ebbed and flowed with stress and external stimulus exacerbating his condition. The king's illness was so debilitating that the birth of the long-awaited heir, Prince Edward, on 13 October 1453, could not rouse him, we are told, from his stupor. As Sally Fairweather posits, that Henry had only a single child may again relate to his illness: difficulties with sex drive and performance are common issues for men dealing with depression, and other psychosis.

With Henry's illness government stopped. Parliament had opened on 6 March 1453 and had closed for an Easter recess on 17 April, reopening from 25 April to 2 July. With the king unable to assert even the limited authority he commanded, it was now impossible for government to continue: no legislation could be agreed, pardons, fines, or taxes levied because nothing could be passed without the king's seal of approval. This allowed slow-burning feuds to escalate as no legitimate royal authority existed to hold them in check.

## Wressle

As we commented earlier, the North of England was dominated by four landowners: Neville, Percy, York and the crown. The crown held land through the vast Duchy of Lancaster centred on Pontefract. York held the Manor of Wakefield centred on Sandal, the largest single administrative unit in the country. The Neville family was simultaneously at war with its self between the children of Ralph earl of Westmoreland's first and second marriage over seniority and with the Percys. The king's mental collapse and the subsequent challenge to Somerset's authority by the duke of York towards the end of summer 1453 led to the paralysis of national government and the exacerbation of local tensions.

In this feud the manor of Wressle figured large. A former Percy holding, it was ceded to Lord Cromwell, along with the majority of the manor of Burwell in 1438. They had been forfeited to the crown in 1403 following the Battle of Shrewsbury and Northumberland's aborted rebellion. The prospect of Percy manors passing to the Neville family directly contributed to the outbreak of open war in Yorkshire between the two families. The Nevilles had reached the apogee of their power by the later 1440s. The handing of Richmond and other land to the king's half-brother limited either family's chance of further aggrandisement. The Tudors' admittance into the royal family marginalised the Nevilles into 'lesser royals'. Both Tudor earls were given precedence over Warwick, the premier earl. For an ambitious young man, the demotion was taken as a personal affront. The era when Salisbury could obtain royal favour for his underage son to inherit was over. The admission of the Tudors to the royal family in a position of seniority signalled the transition of the junior house of Neville away from the inner royal circle and may have been a factor in their alignment with Richard, duke of York and hence in the emergence of the Yorkist party that made the Wars of the Roses possible.

York's own attitude to the Percy clan is best surmised from the fact he obtained the lease of the former Percy town of Doncaster on 3 July 1453 from Sir John Salavin.[3] Salavin had been attacked in May by men loyal to Exeter.[4] Percy retainers like Richard Aldborough fought for Exeter in that encounter, as did John Caterall.[5]

It has long been assumed that tensions boiled over into civil strife with the marriage of Salisbury's second son, Thomas Neville, to Maud Stanhope, the widow of Robert, Lord Willoughby. The fear was that Wressle, held by Lord Cromwell, would pass to the Nevilles, rather than be returned to the Percys. However, at the time, no one knew when this would or could even happen, or even if Maud rather than her sister would inherit the contested lands! The marriage, it is reasonable to suppose, was not the cause of the clash. Why would Egremont initiate a feud over an event that may not happen, years ahead?

The struggle between Neville and Percy grew out of the struggle for regional hegemony. Ralph Griffiths has suggested, rightly in my view, that by the mid-fifteenth century relations between Percy and Neville were 'poisoned by jealousy and resentment'.[6] Michael Hicks has described the roots of the earl of Salisbury's alliance with Richard, duke of York in 1453 as being based on their having 'common enemies'.[7] The alliance of Neville and York created a regional hegemony that was stronger than that of the Percys. The Percys, feeling pressured, sought allies to restore some degree of power balance. Younger sons took the lead in this quarrel which began before the marriage centred at Topcliffe.[8] Thomas Percy (1422–60), Lord Egremont, the son of Henry Percy, earl of Northumberland, and Elanor Neville, daughter of Ralph Neville, earl of Westmoreland and Joan Beaufort: she was sister of both Cecily Neville, duchess of York, and the earl of Salisbury. In theory they should have been allies. Local tensions, however, split familial ties. Egremont was called before the royal council on 8 June 1453 to answer for his actions for raiding into Neville lands. This failed to attend or to curb his behaviour, with further summons issues on 26 June and 7 July. His actions clearly offended Sir John Neville, the earl of Salisbury's son, who retaliated with a violent raid of his own into Egremont's lands, for which he was summoned on 26 June to also answer for his actions. Like Egremont, he failed to attend, and in an escalation of the conflict on 29 June attacked Topcliffe Castle, held by the Percys. It was likely this episode that resulted in a commission of oyer and terminer in the North Riding, on 12 July, in which both earls were named, along with sixteen others including three other peers. The commission was re-issued on 25 July. Salisbury was attending the Council at the time of the issue and re-issue. Two days later both earls were urged to control their sons and a new commission was appointed to inquire into the riots and other incidents that were breaching the king's peace. Of the Percy retainers summoned on 10 August, nine were from the West March, which perhaps shows that Cumbrian manpower was being deployed in the North Riding.[9]

In a further escalation, Heworth Moor became the scene of a bitter stand-off, following earlier raids. This clash, on 24 August 1453, was an attack against the earl of Salisbury. Sir William Buckton was recorded as being *'contra comite Sarum in campo'* (against the earl of Salisbury in the field).[10] Salisbury claimed over 700 supporters of Northumberland were at the skirmish. The figure seems unreliable. Some of those whose names are recorded include Richard Aldborough, John Caterall, Thomas Clapham, Thomas Fairfax of Selby, Thomas Frost of Featherstone, John Hammerton, Stephen Hammerton, John Pudsey, William Rither/Ryther, Thomas Sandford of Doncaster, Brian Stapleton, John Stapleton (killed at St Albans in 1455), Richard Tempest, Henry Vavasour, Roger Warde, and John Clifford.[11] Many of these men, especially from the West Riding were retained by the Percy earls, the majority living within the vast Honour of Pontefract.[12]

Heworth was not the end, but the beginning of broader issues. In September, mediation by the mayor of York, and then Archbishop Booth of York, as well as Bishop Geoge Neville as well as the second earl of Westmorland. Rather than calming the waters, a second clash at Topcliffe took place on 20 October.[13] The duke of York had not been involved in any of these clashes and the deteriorating situation: the Neville–Percy feud developed independent of York and his grievances with Somerset. It was not until 1454 that the two causes coalesced.

# Chapter 10

# THE FIRST PROTECTORATE

By October 1453 Henry's total incapacity could not be concealed. A form of properly constituted authority was required to contain and suppress the growing wave of apparently uncontrollable conflict amongst the disunited nobility. It was impossible for Somerset to continue. No king meant no governance; it meant Somerset had no authority to act.[1] If Somerset had been of that intention, he could have seized the throne and named himself regent: that he did not, speaks volumes about the differences between him and York.

If the Council was to rule in the king's absence, it had to rule by consent, and that meant including York. To this end, York received a letter of summons on 23 October to attend a Great Council. Its purpose was:

> to establish peace and unity between the lords of this land. And since there has been and still is, as it is believed, variance between him and some other of the lords, therefore the king wills that he in all haste disposes himself to come to the Council peacefully and moderately accompanied.

As B.P. Wolffe notes, the birth of Prince Edward on 13 October removed York from his position as heir presumptive, and therefore made it easier to invite him back into government.[2] He arrived in London on 12 November, the date that Parliament was scheduled to re-assemble.[3] York was present at a Council meeting on 5 December 1453 to deal with absolutely essential matters of state, 'until the time their power was more fully declared by sufficient authority'.[4] In proceeding in this manner, government by council, York and those around him were uncertain of their authority to act, as no one other than the king could authorise and legitimise such an act of government. If Henry VI died, as was feared, resulting in an infant king, there was a real need for collective action amongst the nobles. York was best placed to act as regent in the infant king's name. York declared to a Council in Star Chamber on 21 December, which was attended by the Prior of St John, ten diocesan and thirteen lay lords (which did not include Somerset), that he had come to the Council as the king's loyal subject and that he would act with all his diligence towards the king's welfare and that of his subjects. York then used the situation to make it clear that he would not be dictated to, reminding his fellow peers that a number of his previous advisors had been commanded to withdraw from him, 'which is to his great hurt and means that he cannot proceed with such matters as he had to do in the king's courts and elsewhere'. He therefore asked that such men should be restored to his council. The lords agreed to this, considering it 'just and reasonable'.[5] It is reasonable to assume York sought the return of Sir William Oldhall. York's price for his co-operation in the Great Council was Somerset's fall, who was denounced by Norfolk as a traitor and imprisoned in the Tower once more.[6] Also arrested alongside Somerset was his ally Thomas Thorpe, Speaker of the House of Commons. The justification for these arrests that the pair were planning military action against the duke of York to make Queen Margaret regent. Thorpe's imprisonment would set in motion a vendetta which resulted in the duke's death.[7] At the same time, York showed his sensitivity to the need to ensure wider acceptance of his rule in February 1454, when in an effort to force the nobility into wholesale complicity in the setting up of a Protectorate, he ordered lords absent from Parliament without licence to be fined.[8] York was trying to 'keep the show on the road' and form an effective coalition government: yet he had no authority for this from Parliament or Henry.

Gaoling Somerset was vindictive and a lapse of judgement on York's part. Where compromise was possible, York made conflict inevitable. Being gaoled made Somerset an overt threat and destabilising influence. James II of Scotland offered Somerset military aid to lead a coup against York and those who had imprisoned him.[9] John Stodeley, writing in London on 19 January 1454, reported that Somerset had 'spies going in every lord's house in this land' adding that Thorpe was preparing articles of impeachment against York. Stodeley's most important contribution to the discussion of the events at the close of 1453 concern Margaret of Anjou, Henry's queen. Scottish aid would make sense given what the queen was potentially planning, although we only have Stodeley's word for it. He tells us:

The queen has made a bill of five articles desiring those articles to be granted. The first is that she desires to have the whole rule of this land; the second is that she may appoint the chancellor, the treasurer, the privy seal and all other officers of this land, with sheriffs and all other officers that the king should appoint; the third is that she may give all the bishoprics of this land and all other benefices that belong to the king's gift; the fourth is that she may have sufficient livelihood assigned to her for the king and the prince and herself.

He adds that there was a fifth article but he did not know its contents. The queen was seeking to be made regent: no precedent existed in England, but it did in France.[10]

It was perhaps because of the fear of the queen being made regent that the Council agreed on 7 February 1454 that Parliament was to proceed. Yet without a king to call Parliament, who could do so? After much deliberation and hand-wringing, on 13 February, York was given the commission to hold Parliament: it was essential that power to hold the Parliament was vested in one individual and not a committee. York's commission was read out at the opening of the Parliament at Westminster on Thursday, 14 February, including the power to dissolve Parliament 'with the assent of the Council'. All was going well.

Chancellor Cardinal Kemp died on Friday 22 March: Ralph Griffiths has suggested that Kemp's death have been in part because of the bullying and threats he had been subjected to, most 'notably by Norfolk'.[11] The king had to be told of Kemp's death, and no one except the king had the power to appoint a new chancellor. A delegation was sent from Parliament to the king: they visited him during mealtime, but he was unresponsive. After three attempts to elicit a response from Henry during the course of 25 March, there was now no other option than to appoint a Protector.[12] Yet it was by no means a forgone conclusion that York would be named Protector: given that Salisbury and his immediate family constituted the core of his supporters, his candidacy could be very easily construed as a partisan scheme to promote the interest of the Neville faction and Lord Cromwell against Somerset and Exeter. Was York impartial enough to be made Protector? A solution to this came on 15 March, with the creation of Henry and Margaret's infant son as Prince of Wales by York's government. This act indicated York's recognition of Prince Edward as Henry's legitimate heir and in doing so united the nobility behind the duke. Having gained important support from both sides of the fractured nobility, York was named 'protector and defender of the realm' on 27 March

1454, to be succeeded, if necessary, by the Prince of Wales. The lords and magnates, York included, were now formally acting together in public unity, which we ought perhaps not see as the triumph of York but more as the triumph of collective rule in time of protracted crisis after Somerset's failure to address magnate feuding.[13] However, 'to make him protector in the constitutional uncertainty of 1454 might be deemed by some a dynastic challenge on York's part and the duke may have regarded it in precisely the same light,' suggests Ralph Griffiths.[14] Neither conclusion is exclusive: York was at the apogee of his power, and we cannot be certain how he viewed his own success. That he was sensitive for the need to draw the entire nobility into the complicity of his rule to ensure its acceptance, recognised both the need for consensus government and importantly how York viewed his position, and the need to win over hearts and minds. In France, one chronicler noted 'the duke of York assumed the government of the king and kingdom of England'.[15] Parliament chose Richard Neville, earl of Salisbury, as chancellor: he may not have had at this stage had very strong bonds of loyalty. For York's detractors, it smacked of nepotism. Norfolk was asked to join the Council, but he refused, citing ill health. Before Somerset's arrest, Norfolk presented charges against Somerset in Parliament, attacking his failure to prevent the loss of the 'two so noble Duchies of Normandy and Guyenne'.[16]

York was now king in all but name. The appointment was at the king's pleasure, or until Prince Edward came to the age of discretion, assuming that the latter was at that point willing to take up the position of Protector himself and rule in place of his father. York sought, and obtained, the captaincy of Calais and used the opportunity to remind Parliament that his previous services in Normandy, France and Ireland had not been fully recompensed. Rowland FitzEustace was appointed lieutenant in Ireland.

York's position was contested, or at least exposed the underlying cracks in the country which he sought to 'paper over' with consensus rule. Rioters in Derbyshire denounced the new regime. Thomas Scales (1399–1460), Lord Scales, was ordered to quell rioting directed against the king's new college in Cambridge. More seriously, Henry Holland (1430–75), the duke of Exeter, a grandson of Henry IV's sister Elizabeth, and great-grandson of John of Gaunt and first wife Blanche, had joined the Percys against the junior branch of the Nevilles. After the issue of an open letter stating he was acting in the name of the king and 'defender of England', most rioters submitted to York's authority, or fled seeking sanctuary. Exeter was dragged from sanctuary and imprisoned at Pontefract Castle. In imitation of a royal progress, York went on tour during summer 1454, presiding over judicial sessions as Henry had done. Through direct intervention, the duke brought warring factions to heel. But in delivering his justice, he was far from impartial. He sided with the cadet branch of the Nevilles, and proceedings against the earl of Salisbury and Warwick were dropped for their actions in Glamorgan and the North, and in consequence found the Percys guilty.[17] Thomas Percy, Lord Egremont, was ordered to answer for his acts of violence in the North.[18]

The treason trial of Thomas Courtenay, earl of Devon, for his support of York at Dartford was heard, and as could have been reasonably predicted, he was acquitted.[19] Devon and his rival Bonville were bound over for good behaviour or to be forfeit 4,000 marks.[20] However legitimately conceived, York's actions against the Percys and Exeter were bound to be taken as preferential treatment of the Nevilles; a king might have done the same, but York was a subject and a friend of the Nevilles, especially when Richard Neville, earl of Salisbury, was appointed in Kemp's place from 2 April 1454.[21]

Somerset was displaced as captain of Calais at York's behest, who stressed to the peers Calais' vulnerability should the French choose to attack. The garrison refused to acquiesce and York sent his brother-in-law Henry Bourchier (1406–83), the earl of Essex and Lord Treasurer, was sent to Calais to placate the garrison.[22] York at the lord's request was made captain of Calais, and he set out a manifesto to ensure an adequate payment of wages for the garrison, arrangements for victualling and repairs. A loan of 12,000 *livres tournois* from the merchants of Calais that was owing, was to be paid York promised. He also made demands of the lords to promise that there would be adequate assistance if Calais attacked by the French. Somerset's allies Lionel Welles (1406–61), 6th baron Welles, and earl Rivers remained in Calais with a significant body of troops: the fear was they could invade England. York also endeavoured to fund the neglected navy. Yet York would not control Calais.[23]

Through his governance, York could reassure the Commons that he was committed to the maintenance of law and order, a stance which he put into practice by carrying out a judicial progress into Yorkshire in mid-May. He also acceded to merchants' demands concerning abolition of the poundage on cloth exports. Yet we must stress that York was ruling in collaboration with the peers and Parliament, emulating the minority government of 1422–37.

One of York's key goals was to put Somerset on trial. Yet he was in a minority position over Somerset: the greater majority were unhappy with Somerset's treatment.[24] A date was fixed on 28 July for the trial to begin on 28 October. It was to be a show of political strength. A few days earlier, he had obtained authority to deliver the king's livery to eighty unarmed gentlemen, no doubt intended as a personal bodyguard. York set off almost immediately after the trial date was set to York, where he arrived on 3 August. Salisbury and his son, the earl of Warwick, were indentured together as joint wardens of East March for a period of 20 years. By 19 August York was at Sandal, where he remained for six weeks.[25]

## Why Sandal?

What made the duke of York head to Sandal? Sandal had come into his possession on the death of John de Warenne in 1347. Edward III handed Sandal and the vast Manor of Wakefield to his son Edmund Langley, who was subsequently made duke of York. On his death in March 1402, the most lucrative part of Joan's settlement was almost certainly her entitlement to a third share of her husband's entailed exchequer annuities, which it seems was seized by Henry IV along with 'the castle, town and manor of Sandal'.[26]

It would be Joan's second husband, Lord Willoughby, who issued a quitclaim to restore his wife's lands in 1405.[27] Willoughby held lands in East Yorkshire, notably Wressle castle near Hull. We need to remember the duke's familial connections to the Willoughby family. On Willoughby's death in 1409, she married Henry, Lord Scrope of Masham, in 1411. Lord Scrope occupied Sandal Castle in right of his wife until his forfeiture and execution in 1415.[28] Scrope was executed alongside the duke of York's father. The Scropes would become Yorkist allies. Joan claimed the castle, town and manor, perhaps due to a politically useful fourth marriage to Sir Henry Brounflete the following year.[29] The castle, manor and town of Sandal passed to Duke Richard on Joan's death in 1435.

Sandal was something of a 'toy castle': it was never meant to be the permanent or primary residence of a great lord. It provided an administrative space with attached high-status lodgings. Set at the centre of a park, with a pleasure garden attached to it, it was a hunting lodge with pretensions to grandeur rather than an impregnable high-status citadel like Pontefract or Middleham. The castle was both the *caput* of the Manor of Wakefield, but also the centre of its own administrative unit: a graveship. The term graveship and grave translate *prepositura* and *prepositus*. These terms have always been used in connection with the Manor of Wakefield and the other Warenne estate in Yorkshire, the Honour of Conisbrough. Little accounts exist for the administration of the castle and its graveship: the *compoti* (accounts) of 1265–6 and 1270–1 tell us little beyond the castle had 72 acres of arable and 11¾ acres of meadow. By 1275 a park of 40 acres bounded the north-western side of the castle. To the north, south and west were the infields of the demesne, defended by ditches and stock proof hedges since the 1260s.[30] The service buildings for the castle – mill, barns, cattle and sheep pens, blacksmiths, brew house etc — were located at the *manerium* or grange.[31] The castle had its own bailiff manging the graveship, a park keeper and constable, all who lived in the castle.[32] The castle was both a farm, administrative centre and residence. Defence was very much secondary.

## Stamford Bridge

From Yorkshire, the duke was in Derby by the middle weeks of September, and his whereabouts are not known till 7 November when he attended Council at Westminster. The Council met again six days later, again on the 15th, and the 23rd, 24th and 27th of the month. For whatever reason, Somerset's trial failed to materialise.[33]

In the widening dispute between York and the earl of Exeter, the latter allied himself with Lord Egremont and the broader Percy interest to remove York from office, to allow Somerset to resume governance of the king. According to a document in The National Archives, the pair wanted York dead as well as his commissioners who had arrested them. Exeter promptly rebelled, but was captured.[34] He was bundled off to captivity at Pontefract.[35] His allies fared little better: Thomas Percy, Lord Egremont with his brother Richard clashed 30 October 1454 with Thomas and John Neville. In the fighting 'were captured the aforesaid Thomas and Richard, his brother seriously wounded and many of them killed, among whom the brave solider John Salvin'.[36] Benet's chronicle tells us a hundred men were killed.[37] The Nevilles sued Egremont for damages, and were awarded the incredible sum of £11,200. Not even the Percys could raise this sum and in consequence Egremont was consigned to debtors' prison.[38]

By early December 1454 York appeared to be in a very strong position. His main political opponent, Somerset, was in the Tower of London and Egremont was in debtors' prison. York's allies held the main posts in the government. Moreover, Protector York had crushed rebellion and was in effective control of council and royal household. Yet he could not bask in a glow of total success: he had been unable to deal decisively with Somerset and, moreover, he had totally failed to establish his authority over the Calais garrison.

Fate one more intervened when Henry recovered on Christmas Day 1454: by 9 February 1455 the king was well enough to take back his power. York's term of office ended. The great weakness of York's position since taking power was that the nobility justifiably remained anxious about his treatment of Somerset. The nobility was unwilling to see the latter destroyed – just as they had not allowed Somerset to destroy York. This meant that, as soon as Henry recovered, Somerset would be able to achieve once more, a position in control of the king.[39] So far violence had been limited to grievous bodily harm and robbery: that was all to change.

Chapter 11

# COUNTDOWN TO CONFLICT

With Henry restored to something approaching normality, the circle around him proceeded to make it clear that they regarded many of York's actions over the previous months as partisan, which many of them were, and unacceptable. Somerset was legally freed from the Tower on 4 February 1454. It has been suggested that this action triggered York to resign the Protectorate. A month was to pass before the new political situation was made crystal-clear to York. At Greenwich on 4 March Henry personally presided over a council meeting and repudiated all the charges of treason against Somerset. York was stripped of his title as captain of Calais with Henry taking the title for himself before passing it back to Somerset.[1] As Jane Dawson noted in 1997, contemporary comment on how the volte face in politics and the return of Somerset to government was received by the commonweal is almost entirely lacking.[2]

Differences between Somerset and York were placed in arbitration, and both men were bound over on the enormous sum of 20,000 marks (£13,333 6s 8d) to abide by any judgement. Exeter was taken from Pontefract to Wallingford to be tried. Salisbury resigned as Chancellor on 7 March, possibly for the king's actions against Exeter, of whom he had custody. He was replaced by Archbishop Thomas Bourchier, the new Treasurer was to be the earl of Shrewsbury. This mishandling of the Nevilles was a mistake on the government's part: it forged an unbreakable alliance between York and the hugely powerful Nevilles. The earls of Salisbury and Warwick became convinced that a faction at court led by Somerset, which included Wiltshire, Beaumont, Exeter and Northumberland, was bent on their destruction.[3]

It was these decisions which Henry appears to have taken personally immediately after his recovery, which are, with hindsight, seen as the triggers for war. It is undeniable that the greater part of the nobility had been uncomfortable with the treatment of Somerset and his release was a forgone conclusion. The issue over Somerset's treason was closed; he had been pardoned, and moreover it was legally unacceptable to hold him indefinitely in the Tower. The king's actions were taken with consent of the Great Council and marked a return to 'business as usual'. York was acting like Hermann Melville's character Captain Ahab, obsessed to the point of madness with Somerset. Henry had pardoned Somerset: the only way the case failed to 'stand up' was if Henry had not done so, but Kemp had pardoned Somerset in Henry's name. In this reading of events, York had a legitimate case, but it meant further exposing the nullity of Henry. James Ross describes Henry as an 'occasional' king; a man who could, on occasion, assert his royal will and make decisions.[4] It was in these periods of normality that, as Lauren Johnson notes, Henry was 'kind-hearted, charitable, generous to a fault' who believed 'that peace was a cardinal virtue and chastity and self-denial crucial for a ruler'.[5] Griffiths argues Henry was 'over-merciful and compassionate to those at fault' and suffered from 'naively defective judgement'.[6] It was these failings, Henry's second childhood as MacFarlane describes it, related to his fragile mental health, that created Henry the nullity, and led to war in 1455.[7]

York had built his reputation on his oppositional position to Somerset. This madness would lead to his own death. If we question Henry VI's mental capacity, we must surely question that of York who seems to have had obsessive/compulsive behaviour and a sense of entitlement. York was well aware of Henry's nothingness and occasional rule, and benefited from that. As a landowner and great noble, stability in government was needed for administration, delivery of justice and fiscal probity: York's vendetta blinded him to the positive legacy of Somerset in 'keeping the show on the road'. York deliberately destabilised government for his own ends, egged on by Norfolk and then Warwick to override the actions of the king. York had no right to commit treason: he had been shown leniency. Henry was king; whatever he signed was his will, even if his capacity to generate policy and understand the implications of what he agreed to was hugely limited. The solution to Henry was either 'more of the same' with consensus government – which had worked for over a decade – or to replace Henry. Yet in 1455 no one dared suggest this solution. What happened next is shrouded in myth.

Because the Yorkists won, their version of history has become the accepted line. We have to look behind what the victors wanted the commonweal, Parliament and contemporaries to believe to get closer to the motivations that led to armed conflict. Nothing in Henry's actions could be seen at the time as precipitating war. York provoked the conflict: he was the aggressor. He had no right to take extreme and legally treasonable acts to pursue a personal vendetta. York was not entitled to override the legitimate judgement of the king. As Christine Carpenter argues, quite rightly in my view, 'the absence of any kind of real rule, except when York was officially Protector, ensured that there would increasingly be unresolvable conflicts among the nobility'.[8] The broader conflict that was played out was derived from smaller, local disputes, which fundamentally undermined the unity both of the nobility but also government: the root cause lay in the failure of kingship, without which those disputes could not be resolved.

## Fear and paranoia

Most histories of 1455 are written by those emotionally compromised by their loyalty to York or to Henry: in both cases objective history suffers. The truth is between these two differing camps. The council which met at Greenwich on 4 March was well attended: thirty-three peers attended, far more than those who attended during York's protectorate. Henry was resolved to arbitration between Somerset and York. It was agreed at a Council held on 15–18 April, to call a Great Council at Leicester: it was needed to give a final judgement on the issues between York and Somerset. Having left office, York was at Sandal at the start of the year.[9] The three Yorkist earls were summoned to Leicester, in the heart of the duchy of Lancaster, to attend a Great Council which was to commence on 21 May 1455. Yorkist legend implies that, fearing a trap – the precedent with the supposed arrest of the duke of Gloucester in 1447 being more than apparent – York decided to raise an army for his own safety. According to Yorkist chronicles, Somerset wanted revenge, and with support of the king, he sought to exact it.[10] But is it true?

The Yorkist earls, the victors of St Albans, wrote their official history of the events into the Roll of Parliament:

> Edmund, late duke of Somerset, Thomas Thorpe and William Joseph, intending, as it is supposed, the hurt and destruction of our true, most trusty and well-beloved cousins Richard, duke of York, Richard, earl of Warwick, and Richard, earl of Salisbury, and their heirs, prompted and solicited us by various means to mistrust our said cousins, and to estrange them from our favour and good grace, declaring them not to be our true liegemen, and therefore provoked and incited us to proceed with a great force of people on pretence of our own interest, but in fact to advance their own interests and quarrels.[11]

The earls then noted that it was not their intention to fight, but to intimidate their opponents, and:

> reinforced themselves with a large host of men in various counties and a great supply of armour and military equipment, set off towards us, to declare themselves our true liegemen, better companioned for their security, and to resist such malice as they sincerely thought was planned against them, at their coming to us, by the said Edmund, Thomas and William, and for no other reason; and so that we should not wonder or marvel at the appearance before us of our said cousins, or at the manner of it, or have any suspicion or mistrust of their intentions towards us, they wrote letters at Royston on 20 May last, stating their desire, and before coming to us they sent them to the most reverend father in God, Thomas, archbishop of Canterbury, our chancellor of England.[12]

The earls claimed the archbishop failed to deliver their communication to the king: in essence the battle at St Albans was not their fault. They were not traitors; they were reforming government. Action speak louder than words: unlike Dartford both sides clashed and men were killed, and the king wounded.

Yet this assumes that York had the right to override the king – he did not. He always knew the protectorate was temporary, and taking up arms – again – was treason. Yes, a legitimate case could be made that Somerset had faced no charges for his culpability in the loss of Normandy; yet York had faced almost no penalties for Dartford. With both men escaping charges, Henry was being magnanimous to men of royal blood: he was being even-handed. Remarkable as it seems, York felt he was being victimised because Somerset was treated as fairly as he was. As far as Henry and those around him were concerned 'the case was closed'. This was not the answer the duke of York wished to hear. It was also obvious to the nobility that Somerset had reasonable grounds for complaint for his treatment over the last 18 months against the duke.[13]

The Yorkist revisionary understanding of events is repeated by Johnson, that York had to attack at the Great Council as he believed that at this meeting a settlement about the form of government would take if the king had a relapse, was to be agreed. The duke believed that the Council would permanently exclude him from power.[14] Professor Pollard follows this argument, commenting York, Salisbury and Warwick chose to seize power in a pre-emptive strike.[15] Lewis argues Somerset held the reins of power and the three earls were targets of a plot to eliminate them 'with a trademark spitefulness and disregard for the governance of the country only recently so well steadied'.[16] However, no documentary evidence to support this contention exists outside the biased and revisionary Yorkist chronicles. Discounting the Yorkists' own claims to the contrary, the facts as we have them is that York's actions were unprovoked and any other hypothesis is not sustainable. History is what the victors say it is, therefore we must always be cautious when dealing with overtly biased source material.

Did the duke of York really raise troops to simply make sure Somerset faced trial in a re-enactment of Dartford? Was this really a cause 'to kill for'? Many of York's actions were driven by his power base. We remember it was not York who charged Somerset with treason, but according to a letter dated 28 July 1454, it was the duke of Norfolk, although he may have acted at York's request. The appointed date of the trial, 28 October, witnessed no trial: yet the matter was not forced again during the protectorate.[17] If bringing Somerset to trial was the bedrock of York's treason – and taking up arms against the king was treason – and breaking the Dartford accord, York's case was 'threadbare'. It speaks more of the paranoia of York's power base to being held to account or at least made accountable, and underscores 'the fact that it was now principally fear which was driving the Yorkists on', argues Carpenter.[18] Fear of being held to account, fear of losing power and prestige drove events forward. As first among equals, a man who believed he was born to be king by right, a man of great capability than the king, a man to whom no one said no, being held to account was an anathema. But by 1455 how much of what was happening was being driven by the duke? York had always co-operated with others, who often 'did the heavy lifting', as with Dartford. York was, I believe, very open to flattery – ego massaging – and could be ruthlessly exploited by others for their gain, if York felt it would benefit him. Was York a natural leader? We ask this question again later. Was he in charge of his own destiny? Perhaps not. If so, who was?

Top of the list is the young, charismatic Richard Neville, earl of Warwick (1428–71). He had good reason to fight. It was undeniable that Somerset would not have forgotten the recent tussle over the de Spencer inheritance in Glamorgan. For his father, dispensation in his favour of the Percy–Neville feud that York had engineered was likely to be overturned in favour of a more equitable settlement. Fear of loss of prestige, land and honour drove the Nevilles. Warwick and his father believed it was sufficient justification for attacking the king. The duke of York's personal grievance was now magnified through its assimilation with the broader Neville–Neville feud and the Percy–Neville feud. The Yorkist faction was born.[19] Indeed, the duke was without doubt emboldened after Dartford: he had committed treason and 'gotten away with it'. A multiplicity of reasons on the Yorkist side drove events forward. Rather than merely seeing an end to Somerset, York wanted to be back in control. The sabre-rattling outside St Albans marked a point of no return: whoever controlled the king ruled England. The consensus from 1422 was over. A middle ground no longer existed. It was a contest of 'might is right'. Legally, in raising troops against the king, the duke of York was the guilty party, and explains to some degree the amount of Yorkist propaganda generated later to justify his actions. The Yorkists had no real grounds for complaint. York's tenure as Protector was always bound to end. The Nevilles had used the protectorate to further their own ends, a crime that Somerset they considered to be guilty of. Rather than waiting for arbitration, and acting out of paranoia, self-interest, the Yorkists precipitated violence as a way of 'score settling'.[20]

### St Albans

York left Sandal for, we assume, Fotheringhay, and was in Royston by 20 May. He could have swung his forces to Leicester, or proceeded south to intercept the lightly-guarded Henry. The king was at Watford by the 21st, leaving the following morning for St Albans. Somerset we stress was not 'the man of the hour': the duke of Buckingham was Constable.[21] Unable to believe that York could attack him with his banner displayed, the king travelled with only a small escort.[22] The duke of York at this stage on the 21st hoped to merely delay the king and enter negotiations.[23] Perhaps. The three Yorkist earls wrote their apologia into the Rolls of Parliament; how true it is depending on the bias of the reader. Ricardians are keen to point out the bias in Lancastrian propaganda concerning Richard III, in order to justify his actions. As we said, the victors write the history. In the case of the events of 1455 onwards, this is true of the Yorkists.

Perhaps seven contemporary newssheets, all from the Yorkist side, exist. They contain sections of prose and also graphic discussions of the battle they describe. This junction of prose – what was said, or perhaps what was hoped in hindsight had been said – are typical of newssheets of the epoch, which form the basis of the work by Wavrin. There are two sides to every story: since 1455 the Lancastrians, Somerset and Queen Margaret in particular – although she had almost no influence at this stage – have been openly slandered by Yorkist chroniclers and contemporaries to justify their actions. If we are to be objective students of history, we cannot seek to overturn one set of propaganda written by Lancastrians under the Tudors, without challenging the narrative of events from the Yorkist side. Like no other period in history, the study of the Wars of the Roses is dominated by vociferous factions and champions of one side against the other, writing books, presenting TV documentaries and public lectures to argue their case, without stopping to challenge their own bias. We must always check the bias of the sources we use in the creation of the narrative. We do not have a Lancastrian view point for what happened, and the newssheets which were issued within days of the events, if not hours, are entirely Yorkist in view.[24] By newssheets we mean narrations of events created to describe an event with the purpose of informing third parties about important event. The writer was not consciously writing history, and were passing on information they believed to be true. The authors were heralds or secretaries to the protagonists mentioned in the newssheet. This material was an established part of the chronicler's material.[25]

We are traditionally told that the king had no time to muster a large army on his move to St Albans, and he was surprised by the events, yet a letter written within weeks of the event reported (my translation from the Italian):

> 3rd of June. – I have further news of the battle in England brought by one who came here from Calais. They say that on the 21st of May the king left Westminster with many lords, including the Duke of Somerset, to hold a council at Leicester eighty miles from London. They went armed because they suspected that the Duke of York would also go there with men-at-arms. That day they travelled twenty miles to the abbey of St. Albans.[26]

If this was the case, Buckingham, Somerset and Henry were expecting trouble from York. A seemingly anonymous Burgundian commentator reported (my translation from the French):

> When the duke of Somerset and those who were of his party then being in the City of London, head that the Duke of York and many other lords in his company were advancing against the with a force of five thousand men . . . and hastily gathered on the third day after the feast of ascension up to 3,500 people.[27]

Clearly, York's army had not been raised in secret, and his intention of marching to London were known by Henry and his advisors. Yet, if they did not expect York to attack, they were being naïve.

From a European perspective, the duke of York was considered a 'safe pair of hands' to run government. Henry's illness had exposed the weakness at the heart of government. An Italian account written within days of the battle acknowledged (my translation):

> Although it is not good for those who are dead, yet it cannot fail to favour our proceedings, because it will make the French a little more cautious, as during these differences between the English, they had become great and daily became greater.[28]

In terms of geopolitics, Burgundy, allied with the Dauphin, was arrayed against Charles VII. The Yorkist faction were opposed to France and the influence of the Angevins. The duke of York had been allied to Burgundy since 1443. The city-state of Milan was in alliance with Burgundy against French influence in Naples and Sicily. Despite the economic recession, English wool and cloth was in high demand in Europe, particularly so in Venice and other Italian city states. For commercial reasons, much could be gained for Italian and Burgundian merchants if York was back in power, as our writer openly acknowledged.

The confrontation began, like Dartford, with an exchange of letters. The various accounts that have come down to us are an exercise in Yorkist propaganda, many intended for circulation: therefore, the speeches are presented are what the Yorkists either said, or wished they had said with hindsight, while the reply from Henry is perhaps fiction. York, as at Dartford, claimed he was acting out of loyalty to Henry 'praying & besekyng him to take hym as his true man and humble suget'.[29] Yet to act against the king's government was one thing, to act directly against Henry was treason: York went beyond criticism: he wanted justice not on the king's terms but his own. York claimed that Henry had broken promises and was intent 'to destroye us all and theruppon a grete othe hath made that there ys no one othere way'.[30]

Henry condemned the duke of York as a traitor – perfectly believable – as the Dijon relation notes:

> he was unaware of any traitors around him were it not for the duke of York himself who had risen against his crown . . . And thus when the duke of York had the aforesaid reply the battle became more violent and both sides with banners displayed began to fight . . . the battle began at the stroke of ten hours in the morning.[31]

A French chronicle records what happened from a Yorkist perspective (my translation from the French):

The said king of England, by the advice of the Duke of Sombersert, summoned all the great lords of his kingdom, in order to come before him, their simple estate, and in a small company, to order, as he said, high and important affairs of his kingdom . . . And the Duke of York thought he would be there. And in fact, he set out on this subject and left his country [*sic*, lands/estates] with a thousand men-at-arms in his company. Besides which came after him four to five thousand combatants. Of those thousand combatants the king and those of London were well informed, but not of all the others who came after.

The king and the said duke of Somberset deliberated, accompanied by the earl of Northumberland and several other lords, and because of what they feared, hastily collected people in London, and resolved to go against York . . . and still knew nothing of the large company which followed this Duke from afar, as is said. Therefore, the king set out on the campaign and rode, he and his host, so that he met this duke. Then immediately, without bargaining, both parties began to argue roughly and beat each other.[32]

Of the fighting, several conflicting accounts exist. Our Italian commentator writing from Bruges tells us (my translation from Italian):

A great part of the nobles have been in conflict, and the Duke of Somerset, the Earl of Northumberland and my lord of Clifford are slain, with many other lords and knights on both sides. The Duke of Somerset's son, who presented the collars of the king, was mortally wounded; my lord of Buckingham and his son are hurt. The Duke of York has done this, with his followers.[33]

Our Burgundian writer reports that on the 22nd (my translation from French):

Very early the king sent a herald to the duke of York to know the cause for which he had come there with so many men, and it seemed to the king . . . the duke should not be rising against him . . . the reply made that he was not coming against him, was always ready to do him obedience but he was well intended in one way or the other to have the traitors who were about him . . . should be punished and that if he could not have them with good will and fair consent, he intended to have them by force.

The king replied he knew of no traitors and signalled to the duke that he had crossed a symbolic line into treason, by rising in rebellion against the crown. In the wake of this missive to the duke, fighting began.[34] This account is largely drawn from Yorkist sources i.e. what the Yorkists hoped they said, rather than what they may have said. Our Italian commentator, relying on news from Bruges, tells us 'on the 22nd the king set out to continue his journey, but when they were outside the town they were immediately attacked by York's men, and many perished on both sides'.[35] This implies no parlay was offered, which is contradicted by the other accounts of the proceedings.

Reading the sources that exist carefully, even allowing for bias, York mustered an army to negotiate from a position of strength: he had with him perhaps 1,000 men, the king double that. York's position was bolstered by the Neville earls of Warwick and Salisbury with perhaps 2,000 more men. A battle was not inevitable, the earl of Warwick made it so: how right Thomas Basin was to call him perfidious.[36]

Seeing the Percys arrayed in the marketplace, Warwick could not believe his luck in being able to bring his bitter rival, Northumberland, to battle. Following a volley of arrows – one wounded the king, and indeed it may have been intended to kill Henry – Warwick led the attack about 10am against Northumberland. York's retinue moved off about 11am, it seems ostensibly to protect Henry VI from the Percy–Neville feud that was rapidly taking hold in the marketplace of St Albans. In the fighting in the market place Lord Clifford was killed outright commanding the barricades. York's arrival, prevented wholescale massacre by Warwick and took Henry into his protection. Somerset tried to fight his way out. He charged into the street and killed four men before he was fatally wounded.[37] Northumberland also fell in combat. Stowe implies that the 'The duke of York, and the Earls of Warwicke and Salisburie, with their hosts . . . commanded his host to slay all manners of Lords, Knights, Squires, Gentleman and Yeoman.' Of those killed, Ralph Babthorpe, justice of the peace of the East Riding, was seen by the Commons as a profiteering member of the king's household: York sought him removed in 1450.[38] The Herald of Berry reports (my translation from the French):

And the Duke of York killed the earl of Somerset and Northumberland, the duke of York took several prisoners, as well lords, nobles, and others, whom he conducted to London with the king, the whole government was placed in the hands of the said duke of York.[39]

Our Italian commentator tells us what happened in the immediate wake of the battle in a letter of 3 June 1455 (my translation):

The Duke of Somerset was taken and forthwith beheaded. With his death the battle ceased at once and, without loss of time, the Duke of York went to kneel before the king and ask pardon for himself and his followers, as they had not done this in order to inflict any hurt upon his Majesty, but in order to have Somerset. Accordingly, the king pardoned them, and on the 23rd the king and York and all returned to London. On the 24th they made the solemn procession, and now peace reigns. The king has forbidden any one to speak about it upon pain of death. The Duke of York has the government, and the people are very pleased at this.[40]

Stowe goes onto tell us:

the earl of Wiltshire and Thomas Thorpe, lord chief baron of the exchequer with many others fled and cast away their harneis in ditches and woods. This done, the duke of Yorke the Earles of Warwick and Salisburie came to the king where hee was, and besought him on their knees of grace and forgiveness of that they had done in his presence.[41]

The Dijon relation places this scene in Delapre Abbey.[42]

The duke of York, Warwick and Salisbury had committed treason, gambled and won: they again controlled the king. Seemingly God had blessed the righteousness of the duke's cause. York removed the king from power, and attempted to erect a new source of authority based on the will of the commonweal and Parliament. Although York was victorious, the situation was not yet resolved: he had attacked the king's army and killed three important nobles which was a stark change from the peace and stability that he had originally aimed to bring. Professing his loyalty to Henry, York requested that he and Warwick be made his advisors. The defence of the commonweal was no excuse for treason as York claimed. Nor was self-defence against an alleged attack. More than this, St Albans was a watershed, not just because it was the first confrontation between the Yorkists and those with the king which took on a military dimension. Equally as important, St Albans publicly marked the point when it became obvious that whoever controlled the king ruled England. Moreover, St Albans marked the moment when a return to 'business as usual' in consensus rule was made extremely problematic: the two factions had drawn blood, and too few nobles held a central position to act as mediators.[43] Yet the clock was not ticking inextricably to all-out confrontation between the two clans.

Chapter 12

# THE SECOND PROTECTORATE

In the custody of the Yorkists, the king was returned to London with York and Salisbury riding alongside him, and with Warwick bearing the royal sword in front. Because loyalty to the king was the only issue that could unite the nobility, whoever had control of the king could become the focus for magnate unity. In this sense, it was 'business as usual' with York in the place of Somerset, but rather than a consensus, York ruled at the whim of the Nevilles.

On 25 May 1455, Henry received the crown from York in a clearly symbolic display of power. York made himself Constable of England and appointed Warwick Captain of Calais. Parliament was summoned by writs of 26 May. Henry himself opened Parliament on 9 July. There was a respectable turnout of lords: thirty-three lords spiritual and twenty-seven lords temporal attended. Unsurprisingly the duke of Exeter and Thomas Percy, Lord Egremont, who had played leading roles in the Neville–Percy violence and were both in custody, were absent. There were some equally striking attenders. Egremont's brother, Henry Percy (1421–61), who was the new earl of Northumberland, attended, as did John, Viscount Beaumont (1409–1460), who had refused to serve under York in his first protectorate, reminding his colleagues 'that he was with the quene'.[1] As after Dartford, a full pardon was issued by Henry, reinforced with a Parliamentary pardon for those who had fought with York. Responsibility for the battle was assigned, sensibly enough, where it did least harm, to those killed in the battle. This judgement made very good sense, as the battle was effectively removed from the political agenda. Buckingham, the leader of the royal forces at St Albans, was put under bonds but not otherwise punished, and to ensure that bygones were bygones, Buckingham was among the lords summoned to Parliament.

Yet it was not so easy to win over 'hearts and minds'. York was heading government but had no official mandate to rule, he was not Protector. This made dispensing justice problematical. Unlike the first protectorate, York led a narrow faction; St Albans, as could be reasonably expected, exacerbated regional feuds.

## The Courtenay feud

In the West Country, the Courtenay family sought to 'flex their muscles'. Taunton Castle was the home of William Bonville (1392–1461). He was in a feud with Thomas Courtenay, earl of Devon. The Courtenays and their supporters rampaged across the West Country for much of October, Sir William Bourchier being one of their targets.[2] James Luttrell was a key player in this violence and 'clash of clans'.

Thomas Courtenay and his men proceeded to terrorise the neighbourhood of Exeter from their castle at Tiverton. The Michaelmas term sessions could not be held in the city owing to this anarchic state of affairs, and on 24 October the recorder, Nicholas Radford, one of William Bonville's closest advisors, was brutally murdered by the earl's sons in person. They ransacked the town houses of Bonville and Fitzwaryn, and then laid siege to Powderham Castle, seat of Bonville's friend and their own distant kinsman, Sir Philip Courtenay.

Escalating the chaos, Luttrell got into a dispute with one of his feoffees, Alexander Hody. According to a complaint by Hody's wife, Luttrell detained one of Hody's servants at Dunster Castle, Somerset, and then took thirty-five armed followers to the home of Hody's father-in-law Thomas Bratton. The court papers tell us this was for one reason, the 'purposyng to have murderyd and sleyne the seyd' Alexander Hody. On finding Hody was not with his father-in-law, Hody's wife tells us Luttrell and his gang beat and seriously wounded another of her husband's servants, John Toker, who was present. Having learned that Hody was at Taunton Castle, with Bonville. Hody's wife again under oath tells us Luttrell with his gang broke down the doors of the castle made entry and seized goods. Either Luttrell or one of the gang violently assaulted Hody's wife and threatened to stab her to death; one of the gang seriously wounded another of Hody's servants, Water Peyntore; another gang member seized Hody's priest by the hair and beat him whilst others beat him with the pommels of their swords. The origin of this dispute may have been financial – Alexander claimed money from Luttrell; the allegations of violence may have been a legal fiction to bring the matter within the jurisdiction of a court. A settlement was reached in February 1458.[3]

In retaliation Bonville sent a party of armed men to the earl's fortified house at Colcomb, which they looted on 15 November, and then tried to reach Powderham to raise the siege by crossing the estuary of the Exe. Pitched battle was joined on Clyst Heath.[4] Devon's trial was scheduled for 9 February 1456, but never took place.[5] Henry VI pardoned Thomas Courtney in February 1457.[6]

With 'an axe to grind' against Henry and the earl of Devon, it is no surprise William Bonville and his two sons, notably William Bonville, 6th Lord Harrington (1442–60) joined the duke of York: his sons were killed at Wakefield, and he himself was executed after Second St Albans aged about 68. Luttrell, like the earl of Devon, was 'mad, bad and dangerous to know': but one had to be to survive in the Middle Ages. Bastard Feudalism at its most basic pitted the strongest against the weakest in a game of chance. Their family feuds were brought with them to Wakefield: national politics was shaped by personal enmity.

These petty feuds raised the question of York's right to rule. He had no title, or formal position in government.

## The king's illness

When Parliament met again on 12 November, the throne was empty, and it was reported that the king was ill again. A Commons delegation was sent to the Lords, led by one of York's retainers Walter Burley, who requested that an able person be appointed Protector to address the disturbances in the West Country. The Lords agreed to consider the proposal. After a three-day impasse Burley returned to the Lords on the 17th, asking that a Protector be appointed. The Lords reluctantly agreed that York was the only possible candidate and resumed the office of Protector; this time serving solely at the king's pleasure. York stipulated he could only be removed by the Lords and king in conjunction. York was given the power and authority that was lacking in government to bring Egremont, Bonville and others to heel. York was vested as chief councillor: a new form of minority government had begun, which implied that Henry would never be a real king again.[7] As in York's first period of rule, there was no Yorkist monopoly of grants. In February 1456, after protracted negotiations, York was finally able to get a settlement with the Calais merchants and the unpaid garrison, which enabled the merchants to make advances guaranteed by control of the customs revenue. The agreement also made it possible, for a Yorkist, the earl of Warwick, to become Captain of Calais, an appointment that was to have momentous consequences later in the decade. To emphasise that York's rule still rested on what Yorkist propaganda now defined as an honourable tradition, the post-St Albans Parliament petitioned that Humphrey of Gloucester be formally rehabilitated. Indeed, York's conduct at the start of his second period as king in all but name, argues Christine Carpenter, 'makes it clear that he was trying to construct a workable basis for governance from among the nobility. He had no choice, for the Nevilles were still the only substantial noble family prepared to support him in opposition, although Viscount Bourchier remained with him and was appointed treasurer.'[8]

Futhermore, York made sure that his actions over St Albans were rehabilitated and the penalties imposed on his supporters were wavered: the order of resumption passed against the Dartford rebels was cancelled. Sir William Oldhall's attainder, signed by the king in person for offences going back to 1450, was revoked. Penalties again Thomas Young and others were likewise cancelled. York, however, showed a vindictive streak towards Thomas Thorpe and Joseph: their penalties, so recently cancelled, were resumed. Moreover, York sought to curb the influence of the king's household, and cut its spending and numbers. York's justification for his actions was to restore domestic peace and quash rebellion at home which his own actions at St Albans had triggered.[9]

As far as legal recriminations were concerned, bygones were to be bygones, yet history was to give the lie to this.

### Protector York

The nobility was lukewarm to York's resumption of office. Why? His opposition to Somerset, and inter alia the king, was not considered to be the loyal opposition as York claimed, but was seen by the majority as treason, which St Albans was. Those who tried to take power from the king or dictate to the king were considered suspect in their motives, especially when they did so by force. Even with York in power, the 'elephant in the room' as it were, was Henry VI himself. No legitimate mode of governance existed to cope with an inadequate king despite what York said or tried to enact. York compounded this issue: many of the nobility still felt, despite Henry' obvious failings, that he had the right to have men of his own choice around him and was the anointed king. In this regard, Somerset replacing Suffolk in 1450 was, by and large, business as usual. York, appealing to the commonweal for his legitimacy and rule through council, was construed as illegitimate.[10] Yet York tried to govern from the centre, to make government work.

In terms of domestic policies, York aligned his regime with the protectionist stance of the London merchant community. Foreign merchants were blamed for the economic crisis, and York took steps to restrict their trading activities and the export of bullion, in the form of coin. Italian merchants were restricted from travelling beyond specified ports. By 1457, thanks to the Yorkist reforms, 93 per cent of all wool exports passed through London.[11] Such monopolisation of trade into London, and inter alia Gloucestershire and Norfolk, crippled the woollen trade of York and Beverley.[12] York's protectionist regime, coupled with economic stagnation, meant that by 1468–9 York was recorded as producing 1,809 cloths, down from 3,200 in 1395: the downward spiral continued, with 922½ cloths being stamped in 1475. Cloth production had dropped by two-thirds in 80 years.[13] Such actions hardly endeared northern merchants to the new regime, but it did win loyalty of London and Calais to the Yorkists. Customs were used to cover debts rather than current costs. York's economic policy was one likely not to succeed: how could the costs of Calais be funded if not by customs? Protectionist policies risked similar measures from Burgundy, Milan and elsewhere.[14] Trade wars are always ill-advised.

York's vision of himself and his long-term position as Protector is best summed up by his dealings with France. Soon after seizing power, the duke hoped to use war with France as a method of drawing allies to him, and his government: nothing like a war to bring a degree of unity to the magnates and peers, as Henry V had learned. By June 1454, the French king feared for an English army to land: the English threatened the coasts of Saintonge and Guyenne.[15] The Bailiff of Caux brought news on 21 August 1454 that the army from England was at sea.[16] Fear of invasion did not abate till new year 1455.[17]

York's aggressive foreign policy was seeking to exploit the rupture between Charles VII and his son the Dauphin. The pair faced civil war between them by 1456, into which real life 'game of thrones' came the Yorkists, the Milanese and the duke of Burgundy. In June 1455, an English herald sent news to Jean duc d'Alençon that his ally, the earl of Somerset, was dead at York's hands. The herald was from the retinue of duke of the Exeter. Sensing an opportunity, d'Alençon sent an embassy to Calais at the end of July, from whence they were in London by the close of August. The sergeant-porter at Calais was Andrew Trollop, who became involved in the event planning that followed. He had served his apprenticeship in in Lancastrian Normandy, arriving in Normandy with Edmund Beaufort and Osbert Mountford, whose lieutenant he had been at Fresnaye in 1451. From 1436, Trollop had been in Fastolf's retinue at Fresnay, as a man-at-arms. At Calais when he joined the garrison in 1451 under Edmund Beaufort, he was also a mounted man-at-arms, listed first among them.[18] Having dealt so far with the negotiations, Sir Richard Harrington told the duke of

York on 23 November that d'Alençon had offered military support if York sent an army to Normandy to re-conquer lost territory. The duke met d'Alençon's embassy on 28 November. As well as consulting with the York, the chancellor and treasurer Buckingham was part of the negotiations, so too Salisbury, Warwick and Wenlock. Part of the negotiations centred on a marriage between York's son Edward and d'Alençon's daughter. Re-conquest was an attractive proposition: if he regained Normandy, his position was secure. Charles VII seriously feared, York was told, that Normandy would support a return of the English: officials ousted from office as well as minor officials and the remaining English colonists resented French rule, and would rise in rebellion if English soldiers landed. York also made aware of lingering loyalties to the English in Maine. D'Alençon was drawing York into his own feud with Charles VII: reducing Charles VII's power and curtailing the French monarchy, as we discussed earlier, was a key feature of English policy. For York, a chance to win back France was incredibly tempting: furthermore, a war with France would allow him to levy taxes and unite the nobility behind him against a common enemy. It seemed an ideal opportunity to cement his power and to overturn Somerset's failure.[19]

York met Alençon in Bruges, and promised to land in Normandy in 1456. York demanded 30,000 ecus to pay his army. For his part Alençon was to provide York with artillery and offered to open the gates of Le Mans to the Yorkists, telling York that if he offered to drop new taxes levied by Somerset and the French, and more overkeep his army disciplined, Caen and Rouen would also open their gates. Richard Wydeville, earl Rivers, and Lord Welles were part of York's diplomatic team, along with the duke of Buckingham. York and Alençon both agreed that if Henry VI was seen to lead the English army, Normandy and Maine would submit once more to English rule. Alençon wanted revenge on Charles, claiming 'by Gods death! I will keep to the duke of York and the other lords of England what I have promised them.'[20] In October, Thomas Gille went to Calais on behalf of Alençon, to speak with Richard Wydeville, before crossing to England to speak with York, where he arrived 23 November.[21] Wydeville was told that the Normans insisted that the duke was their lord, and would fight for the English. Alençon demanded from York 10,000 francs to defend Normandy from the French, 30,000 francs to pay for artillery he had already had cast, as well as a further 30,000 francs for his own expenses, a duchy in England, all the taxes from his seigniory. Wydeville was also told that Normandy was almost total undefended, only Pierre de Brezé and 100 lances remained.[22] When Gille arrived in London, rather than meeting York, he met on 26 November the earl of Warwick. Warwick pledged on oath that he would live and die to accomplish the will of 'the noble prince of Alençon' and offered to sell all his land to fund the expedition.[23] Warwick took Alençon's information to Parliament: which, we are told by Warwick, voted for a tax to fund the army, and promised to descend with 40,000 men. This was detailed verbally to Gilles by John Wenlock, chamberlain to Queen Margaret. John Cley, York's treasurer, also sent a letter to Alençon via Gille confirming what Wenlock had spoken about. The King of Aragon and the count of Armagnac (brother-in-law of Alençon) pledged 10,000 men. France was to be carved up for the gain of England and others.[24] Whatever was being discussed was handled by Warwick. York was away from London in Huntingdon, hunting: Warwick, to use the vulgate, was 'in the driving seat'. York and the chancellor eventually received Gille on 20 December: yes, York said, the English would land, and Alençon would be compensated with 30,000 francs for the artillery he had had cast. Edward, York's oldest son, would be married to Alençon's daughter, whose son would marry one of York's daughters. He gave no time scale. York also acceded that all of Maine would be handed to Alençon on a successful conquest of Normandy.[25]

Thomas Gille was back with his master on 6 January with a tentative agreement. York had given serious consideration to an offensive in Normandy. He was following a very different policy to Henry, which moreover implies that he felt secure enough in his position to embark on such a policy, which was reliant on still being Protector in 1456 and beyond. The negotiations with d'Alençon and the potential threat of English incursion onto French soil understandably angered Charles VII. Fate, however, intervened before any commitment to d'Alençon could be made.[26]

In November 1455 Queen Margaret had appealed for military aid from Charles and James II of Scotland. Charles would besiege Calais and James would attack Berwick.[27]

Chapter 13

# YORK ASCENDANT

By December 1455 York's rule was beginning to founder. The Commons had demanded an Act of Resumption to re-establish the finances of the royal household on a new footing. York was committed to its effective implementation as curbing royal excess had been a central tenant of his manifesto since 1449. Under the Act, the queen was to have her expenditure limited to the large sum of 10,000 marks a year. Furthermore, the Duchy of Lancaster was no longer to be used to finance patronage and the king's own personal projects, which primarily meant the abandonment of the controversial Eton and King's College Cambridge. York hoped to persuade the Lords to agree to further resumptions, but without success. Unquestionably, York had never been able to achieve a broadly-based consensus government despite his best efforts. For example, the earl of Wiltshire had flatly refused to co-operate. Faced with opposition, all of York's major officers were men whose loyalty he could count on.[1] That meant primarily the Nevilles or the Bourchiers: York was admitting he was incapable of creating unity amongst the nobles and magnates.

York had almost no influence over the royal household. Those gathered around Henry refused to agree to the Act of Resumption, and drew allies from the nobles who were opposed to York's rule in principle. The Lords moreover, would not sanction the Act as it represented a radical restructuring and restriction of the crown's power to make grants. Whether Henry was *compos mentis* or not at the start of February 1456, he instructed the lords to reject the bills from the Commons.[2] Realising 'the game was up' – Margaret had brokered a deal with Scotland and France for armed assistance to restore her husband to the throne in an alliance supported by the Papacy[3] – York tried to overawe Parliament with a military coup, before Margaret could strike. York and Warwick arrived in London on 9 February with 300 men-at-arms.

The coup failed. Benet tells us 'almost all the lords resisted them and went to fetch the king and accompanied him to Westminster to persuade him to refuse a resumption'.[4] York could not control the lords and it seems had never fully enjoyed their consent to his second term as Protector.[5] Indeed, two days later, York told Alençon that the King of England was coming to remove the government from him and that he could give no answer if an English army was to land.[6] York had to turn his attention to domestic affairs rather than the conquest of Normandy. Despite Margaret placing her husband back at the head of state, politically her efforts to oust the Yorkists were in vain when she tried to reclaim the reins of government.[7]

Despite having resigned as Protector on 25 February 1456, York was still effectively in charge of the government. It is no surprise therefore that Salisbury and Warwick continued to serve as councillors, and Warwick kept his position as Captain of Calais. In May York was still sufficiently in command to respond to the king of Scotland's threats and to deal with other matters of foreign policy.[8] If anything, the Yorkist factions were the winners of 1456. York had committed treason, but faced no repercussions and, for the time being at least, controlled Henry and would so till early summer 1459 in one form or another.

In terms of foreign policy, York had to deal with the fallout from his bid to reconquer Normandy. In France, d'Alençon was arrested on 27 May 1456: he was charged with treason for aiding the king's enemies. This was perhaps understandable, as Charles was in conflict with his son, the Dauphin and future Louis XI, who had sought Burgundian aide to topple his father. So serious was the rupture, that on 30 August 1456, the day Charles gave orders to Antoine de Chabannes to invade the Dauphine, Louis fled, his excuse being that he was seeking to join the duke of Burgundy on crusade. Charles blamed the comte d'Armagnac, who had also been sounded out at the end of 1455 over his support for an English re-conquest of Normandy, for this final rupture between father and son.

In consequence of the Franco-Scottish treaty, in June York was sent north to defend the border against a threatened invasion by James II of Scotland. The Franco-Scottish alliance was destabilised by the formal rupture of Charles VII and the Dauphin: by October James II expressed his disgust that the French had not held up their part of the agreement in face of English raids.[9] York used Sandal Castle as his northern power base.[10] Were Duchess Cecily and their youngest children, who included the future Richard III, with him? Cecily certainly visited the city of York, but the whereabouts of the children and where she lodged are not known.[11]

Based at Sandal for several months, the duke no doubt hunted in the park around the castle, as well as the Old and New Parks of Wakefield. He would also have been able to gauge local loyalty to himself and the Yorkist faction: he may have made assumptions four years later on what he learned now about the loyalties of local families, such as the Watertons of Methley, the Pilkingtons at Snapethorpe, the Nevilles at Chevet and others. Snapethorpe was home to Sir John Pilkington (c.1425–79) who fled with Salisbury and Warwick to Calais in 1459, but following Towton was rewarded for his loyalty. His involvement in the events of December 1460 is, however, not known.

It would have been on these hunting parties that the duke would have become well acquainted with the landscape around the castle, as well as the castle's defensive capabilities. Who visited the castle and what was discussed are lost to history. Warwick meantime, based in Calais, was testing both his military strength and his alliances. Over winter 1456, he launched a series of raids into Burgundy, with the duke of Burgundy deploying troops on the border with Calais in reply: it brought Warwick, the duke, Philippe le Bon and his half-brother Antoine de Bourgogne into negotiations. An Anglo-Burgundian strike into France in aide of the Dauphin was projected. The friendship between Warwick, Louis de Valois and Duke Philippe would shape the next decade.[12] In retaliation, Charles VII and James II were planning their own revenge.

## The Loveday

Following rioting in London during August 1456, the court moved to Coventry: this made a lot of sense. Removing government from a potentially dangerous and threatening situation was a logical course of action. However, this event is traditionally understood to have been inspired by the queen to take Henry away from Westminster and to administer 'abnormal' governance. These views, propagated primarily by London-based, pro-Yorkist chroniclers are not representative of political reality. Henry had not been sedentary: government was peripatetic, but for Londoners, who considered their city the centre of governance, Henry's absence was considered by these biased writers to be abnormal. London-centric, Yorkist sources, often written after the fact, are to exonerate the Yorkists and provide a false narrative to justify usurpation. Any move of the court away from London must have had some darker meaning as it detracted from London and its pre-eminent status. The history presented by these writers, often reliant on hearsay, is unreliable at best. Indeed, most of these London chronicles were written with hindsight to prove armed conflict was inevitable because armed confrontation *had* taken place: the circumstances of 1459 were backdated to the fall of the second protectorate.[13] York was still in power in summer 1456. No rupture had occurred with Margaret or anyone else at this stage. This does not mean, however, that York faced no opposition.

Over the summer of 1456, whilst York was at Sandal, two of his principal retainers involved themselves in their master's affairs in Wales, and in doing so 'stirred up a hornet's nest'. York had appointed himself Constable of Carmarthen and Aberystwyth in 1455, but effective control remained with Gruffydd ap Nicholas. Gruffydd was ousted by Edmund Tudor, the king's half-brother whom York had sought to have disinherited. Tudor occupied the two castles that York was keen to hold. In reply Sir William Herbert and Sir Walter Devereaux intervened. They had already caused havoc by Devereaux seizing the mayor of Hereford in April and Herbert attacking the property of the earl of Wiltshire at Orcop: the two then planned to attack Kenilworth and murder the king.[14] Combining their efforts, in August the pair raised 2,000 men, marched through Wales and took over the castles so recently occupied by Edmund Tudor. On 25 October Herbert raided Glamorgan and Llandaff. James II of Scotland implied this was part of a coup by York to oust Henry.[15] Edmund Tudor died on 3 November, leaving a pregnant wife. The marriage of Edmund to Margaret Beaufort on 1 November 1455 united the Beauforts and the king's half-brothers into a powerful alliance against York. On 28 January 1457, the 13-year-old Margaret gave birth to a son, Henry Tudor, the man who would remove York's son from the throne of England in 1485. But all that was in the future.

As Christine Carpenter notes 'the disturbances of August to October 1456 should have been the moment from which a rapid descent into armed conflict resolution occurred: why this did not happen is not clear.'[16] The royal household and the queen exploited the situation to their own benefit: the queen's coup was complete by October when York's nominees in the major offices of state were replaced by men loyal to the queen. One factor that seems to have precipitated civil strife and conflict was that a sufficient percentage of the nobles and magnates were opposed to partisan rule: therefore, they did not object to the reshuffle of the great offices of state. Buckingham and Shrewsbury are reported to have objected to some of the dismissals among the great officers, but their voices were in the minority. Certainly, Buckingham would have been delighted at the removal of the Nevilles: he was in dispute with Warwick in the Midlands, but he was also aware that further conflict was damaging and perhaps futile. At the same time, the

Nevilles, with their primary opponents dead and Egremont contained, felt secure enough not to take up arms to defend York. In essence, neither side was strong enough militarily, or willing to risk all-out war. Stalemate ensued. Yet, efforts were made to 'keep the show on the road'. The minority council still functioned, and represented the continuing aspirations of many of the nobility towards unity around the king.[17]

If any rift existed between York and the queen at the end of 1456, no evidence of this can be found from contemporary sources. With relative 'peace and plenty' York looked to the future, planning the marriage of his daughter Elizabeth to John de la Pole, the young duke of Suffolk. The marriage seems to have been agreed in February 1457. It further cemented York into the Lancastrian dynasty.[18]

In September 1456, Herbert and Devereaux along with Gruffydd had submitted to Henry. This event was followed by a Great Council being held at Coventry on 28 September which ordered Devereaux to imprisonment at Windsor and then Marshalsea, from whence he was pardoned on 7 June 1457, along with Herbert.[19] York was forced to hand over Carmarthen and Aberystwyth to Jasper Tudor, earl of Pembroke. Bishop Wayneflete, the Lord Chancellor, as well as the duke of Buckingham reprimanded the duke in the presence of the king for his behaviour: if York rebelled again or stirred up trouble, he would have to face the consequences of his actions.[20] York sensibly 'kept his head down'. That York did not attempt a coup, or more violence break out, in 1457 again shows that the Nevilles and the majority of the nobles were more concerned about managing their own estates and 'keeping the show on the road' than factionalism. Moreover, it shows that these events, were not triggers to further escalation. The few episodes of disturbance are a-typical: fighting and conflict was not the majority experience of the period. Yes, disturbance happened, but were of a scale nature that did not unduly 'rock the ship of state'.

International events changed domestic policy and put York and the Nevilles once more back centre stage. York brokered a peace treaty with Scotland on 6 July 1457: in Europe Charles VII had broken with the duke of Burgundy, York's ally. Some form of alliance had been brokered by Warwick with Antoine de Bourgogne, the comte d'Etampes, almost simultaneously.[21] That Warwick was openly negotiating from March to early August, rather supposes that the Yorkists still held control. That Warwick was now openly supporting the Dauphin and Burgundy against France, perhaps resulted in what happened next.

On 28 August 1457, Pierre de Brezé attacked Sandwich. The French fleet had left Honfleur on the 20th, carrying 5,000 armed men provided with ladders and other siege equipment. The town, then a major port, was destroyed, three English ships were sunk and 300,000 livres of goods taken from the warehouses in the port. It was a devastating raid, and one that could have led to all-out war.[22]

Rather than Sandwich, de Breze had been heading for Burgundy: pushed by wind and a hastily assembled fleet led by the Dauphin, de Breze attacked England.[23] Sandwich was the primary port from which Warwick supplied Calais: in attacking the port, de Breze hoped to deny resources to Warwick, who himself expected to be besieged since April, and took measures to re-supply the garrison.[24] In reply, Warwick was appointed Keeper of the Seas in December 1457. His appointment was part of the Great Council which met at Westminster between 12 October and 29 November 1457. The goal was to set aside the differences between York, Salisbury – inter alia the Nevilles – and the sons of the dead of St Albans, Henry Beaufort, the new duke of Somerset, and his allies, who may have attempted to assassinate York.[25] Thomas Thorpe was made Keeper of the Privy Wardrobe, and Somerset was given a 12-year lease of the Isle of Wight. The earl of Devon was rehabilitated. Henry was being magnanimous, rewarding both sides.[26] This event became known as the Loveday. As well as healing rifts, it exposed, and formally recognised, that there were two opposing camps around Henry.

The king ordered a further council to meet on 27 January 1458, for concluding the matters that remained outstanding from the previous council. The lack of armed conflict following the previous council gave Henry much to be thankful for. The high-status deaths at St Albans were always going to be contentious. Thomas Clifford (1414–55), 8th baron Clifford, had commanded Henry's troops in St Albans' marketplace securely placed behind barricades. As Warwick's men surged into the market place, Clifford became a casualty of this fighting. It cannot be seen as murder, but his son John Clifford (1435–61) understood it to be so. Northumberland, as far as we can tell, died in battle and Somerset died of his wounds. It is possible all three were deliberately targeted: but it seems unlikely. They were killed in an act of treason, and as such, their deaths were unlawful. The grudges that John Clifford, Henry Beaufort (1436–64), 3rd duke of Somerset, and Henry Percy (25 July 1421–29 March 1461), 3rd earl of Northumberland held, did indeed precipitate war. At the same time the royal household had good reason to resent and opposed York and his Neville allies for attempting to 'clip their wings' with the Act of Resumption. Slowly but surely these tensions would lead to war. Yet, those around Henry worked tirelessly to keep some form of consensus non-partisan government working.

York arrived in London with a retinue of 400 armed men on 26 January 1458. Salisbury had already arrived. Somerset arrived on the 31st, and Exeter, Egremont and Clifford in the first days of February. According to Yorkist accounts, Somerset attempted to ambush York as he rode from Banyards Castle to Westminster.[27] Northumberland arrived on 26 February. In the negotiations which followed neither York nor Exeter was present. The 'angry young men' of St Albans, Somerset, Clifford and Northumberland, ambushed Warwick on 9 March, prompting the king to lead a public procession for peace at Westminster a few days later on 17 March.[28]

The king had long abandoned any demand for justice for the perpetrators of Dartford and St Albans, but the widows and heirs wanted retribution. The Yorkist earls had no case against the angry young men. Through the king's arbitration, the Yorkists were bound to endow a chantry at St Albans Abbey for the souls of the dead compensate Somerset's widow £5,000, Clifford's heir £666 13s 14d. the damages in the Percy–Neville feud estimated to be £15,000 were cancelled. Egremont was bound over to keep the peace for ten years. In response all heirs were to withdraw their demands for vengeance.[29] The Loveday restored the political system which welcomed York back into public life once more after his rebuke months earlier by Wayneflete. As Michael Hicks makes clear 'there was no inevitability to the progression to further conflict'. Henry had achieved his stated objective.[30] All parties accepted the terms, and on 23 March 1458, the feast of the Annunciation of the Blessed Virgin Mary, the king and queen with reconciled parties attended mass at St Paul's in London. York walked alongside the queen, Salisbury with the young Somerset, Warwick with Exeter. For Henry it was 'peace in our time'. Further conflict was not inevitable.[31]

Once Henry and Margaret had left Westminster, York and the Nevilles remained in London. Having been rehabilitated back into public life, York was able to act as chief councillor, and attempted a form of rule based on noble co-operation: it was in fact the only way they could proceed.[32] Under the terms of the Loveday, the Yorkists were bound over to pay compensation for St Albans, payment of these sums was to be by reassigning royal debts; very little hard cash actually changed hands. York had been bound over to pay Somerset's widow £1,666 66s and the new duke the remaining balance. York had driven a very hard bargain: the payment would be in tallies – albeit yet to be issued – from his owed pay as lieutenant of Ireland. By agreement, these tallies were transformed into a licence to export wool up to a value of 10,000 marks. This left York with 50 per cent of the exports assigned to him to cover his owed pay. We cannot say if York ever shipped any wool. York and the Nevilles had to promise to settle land valued at £45 per annum: this amount to providing land costing £900. A two-year respite was allowed, if the Yorkists paid £45. Clearly the Yorkists had agreed to amortize their land, and stood by the agreement.[33]

For Egremont, still angry about the loss of Percy lands to Neville and his own treatment by York, believing that the time was now right to right the wrongs of 1453-4, petitioned Henry to restore the manor of Wressle to the Percys. The King agreed, and on 10 June 1458 handed Wressle back to Lord Egremont.[34] Ralph Griffiths argues that this was all part of a plan by the queen contain York and the Nevilles' influence.[35] I am not so sure.

William Plumpton (1404–80) seneschal and master-forester of the honour and forest, constable of the castle of Knaresborough from about 1439 to 1461, and seneschal of all the earl of Northumberland's manors in Yorkshire, now enters the scene. Plumpton issued arrest warrants against supporters of Salisbury for inciting rebellion when they refused to vacate Wressle.[36] At the same time, the queen had bolstered her position, when she had placed Lawrence Booth, Keeper of the Privy Seal and her chancellor, into the vacant office as Bishop of Durham, a diocese that covered much of the Neville lands. Booth proceeded to withdraw annuities that his predecessor had granted to Salisbury's branch of the Nevilles. Reignition of the Neville–Neville feud, pushed Salisbury and his son into full military alliance with York.[37] Trouble was brewing but conflict was not inevitable. None of these events were triggers for 'civil war'.

Indeed, York, heading the government, invited Philippe le Bon to England to negotiate a trade treaty and more formal peace treaty: this had been brokered since 1457 by Warwick. The treaty was to be negotiated by York and Somerset.[38] John Wenlock was party to the negotiations, who was met at Mons. The contingent from England was a veritable Neville family affair: we find the bishop of Salisbury – Warwick's uncle and confessor to Monsieur, the second son of Chares VII – Henry Bourchier, William Bourchier, as well as Warwick's brothers John and Thomas, all headed by Warwick.[39] It was a Yorkist delegation like no other. As Schofield notes, 'in the course of the negotiations, Warwick succeeded in establishing a secret understanding between Philippe and the Yorkist leaders'.[40] This 'understanding' between Burgundy and the Yorkists would come to define the next decade and shape English politics like no other. In May 1458 Warwick and Antoine de Bourgogne (brother of the duke) met at Etampes. They had met at Andres in 1457, charged with negotiating a peace treaty and economic treaty since October that year. His diplomatic skills and link with Burgundy gave Warwick allies, influence and money: what happened next was driven by Warwick.

The young and charismatic Warwick, as Captain of Calais and Keeper of the Seas, embarked on what his detractors considered to be piracy, to pay his own men and enrich himself. The reality is somewhat different. In France, the English in Calais – for this we need to read Warwick – were charged with espionage by Pierre de Brezé, Seneschal of Normandy, and ordered the arrest of English merchants in Gravelines and Bourbourg, and seized English shipping. In reply, the duke of Burgundy enacted similar measures.[41] On 29 May 1458, Warwick, using his small fleet, attacked a Castilian convoy of twenty-eight ships near Calais. The battle started at four in the morning and went on for six hours. Warwick's fleet lost 80 men, while another 200 were wounded. The Castilians lost 120 men with another 500 being wounded. In total, Warwick's fleet captured six ships, one of which was at least 300 tons which was taken into Calais. Later that summer, Warwick's forces attacked a convoy from the Hanseatic League comprising seventeen vessels returning to La Rochelle. In a short action Warwick's fleet captured a number of them. The Hanseatic League was outraged, and in reply Henry VI organised a commission at Rochester to report back by August on Warwick's affairs. Unabashed, Warwick attacked another convoy on or by 7 September. With complaints about Warwick and 'piracy', the government mooted Warwick's replacement.[42] In reality, much of the so-called piracy was enforcing customs and impressing ships into the navy as he was legally allowed to do. Indeed, the exchequer plea regarding the seizure of ships in 1457 shows Warwick and Trollop impressing ships for the king's navy.[43] Indeed, on Henry's orders, Warwick impressed Burgundian ships on 10 March and 8 July: one ship from Kampen was returned in exchange for two English ships taken by the Burgundian fleet.[44] These were ostensibly policing operations to prevent smuggling of woollen cloth and other goods.[45] The use of the charge of 'piracy' towards Warwick was one means of his detractors to remove him from office: behind these charges lay Admiral Exeter, who hankered after the title Keeper of the Seas. Richard Wydeville, earl Rivers, was placed at the investigation to Warwick's conduct. We assume, in revenge, Warwick paraded him through the streets of Calais in early 1460, berating him for his low birth after the attack on Sandwich. Warwick harboured grudges.[46] The claims of piracy were all spurious. Castile was a French ally, an important one for Charles VII in his escalating conflict with Burgundy and England. Charles was also brokering an alliance with the Holy Roman Empire, and presented his son Charles as candidate for the vacant Bohemian throne, supported by the king of Aragon and of Denmark.[47] Two power blocs were slowly emerging: France, Aragon, Castile, and Germany against Burgundy, Milan, the Dauphin and the Yorkists.

As Penny Tucker convincingly argues, Warwick was innocent of charges of piracy, stating 'there is no good reason to believe that he was disobeying his orders or engaging in piracy'.[48] Warwick, if guilty of anything, was of obeying his orders to enforce customs. If, as Yorkist apologists of today claim, in the 1460s the queen was intent on the destruction of the Yorkists, it seems rather a surprise for Warwick in May 1458 was to lead a delegation to discuss the faltering truce with Burgundy? That delegation included his brothers, Thomas and John, as well as his Bourchier cousins and Henry Scrope, who would become leading Royalists cum Lancastrians.[49] Indeed, on 14 May, Henry himself gave Warwick powers to negotiate with the duke of Burgundy, and a safe conduct to the duke's ambassadors.[50] The negotiations ran from 27 May to 1 July.[51] Negotiations centred on Warwick continued from 12 July well into August.[52] This rather suggests that Warwick's supposed 'piracy' was politically awkward, but not sufficient to have him ejected from Calais or his other posts. Indeed, by early August 1458 an invasion of Normandy was feared by Charles VII:

> our lords of Narbonne and great seneschal of Normandy, to carry letters to the officers of the king, captains, burghers and inhabitants of the said towns and places, mentioning that the English were on the sea with great power and army, and that each one should keep his guard, with what the noble and frank archers of the country had assembled.[53]

York had begun negotiations with Charles almost as soon as the Loveday had been agreed, to solidify a peace with France.[54] Clearly York's optimism had become misplaced by the summer. To resolve the tensions, on 29 August Sir John Wenlock, on York's agency, landed in Antwerp. Wenlock was to meet the duke of Burgundy, and then rendezvous with Charles' agents at Rouen.[55] Clearly, York and Warwick were not outside of government, as mythos implies, but very much heading it.

Indeed, safe conduct was given to Philippe le Bon, Antonio de la Tour and William Caxton on 20 August as part of a commission from Henry VI to assemble at Bruges. Both York and Somerset were entrusted by Henry on behalf of the aldermen of London to negotiate. The two delegations met at Calais on 24 October 1458.[56]

Chapter 14

# BEGINNING OF THE END?

As winter 1458 began, some form of consensus government was still being attempted. Superficially the major differences between the two parties had been healed. No formal rupture existed between York and the queen as a letter written in October 1458 tells us (my translation from Italian):

> The Englishman told me that the queen is a most handsome woman, though somewhat dark and not so beautiful as your Serenity . . . She has a most handsome boy, six years old . . . The following noblemen serve her: the Dukes of Somerset, York . . . Exeter, Buckingham, Norfolk, and Suffolk. Their wives are at Court also, and when . . . the king's son and all the duchesses speak to the queen, they always go on their knees before her.[1]

York was not outside of government: York was heading the government. That Warwick did have political enemies, which included the duke of Exeter, who sought to remove him from office is a given.[2]

Chancellor Wayneflete called Warwick to account at a general council summoned at Westminster on 11 October, to ostensibly to discuss his actions in the Channel concerning shipping from Portugal, Castile and the Hans. Warwick suspected it was to deprive him of the captaincy of Calais and delayed his attendance. York did not attend. Warwick was in London by the start of November: a second summons had been issued on 6 November. On the 9th, when leaving Council, he became embroiled in a fight with members of the household staff. All the chronicles present the same story: one of Warwick's retainers struck a royal servant – why is not recorded – an offence against the king. The situation rapidly escalated as cooks and other servants arrived from the royal kitchens armed with spits. In the ensuing chaos, Warwick himself was bundled out of Westminster by other lords at the Council.[3] He alleged a year later – on slim evidence – that it was a plot to assassinate him.[4] Escaping by boat to Greyfriars and then Warwick, with permission of the king to return to Calais, he avoided being held to account for his actions. IF this happened.

Against Warwick's pleadings, and later assertions to the contrary, York in late 1458 felt sufficiently secure in his position to act in foreign policy.[5] York, via Henry and we assume Margaret, embarked on an ambitious negotiation of a peace treaty with France, to end the stalemate truce. Whatever negotiation were being made, they were being conducted at the court of Burgundy with Pierre de Brezé acting as proxy for Charles VII.[6] John Wenlok was one of the official ambassadors, given safe conduct on 26 October 1458, and he was in France at Rouen on 3 November.[7] Wenlock's commission is given in Stevenson.[8] The delegation was in France on 31 October as a Quittance of 1 November confirms: 'for the journey he is now making, from the city of Rouen to Calays, to bring a safe-conduct from the king to Messeigneur Jehan Wanelock and Messire Loys Galet, Anglois, being in the said Calays 18 livre tournois'.[9] York sought to arrange a marriage between Edward Prince of Wales and a daughter of Charles VII as part of a peace treaty with France, and the marriage of his son Edward to a royal princess and likewise Henry Beaufort, duke of Somerset.[10] That Henry Beaufort was allied to York at this stage and part of the Burgundian negotiations is confirmed by Philippe le Bon.[11] The initial negotiations concerning the marriage of Edward Prince of Wales, Edward earl of March and Somerset to the daughters of the comte de Charolais, duc de Bourbon and duc de Gueldre coming to nought the daughters of the duc d'Orleans and comte du Maine was proposed. The comte du Maine was Charles d'Anjou, uncle of Queen Margaret. The duchess of Burgundy, Isabelle of Portugal, was sounded out by Wenlock as to how Burgundy would react to such marriages. Margaret hoped to cement alliances with France and not Burgundy.[12] Making the existing treaty into a lasting peace was a dividing line between York on the one side and Margaret and her allies on the other, which slowly but surely exacerbated tensions.[13] Yet a poem written at the time shows a degree of unity between both factions.[14]

That York was involved and named as controlling government rather shows that the Yorkists, contrary to their own pleadings, were not ostracised and continued to be directly involved in government as new year 1459 dawned. Indeed, on 31 December 1458 Charles VII accepted the terms that Wenlock had brought.[15] On 15 January 1459 the terms were sent to Henry VI, and Wenlock returned to England via

Burgundy to agree terms with the duke. The duchess of Burgundy was prepared to continue negotiations so long as York sent men skilled in negotiations – an obvious slight to Wenlock.[16]

Indeed, the Loveday was 'Peace in our Time'. We see that on 11 February 1459 the Yorkists made their payment of £45 towards the chantry at St Albans, and the same day Warwick secured new assignments for bad tallies. A month later the royal commission was preparing his fleet as Keeper of Seas. Salisbury received payment of £9 5s on 22 June, so too his son, as wardens of the West March.[17] Neither the queen nor anyone else for that matter was set on destroying the Yorkist lords, at least openly. Indeed, whatever charges levelled at Warwick by Wayneflete and others were 'his maritime misconduct in 1458 and 1459' did not cause the Loveday arrangements to collapse.[18] We need another reason.

Reading between the lines however, two negotiations were being conducted: one from Henry for the marriage of his son, led by Wenlock and which involved York, and another centred on Warwick and his uncle Richard Beauchamp (?–1481), bishop of Salisbury. We already noted that the Burgundians were not happy with Wenlock or the negotiations. War between Burgundy and France seemed imminent. What had caused this?

We may find an answer in the Bibliothèque Nationales de France. A report written to Pierre de Brezé by his secretary concerns the bishop of Salisbury. In this document, we find that Henry had decreed that the bishop of Salisbury should be authorised to make journeys to France under the pretext of seeking information about St. Osmond, who had been canonised the previous year and had been the first bishop of Salisbury. He was to travel incognito so that the co-ambassadors would have no knowledge about his journey or involvement. The bishop requested he involve his nephew, the earl of Warwick, in the negotiations, and swore on oath that nothing was to be decided with the ambassadors of Burgundy to be prejudicial to the king and kingdom of France until he had brought a commission from Henry. The Bishop of Salisbury stated on oath that he had been tutor to Henry VI, that he was 'a man whom the king loved most in the world' and that he knew 'as much of his secrets and privy counsels as anyone in the world'. The bishop added was 'principal ambassador, with the earl of Warwick, of a mission now sent to treat with Burgundy for the prolongation of the truce' and that the duke of Burgundy had sent his terms to Henry 'about Christmas.' The bishop continued: 'But the king of England had declared to him that he did not like to treat with Philip the Good because of the latter's great falsehood, that he would much prefer to come to an understanding with Charles VII.'

Henry feared that war with France or Burgundy was inevitable, and preferred an alliance with France 'than the false duke of Burgundy.' He stated that:

> the prelates of England, the Dukes of York and Norfolk, the Earls of Salisbury and Warwick, and the other lords of their family, who formed the most numerous party and is well informed of their good will in this matter . . . and also told me that all the merchants and all the peasant's demanded peace with France.[19]

What was going on? Clearly some around Henry favoured peace with France and not Burgundy, and sought peace with France, no doubt against Burgundy. Whose side were the Yorkists on? York was involved with the negotiations with Burgundy, but also 'name-dropped' by Bishop Beauchamp. The Dauphin seemed certain that a truce with Burgundy would allow an English army to land to aid the duke of Burgundy if attacked by France.[20] For his part, the duke of Maine travelled to London around 19 January.[21] He is named in contemporary documents along with Wenlok tying to hammer out a deal between France and England.[22]

For whatever reason, by March negotiations over peace and a marriage between the king's daughters, and those of the count of Maine and duc d'Orleans, had broken down, despite the request for personal intervention from the duke of York, despite an apparent agreement at the start of the year.[23] On 16 March, Maine informed Henry that Charles was preparing to invade England.[24] Judging from archive documents in France, he seems to have left London around the 19th of the month and was paid 50 livres and safe conduct to bring back the ambassadors from England.[25] The English embassy in Rouen left around 20 March.[26] Peace had been brokered, but not with France: we remember the Bishop of Salisbury 'swore that nothing should be decided with the ambassadors of Burgundy to be prejudicial to the king and kingdom of France'.[27] Presumably, this also meant nothing was to be prejudicial to Burgundy. That the duke and the Dauphin – better known as the Universal Spider for his spy network – was engaged in 'secret matters' is preserved in his papers.[28] Whose side were the Yorkist lords on? Who stood to benefit from war with France? Georges Chastellain (1405–75) notes:

> the Count d'Estampes, the Bishop of Toul, the Mareschal of Burgundy, had gone to Calais to hold a Parliament with the English the Count of Varvyc [Warwick ed], and any others, for the renewal of the truces between the king of England and the duke, with some other secret understandings

which they had together . . . the king was afraid of this Parliament held at Calais, and that Warwick was on the side of the duke of York, who was more inclined towards Burgundy than towards France.[29]

Chastellain tells us that Charles VII was so concerned about the Yorkists' true intentions that he sent spies into England and Flanders, which is confirmed by an existing report sent from the Burgundian court.[30] One of Charles's agents also found letters and other documents hidden on a wool merchant lodging at Gravelines, who had come to the town from Calais. Chastellain adds that Charles prolonged the talks until he had come to a firm conclusion about the trustworthiness of the Yorkists. The blame of failure was placed on the duplicitousness of the Dauphin and the duke of Burgundy.[31] Inter alia, Warwick and the Yorkists and indeed the duke admitted on 7 March 1459 he had made truces with the English, which were counter to the will of Charles – and Queen Margaret no doubt whose aunt was queen of France – who openly threatened war.[32] Economically both England and Burgundy needed a 'free trade agreement': economic necessity drew this alliance closer together against France.

If Margaret had wanted a deal with France, her kith and kin, and the Yorkists with Burgundy, one can easily see how, if held to account for destabilising a treaty with France, Warwick would overact, especially when one takes into consideration the attempt on his life, a new bishop in Durham and also the issue of Wressle. Certainly, Warwick and the duke had agreed terms on 9 February.[33] Henry – controlled by York? – agreed to meet Burgundian emissaries Jacques du Vingage and Simon de Moerkerke in London, exploring damages and liabilities between both sides since 1458.[34] Some form of Yorkist administration collapsed at the end of May when Warwick recalled the ambassadors on the 21st.[35]

With the count of Maine withdrawing from negotiations, France and England were in dispute, with a phony war being played out at sea, with Warwick once more centre stage. English ships were captured on the Gironde.[36] On 25 May French goods captured from English merchantmen whilst at sea were to be returned.[37] Henry for his part exchanged Norman merchants for English sailors taken prisoner at Queensborough and imprisoned at Dieppe on 22 June.[38] So serious was the threat of war, that invasion was feared from France:

they have entirely raised the coast from the north to the west, saying that the army of France was prepared to come thither in force; and to do this, there are commissioned, with a great number of soldiers, the archbishop of Canterbury, the lord of Rieveres, and Sir Girvais Clifton.[39]

No doubt these events – and NOT a Yorkist rebellion – explain why East Anglian squires were summoned on 26 April to be in Leicester by 10 May with as many men as possible, arrayed for two months service. On 7 May 3,000 bow staves and as many sheaves of arrows[40] were ordered from the Tower. The document authorising the armament explains why such steps were necessary, because 'the enemies on every side approaching us, as well upon the sea as upon the land'.[41] Not Warwick invaded, as history books have us believe, but the French. That York's failure would lose him prestige and credibility is perhaps a given: was he held responsible with Salisbury an Warwick for the failure of peace talks and resulting conflict? I suspect they were. Was war a good enough reason to remove York? Perhaps.

Yet, we must admit, no one knew in spring 1459 that conflict between York and the King was inevitable. We know in 2025 it was coming, and it is all too easy to read into events an interpretation of events once conflict had started. Clearly therefore, raising troops and arming them was not to guard against Yorkists, but the French. We must seek another trigger for war. It is in this context of Neville 'double dealing' that we need to read a letter sent to Queen Margaret via Prior John Bromley of Arbury. From this letter, the earl of Salisbury or perhaps the Yorkists en mass, had committed a rebuttable offence, possibly treasonous, which Salisbury flatly denied in a letter to the queen:

> as for myn own partie as I wol aunswere to our lord I nevere ymagined, thought ne (or) saied eny suche matter or any thing like therunto in my dayes. And in like wise I dare well say for my said lord and son as ferre as ever I herd or in eny wise knowe (knewe) unto their honire (this houre) as I doubt nat thai wol at al tymes right largely declaire for theim silf. And therfore therin or in eny othere, concernyng my trough I pray yow alway to aunswere largely for me. And if there bee thing that I may doo fo (to) your wele cretifieth em, and ye shal to the performing therof fynde me right hertly dispoed as our lord knoweth, which have yow ever in his blessed keping.[42]

The exact date of this letter is not certain, with various hypotheses given by various historians.[43] IF we accept Hick's argument that the letter is dated 7 March 1459, it correlates very well with a degree of fallout from the failure of negotiations with France due to Warwick. In response to Warwick's subterfuge, he was to be removed from Calais, resulting in his claims that he would lose his English lands rather than Calais.[44] The important passage is that *someone* was accusing Salisbury, Warwick and York of releasing information that was potentially damaging, now being aired in the context of negotiations for peace: the lack of reprisals in the wake of the attack on Sandwich was the queen's fault and she overstepped her authority? This was a claim made later that year, but what the accusations were, we shall never know. We are not even confident the letter is from 1459, but its contents, as we said, do correlate with pollical events of that year better than 1458. Given Warwick's enemies, and his sense of victimisation, Warwick's alienation and the crown's justifiable anger at him at causing war with France, was a defining moment. Warwick harboured grudges, and his experience of the events at Westminster Hall meant that the clock was now ticking down rapidly to armed confrontation.[45] A writer close to Warwick elaborates – perhaps wrongly – that Somerset was to blame, who with others:

> It seemed to them that if he were slain, the party of Yorc would be easier to put down. So they concluded that, the next day, they would summon the count of Warewic to come to the king. And in the event of this, a gentleman who was very careful to stir up the debate between them while the said de Warewic was before the king, who had died there if a knight had not been adverted to. When the count of Warewic thus escaped from this peril and great treachery, as much as he could have ridden against the duke of Yorc and the count of Salsebery, his father, he told at length the manners that had been held to him or by king Henry, of which they were much amazed. If they held a council together, or they concluded to wage war on those who governed the king. And to do this, as soon as they were able to write and command all those who were of their party and to join them, that, on a day appointed, they should be present, and that it was for the good of the king and the public thing of England.
>
> After this conclusion, the count of Warewic took the summons to the duke of Yorc and his father, and then went to Callaix to his people, who had already been informed how they had intended to kill him. And there was received from his uncle the count of Fauquembergue, and from the Sauldoyers of the town, with the burghers and merchants, whom they all made a great deal of trouble with; then the next day he related all his case to his said uncle de Fauquembergue, in order to have his advice on this to know what he had to do with it, and then they concluded that it would be good for him to return to Monseigneur d'Yorc, and the said de Fauquembergue would keep the town of Callaix. And then the Count of Warewic summoned all his men-at-arms, especially Adrien Trolot.[46]

## Paranoia

Quite what happened, had to happen, is lost to history, though we are sure fear and paranoia played a major part. Warwick felt himself set apart from other nobles: he was the premier earl after all. In Calais, he was king in all but name of an independent state, with little Henry could do to check his avaricious nature. Warwick believed he and the Nevilles were to become victims of the queen's revenge, leading to the possible destruction of his estates: what was given by Parliament could be as easily taken away. Warwick believed that he had been the victim of an assassination plot, and that the queen was 'hell bent' on his destruction. If such a plot existed does not actually matter: it matters that Warwick believed one did exist. If a plot did or did not exist is immaterial to what followed. Exeter and Warwick were at loggerheads: Exeter was an ambitious trouble maker. His claim to the crown, was strengthened by his marriage to York's daughter. Any offspring had thus the claims from both sides of the argument to use the vulgate. That Exeter in summer 1460 was close to the queen, if not her principal councillor, suggests he imagined himself in such a pre-eminent position before the events at Northampton. Another trigger for Warwick may have been the sea battle in the straits of dover in late June when Warwick's ships from Calais captured two or three ships from Castile and two Genoese carracks in the Straits of Dover. The Castilian ships were enemy ships, so a legitimate target: that the event was weaponised by the duke of Exeter who objected to Warwick as Keeper of the Seas, because as admiral of England he felt he should have the job, which was owed to him by right, as a prince of the royal blood, as much as it was to Henry Beaufort.[47] This is of course all speculation, but it may be a fruitful avenue for future research.

Warwick was convinced that the time of retribution by the 'angry young men' of St Albans had come, implanted this fear in the mind of his father and York. Why York at the apogee of his power became involved with Neville politics is lost to history. It may be down to York's own personality.

If York was one to panic in a crisis point, he had Warwick to egg him on: Warwick was the *éminence grise* and had been since 1455 and during the following decade. Warwick had little to gain and everything to lose from the status quo: York as king opened the way for undreamt-of superiority for the Nevilles, and Warwick of course. Removing Henry was the only way to secure the Neville and wider Yorkist interest. Without a shadow of doubt Warwick was a destabilising and unstable influence on York and his father, Salisbury and Europe. If York is seen not as a born solider and leader, but more as a born subordinate, then the events from 1450 start to make more sense. York and Norfolk's failure in 1450–2 only turned to success through the Nevilles, and Warwick in particularly. York acting on his own initiative, with his lack of clear focus and objective beyond the destruction of Somerset, implies a man somewhat out of his depth and lacking clarity in what he was seeking to do. His hesitant steps in endeavouring to reform government were singularly replaced with direct action for usurpation: a change of modus operandi that speaks of a change of dynamic in the Yorkist position, and the proposal of a different solution to the one York had originally proposed. Only with Warwick taking the lead does the Yorkist cause gain momentum: York surrounded by others to urge him on – who had a vested interest in regime change – were as much in charge of what happened from 1454, as York.

This is of course all supposition and my opinion, which may be far off the mark, but it is the historian's task to offer insights and ideas about events. We cannot reconstruct the past exactly; we can merely offer commentary on what we take the primary source material to tell us. No two historians will interpret the same document the same way. Again, as historians we are free to change our minds: the perils of putting ideas on paper and not water, means that we can be accused of hypocrisy when our thinking changes based on reassessment of source material and access to new archive documents. History is constantly changing, so too must ideas about past historical events.

Perhaps we will never know what finally precipitated armed confrontation in summer 1459. That the Yorkists suffered a spectacular reversal of fortune is given, but the causation is not clear; perhaps petty local grievances, jealousy, ego, simply 'boiled over'.

Chapter 15

# OBLIVION

At the moment when the country needed a sense of national unity in face of invasion from France, factionalism took centre stage. For the queen, preventing war against her family was her priority. We may sense her influence in the failure to react against the attack on Sandwich. That York was blamed for the breakdown in negotiations, and his pro-Burgundian support added 'fuel to the flames'. Those opposed to York, whatever their true feelings about France, backed Margaret. Without a king to act as mediator, paranoia led the duke to oblivion. In June 1459 a Great Council was summoned to meet at Coventry on 22 June, presumably to discuss the war with France and negotiations with Burgundy.[1] What happened next is shrouded in myth and 'fake news'. York, Salisbury and Warwick, as well as the archbishop of Canterbury, the bishops of Ely and of Exeter, the earl of Arundel, Lord Bourchier and others apparently, failed to attend.[2] For what happened next, we have to trust a single document, written after the fact by a Yorkist partisan. We do not know what happened beyond a great deal of supposition from this single, unreliable source. It seems the duke of Buckingham and Chancellor Wayneflete laid formal charges against York, about which we know nothing, and he was judged by his peers in his absence and found guilty. Henry refused to punish York, Buckingham and the lords then begged the king to show no more clemency to York, and Henry bowed to that pressure. York was bound to swear an oath that bound him to refrain from rebellion, which he signed. It was a very public humiliation: because they had submitted to Henry's will, York, Warwick and Salisbury were allowed to go free.[3] What were the charges? Was York held personally responsible for the breakdown in the negotiations with France? Not obeying a royal summons was technically treasonable. We do admit that the reasons for York not attending the king's summons, the specific charges laid and why, seem impossible to determine with any degree of certainty: this has not stopped much myth making. We can be sure that the troops levied earlier in the year were to guard against the threat of French aggression and NOT to arrest York.[4] Whatever the cause of the rupture, armed confrontation was the response between York and the king, and in Europe, France was set to go to war with Burgundy and Burgundy's ally, England.[5]

Whatever had caused the rupture between York and Margaret – and we know nothing for a fact despite what chronicles and historians say about the cause and our supposition may be totally wrong – the news was rapidly propagated. The duke of Burgundy was informed on 8 July that the reconciliation between the duke of York and Queen Margaret had come to an end, and violence between the two opposing factions seemed imminent.[6] The duchess of Burgundy still hoped for some form of reconciliation could be achieved between England and Burgundy as August began, as had been hoped for in May.[7] It was not to be.

By the time the Great Council met, the young Margaret Beaufort, sole heir of John Beaufort, duke of Somerset who had died in 1444, was again a widow. Her marriage to John de la Pole, son of the duke of Suffolk, had been annulled in 1453, she married the king's half-brother Edmund. The marriage was seemingly to strengthen Edmund's claim to the throne should Henry be forced to designate him his heir. Margaret was 12 years old at the time of her marriage in 1455. De la Pole had married Elizabeth of York in 1458. Edmund was dead at the end of 1456, as we noted earlier, and on 28 January 1457, the 13-year-old Margaret gave birth to a son, Henry Tudor, at Pembroke Castle. She later married Sir Henry Stafford (c. 1425–71), the second son of Humphrey Stafford, 1st duke of Buckingham, on 3 January 1458, at the age of 14. A dispensation for the marriage was necessary because Margaret and Stafford were second cousins; it was granted on 6 April 1457. Her father-in-law was the prime accuser of York's misdeeds at Coventry. On 29 July, Henry was vested with a livery dower of £600 for his wife.[8] This act brought Margaret and her son, Henry Tudor, into public life and the court. Beaufort and Tudor blood, and status from Buckingham, meant the young Henry had a claim to the throne, one as strong as York's if Parliament could be persuaded to legitimise the Beaufort claim from John of Gaunt. If the king relapsed in his illness, it could be reasonable to suppose it would not be York who would be Protector. If Prince Edward died, the young Henry Tudor looked set to be king, surrounded by his Beaufort kin as a regent.

## Blore Heath

According to evidence presented to Parliament later in the year, Sir William Oldhall had allegedly begun plotting with Thomas Vaughan in London on 4 July to overthrow Henry and replace him with York. The same evidence reports that Alice Neville, duchess of Salisbury, at Middleham in conjunction with the bailiff of Bawtry, near Doncaster, Henry Walron, during late August was also plotting armed rebellion.[9] On 18 September the earl of Salisbury was at Borough Bridge with an army of perhaps 5,000 men drawn from across the West Riding.

A writer close to Warwick – or even Warwick himself – placed the blame on what happened next squarely on the shoulders of Exeter, rather than the Yorkists:

> After the duke of Yorc had taken the administration of the kingdom of England, some of the lords were not satisfied with it . . . such as the duke of Excestre, the children of the late duke of Sombresset, the lord of Beaumont, and others: so de Beaumont and Excestre made a large army, with whom were joined the Count of Willechier,[10] the Count of Denchier,[11] Monseigneur Fidelan, the Lord of Welles, and others; All these lords could have in their company fifteen thousand men, all on horseback. From whence the news reached the of the Duke of Yorc, he promptly assembled what people he had to resist the enterprise of the Duke of Excestre and his allies, giving the charge and conduct of his men, to the counts of Salsebery and Warewic.[12]

Our writer gives the Yorkist army as 25,000 which is exceptionally unlikely. In another account, Salisbury had barely 400 men, which is more reasonable. Whatever sparked confrontation is lost to history and has been obscured by 565 years of myth and propaganda propagated by both sides.

Salisbury raising his banner in defiance to the king alienated all but the most committed Yorkists. Few were prepared to fight for the cause York espoused: the majority of the nobility and gentry were not invested in York's vendetta, fear and paranoia, and fewer still were prepared to commit treason.

In Calais, Warwick had put to sea with the garrison and issued a manifesto explaining his treason. As before, the Yorkists were at pains to show themselves as true and loyal subjects, ejecting disloyal subjects who had abused their position of trust close to the king. Such evil council could only be resolved through the intervention of:

> The advice of the grete lords of his blood that it will lyke hym to put his moaste truste noble persons in devoure to the redresse of the same and to punyshe evenly the causes of the sayde myscheves aftar theyr desawetes

and demerites in example of all other here aftar, and that it will please his good grace tordeyne suche governaunce for thobservynge of his lovars here aftar reste of his land and subiects for supportinge of his sayde royall estate for the course of merchaundise and for the chastisyng of suche errours and mischeves afore rehersed to thentent that his subiects love, obeye, and drede his estate and lawes as ever aforne they have done, and his enemyes to be put in as greate fere of his might as ever they were of any of his progenitors wherby he his land and people may growe to as greate worshipe and profyte as they have bene holden of aforene amonges all cristen Realmes, where vpon we notifie vnto you that to this entente we woll employ our persons and labours about the Kyngs moste noble person and there to be assystaunt yf it be his pleasure nor presuminge to take vpon vs any private rule or entre into eny mattar betwene eny estate of this land and any of vs or to eny quarelle or revengement othar then lawe woll but only entendynge with gods mercye to the performinge and accomplishinge the causes afore seyde, etc.[13]

Warwick arrived in London on or around 20 September. The manifesto said nothing that had not been said already over the previous decade.[14] A war erupted to win 'hearts and minds'. Henry issued a similar manifesto:

Trusty and well beloved, We have understande by dayly report made to us how divers persons of the northe partes of this our Beaume make great assembles and gaderyng of people for what cause we understande not, How be it that it cannot be thought but it sowneth greetly to the trouble and subverting of our pees and lawes. Forsomuch we, of the greet and singuler truste that we have in you, wil, desire, pray you specially, and also charge you, that with alle thee might and strength that ye can make ye addresse you towardes oure persone in alle haste, to entende and assiste us with other our trewe subyects to the rebuking and setting of parte of thothat wold anything presume to attempte ayenste oure persone or our saide pees and lawes . . . yeven under oure prive seel at oure castel of Kenilworth the xi day of Septembre. To oure trusty and well beloved the Bailiff and Burgeys of the toune of Beverlay.[15]

As Michael Hicks states, 'contemporaries recognised treasonable insurrection when they saw it'.[16] Beverley was staunchly loyal to Henry, and would send an armed retinue to fight for the king at Northampton. The Yorkists had started to arm themselves and Henry took all precautions to prepare an army to oppose the coming insurrection by a minority faction.

As both sides 'rattled their sabres' York's own involvement is not so clear. He had been at Sandal sometime that summer, as the castle accounts completed on 29 September 1460 record:

10s are allowed to him for the benefit of John Sprigonell' grave of Sandal in the 38th year paid for the price of one bull for the household of the late Duke by Thomas Gayton' clerk of the said household . . . £4 15s 1½d half farthing on John Sprigonell' grave there in the 38th year for his arrears.

£10 8s 4d on John Erle grave there in the immediately preceding year with 9s 4d for perquisites of the court for the same year charged above.

112s 3d on the lord accounts this year from which ......................paid to John Clapham in the castle there in various .......... 74s 9½d.[17]

The accounts cover the period from Whitsun (7 June) to St Michael's Day (29 September). Did York travel north and then head to Ludlow? We assume so.[18] Why was he in Yorkshire? To meet Salisbury? He was certainly recruiting from his Manor of Wakefield and the neighbouring Honour of Pontefract. We only know this from pardons issued in 1460. The Harringtons (Thomas and James) from Brierley were part of Salisbury's network who were present at Blore Heath, but it seems York had his own retainers at Ludford, if not Blore Heath. John Saville esquire, son of Sir John Saville of Thornhill, constable of Sandal, was involved in the attainder process in winter 1459. He was pardoned alongside Thomas Harrington on 18 November.[19] Saville's loss of his three offices in the Manor may have been sufficient punishment.[20] Sir Richard Welles was charged on 14 October to confiscate the lands of York, Warwick, Salisbury, Thomas Harrington, John Conyers and both John Saville father and son as 'traitors and rebels'.[21] Also present at Ludford and we assume Blore Heath was John Pilkington of Pilkington, Lancashire, steward of Sowerby in West Yorkshire since 1442. A convicted rapist and thug, he fled to Calais with Salisbury, and took advantage of a pardon in March 1460.[22] Sowerby was granted to John Talbot, earl of Shrewsbury on 9 December 1459, who also became steward of the Manor of Wakefield and constable of Sandal Castle.[23] After his marriage, John lived at Wakefield; his father Robert Pilkington was listed third amongst those accused of extortions, oppressions and the like by the parliament of 1459. John on returning from Calais, and we presume participating at Northampton, on 30 July 1460 was made a controller of the port of London.

Locally, William Wakefield of Pontefract was pardoned on 5 December.[24] Wakefield was named in local legal action regarding support for Salisbury in rebellion in Knaresborough. Also named in this case were John Wakefield and William Wakefield junior, James Wilsthorp, the leader being Robert Percy of Scotton, who we come to later. Salisbury (or York from Sandal?) clearly mobilised tenantry within the honour of Pontefract. Another so named was John Bere, pardoned 29 March 1460.[25] Bere, from Berwick-upon-Tweed, sat as an MP for Carlisle from November 1449 with another Neville man, Thomas Derwent alias Derwentwater. A close associate of Thomas Neville, son of the earl of Salisbury, he may have been killed at Wakefield, or equally Towton.[26] Derwent had been at Blore Heath and Ludford.[27] We meet him again later. Clearly the interplay between Salisbury's retainers and York's overlapped to some degree. Others from York's household included his receiver general John Mylewater of Stoke Edith, Herefordshire and Walter Mymme of Fairford Gloucestershire, who had been auditor of York's lordship of Denbigh in November 1458.[28] Pardons were also obtained by a group of yeomen with similar connections in Yorkshire and elsewhere in the North: Thomas Bone alias Boon of Penrith yeoman; Thomas Sclatter of Kendal yeoman; John Withes of Aismunderby (in the Parish of Ripon) yeoman; and a merchant, John Robinson of Scarborough.[29] We meet Sclatter later.

York we assume, travelled to Ludlow, not in the company of Salisbury, but in an act of hubris, marched to Ludlow from Sandal. This supposes that York had some degree of involvement in this Neville feud: at one moment he was at the heart of government, within weeks of the peace negotiations failing, York was 'enemy number one' and I am not sure why. York had everything to lose by rebelling. He had no need to, unless fate – Warwick – intervened. The Roll of Parliament records what happened next:

> the earl of Salisbury set off . . . from the castle of Middleham in your county of York, and of your knightly courage you took the field without delay with those of your lords who were then about you, and in a princely manner with great speed you hastened towards the region upon which the earl of Salisbury was advancing, which caused him to depart from his original plan, and take another route to meet with the said duke of York and the earl of Warwick, so that their coming together might make a mightier army.
>
> In which progress the said earl of Salisbury with Thomas Neville, John Neville, knights, sons of the said earl of Salisbury, Thomas Harrington, knight, John Conyers, knight, Thomas Parre, knight, William Stanley, esquire, son of Thomas, late Lord Stanley, and Thomas Meryng, late of Tong in the county of York, esquire, accompanied by a great multitude of people, numbering five thousand or more, arrayed for war, with their standards displayed, intending to destroy your most royal person, on the Sunday after the feast of St Matthew the apostle, in the thirty-eighth year of your most gracious reign [23 September 1459], at Blore in your county of Stafford, in the fields of the same town called Blore Heath, falsely and traitorously raised war.[30]

Salisbury could have withdrawn or disbanded his forces: he chose to fight, and his forces 'there slew James, Lord Audley, and many other knights and esquires, and others of your liege people, and did more besides, cutting the throats of many of those who had been sent there'.[31]

Salisbury had precipitated war, and when his son, Warwick, brought the Calais garrison ashore, an act in itself which probably treason and certainly a breach of trust and gross misappropriation of national armed forces, there was no going back. The Nevilles had chosen to escalate familiar grievances for a second time into all-out war.[32] The Yorkists could no longer portray themselves as reformers of royal government, who were anxious to protect the king and the realm from what they saw as 'evil' councillors. Accounts of Blore Heath are drawn from Wavrin primarily. He copied into his chronicle two differing accounts: a longer text, which was presumably from Warwick's pen, and a shorter account that may also be from Warwick, or preserve a lost contemporary newssheet. Wavrin studiously copied these texts written by others: he is not the originator of these lost documents. The first, shorter, and possibly the most reliable of the two accounts provided by Wavrin describes events that lead to the earls of Salisbury, Warwick and March leaving York to head for Calais, and in doing so encountered an army of the queen's men, led by Audley. The earls defeated the queen's army, killing Audley and the death of lords of 'Charinten and Kindreton'. Taken prisoner was 'the baron of Duclay and Messire Thomas Fiderne.' The victory was in spite of the earls' force being only 400 strong while the royal force was 6,000 or 8,000. Audley's son, Humphrey, was granted the castle of Snodell and park from the earl of Warwick.[33]

The second text by Wavrin, which discusses the battle of 'Blouher', describe the desertion of royalist troops on the sighting of cavalry pennons. The unknown writer – presumably Warwick or someone from his circle – locates the encounter it 'prez dune forest', and makes the royalist commanders Lords Welles and Beaumont and the duke of Exeter, and indicates that Warwick was the leader of the opposing side. This account has been considered to be a confused amalgam of reports about other battles and 'demonstrably wrong'.[34] It may be, but it is clearly crafted as a piece of propaganda, setting the stage for retribution against Welles at Towton, Beaumont at Northampton and Exeter is named for his opposition to Warwick as keeper of the Seas. Undoubtedly, this forms part of Warwick's 'Apology', edited by Wavrin in his compilation of newssheets in the mid-1470s to make his chronicle. All three men were involved in the Ludford campaign and probably led that encounter: Exeter was rewarded 'for good service against the rebels' being handed York's principal seat of Fotheringhay on 19 December 1459 at the Coventry Parliament.[35] John, lord Neville, was granted Middleham in recognition of his service against his half-brother, the earl of Salisbury.[36] Beaumont, for 'his labours against the rebels and traitors Richard duke of York, Richard earl of Warwick, Richard earl of Salisbury and their accomplices', was given the stewardship of the manors of Grantham and Stamford, seized from York by the crown. We find Richard Welles was rewarded 'for good service against the rebels of 40l yearly' on 21 March 1460. Also rewarded was Thomas Roos of Helmsley, awarded the same fee earlier on 10 March 1460.[37] Most of Salisbury's retainers at Blore Heath would be at Wakefield, and it seems, provide him with very few soldiers.

Had that battle not taken place, and had Salisbury withdrawn without giving battle, a workable compromise could have been found between York and the royalists. Salisbury's clash of arms changed that. The Yorkists had exposed themselves as driven by power more than reform. If the Yorkists had hoped for a mass uprising in their support, they were sadly wrong. Salisbury's decision to turn and fight gave Henry the initiative. Salisbury's hollow victory did little to disguise the weakness of the Yorkist position. They now appeared as traitors in open rebellion. This might not have mattered so much had they not been seriously outnumbered by the main royal army. A series of manoeuvres followed in which Salisbury and his son, seeking to avoid battle, headed to Worcester.

A war of words erupted between the two sides. The Lancastrian tract, the *Somnium Vigilantis*, tells the reader or listener that:

Lord God, what reasonable answer may be given by the [Yorkist] lords if they are questioned about why they came against the king, first at Blackheath, afterwards St Albans? [That] their intention was subversive to the commonwealth may be expressly proved by their behaviour towards the king's people ... Everyone knows well what extortions, what injuries and oppressions, what faction making and division, they caused, how their behaviour has subverted many men and resulted in the king's people being daily slain and murdered . . . If the public good of this realm has been deficient in any way and in peril of decay, what authority and power had they to reform it without the king's commission? . . . no need to them pardon or mercy; rather exercise all rigour against them conducive to their irreparable destruction.[38]

The writer set out to make the case that Yorkists had been guilty of treason since 1450, and the deaths at St Albans and Blore Heath were contrary to the very principles which they professed. York, his opponents asserted, could not pretend to represent the common weal because only the king could do this: the person of the king united the differing poles of authority.[39] It was only through obedience to the king, his appointed ministers and his laws that the common weal, the *communitas*, which York claimed to cherish, could be served: if disagreements existed, they were to be placed before due process, and the appellants content with what was ordained. In not accepting the due process which had cleared Edmund Somerset, York showed that he would never accept the judgement of the king or those who ruled in his name that he did personally not agree with. In doing so he literally took the law into his own hands which was a subversive act, if not treason. The Yorkists' activism on behalf of the communitas was a façade for a bid on powers as the contemporary writer noted: 'they did pretend a reformation of wrongs and extortions used, as they said, in this realm and the sovereign, the most endless misrule of all the sinners of the world did rest in them and in their servants.'[40]

The writer of the *Somnium Vigilantis* further more noted that the Yorkists said 'it belongeth to every person of the community to oppose himself to the ruin of the public good. But it is not so when authority lacketh . . . Who made [the Yorkists] judges?'[41] The *Somnium Vigilantis* provided the royalists with a simple and authoritative statement, that even if the king's judgement could be called into question, attempts to depose the crown, no matter how well intentioned, were treason.

Indeed, the Coventry declaration had bound both parties to keep the peace: the Yorkists had broken their oath and disobeyed their king. Yet, in a last diplomatic effort, Henry offered pardon to York and Warwick and preservation from attainder: they refused the offer as Salisbury was not included in the pardon. The Yorkist earls were now outside the king's protection and committed themselves to stand together and sent a proclamation to the king and Lords that they were acting to safeguard the crown and their conduct was not treason. If York and Warwick had hoped to placate the king, the tactic failed.[42] Henry, ever magnanimous, gave York six days to surrender. The violence of Blore Heath had removed the option of a surrender on terms, such as had ended York's Dartford rising of 1452, for the King was not prepared to extend his pardon to Salisbury. Warwick would clearly not abandon his father, and complained that they had been unjustly treated. York and Warwick sought to include Salisbury in the pardon. Warned of the advance of the royal army, Salisbury retreated to Ludlow.

## Ludlow

On 10 October, Salisbury, Warwick and York issued their Ludlow proclamation.[43] They claimed that law and order had broken down, the economy was faltering in consequence of this, impoverishing the people, and to make matters worse the earls claimed justice had been perverted. The earls placed the blame for all the nation's woes on unnamed councillors, and in asserting their loyalty to the king, sought to save the king and country from these unspecified persons. As before, the Yorkists presented themselves as loyal to the crown, offering advice and not condemnation, who sought to clear their names. The profuse exaggerations of loyalty and reiteration of bad governance by evilly-disposed men about the king was in essence a re-working of the Ludlow Manifesto of 1452, but made it rather more obvious than before about the defects of Henry himself. Not blamed were the princes of the royal blood, Somerset, Buckingham and Exeter, and the queen was protected by laws of treason. The Yorkists were targeting those in the king's household, as they would in 1460, the earls of Shrewsbury and Wiltshire and viscount Beaumont. Why? Government by faction meant that trust was one of the first casualties between the ruled and the ruler. Edward I, or even Edward III, had absolute power, moreover their power was public and all their subjects were bound to uphold it. Henry VI was no Edward III. With rival claimants to power, and a breakdown of trust between the gentry and the crown, the gentry were increasingly less willing to commit themselves to public office as the 1450s drew on. In order to enforce royal authority and power, the government had to resort to the appointment of household men as sheriffs and other office holders in the shires. Rather than being understood as a deliberate policy, such actions represent an act of desperation:

> The government had to resort to the appointment of increasingly unsuitable local officers, including men who did not even meet the official qualifications and household men who had often become cut off from the places of origin where they were now trying to enforce the king's rule.[44]

This had two effects: firstly, it fostered local resentment, between an already fractious gentry, secondly, the increasing reach of the royal household beyond its traditional remit, and thus increased costs, became a target for criticism by both the gentry and *communitas*. The very real desire to curb the power, influence and cost of the royal household and return it to what was perceived as the status quo was a very real and pressing need of the gentry and York. York and Warwick's critique of how the government operated was very real and based on legitimate grievances.

The same concerns are addressed in Warwick's manifesto. He echoes these fears that the household, in appointing men of low birth, lack of education and qualification from its own body corporate, had led to these evil councillors hiding the truth from the king. Warwick, in claiming royal patrimony had been abused resulting in lawlessness, represented very real fears of the gentry and *communitas* about the dispensation of local justice by unqualified justices and sheriffs. Imposed sheriffs and justices from the household was considered an abhorrence by those who traditionally held these posts. That justice as abnormally administered therefore justice itself was under threat. Warwick had 'read the room well' in creating his list of demands. By 1459, trust in Henry's government had totally broken down, no matter who ran it.[45] The attack on Warwick showed the nothingness of Henry's word.

Without substantial research in regional archives, we cannot say if, as the Yorkists claimed, the late 1450s was more lawless than a decade earlier: what is important though is the perception of it being so, and moreover, how justice was implemented, as we touched on above, at local level. The gentry and squirearchy needed the reassurance derived from a single, central authority to enable the continued functioning of the complex interweaving of power at the local level which ensured the peace. The factionalism which increased in the last 18 months of the 1450s meant that a friend today could be tomorrow's enemy because their lord had changed sides. This this meant that, at the local level, for the gentry and squirearchy that if your overlord suddenly became persona non grata to the government, this action had a major impact on the security of your estates, it broke down bonds of trust and patronage as we have noted. With household men occupying local positions of law, order and administration, separate to noble–gentry patronage, and loyalty to the nobility questioned – did you follow your lord into treason or not was a question many landowners asked themselves – it meant that the shires and their gentry could not function.[46] Unlike the great magnates and landowners, the gentry could not afford to be in conflict with their neighbours: they lived and moved in a much smaller world that York, Suffolk or Somerset where ties of loyalty and breaking that trust had a much more immediate effect. Yes, marriage alliances united great families, but at the macro-level these bonds of marriage were as important, if not more so. Changing noble allegiances threatened the disintegration of traditional gentry lines of patronage and marriage: the son of your neighbour, who married your daughter, might owe allegiance to a different lord, who supported a different faction to your own lord. Moreover, unlike the great nobles, the gentry had much narrower margins of financial safety and could not absorb the loss of a small proportion of their income if an armed retinue devastated their estate as easily. The factionalism and division amongst the nobility was extremely damaging to the gentry: it forced gentry networks into the same system of polarisation which undermined the system of mutual favour and obligation which held gentry society together. The nobles forced a pattern of loyalty onto the gentry, which was often resented. That Henry was deposed speaks volumes about his lack of support from the gentry and shires.[47]

With traditional lines of patronage, loyalty and administration breaking down, for many the only solution to a weak king and overmighty household and thus to save the country from bad government, was for York to be king: it was these voices that York and Warwick articulated in their manifestos. This was until October 1460 only ever hinted at, but the underlying message was York at the head of a reformed government headed by likeminded lords, following the reform policy outlined at various times in 1449 and 1445, would resolve these grievances, so much so York and his allies made the claim of superior governance the centre piece of their justification.[48]

Yet it is undeniable that none of the grievances raised were justifications for treason: if Henry had not been a nullity, nominally at the head of a faction, these issues could have been addressed; as it was, the very absence of strong monarchy by 1459, free from factions, meant that revolution was the only solution. Therefore, it is important to note, that claims the Yorkists made to the gentry and *communitas* could not have been made unless Henry had already lost the natural loyalty of a large section of his subjects: the Yorkists' challenge was transforming this lack of loyalty into armed support. York's power base was London, the south-east and the Nevilles: he, like the queen, derived power from a small faction.

How much of York's position below the level of the nobles and magnates, was owed to economic decline and social changes rather than to political events needs to be further studied. The main aim of the manifesto was to garner public support, to say to the gentry – who were territorially more powerful than the nobles – we are listening to your concerns, and prepare the ground for what happened next: York was planning a coup and as in 1452 and 1455 needed justify his actions. Cade's rebellion shows a far more mature and sophisticated understanding of the mechanisms of local government than the vague statements issued in 1381. The *communitas* and gentry were able to bypass the nobility and appeal directly to the king. It was in this changing social dynamic that York operated and sought to exploit to this own ends.

As Dr A.J. Pollard makes clear, despite Warwick's protestation that no grudges were behind the Ludlow manifesto and events leading up to it, the aim of the Yorkists was to 'seize power, by force, if necessary, in the king's name'.[49] The killings at St Albans and the reconciliation at the Loveday, had not solved the inherent issues that had become obvious since 1450. When faced with a perpetual minority, those who accepted the task of substitute rule failed to take responsibility for their shortcomings. York and Somerset, who both proposed themselves for the job of standing in for the king, rendered any solution impossible as neither man would give way. In this constitutional crisis, ironically, only a strong king heading a unity government could have adjudicated a confrontation of this order: Henry was incapable of this, further reinforcing the impossibility of a solution within the existing constitutional framework. Indeed, no solution existed to contend with an inept king other than deposition, and it was the only possible answer to this conundrum. The events of 1327 and 1399 became the new framework in which a solution had to be found. The succession internal disputes throughout the 1450s, pushed the nobility to one side or the other, seeking to maintain an illusion of unity with collective responsibility. It was the queen's intervention from 1458 that inexorably pulled the nobles away from the centre where most wanted to be; it made the Yorkist revolution inevitable.

In defending their actions, York, Salisbury and Warwick stated under oath that they had never intended treason, but failed to explain why they had failed to obey the king, nor accept his offer of pardon. As we have noted before, in the medieval idea of state and kingship – polity – emphasis was quite rightly placed on unity under the single apex figure of the king; such a system did not allow for legitimate opposition. As we have said, the king was free to choose his advisers, therefore no-one could dictate to a king, however inappropriate his choices and decisions. The Yorkist position was always treason within the medieval polity. The nothingness of Henry, as we noted before, meant that whoever controlled the king controlled the nation. In order to remove opposition – which the queen, her allies and household never understood as nothing less than treason – allowed (perhaps tuned a blind eye?) to the attack on Warwick at the end of 1458 in an exercise of problem-solving. The murders at St Albans were a problem-solving exercise after all! Such factionalism however, showed pardons were worthless: a point Warwick himself argued with some degree of fluency. It marked the breakdown of the illusion of unity government, and moreover showed that the word of the king was meaningless. The extermination of one side by the other, even if protected by oaths and pardons, precipitated war. It is hardly surprising, that lacking any trust in the offer of pardon from Henry – any such pardon could be rescinded anyhow – it was allowed to lapse:

> And on the Friday, the vigil of the feast of the translation of St Edward, king and confessor, in the thirty-eighth year of your most noble reign [12 October 1459], at Ludford in the county of Hereford, in the fields of the same, the said Richard, duke of York, Edward, earl of March, Richard, earl of Warwick, Richard, earl of Salisbury, Edmund, earl of Rutland, John Clinton, Lord Clinton, John Wenlock, knight, James Pickering, knight, the said John Conyers and Thomas Parre, knights, John Bourchier and Edward Bourchier, esquires, nephews of the said duke of York, Thomas Colt, late of London, gentleman, John Clay, late of Cheshunt in the county of Hertford, esquire, Roger Eyton, late of Shrewsbury in Shropshire, esquire, and Robert Boulde, brother to Henry Boulde, knight, with other knights and people whom they had blinded and brought together by wages, promises and other carefully calculated methods, brought certain persons before the people to swear that you were dead, causing mass to be said and attending it, all to make the people less afraid to give battle.[50]

## Ludford Bridge

The evening of 12 October found the three Yorkist earls drawn up in a defensive position at Ludford Bridge on the river Teme, below Ludlow Castle. Ludford was an almost non-battle but it marked a significant turning point. Gregory's chronicle notes:

> Ande thys same yere there was a grete afray at Lodlowe by twyne the kynge and the Duke of Yorke, the Erle of Salisbury, the Erle of Warwyke, the Erle of Marche. The Duke of Yorke lete make a grete depe dyche and fortefyde it with gonnys, cartys, and stakys, but hys party was ovyr weke.[51]

Defensive position or not, York, Salisbury and Warwick had no doubt that they faced defeat; as the writer of the chronicle observes, they were outnumbered.

Henry himself was present with his banner displayed. The Yorkist artillery opened fire, supported by archers. Fears about taking up arms in face of the king's person perhaps lay behind the demonstrable lie that Henry had been killed, and the Yorkists celebrated a mas for his soul.[52]

The implications of this are important. York had no practical basis for power unless he and his allies could capture the king, or kill him: in the event of the king's death a regency council would be declared, and York as a prince of the royal blood would have to have been included. Other than the Tudors, York was closest in line. This may have been contemplated at St Albans, where the king was wounded but not fatally.[53] It means York, Salisbury and Warwick were prepared to commit regicide: had they been prepared to do the same at St Albans? The archers' opening volleys of arrows had wounded the king; with the expectation he would be killed? To even consider such an act – to imagine the king's death – meant that York was not after a mere third term as Protector, he wanted the crown. Succession was by descent or by conquest as Edward IV and Henry VII would prove. York was prepared to bid for the throne through conquest. This went beyond seeking to reform government and replace 'evil' councillors from around the king: this was not restoring good governance and reforming abuses; it was an out-and-out bid for the crown. When they wrote to the king, that they sought his prosperity and his advancement, they were perjuring themselves. The lie was exposed when Henry showed himself to be alive and offered pardons to those who submitted. A writer close to Warwick adds:

> Monseigneur de Warewic ordered his battles: it was to be known to Andrieu Trolo to lead the vanguard, for he trusted more in him than in any other. Which Andrieu had received news of by a secret message from the duke of Sombresset, who was much languished, who showed him how he had come to wage war against the king, his sovereign lord; saying, also, that the king had caused it to be published among his host that all those who were adherents to his adversary, come and serve the king, he would forgive them everything, and give them great willows, and do them many good. Then the said Andrieu Trolot secretly went to all the men of the garrison of Callaix, and so horrified them that he tore them out of his party, so that all together came to the count of Warewic and told him that they did not wish to fight against the king, their sovereign lord: and immediately turned to the other party, without what anyone can retain.[54]

The direct consequence was that 'in the nyght Andrewe Trollop and all the olde souldyours of Calays with a grete felawshyp sodeynly departed . . . and wente strayte unto the kynges felde where they were receyved joyously'.[55] On learning of Trollop's defection, assuming it is not Yorkist propaganda to hide the fact most of the Yorkist army when offered pardon remained loyal to Henry, the Yorkist earls fled.[56] York, Warwick and Salisbury had failed in their bid according to:

> Robert Radcliffe, one of the fellowship of the said duke of York and the earls of Warwick and Salisbury, confessed at the point of death that they would have translated both the crown of England and the duchy of Lancaster at their will and pleasure.[57]

Trollop's defection showed the immense power conferred on those who controlled the king, and moreover, the respect for monarchy even after a decade of far from unity government led by factions around the nullity of Henry. Treason, after all was treason and moreover a mortal sin: few would imperil their soul. Neville politics had become intwined with those of York and the nation.

York could hardly have suffered a greater humiliation, not only abandoning his town of Ludlow to the plunder of the Lancastrian army but leaving his wife to fall into Lancastrian hands. How much of what had happened was purely down to York, and how far he was in control of his own destiny is hard to say. 'Perfidious Warwick' had driven the events forward through fear and paranoia. Salisbury was approaching 60, York almost 50, both men were past their prime, Warwick was just entering his. He had the energy, dynamism and ego to drive events forward. The Yorkists had gambled and lost. A 'line had been crossed'. Blore Heath and Ludford had shown the duke of York was unwilling to compromise and a refusal to submit to the king's mercy was easily understood to be treason; indeed, the only terms on which York, Warwick and Salisbury were prepared to become peaceable subjects was if they took over government.[58]

By the morning of 13 October, York was seeking sanctuary in Ireland. Warwick and Salisbury, with the young Edward earl of March headed to Calais, aided by John Dinham, or Dynham, a Devonshire squire.[59]

## Attainder

Queen Margaret had two options: seek revenge and further narrow her support base, or to try and create some semblance of unity government around the inept Henry. Hoping that this was the end of York, Salisbury and Warwick, we can see her desperately working to create a sense of noble unity. Henry, more likely Margaret and her immediate circle, had called Parliament in the wake of Blore Heath on 9 October as he made his way to Ludlow. The fact that Parliament was to meet at Coventry on 20 November speaks volumes about the confidence that the queen and her inner circle had that they would defeat York. Moreover, there can be little doubt that the decision to confiscate the estates of the Yorkists through the Parliamentary process of attainder had already been taken. That Margaret was trying to occupy a central position and create a unity government can be seen in that of those sitting in Parliament we find the duke of York's receiver-general, John Milewater, and Thomas Bromwich, the latter being of the leaders of the local Yorkist faction. Clearly, after Blore Heath support for York had dwindled, few being willing to contemplate treason. This inextricably drew allies to the Royalists. The Yorkists had always occupied a minority position, and represented few people outside themselves but this, not even York's Bourchier in laws supported his bid for the crown. As a minority faction, quite who supported them, as they claimed in their manifestos, is obscure. At this stage, it seems the queen and her inner circle wanted a truly effective government based on all the remaining magnates. This was only possible by relinquishing both total vengeance and wholesale reliance on the faction that she had helped form. Margaret's period of rule shows that, once the Yorkists were attained, there was still room for all the lords; even the duke of Norfolk is found on commissions. In essence, it was 'business as usual'.

With the earls in exile, in December 1459, Alice, duchess of Salisbury, William Oldknow and Thomas Vaughan were victims of an act of attainder on an unprecedented scale. In legal terms, at least in respect of most of these victims, their condemnation was justified for an act of treason. Parliament recorded the names of others forfeiting their lands:

> Wherefore may it please your highness, considering the foregoing, by the advice and assent of your lords spiritual and temporal, and of your commons, assembled in this your present Parliament, and by authority of the same, to ordain, decree and enact that the said Richard, earl of Salisbury, Thomas Neville, John Neville, Thomas Harrington, John Conyers, Thomas Parre, William Stanley and Thomas Meryng, for their said traitorous raising of war against your highness at the said town of Blore, in the field of the same town called Blore Heath, in the manner described above; and also that the said Richard, duke of York, Edward, earl of March, Richard, earl of Warwick, Richard, earl of Salisbury, Edmund, earl of Rutland, John Clinton, Lord Clinton, John Wenlock, James Pickering, John Conyers, Thomas Parre, John Bourchier, Edward Bourchier, Thomas Colt, John Clay, Roger Eyton and Robert Boulde, for their said traitorous raising of war against your said most noble person

at the aforementioned Ludford, in the fields of the same, in the manner described above, be reputed, taken, declared, adjudged, deemed and attainted of high treason, as false traitors and enemies to your most noble person, high majesty, crown and dignity.[60]

Of the thirty-seven attainted, nineteen, including the three principal Yorkist lords and York's two sons, the earls of March and Rutland, had been in arms at Ludford Bridge with banners displayed in the face of the king, a treason of which they could be convicted by the king's record alone, and a further eight had been at the Battle of Blore Heath, an act of open war, which was itself enough in itself to condemn them as traitors. Their lives were forfeit, and their lands reverted to the king; their heirs would not inherit. This was the most extreme punishment a member of the nobility could suffer, and York was now in the same situation as Henry of Bolingbroke (the future King Henry IV) in 1398. Yet, we must remark, that no one was executed for waging war against Henry, and only thirty-seven out of surely what would have been thousands suffered attainder. Devereux submitted for a third time, and saved his possessions and life. The three Bouchier brothers swore allegiance, so too Bishop Grey, Salisbury's brother Begavenny and brother-in-law Humphrey Stafford, duke of Buckingham, as well as Warwick's brother, Bishop George Neville, and his cousin Norfolk. The Yorkists' claims in 1460 that their enemies had sought their destruction to gain their lands was categorically a lie: York, Warwick and Salisbury occupied an extremist position that would never secure a large following. They had committed treason: yet the Yorkist propaganda machine since 1461 has painted - and still does - the three men as 'hard done by' an evil queen and incompetent king. York had no right to rule, he had no right to dictate who the king surrounded himself with as advisors. York and Warwick destabilised the kingdom to feed their own apetite for ambition and ego. York, like his son, would stop at nothing to be in charge, Father and son had ruthless ambition and refused to accept their actions were treason. If Warwick thought the only way to protect his possessions was to commit treason, he was badly mistaken. Quite why Henry let the three men slip away rather than execute them we shall never know. That should have been their fate. Henry VI, more reasonably Lord Treasurer Wiltshire, planned to keep the lands from the attained Yorkists to supplement his own revenue. It did make good propaganda, however. It is reasonable to suppose that is York, Salisbury and Warwick had showed true contrition, they could have been forgiven. The author of the *Somnium Vigilantis*, however, urged the Yorkists' lands to be disposed of and to banish the leaders as they had proven to be oath breakers, and defined Richard and his associates' behaviour as outside the law, indefensible, and proactively subversive:

> what reysonable answere may be yef for the lordis, if they be questioned for what cause they cam first ayenst the King into the Blake Heth, afterwardys to Sent Albonn . . . Trow ye they will have procured the commone welth? Certenly I hold him not very tru that thynketh other wyse but that thaire intent was so subverted to commone welthe as it may be proved expressly by thairgument of thar demynynge towardis the kynges peple . . . All the centres aboute knowen well what extorcions, what injuries and oppressions, what partie makynge and division thay did and caused to be done. How many prive conventicles undir thaire tuicion and support have ben made to the subversion and misdrawynge of many men, and at whos occasion the kyngese peple was daily slayne and murdred.[61]

The Yorkists were a minority faction, who had destabilised the kingdom for a decade. Many no doubt thought as the writer did. The lack of men willing to stand and be killed with the Yorkists at Blore Heath and Ludford is striking: no glittering array of thousands of men willing to die in combat against the king.

At a local level, there was a comprehensive redistribution of territorial power. In the West Riding, Shrewsbury replaced Salisbury as steward and constable of Pontefract. Of former possessions of York, Shrewsbury's son, John Talbot, succeeded Sir John Saville as steward of Wakefield and constable of Sandal Castle Egremont gained Conisbrough. Local administration was of justice in York's lands witnessed William Bradford, Sir John Tempest and Sir William Gascoigne (killed at Towton) named justices of the peace in December. York's lines of patronage in the North were dismantled.[62]

The flight of York, Warwick and Salisbury meant they personally escaped being held accountable. Henry, as ever, sought to heal wounds. The conclusion that York came to was that only a successful invasion of England would restore his fortune. Assuming the invasion was successful, York had three options: become Protector again, disinherit the king's son so that York would succeed, or bid for the crown for a fourth time. In January 1460, Henry VI issued a proclamation to the City of London to ensure that York, Warwick and Salisbury received no support:

> We verraily perceive the naturell love true obeissaunce and feithfull ligeance that ye owe and bere unto us and can you þerfore right singler thank and so according to yor desertes we accepte and repaie [?] you as

our feithfull and true subgettes and over this whereas we also nowe late directed unto you oure l'res of commission for to have yor aid [?] and assistence at this tyme to the suppressing of our Rebelles and traitours of this oure Royalme We have understand by the said declarac'on the goode disposic'on and towardnesse that ye have tobeye and accomplissh oure intent [and plai]sir in that partie so þat it shuld not be or redounde to þe derogac'on or breche of yor franchises privileges and libertees in any wise.[63]

The mayor, aldermen, and sheriffs were ordered to put in array a force to oppose the duke and his allies, wishful thinking as it would turn out to be. Henry VI may have been on the throne, but he did not lead a unified country. Clearly by new year 1460, his grave error in allowing York and his allies to escape was a point of concern: fearing invasion, Henry began mobilising his own supporters. War was coming, one that Henry could ill afford to lose. Part of this planning was to parcel out lands seized from York, Salisbury and Warwick. On 20 January 1460, 2,500 marks was granted to Alianore, duchess of Somerset, in settlement of debts owed by York for Loveday. A further 2,500 marks was granted to her son, Henry in addition to the 5,000 granted by the earlier settlement concerning the deaths at St Albans.[64]

Chapter 16

# WARWICK THE KINGMAKER

From England our scene shifts to Europe. If Henry and Queen Maragret had made one mistake, it was allowing the Yorkist earls to escape. Chronicler Wavrin offers Warwick's own version of events:

> when they had gone to sea, my Lord of Warwick asked the captain and the others whether they knew the way westward, and they answered they did not, they did not know these waters for they had never been there. The whole noble company then became fearful, but the Earl of Warwick, seeing his father and all the others were afraid, said to comfort them that if it pleased God and St George, he would lead them to a safe haven. And indeed, he took off his pourpoint [tunic], went over to the rudder and had the sails hoisted. The wind took them to Guernsey, where they waited for the wind, until by the grace of God they reached Calais.[1]

Warwick, despite his personal failings, was one of the most gifted politicians of his generation: drawing on his network of contacts in the centre of power in Burgundy and Europe, he quickly and effectively built new alliances to sweep away Henry, and to grasp power for himself by installing York as the new king, with whom he would share power. Warwick's ambition was limitless and would ultimately lead to his death. The merchants of the staple of Calais were easily won over because of Warwick's 'good government of the town and the citizens' love for him'.[2] Warwick and the earl of March arrived in Calais on or around 2 November 1459. They were met by Warwick's uncle, Lord Fauconberg, and both men went to Notre Dame de Saint Pierre to give thanks to God for their safe arrival, and the merchants of the staple, the mayor and the soldiers feasted them.[3] Queen Margaret was well aware of Warwick's destination. She wrote to the duke of Burgundy on 6 November describing Warwick as a perjurer, that he was banished from the country and not acting in the name of Henry. York was a 'fals traitour' driven by selfish motivation, and she was thankful he could no longer blind the people with his lies.[4] The duke was not moved by her petition.

The Duchy of Burgundy had long been involved in English politics: the dukes had backed Henry V in 1415 as part of their military ambitions against France. This ambition informed the political outlook of the current duke, Philip the Good (1396–1467). Charles VII and his successors as kings of France felt the Burgundian state to be a serious impediment to the expansion of royal authority in France, and for this reason they would permanently try to undermine Burgundy, so as to subordinate it to French sovereignty. As we said earlier, the duke of Burgundy therefore looked to England and other European allies to curtail the power of France. An important consideration in all of this was trade. English wool was traded in Genoa and Venice, Burgundy acting as the clearing house for goods shipped into Calais. When trade with Calais was suspended from London, because it was held by Warwick, Fauconberg and the earl of March, London merchants blamed the king for their misfortune. Henry also sought to limit or end trade into Calais from Burgundy. In consequence, the wool trade fell by a fifth, with prices plunging to below 2s a stone: exports fell by 34 per cent to 2,119 sacks. For London merchants, the only hope for an upturn in business was a Yorkist victory to oust Henry VI and his advisors. The Yorkist earls now launched 'a charm offensive' to win the propaganda war, expressing many of the merchants' grievances and popular discontent.[5]

The existing Anglo-Burgundian truce was set to expire on 26 November. When Henry sent his delegation to negotiate an extension, they found that Warwick had held discussions already with the marshal of Burgundy. Indeed, the duke of Burgundy's emissary arrived with Warwick on 5 November, by which time the duke of Milan had broken with France and was seeking an alliance with Burgundy.[6] The end result of these negotiations was that the duke and Warwick had agreed a three-month truce. Burgundy was allied not with Henry, but the exiled Yorkists.[7] That Warwick had achieved this within days of his landing in Calais speaks a great deal about his abilities as well as his long-standing friendship with the duke of Burgundy.

## Ireland

The duke of York landed in Ireland in early November with the duchess of Salisbury. It seems reasonable that York and Warwick had planned 'to go their separate ways': Calais was the obvious sanctuary for Warwick and Ireland for York. York and Warwick were not isolated, as I discuss later. York's retinue numbered at least twenty-one other exiles, including Sir James Strangeways, Thomas Colt, Sir James Pickering and John Bourchier.[8] Having being Lieutenant of Ireland since 1447, the duke ignored his removal from office on 20 November 1459 in favour of James Butler fifth earl of Wiltshire and of Ormond, and called his own Parliament which met at Drogheda on 8 February 1460. News of York's resumption of office reached the king and his inner circle and by 3 March, it was reported that king – or at least his closest advisers – had sent emissaries into Ireland to urge rebellion against the duke. These documents carried the king's seal, and had we assume been issued at the instigation of Butler.[9] Wiltshire's father had been killed at St Albans in 1455, as had his brother-in-law John Talbot, earl of Shrewsbury. Talbot was earl of Waterford since 1446, and was displaced in February 1460 by the duke of York. With powerful Lancastrian lords holding land in Ireland with a considerable degree of patronage and influence, even in Ireland, the duke knew he was not safe. The only way he could guarantee his own safety, and that of his family, was to organise resistance. York needed three things: to recruit allies, secondly an army – Warwick commanded the only professional force available at the time, the Calais garrison. Thirdly, he needed a line of communication to Warwick. York – or his allies in London – recruited a wine merchant, Thomas Desseford, as a messenger between Dublin and Calais. He had legitimate business to sail from the north coast of France and the Low Countries to London and Ireland. Clearly someone on the Lancastrian side became aware of this, and Desseford was arrested at Ostend whilst making his way to Calais. York and Warwick had to meet in person.[10] In a harbinger of things to come, John Higham, in York's immediate circle of exiles, was murdered in April 1460.[11]

## Calais

Both York and Warwick were in the same position as Henry Bolingbroke had been in just over 60 years earlier. The only way they could reclaim their birthright was to depose Henry VI at the head of an invading army. For that Warwick, like York, needed allies and money. However, unlike York, Warwick was in Calais and could easily connect with those in Europe sympathetic to his plight. Another key ally was the duke of Milan, who we mentioned earlier.

Francesco I Sforza (1401–66) ruled the state from 25 March 1450 till his death. In the power politics of the era, he had initially supported Rene of Anjou in his bid for the crown of Naples in the 1440s and had brought Venice into the Milanese sphere of influence. During Sforza's reign, Florence was under the command of Cosimo de' Medici and the two rulers became close friends. This friendship eventually manifested in first the Peace of Lodi and then the Italian League, a multi-polar defensive alliance of Italian states that succeeded in stabilising almost all of Italy. In the long term the league would go to war with Francis I of France. Due to the League's influence, Sforza was able to abandon his former Angevine allies in Naples, and sought instead to claim the crown for himself and conquer Genoa, which he occupied in 1464. Sforza was the first European ruler to follow a foreign policy based on the concept of the balance of power, and the first native Italian ruler to conduct extensive diplomacy outside the peninsula to counter the power of threatening states such as France. Edward IV made him a Knight of the Garter. Sforza was a key power broker. His influence and money counted for a great deal in European politics, especially in his power bid for Naples.[12]

As well as the dukes of Burgundy and Milan, the third person of influence in European affairs was the Pope. Both head of the church and secular ruler of the Papal States, the Pope exercised spiritual influence and political power. Well aware of the rising tension in England, Francesco Coppini (1415–64), bishop of Terni, was appointed as nuncio – personal representative to some extent – by Pope Pius II with support from Francesco I Sforza, duke of Milan, on 7 January 1459 to bring political turmoil in England to an end. In bringing peace, the Pope hoped Henry VI would back his call for a crusade. Coppini arrived in Dover on 4 June 1459, then travelled to London, where he initially opened negotiations with Henry VI and delivered his invitation to the Council of Mantua to where Henry had already sent a small and ineffectual delegation on 16 May.

One of the stated goals of the papal mission was to end the civil unrest in England, and fund a crusade against the Turks: in the first goal Coppini found a very willing ally in the Calais earls. Using Coppini as a facilitator, Warwick was able to network into the broader Milan-Burgundian sphere of interest. Warwick realised his own ambition of regaining his inheritance and fulfilling the Papal mission were bound into the same course of action. In this the rich merchants of Calais bankrolled his activities.[13]

In terms of realpolitik, if York took the throne, it meant that Burgundy would have a new ally against France. It also meant for the Italian league headed by the duke of Milan and bankrolled by the Medici would have a new ally in the battle for the crown of Naples and control of Genoa. The Pope would get funding for his crusade. For London merchants, trade would return to previous levels. Both at home and abroad, a Yorkist victory was a 'win-win' situation for all of those who backed the duke and Warwick. In the unfolding European 'game of thrones', removing Henry VI and his replacement with York outweighed Henry VI remaining king. The Hundred Years War was starting to heat up again into a period of phoney war: it was only a matter of time before the two sides clashed.

## Somerset's failure

The biggest mistake Margaret and her advisors had made was allowing the Yorkists three weeks' grace to leave the country. It allowed them to organise resistance. On 5 October, Somerset, now appointed Captain of Calais in rivalry to Warwick, was ordered to capture Calais: he sailed with a small army in November 1459. He was aided in this by Andrew Trollop. As Somerset's small fleet approached Calais, Warwick's artillery opened fire from Rysbank tower and they were forced to land at Wissault. Somerset was admitted to Guines on the promise he would pay the garrison their owed back pay, outstanding since 1456. Somerset carried with him £133 33s, hardly sufficient to meet the demands of the garrison, but enough to buy a degree of loyalty. Loyalty was always fickle if men were not paid: the *Brut Chronicle* notes that some of the ships' companies that Somerset had employed mutinied and joined Warwick in Calais. Stranded, Somerset endeavoured to take Calais by force but was beaten back. Somerset's failure made it clear that additional manpower was required. To transport reinforcements Buckingham as Warden of the Cinque Ports, was ordered to seize Warwick's fleet that was in Sandwich. Learning of Buckingham's intention, the Yorkist earls decided to launch an audacious attack.[14] The *Brut Chronicle*, published in 1480 and written perhaps a decade or more before, reports:

> The lords at Calais sent over Master Dynham with a great fellowship, to Sandwich and [he] took the town, and Lord Rivers, and the Lords Scales his son, and took many ships in the haven and brought all 32 to Calais; with which ships, many mariners came to Calais to serve the Earl of Warwick.[15]

As our chronicler notes, sometime on 15 January a small fleet had left Calais and made its way to the haven at Sandwich. The Yorkist fleet caught the Lancastrian fleet unprepared and wholly unaware of the imminent threat. The result was that the 800 men on board Dinham's flotilla managed to capture Lord Rivers, who was commanding the expedition, and his son Lord Scales and, as our chronicle states, thirty-two ships. The Paston Letters report:

As for tydyngs here, I sende som of hend wreten to you and othyrs how the Lord Ryvers, Sir Antonye, hys son, and othyrs hafe wonne Calais be a feble assault made at Sandwich by Denham, Squyer, with the nombre of viijc. men, on Twyesday betwene iiij. and v. at cloks yn the morning.[16]

Pope Pius in Rome was kept informed of Warwick's activities by Coppini. The Pope wrote that the:

Earl of Warwick a bold energetic character, had taken refuge from the anger of the King. Some days earlier, on learning that a royal fleet was being equipped in the port of Sandwich and would soon sail against him, Warwick himself set sail at night with 800 men; he caught the enemy by surprise, and after killing many men and taking may captives, including the admiral returned victorious.[17]

Warwick lost one prized vessel, the *Grace Dieu*, due to her becoming beached at low tide. The result was Warwick now had a fleet of thirty-two ships and had safeguarded Calais. It also meant that Somerset, who had been sent by Henry to capture Calais, lost vital support.[18] Dynham's victory was both a significant boost to the garrison militarily, but also in propaganda terms. Once in Calais, as we noted earlier, Earl Rivers was paraded through the town by the light of 160 torches culminating in a very public humiliation by the three Yorkist earls, who branded Rivers a parvenu compared to their own noble lineage.[19]

### The queen's response.

No longer the child bride she had been when she came to England, by 1460 Queen Margaret was a force to be reckoned with in a way that her husband was not, or as the contemporary 'Gregory's Chronicle' put it, 'more wyttyer then the kynge': the Queen had a grasp on reality unlike the king is what the chronicle is saying, and she remained determinedly unreconciled to the new dispensation.[20] The continued resistance of Queen Margaret and her allies meant that the day when the duke of York would be crowned king would never come.

Fearing this raid was the precursor for an invasion, the crown sought to organise coastal defences. Henry VI – I am absolutely sure Henry was a proxy for his wife – ordered on 15 February (my translation from the Latin):

The King, to his dearest Kinsman, John Duke of Norfolk, and to his Beloved and Faithful Philip Wentworth the Soldier, and also, to his Beloved, Robert Willoughby, John Hopton, William Tyrell, Thomas

Brewes, Gilbert Debenham, John Clopton, William Jenney, and Reginald Rous, Greetings. Because it is quite evident that some of our Rebels, Adhering to *Richard*, the late *Count of Warrewick*, the Traitor and our Enemy, have already entered our Town of Sandwick, and there they have done and perpetrated the greatest number of Mischiefs to Us and our Faithful Liegemen, and other Mischiefs . . . in different Parts of the Counties Our Suffolk . . . . we give and undertake full Power and Authority, to Summon before you each of our Liegemen of the aforesaid Counties . . . to march with you against the aforesaid Enemy ours and their aforesaid accomplices . . . our Enemies and Rebels, to be Defeated, Conquered, and Destroyed.[21]

The queen, knowing full well the danger that Warwick posed, saw that he had to be contained in Calais: to this end a new naval force needed to be raised and alliances made against him. For the former, Sir Baldwin Fulford was commissioned to raise a naval force for three months and in March the Lord Admiral, Exeter, was charged to raise a second fleet. In addition, the Lord Treasurer, Wiltshire, was charged with providing a small squadron. As Warwick had captured the majority of the English royal fleet, these officials of state had no option but to impress foreign ships and sailors. Genoese carracks were hired, and offers were made to hire Venetian galleys. However, limited financial resources were quickly depleted, which hampered the queen's' plans.[22]

Realising the exchequer was almost empty, she turned to support from 'family': Charles VII. The king of France reassured his niece that he would contain Warwick both at sea and support Somerset from the land.[23] Somerset's attempts to seize Calais from Warwick won the respect of both Charles VII and Charles, count of Charolais, the heir to the duke of Burgundy.[24] Support for York or Lancaster was at the heart of a family civil war: Charles VII and the son of Philip the Good were in conflict with Philip and Charles's son, Louis, the Dauphin. Simmering tensions were boiling over into armed conflict. The Dauphin, allied to Milan and Burgundy, sought to topple his father Charles, and found willing allies in Warwick and the Pope. At the close of 1459, the duke of Burgundy censured Charles 'for the truces taken with the English . . . the Kings people, formed in large companies, were throwing themselves upon his lands'. Charles for his part detailed alliances made by the Dauphin with the English, without the king's consent, resulting in twenty-eight attacks into France by the English and thirteen enterprises against the king and twenty-nine cases of disobedience. A strong European alliance threatened to topple Charles and Henry.[25]

Simultaneously, the queen and her ad hoc government had to deal with internal threats from Yorkists. York's castle of Denbigh still defied the crown, as did his lordships of Usk and Caerleon. Warwick's lordships of Glamorgan and Abergavenny likewise were proving recalcitrant. Henry told his half-brother Jasper Tudor that York and his allies 'once again enter into our Kingdom of England and propose to raise and stir up Insurrections, Rebellions, and other Evils, worse than the former . . . We, therefore, wishing to provide for the resistance of the obstinate malice and enmity of the aforesaid . . . and having as much confidence as possible in your faithfulness and provident circumspection' was to raise an army to ensure 'our Enemies and Rebels, to be Defeated, Conquered, and Destroyed.'[26]

In the Midlands:

The earl of Wiltshire Treasurer of England, the Lord Scales, and the Lord Hungerford, having the kings commission went to the town of Newbury, the which longed to the Duke of York, and there made inquisition of all them that in any wise had shewed any favour or benevolence or friendship to the said duke, or to any of his; whereof some were found guilty and were drawn, hanged and quartered, and all the other inhabitants of the foresaid town were spoiled off all their goods.[27]

How true this is, we cannot say. Our source is a Yorkist supporter and rather sensational in many details.[28] If the Lancastrians had hoped to intimidate Yorkists into acquiescence, they were mistaken.

# Chapter 17

# WARWICK'S REVENGE

Fear and paranoia drove events forward. The terror unleashed in England drew allies to Warwick, who were to prove vital in what he was planning:

> The commons of Kent, dreading the malice and tyranny of the foresaid Earl of Wiltshire and of others, lest he should exercise his vengeance upon them, as he had done upon them at Newbury, sent privily messengers and letters to Calais to the foresaid earls, beseeching them, that they would in all hast possible come and succour them for their enemies, promising they would assist them with all their power.
>
> The said earls would not anon give credence to their writing and words, but sent over into Kent the Lord Fauconberg, to know whether their promise and deeds should accord: and anon the people of Kent and of other shires about resorted to said Lord Fauconberg in great number abiding the coming of the earls.[1]

Warwick now knew he could be sure of 'boots on the ground' waiting for him when he landed with the Calais garrison. Warwick now had ships and allies in Kent to aid his coup, what he needed now was hard cash to pay the garrison. To that end, Warwick launched the Calais garrison across Burgundian territory into France in a series of chevauchée, and resumed attacks on French, Castilian and Genoese shipping. In a stroke of luck, on 16 March he captured a shipment of pay for the garrison of Guines. Piracy and loans from the merchants of Calais, who advanced him £18,000, funded the garrison, and beyond reasonable doubt the invasion of England when it came.[2]

When and where Warwick initially met with Coppini we do not know, but towards the end of March they held a conference in camera, the contents of which were shared with the Pope and Sforza. We cannot be certain what was discussed, but Warwick clearly already had in mind usurpation. Warwick was well aware of the strength of York's claim to the throne both through his father, but also the Mortimer line via the Salic law – this law had allowed Henry II to succeed to the throne after his mother, Matilda. Legal precedent favoured York's claim. Coppini writing on 22 March to the duke of Milan from Bruges:

> Although we have no actual certitude, it is believed, nevertheless, that the newly appointed one together with Warwick will perform marvels . . . to effect the greatest and most noteworthy achievements ever heard of in these parts for five hundred years, if God wills it so. I am leaving for a while because it is necessary and also by Warwick's advice. I expect to return any day according to the encouragement received from thence, and we have no doubt of success if we have help.[3]

Coppini was drawing Milan and Burgundy into Warwick's coup. As noted earlier, attempts by York to communicate with Warwick through messengers failed, therefore to make their plans securely, Warwick had to meet the duke of York in person. That meant sailing to Ireland. He left Calais in early March.[4]

Warwick met York at Waterford on 16 March. They were received by the mayor and burgesses of the town with 'pomp and ceremony'.[5] That York expected Warwick is presented in a document in Lambeth Palace. It tells us York sailed into the Irish Sea, and met Warwick who had twenty-six ships, and they then both sailed into Waterford harbour together.[6] It is almost impossible to believe that such an event was not co-ordinated by letters between the two men. Therefore, York taking the throne was planned at Ludford, and the plan matured and developed in Calais and Ireland. Warwick in Calais could bring his contacts with European princes to bear, to ensure success of his venture. Reliant on loans from the Calais staple, outnumbered militarily, the tiny Yorkist faction – remember, less than thirty men – gained immeasurably through finding willing allies in Europe as part of the political fallout between France and Burgundy. A writer close to Warwick adds that the earls in Calais:

> concluded that the count of Warewic should be expedient, he should be transported to Ireland to the duke of Yorc, to have an arrest and consultation as to how they would make their present war . . . When the Duke of Yorc really heard of the coming of the Count of Warewic, he was very glad; for he had had no news of them from their department of Ludelo. When he had gone ashore, the reception which was given to him and his family was very great, according to the fashion of the country. On that very night, the duke of Yorc, the count of Warewic, and all the lords who were with him, stood apart in a chamber, to discuss

their affairs; looking if they could find any alyance in the said country; begging some lords that they would help them this time, remonstrating with them that it was not to go against the king, but to make war on the duke of Sombresset, who was waging a very great war against them at Callaix and wherever he had power, because it was necessary for them to remedy it . . . In this consultation, these lords, considering how they could return to the kingdom of England, advised each other that they had several good ports in the country of Kent, which if they could arrive at and enter, it seemed to the duke of Yorc that they would conquer all the kingdom of England if necessary. And then the Count of Warewic asked the duke whether there would be any men-at-arms to be found in the country of Yrland. To which he replied that if he could enter England by the country of Kent, he would go down from the north, and do as long as he had sufficient men and ships. So the said lords of Yorc and Warewic concluded to do so.[7]

On the voyage, Warwick's fleet overpowered several merchantmen, adding ships to his growing flotilla and gaining much-needed supplies.[8] Warwick's actions could be described as piracy, but were essential in aiding Warwick's 'great journey from Calais to Ireland, and detained to help conduct the late Duke of York, and so lost the voyage'.[9]

## Scotland

As well as negotiating with Burgundy, Milan and the Papacy, the Yorkists sought to further isolate Henry. Royalist power in the North of England was centred in Northumberland and Westmoreland, controlled by the Nevilles and Percys. York and Warwick reasoned at Waterford that if royalist forces could be prevented from marching south to London, that would almost guarantee their invasion would be successful. Therefore, it was important to draw James II of Scotland into their sphere of influence. Based on later texts it seems reasonable to propose that York offered to hand Roxborough and Berwick-upon-Tweed back to Scotland, and agree a marriage to Edward, earl of March to unite both crowns. To broker the alliance, York sent one of his clerks, John Kingscote, who arrived in Edinburgh on 30 March.[10] James agreed and a Scottish envoy was sent to Ireland, where a treaty was concluded. It was to be sealed with a marriage alliance between one of York's sons and a daughter of the king.[11] The news of the treaty was transmitted to France in June:

For we have heard of the great and serious quarrel there is between the King of England on the one side, and the Duke of York, the Earl of Salisbury, and others with them, on the other . . . for these causes and on account of this quarrel, it seems to us a suitable time to send a hostile force into the realm of England to the advantage of the kingdoms of France and Scotland . . . and if we now let this opportunity slip away, it is not to be hoped that such a one will ever be presented to us again. For this, and for other reasons which have weighed with us, we have promised the most renowned Duke of York aforesaid to help and assist him in this quarrel concerning the insignia and crown of England, as he has tenderly desired of us by sending to us honourable ambassadors and letters.[12]

James II also informed his ally, Francesco Sforza, Duke of Milan on 28 June (my translation from the Latin):

Most loving brother: we have renounced the truce between us and the King of England, with certain and reasonable causes moving us.

Moreover, a division has arisen between the King of England and the Duke of York in the Kingdom of England.

At the humble request of the aforesaid Most Illustrious Duke of York, we understand the clear right which he has to the crown and diadem of England, we have promised him our assistance in the prosecution of the aforesaid complaint against the King of England, and we intend to attack the aforesaid Kingdom in the aid of the aforesaid Most Illustrious Duke.[13]

It is clear that most of Europe knew what was being planned. James had married the niece of the duke of Burgundy, Mary of Guelders. In backing Warwick, James aimed to remove English possessions from Scotland. Roxborough was high on his list of land to retake: Warwick and York had not expected the garrison to hold out for Henry. It could only be taken by siege: to ensure James took Roxborough, the duke of Burgundy supplied a siege train of artillery. On 3 August, he was standing near one of these cannons when it exploded and killed him. Rather than supporting her husband's alliance with Warwick, his queen found consolation with Queen Margaret.

Moving back to Warwick and his ambitious plans to topple Henry, how much of this plan had already been arranged before Blore Heath? How involved in this process of broader European alliances was the duke of York? It is hard to say. Usurpation was being planned, backed by Florentine money and Burgundian soldiers.

Despite Warwick's own apologist and propagandists' pleadings, he was central to what happened.

### Somerset's defeat

The queen and her entourage had hoped to profit from Warwick's absence in Ireland, and ordered Somerset to take control of Calais. They had underestimated the ability of their opponents. Earl Fauconberg and the earl of March defeated Somerset in open battle at Pont de Neuilly close to Calais, forcing Somerset to retreat back to Guines on 23 April. Somerset and Trollop's failure resulted in them being effectively prisoners. It was now, according to Warwick or someone very close to him – and therefore we cannot be sure this actually happened – Somerset made a promise given on the bible at Notre Dame de Saint Pierre that he would not take up arms against Warwick and the Yorkist earls. On hearing the news, the merchants of the Staple rejoiced at Warwick's good fortune.[14]

In the wake of the victory, the Milanese ambassador to the Papal court reported Warwick's and the Calais earls' intentions:

> The ambassador of the Duke of Burgundy hears that a certain English lord, enemy of the King of England, who had gone to Cales [sic: Calais] with a great following of other Englishmen . . . and it is hoped that he will deprive the king of that lordship and that the said lord is a very great friend of the aforesaid duke.[15]

Warwick's goal was clear enough: usurpation. It had been his goal since the beginning of the year, if not the whole basis for the Battle of Blore Heath: attack was the best form of defence. Warwick was driving the first stage of his projected coup forward, which was increasingly common knowledge amongst his allies. Indeed, Warwick had told the Papal legate in March:

> Our king is a dolt and a fool is ruled instead of ruling. The royal power is in the hands of his wife and those who defile the King's chamber. Because I could not endure this state of things and desire another form of government I was banished from the King's presence. My time of exile will be short. Many feel as I do, chief among the Duke of York, who would now be on the throne if there were any regard for justice. We shall soon have armed forces and shall put our fortune to the test of the sword.[16]

Warwick added that 'the King will retain only the bare name of sovereign' implying that Yorkist policy – more correctly we suppose the Neville policy – was that they rule through Henry. The Yorkist faction had no objection to his rule, as long as Henry could be reduced to a mere figurehead, who 'could be wheeled out' as necessary to legitimise their authority. Indeed, in early 1461 the Pope commented 'the king of England was Henry VI, a man more timorous than a woman, utterly devoid of wit or spirit, who left everything in his wife's hands'.[17] It benefited Warwick's allies if the king was replaced, but all that was in the future. Warwick was a friend of Philip, duke of Burgundy, a seemingly eager supporter of the papal crusade, and thus papal support, however tacit, to a decisive victory by the Yorkists, it was hoped, would lead to England's participation in the crusade.

Warwick returned from Ireland in late May:

> After Easter 1460, about the feast of St Aldhem, the duke of Exeter went to sea from Sandwich with fourteen ships and 1,500 men, and was making for Dartmouth when he met the Earl of Warwick, who was coming from Ireland with his mother.[18]

The *Brut Chronicle* adds that duke of Exeter, as Admiral, flying his flag in the *Grace a Dieu*, met Warwick in the Channel, but lost the action when a number of his ships defected to Warwick. It must have become increasingly clear to Henry – or at least his inner circle – that Warwick was a major threat who needed to be contained. It must have been obvious that as the summer began, Warwick was going to land. It was impossible to defend the entire south coast. Henry drew his court to the Midlands, and resorted to occupy a central position at the cost of losing London: Warwick could land at liberty along the south coast. Yet what if York landed first into his Marcher strongholds? What if Salisbury landed on the Yorkshire coast and sought to raise his tenants at Middleham? Henry VI was forced to occupy a central position, fortify it and wait for battle. The tactic failed for Edward IV in 1470 and Richard III in 1485, and in 1460 stood little chance of succeeding.[19] Correctly believed that Warwick would cross the Channel as close to Calais as possible, Sandwich was garrisoned by 'one Mounteforte, Capytan of ye town, & warned that no man' including merchants to sail to Flanders – i.e. Burgundy – or Calais.[20] By May, Henry and his councillors were expecting Warwick to land with Burgundian support, and reminded the *communitas*, that helping the invaders was treason under the statute of 1352.[21]

## Irish problems

Warwick was back in Calais about 27 May, with a fleet of twenty-six ships. He was expecting York to join him, but fate intervened in Warwick's planning. Lancastrian supporters in Ireland knew the duke of York could only return to Dublin from Waterford with any degree of safety via the sea. James Butler realised he had a window of opportunity to attack York once he had put to sea. If York could be captured or killed, the Yorkist claim to the throne was over. Butler with his Irish allies attacked on 3 June, in what was primarily a naval contest:

> the Odriscols w[i]th their Galleys arrived at Tramour[e] / in the Countie of Wat[e]rford being drawen thith[er] by the poers all / co[n]tinewing[e] their former ranker & malice. The Maior &Citize[n]s of Wat[er]ford in warlik maner salied forth to encounter w[i]th / them. at Bally Mac Daviethey mett. the fight was hott resolut / of both sides. the victorie fell to the Maior & Citizens & / a fewof their side slaine, but of the Odriscolls & poers / were slaine eight score, many p[ri]soners taken ofw[hi]ch nu[m]ber the chief was Odriscol oge w[i]th six of his sonnes & iij galleys. / The reason of thisoverthrowe I fynd was that the Odriscolls & poers had bene drinkinge of Aqua vitae at Balla macDavie & when the Citizens cam they found them all no bett[er] than drunke, sett upp them in theheate of the Day when many of them \scarse/ knewe where their armes were.[22]

The attempt to seize York on the high seas as he made his way back to Dublin from Waterford failed, but it also meant he was blockaded in Ireland. From this point onwards Warwick was in control of what happened next and not York. Politically, the Yorkist earls were isolated: the queen had not just the king but the claim of legitimacy, as she had the support of most of the Lords, uniting the rival poles of authority that had existed since 1450, in the person of the king. The Yorkists were a minority faction, backed by a minority of the *communitas* but it was a minority that mattered: London and the weald of Kent, which perhaps caused by the royal household's move to the Midlands in the case of London. Whoever controlled London controlled the country.

# Chapter 18

# WARWICK'S VICTORY

On returning to Calais with York's agreement to the coup, Warwick began preparations to invade. He had ships and men enough, but if he was to land, he needed to control the Channel. Like all invaders since 1066, whoever controlled the Channel, controlled England. Unlike the Normans, Warwick had the French navy to contend with. He had to find the French fleet, engage it and most importantly win. Aware that Warwick was planning to land with the Calais garrison, Henry VI offered pardon on 5 June to all soldiers in the garrison, except Warwick, March, Fauconberg, Salisbury, John Dynham, Richard Anson and others, because they had 'by false and fraudulent words and colours fabricated and imagined by their Leagues, which they owe to us, have led them to incline and adhere to the most nefarious purposes and intentions of our Traitors, Rebels, and Enemies'.[1] Anson had presumably fought at Ludford and fled to Calais. taking with him 500 marks which he had collected in customs' revenue at Hull. It is tempting to suggest that he had taken these funds directly to Calais, where Warwick was captain.[2]

Four days later, aware that invasion was imminent, Henry ordered the Sheriffs of Oxford, Berkshire, Southampton and Wiltshire, that all persons assisting:

Richard late Duke of York, Edward late Erle of March, Richard late Erle of Warrewik, Richard late Erle of Sarum, Edmund late Erle of Rutlond, John Clynton late Lord Clynton, Thomas Nevyll Knyght, John Nevyll Knyght, Sonnes of the said Erle of Sarum, Thomas Haryngton Knyght, John Wenlock Knyght, James Pykering Knyght, John Conyers Knyght, Thomas Parre Knyght, John Bourgchier Squyer Nephew of the said late Duke of Yorke, William Stanley Squyer Son of Thomas late Lord Stanley, Thomas Meryng late of Tonge in the County of Yorke Squyer, Thomas Colte late of London Gentylman, John Cley late of Chesthunt in

the Counte of Hertford, Robert Eyton late of Shrewsbury in the County
of Salop Squyer, Robert Boulde Broder of Henry Bould Knyght, Alice
late Wyfe of the foresaid Erle of Sarum, William Oldhall Knyght, and
Thomas Vaghanlate of London Squyer,

were also to be considered traitors. A similar appeal was made on 23
June to the Sheriffs of London, Essex, Hertfordshire, Sussex, Middlesex
and Canterbury.[3] For men loyal to Henry, it was their moral duty to
'destroy' the duke and his allies. Invasion seemed imminent.

Fate, though, intervened. In a letter to Thomas Thorpe – not the
Speaker of the Commons of the same name – a Yorkist supporter
known as Simon L on 17 June reports:

The Friday after Whitsonweke, my lord Warwick sent into the sea
diverse carvels and balingers[4] and in front of Dunkirk they met
with [illegible] French ships of war, and they had taken a hulk laden
with . . . merchandise and when the French spotted our ships they fled
and our men captured a pinnace from them and the other ships and our
men after them to Boulogne and there before Boulogne our ships fought
pell mell with them but the men of Boulogne defeated our own men
with guns from their ships . . . and the French took our ships . . . thus
daily does my lord have daily knowledge of the enemy,

Good to his word, the French king had ordered his fleet to sea to defeat
Warwick. The queen's alliance with France meant that Warwick's plans
were starting to unravel: York was trapped in Ireland, and the defeat
by Charles VII meant his invasion was delayed, perhaps for months.
Margaret and Warwick were using their broader networks to achieve
their own goals: they were well-matched adversaries.

Warwick, astute politician as he was, worked hard to downplay the
situation: our writer tells us Lord Fauconberg was expected to land in
London imminently. Warwick must have felt confident enough that
the French would not set sail again. Our writer adds 'and on the eve
of the feast of Corpus Christi their came to Calais the Captain of Ardre
and a herald from the duke of Burgundy'.[5] This episode is potentially
significant in understanding the international politics of summer 1460.
The political situation at the Burgundian court was curious. Phillip,
duke of Burgundy and Louis, the Dauphin, then based in Genappe,
were hand in glove with the Yorkists; however, Phillip's heir, Charles,
Count of Charolais, was an equally ardent Lancastrian. The Dauphin,
and the duke, both supported a Yorkist invasion of England to widen
their conflict with Charles VII of France. Charles, opposed to his father's
Yorkist alliance, made much of his descent from John of Gaunt, duke

of Lancaster, and formed a friendship with Henry, duke of Somerset, his distant cousin. Charles is reported to have helped Somerset while away his imprisonment at Guisnes by treating him to lavish banquets at Ardres and taking him hunting. The Captain of Ardres was effectively the gaoler of Somerset and Trollop. Charles hoped to encourage Charles VII to invade England in support of Queen Margaret. Adding another layer of complexity, Phillip, duke of Burgundy was uncle to the Queen of Scots, Mary of Guelders: despite the best efforts of the Yorkists, was seeking an alliance with Charles VII.[6]

The French fleet did not put to sea again – as far as we can tell – and despite being forced to relinquish the captured pinnace, Warwick had control of the Channel. Warwick now needed favourable wind and weather. Sometime on 20 June, it must have seemed that his prayers were answered: the weather and tide was set faire for the invasion fleet to set sail. So far, Warwick's coup had achieved all its objectives: it must have seemed that God was giving his blessing to remove Henry VI. Before they left Calais, the Yorkist earls issued a list of grievances, declaring they were loyal subjects of King Henry and the Pope. The Calais Manifesto, as it came to be known, singled out Beaumont, Wiltshire and Shrewsbury for punishment, and implied that Yorkist loyalty lay only with Henry and not the queen or her son, Prince Edward. The Calais earls did not recognise the queen's government as representing legitimate authority. The letter set out twelve points of complaint: it was excellent propaganda, as they tapped into public concerns and awareness: France had been lost for dubious reasons despite high taxes, the church was being debased, the rule of law was being debased, the king and his lords by not supporting Calais were intending to hand the entire nation over to the French.[7]

## Invasion

Fauconberg seized the port of Sandwich on 21 June, employing the commandeered ships.[8] Master Dynham (Denham) who had led the earlier raid, we are told by the *Brut Chronicle* 'assayled the town by water & by land & gat it'. Sir Osbert Mountford, who was to lead the expedition, was captured and beheaded once he had been taken back to Rysbanks in the Calais Pale. Andrew Trollop had married Mountford's sister: revenge for Trollop's defection at Ludford seems behind this judicial murder. Did Fauconberg land troops, or had he co-ordinated the attack with allies in Kent? Arguably the latter.

Warwick needed a bridgehead if the invasion was to succeeded. The crown lacked any military leadership: all the key commanders were Yorkists, who had the military initiative and were prepared to risk the penalties of treason and attainder to obtain their goal. Pius II notes that:

> twenty thousand men were waiting for him, an army which soon doubled in size. Here the bishop raised the standard of the Church of Rome because they were going into battle against enemies of the faith, granted plenary remissions of sins to those who were to fight on the side of the Warwick.[9]

As the Pope notes, unlike 1459, Warwick had popular support, backing from key allies – the archbishops of York and Canterbury, for example – and his forces had at its core the Calais garrison which stiffened the levies from Kent. It was a repeat of Cade's Rebellion, but this time led by politically and militarily experienced men of influence and power. Through the envoy, Warwick pledged loyalty to Henry:

> On arriving at Calais, I found everything in confusion, in consequence of a new state of things and fresh accidents, and that the lords were on the point of crossing over to England, saying they could wait no longer by reason of emergencies. I found them disposed to be devoted and obedient to your Majesty, and desirous to maintain and augment the commonweal of the kingdom, but they wished to come to your Majesty and to be restored to favour and their former position, whence they declared themselves ousted and expelled by the envy of their rivals.[10]

Our writer Francesco Coppini wrote to Henry, imploring to him 'to open your eyes to the fact that these evil speakers are the clerks and ministers of the devil, who wish not the welfare and unity of your realm', concerning Somerset, Northumberland and others. The full letter from Coppini to Henry was published at St Paul's Cross, London with full support of the English clergy. The support of the legate and inter alia the Pope no doubt added considerable prestige to Warwick and the Calais earls demands. Moreover, Coppini's presence among the Calais earls enhanced the chance of some form of negotiated settlement: it seemed unlikely the deeply devout Henry VI would stand in the way of the Pope's emissary. Like Henry Bolingbroke in 1399, the earls wanted to return to clear their names and restore their inheritances. Their pledge of loyalty, like that of York and Norfolk at Dartford, was to make them supporters of the king, critical of the government.

Armed confrontation was not necessarily considered at this stage against Henry: having an army at their back gave the Yorkist earls a stronger bargaining position. Bringing the Calais garrison ashore was, if not treason, very close to it when they landed five days later.[11] One contemporary source relates:

> The noble Earls of March, Warwick and Salisbury, having wind and weather at their pleasance, arrived graciously at Sandwich; where he met with them Master Thomas Bourchier Archbishop of Canterbury, and a great multitude of people with him; and with his cross before him [he] went forth with the said earls and people toward London.[12]

From Sandwich, they took the London Road and headed to Canterbury. John Stone, a monk at Christ Church Priory, Canterbury, tells us [my translation from the Latin] 'on the 7th Calends of July [Thursday, 26 June] three earls came towards Canterbury from Calais' and reaching the gates to the city, the Yorkists were met by Robert Hoorne, John Scot, and John Fog. These three local elites had orders from Henry to resist the Calais earls our monk tells us. Warwick's plan could have ended if Canterbury held out. Our monk continues: 'these three men passed after outside the city to the aforesaid counts at St. Martin's . . . and there they negotiated with the counts about peace, and they were agreed . . . and thus they entered the city, and went to the tomb of St. Thomas'. The following day, after praying over Beckett's tomb, Warwick seems to have won over the city leaders. If any lingering doubts remained about the justness of the Yorkists' cause, the arrival of Coppini later that day with pomp and ceremony swayed the argument. Coppini was the personal representative of the Pope to foreign nations, and was one of the highest-ranking visitors to the city after a monarch. Coppini and his retinue were housed in the Benedictine monastery dedicated to Saint Augustine. On Sunday, 28 June, he 'was received at the entrance to the church by Henry Barham, the sub-prior, and the convent in their cowls, with crosses and thuribles and holy water, with the response Sint lumbi. After the procession, blessed by the monks and clergy, they left Canterbury for London.'[13]

Warwick was at Rochester 24 hours later: the strategically-important castle capitulated with no resistance, and the earl entered London on 2 July: this was a morally and militarily significant outcome. Whoever controlled the capital controlled the country both economically and politically.[14]

## Northampton

John Watts points out that for London and the south-east, the ferment of the commonweal in support of the returned Yorkists approached that of 1450, reflected in the re-use of propagandist material from a decade earlier. In many regards, it was a replay of 1450 where aristocratic grievances had aligned with those of the commonweal, the *communitas*, of Kent, in an uprising which had secured power for the Nevilles. The queen, her son and allies were now in the same position as the Yorkists had been following Ludford.

The obvious question for the three earls was, what next? Despite holding London and the south-east, it was extremely unlikely that Henry would agree to restore their lands. That they had popular support is undeniable: they were claiming what was rightfully theirs, as Henry Bolingbroke had done in 1399. But unlike Bolingbroke, it was also obvious that the royalist position was much stronger than 1399. It was not a forgone conclusion the Yorkists would win an open battle, and if they did, the outcome was potentially reversible by a counter-blow.[15] Warwick chose to 'up the stakes':

> Then was a convocation of the clergy holden at St Paul's in London and thither came the said earls: the Earl of Warwick there purposed and recited before all the convocation and innumerable people standing about the causes of their coming into this land; and misrule and mischieves thereof; and how with great violence they had been repelled and put from the king's presence. . . . to declare their innocence or else die in the field; an there they made an open oath upon the cross of Canterbury.[16]

Seeking to win the propaganda war, Warwick told the assembled masses that bad counsel – sound familiar? – of the king had caused the recent economic distress, adding moreover, that the three earls had returned to help the king and remove bad councillors from his presence. This was Dartford all over again! Moreover, Warwick told the throng of commoners and merchants around him that he was no traitor, and he, Salisbury and March sought to regain their birthright. To the assembled audience, claiming a lost inheritance and birthright was acceptable and reasonable: after all, Parliament could change its mind. Inheritance was viewed at the time as a sacred right that could not be denied. Warwick, in appealing to justice and promising to resolve economic distress, won the propaganda war, especially as the Yorkist cause was supported by the Church.[17] The papal envoy hoped Henry VI would step back from fighting, and if fighting broke out, as far the Papacy, Burgundy and Milan were concerned, Henry would be held responsible.[18]

Was Warwick already thinking of replacing Henry with York at this stage? It is undeniable that such public demonstrations of loyalty to Henry meant that when the final stage of coup was initiated, it made a change of allegiance more difficult, if not utterly unacceptable to the *communitas* and nobility. In a world where giving an oath was a solemn undertaking, Warwick and his coterie were seen as perjurers. Breaking an oath was crossing a line in medieval society that few sought to do.[19] That Warwick claimed to be restoring his own birthright and then sought to disinherit Edward, prince of Wales, showed to many his lack of morals, opportunism and double standards; that Warwick, Salisbury, March and York were perjurers was in no doubt. York's actions at Ludford in declaring Henry dead, showed his intent to take the crown, but of Salisbury and Warwick? As it was, they held London, but had no legal basis for rule, and were technically 'outlaws'.

Knowing full well that the queen would sacrifice unity governance for vengeance, even if it meant losing the support of some Yorkists, Warwick had to act quickly. Warwick had no basis for governance without the king. Henry had to be captured or killed.[20]

Warwick knew that time was of the essence: he had to strike before the queen had the opportunity to consolidate her position and increase the number of men who had already rallied to the royal banner. Judging that the earl of Salisbury had men enough to besiege the Tower of London, on 5 July Lord Fauconberg led out an advance guard; Warwick and March followed with the main body soon after, given as 60,000 men which is exceptionally unlikely. Warwick financed the army with a £1,000 loan from the merchants. With Warwick and Edward was a growing number of Yorkist supporters, including Henry Bourchier (earl of Essex), William Fiennes (Lord Saye), Henry Mountford, Sir John Mowbray (duke of Norfolk), Edward Neville (Lord Bergavenny), John, Lord Scrope of Bolton, Sir John Stafford, Lord John Clinton, and John Tuchet (Lord Audley). An impressive array of clergy headed by Thomas Bourchier, Archbishop of Canterbury, Coppini, the papal legate, Richard Beauchamp, bishop of Salisbury and the bishops of Ely and Exeter also accompanied the army. Robert Horne, John Scott and John Fogge, who along with their men had changed sides at Canterbury, were no doubt with them as well. Of the ordinary soldiers, we only know for certain of the men from Rye and Winchelsea, but many towns and villages in Kent must have also sent contingents. He probably had a considerable artillery train.[21]

The court was at Coventry, but on hearing of the Yorkist advance Margaret moved the court from Coventry to Northampton, and encamped an army in the fields south of the town, between Delapre Abbey and the village of Hardingstone. The encampment was an attempt to build an artillery fortification (*Dominus Rex suam posuerat castrametationem*) such as the French used at Castillon in 1453. Indeed, having learned the lessons of Castillon the royalist forces placed their reliance on gunpowder rather than the longbow in hope of certain victory. On 10 July two armies faced each other, yet at first no fighting took place.[22]

Warwick sent the bishop of Salisbury to negotiate with the King but the queen and her Lancastrian nobles refused to negotiate, believing that their artillery and field works[23] gave them both the advantage and the opportunity to crush Warwick's forces.[24]

With any chance of negotiation ended, following a council of war, the battle opened with a skirmish probably between both sides' light horse or 'scourers'. The Lancastrians led by 'Lord Greriffin' were defeated by the Yorkist cavalry, led by Lord John Scrope of Bolton, who went on to set fire to the town. In the wake of the cavalry, the Yorkist forces attacked in three divisions, the first was led by the earl of March, the second by the earl of Warwick, and the third by Lord Fauconberg. The Abott notes that thanks to the treachery of Lord Grey[25] the assault was successful:

> for as the attacking squadrons came to the ditch before the royalist rampart and attempted to climb over it, which they could not quickly do because of its height . . . the lord [Grey] with his men met them and, seizing them by the hand, hauled them into the embattled field.[26]

Heavy rain over night and during the start of the battle meant that the king's artillery was almost useless. Following their defeat, many of the fleeing Lancastrians were drowned in waters swollen by the unseasonal rain.[27] Grey, superficially, seems an unlikely turncoat. Remember the furore over Wressle and the Cromwell inheritance: Grey had agreed to purchase from Ralph, Lord Cromwell, for the staggering sum of 6,500 marks, the great castle and lordship of Ampthill in Bedfordshire, shortly before Cromwell died in 1456. Ampthill stood a few miles from his main residence at Wrest. So far so good. Yet as with Wressle, Cromwell's claim to this extensive property had likewise been, violently and without justification, claimed by Grey's cousin, Henry Holland, duke of Exeter. In this conflict, Grey had supported Cromwell, thereby the Nevilles. If the Lancastrians won, Exeter would Grey feared – according to Leland and a reasonable supposition to make – seize the property: Grey therefore felt a Yorkist–Neville victory would secure the property for himself.[28] Of course, it helped Warwick that it was so wet that the Lancastrian artillery was nullified. In the wake of the battle, that the Lancastrians probably did not need to fight, Henry was made prisoner as a French account states: 'And with regard to the fact of England . . . at the Battle of Northampton, when the king of England was taken.' [29] A Burgundian writer observes:

> Henry the king of England submitted to the earl of Warwick. In the presence of the king Henry the same earl pledged loyalty to the to the king. Ater this the earl of Warwick ordered two or three of the principal governors to have their heads cut off, we do not know their names.[30]

Chronicler Benet records Warwick, Salisbury and the earl of March:

> on Wednesday, the 6th nones of July [2 July 1460] they entered London with a great number of men of war. And they brought with them a legate of the Roman Curia with papal bulls specifying the pope had openly excommunicated three English Lords, namely the Earl of Wiltshire, the Earl of Shrewsbury and Lord Beaumont, and all those resisting the Lord Duke and the lords of March, Warwick and Salisbury.[31]

As Jane Dawson notes, in January 1461, Queen Margaret believed that the Lancastrian dead from Northampton could not be buried due to being excommunicated. Wiltshire, according to a document from July 1461 housed in the Archives Nationales de France, fled to Zeeland. Wool and other property of his in Calais, valued at 300 marks, was seized by Warwick. He was joined by other Lancastrian merchants from Calais, notably Richard Heyron, who petitioned the duke of Burgundy for redress. Wiltshire spent most of summer and winter 1460 in Utrecht, along with his brother, John Butler (1422–76). Wiltshire played little military role in what was to happen.[32]

Warwick, now the most powerful man in England, placed Neville and Bourchier allies in major political positions. A Yorkist ally writing from Bruges on 7 to 10 July on news from London noted to the court of Milan that:

> the Duke of York will descend upon the country with a large number of troops, as well as the King of Scotland with quite 30,000. That king has given one of his daughters to wife to a son of the Duke of York[33] . . . other lords, and thither also the Duke of York . . . and all their friends . . . will gather for mutual support and appoint new offices and arrange the government of the country. This will remain in the hands of Warwick. It is not thought that he will stay his hand, but will put to death all those who have acted against him. It is thought they will make a son of the Duke of York King, and they will pass over the King's son, as they are beginning to already to say that he is not the King's son.

If we had been questioning Warwick's ultimate goal, it is here for all to see, and was clearly 'common knowledge.' The heir to the throne was to be Edward, earl of March. Usurpation by York was not yet 'on the cards' but his return was. The writer adds 'everything is in Warwick's power and the war at an end, and that he has done marvellous things. God grant him grace to keep the country in peace and union!'[34] On hearing of Warwick's victory, the duke of Burgundy sent the Marshal of Burgundy and Sire de Lannoy to Warwick, with Henry appointing commissioners regarding peace negotiations.[35]

In France, Pierre de Brezé at the court of Charles VII lamented in a letter dated 26 July:

> For certain the King is in the hands of the Count of Wawrick, and the Queen is heading towards the marches of Wales, her son with her, accompanied by the Duke of Excestre and a large number of people. The great Tower of London still stands for her, the Lord of Scalles inside and other great lords.[36]

The French court was in a state of panic: the cold war between King and Dauphin looked set to turn 'hot'. On 19 July, the garrison of the Tower were starved into surrender. In part this was thanks to Sir John Wenlock, who it seems had been with Warwick in Calais and had been with the duke of York for a time in Ireland. Initially fighting for Henry VI at St Albans, influence from Warwick led him to change sides, and it was as a Yorkist that he served as Speaker of the House of Commons later that year in the Parliament of 1455. He was present at Blore Heath in 1459 and Wenlock fought under the Yorkist banner at Sandwich, Mortimer's Cross, the Second Battle of St Albans and the Battle of Towton.

With the Tower captured, Scales attempted to escape in disguise by boat, but was recognised and butchered by a mob. Warwick was king in all but name. In London with the hapless king in tow, Warwick had the act of attainder overturned. He and his father were free men.[37] The King of France believed that the Pope had engineered the coup – which he had – and had betrayed the trust of the Kings of England and France. A French ambassador reported on 31 July 'the queen and her son are safe'. Charles used his emissary Morice Doulcereau as intermediary with his niece.[38] He had been present at Northampton. Presumably an account by him exists in a French archive.[39]

Warwick, secure at least in the short term, had widespread international backing: from Milan, the Pope, the duke of Burgundy, the Dauphin, alienating Charles VII and the duke of Burgundy's

Richard, duke of York, from a contemporary manuscript. Very few representations exist of the duke, and we cannot be certain of his appearance.

Henry VI and Queen Margaret from a contemporary depiction.

Funeral effigy of Ralph, earl of Westmoreland, and his two wives. The children from these two marriages created the Neville feud, which destabilised the north of England for a generation.

John Beaufort, duke of Somerset, funeral effigy, created after his death in 1444. His grandson would become Henry VII.

Rouen, Normandy. The town possesses many fine fifteenth-century buildings, which the duke of York would have known.

Rouen Cathedral where Edmund, earl of Rutland, was baptised. His elder brother, Edward, was baptised in the chapel of Rouen castle: likely sickly, in case he died he was baptised soon after birth, which meant no time existed to organise a magnificent ceremony. This fact, combined with insufficient research, has led some to speculate Edward was illegitimate. There is not truth at all to these claims.

Almost all that remains of the duke of York's castle at Fotheringhay. This once sumptuous residence now exists only as a few 'bumps and lumps'.

Ludlow Castle, home to the duke of York, and from where in 1459 he sallied forth for battle, only to flee to Ireland.

Sandal Castle, the caput of the Manor of Wakefield and home to Richard, duke of York's grandfather, Edmund Langley. This eighteenth-century engraving shows the castle as it was in the 1560s.

The remains of the mighty keep at Sandal. It was here that the duke of York's retinue were housed in December 1460.

All that remains of the great hall and great chamber at Sandal. It was here in summer 1459 that the duke of York gathered retainers from the Manor of Wakefield to his banner, who included John Saville of Thornhill and John Pilkington (a convicted thug and rapist) from Halifax, to lead a coup against Henry VI, in which he failed.

Richard, duke of York, from a contemporary manuscript. Very few representations
exist of the duke, and we cannot be certain of his appearance.

Henry VI and Queen Margaret from a contemporary depiction.

Funeral effigy of Ralph, earl of Westmoreland, and his two wives. The children from these two marriages created the Neville feud, which destabilised the north of England for a generation.

John Beaufort, duke of Somerset, funeral effigy, created after his death in 1444. His grandson would become Henry VII.

Rouen, Normandy. The town possesses many fine fifteenth-century buildings, which the duke of York would have known.

Rouen Cathedral where Edmund, earl of Rutland, was baptised. His elder brother, Edward, was baptised in the chapel of Rouen castle: likely sickly, in case he died he was baptised soon after birth, which meant no time existed to organise a magnificent ceremony. This fact, combined with insufficient research, has led some to speculate Edward was illegitimate. There is not truth at all to these claims.

Almost all that remains of the duke of York's castle at Fotheringhay. This once sumptuous residence now exists only as a few 'bumps and lumps'.

Ludlow Castle, home to the duke of York, and from where in 1459 he sallied forth for battle, only to flee to Ireland.

Sandal Castle, the caput of the Manor of Wakefield and home to Richard, duke of York's grandfather, Edmund Langley. This eighteenth-century engraving shows the castle as it was in the 1560s.

The remains of the mighty keep at Sandal. It was here that the duke of York's retinue were housed in December 1460.

All that remains of the great hall and great chamber at Sandal. It was here in summer 1459 that the duke of York gathered retainers from the Manor of Wakefield to his banner, who included John Saville of Thornhill and John Pilkington (a convicted thug and rapist) from Halifax, to lead a coup against Henry VI, in which he failed.

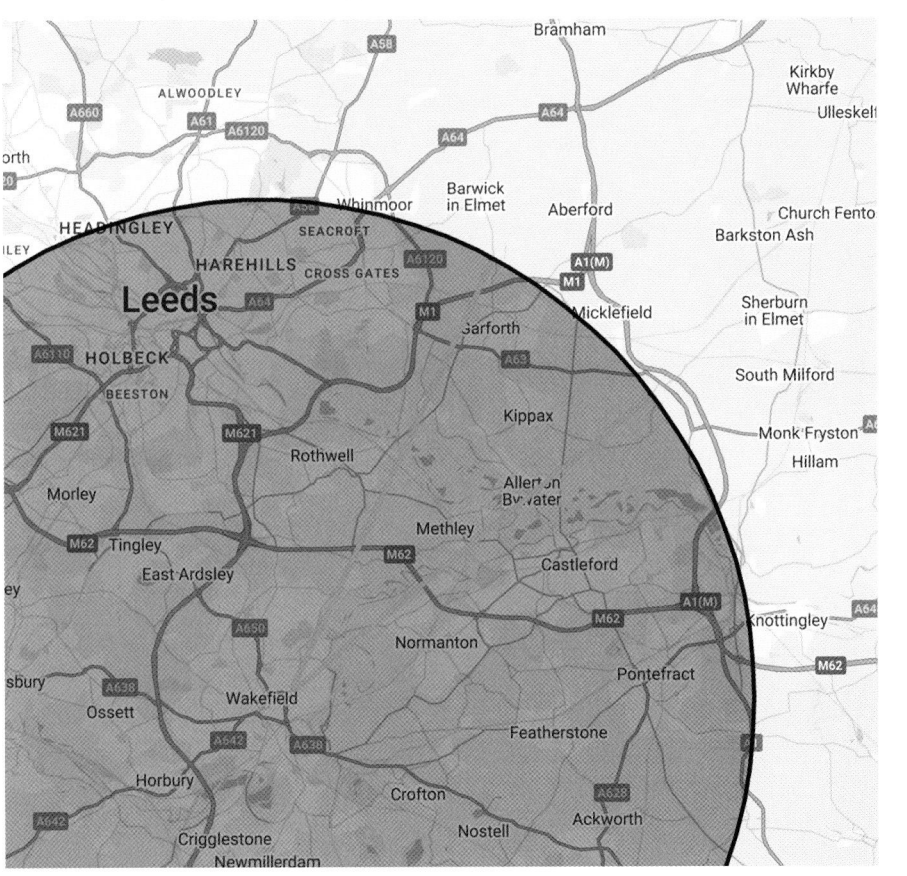

Sketch map showing the likely combat zone on 29 December 1460. The circle is a distance of 10 miles from Wakefield. This assumed York was moving at two miles an hour. He may have been moving much faster: it raises the possibility that two battles were fought at Towton. The triangle shows the likely line of march to York via the bridge at Methley or Woodlesford over the river Aire. Sandal Castle nor the traditional battlefield site at Manygates had any involvement in the Battle of Wakefield.

Monument to the duke of York in Sandal. Said to be on the place where he fell in battle, there is no historical or archaeological evidence to support this notion. The battle was fought north of the town, its location lost to history.

Wakefield Parish Church of All Saints as it looked in 1460. In 1479 the two right-hand bays of the south aisle became a chantry for the soul of Richard, duke of York. A priest would sing the mass every day for the duke's soul, and hold masses for the soul of his son Richard III on a daily basis. No mass has been held since 1541. The roof bosses of the chantry – today the Lady Chapel – carry the badge of the dukes of York.

Long associated with the Battle of Wakefield, the chantry chapel of St Mary the Virgin probably played no part in it. The earl of Rutland was very likely killed with his father in the chantry of St Nicholas within the Walls at Sandal.

The ruins of Pontefract Castle stand as a reminder that this castle once dominated Yorkshire like no other. The castle was used by the earl of Northumberland as a regional power centre in the last weeks of December 1460. The principal seat of Lancastrian authority and power in the north was Beverley.

The gatehouse to Middleham Castle, dynastic home of the earl of Salisbury, and later Richard III.

Ludford Bridge, the scene of the Yorkists' nadir in 1459.

The funeral effigy of the earl of Salisbury and his wife Alice. Formerly housed at Bisham Priory when he was re-buried in 1463, these monuments were saved at the time of the Dissolution.

The funerary monument to Richard, duke of York, erected at Fotheringhay when he was re-buried in 1476, being exhumed from St Richard's Priory, Pontefract. The duke's embalmed heart remained at Pontefract in a lead casket and perpetual mass and prayers for his soul were sung in the priory through to the dissolution. Richard III personally paid for these masses.

The Dominican Friary of St Richard of Chichester, reconstructed from archaeological evidence. This was the burial place of the duke of York, and the earls of Salisbury and Rutland and likely their place of death. (Courtesy Pontefract and District Archaeological Society)

The duke of Milan, a key Yorkist ally.

Francesco Coppini, Papal Legate and key member of the Yorkist coup of 1460.

Edward IV, son and heir of the duke of York, who was king 1461–70, 1471–83.

Richard III, youngest son of the duke of York, reigned as king 1483–5.

Henry Tudor, reigned as king 1485–1509.

heir, the future Charles the Bold. The new administration was to be a display of Neville power. George, bishop of Exeter was chancellor, Viscount Bourchier resumed the treasurership. The power based was narrow and partisan: a minority had defeated a better equipped and popular majority. Governing by the centre would have alleviated many problems, but if the goal was usurpation, filling offices of state and the king's household with Neville family members or retainers made the plan perhaps, a foregone conclusion. Nor was the new regime committed to reform: no attempt was made to introduce reforms to Parliament, no taxes were levied. It was a power grab and nothing more. The failure to bring about reform would bring the regime to collapse a decade hence. This was a Neville coup pure and simple: two pairs of brothers held total power. If they were to retain their power, lands and patronage, all roads led to York usurping the throne. Yet York was nowhere to be seen.

## The Percy-Neville feud re-ignited

Warwick's coup, predictably, alienated and angered a swathe of royalist nobles. Maybe he had planned for this eventuality: he needed a hero on a white charger to come and save the crown from chaos and dissent. The hero was York: the villains readily supplied themselves, harbouring old grudges. The royalists who had escaped Northampton fled abroad as a Milanese merchant reported:

> The Duke of Somerset has scarce a party to follow him . . . when he heard that Warwick had arrived near London, went on board a Genoese ship with many others, and it is thought that he will have himself taken to France, because they say that he has a safe-conduct from the King of France, with whom they had great dealings. It is thought that a truce would have ensued between them; all in order to hurt the lord here [the Duke of Burgundy], who can hardly have received more welcome tidings than that of Warwick's arrival as related above. This will give the King of France matter for reflection, that before much time has passed the English may land troops in Normandy and Gascony to recover the lost lands.[40]

The scattered royalist leadership sought to build alliances, to counter Warwick and the Burgundian-Papal-Milanese pact supported by the Dauphin.

Despite gaining the capital, the Yorkist government had not gained the kingdom.[41] Warwick's coup was part of a larger re-shaping of geopolitics. York had long harboured the goal of restoring Henry V's conquests in France, and clearly Philip the Good, duke of Burgundy, as well as the court of Milan harboured these ambitions in their power struggle over Sicily. Warwick now had to build a government and deliver on his promises.

At the end of July, Henry and the senior Yorkists headed to Canterbury, where he was received by Archbishop Bourchier Henry was accompanied by Thomas Kemp, bishop of London, Job Arundel, bishop of Chichester, and George Neville, Lord Chancellor and bishop of Exeter, as well as the earls of March, Salisbury and Warwick. Henry was still in Canterbury on 14 August, where he prayed in vigil on the eve of the Assumption, and participated in the solemn procession and mass on the following day. Henry left Canterbury sometime after 18 August. One monk, an eyewitness to these events, believed he had been uncrowned.[42] For a monk to be convinced of this – it seems unlikely for him to invent this, but NOT impossible, depending on what he had read and was told – some form of discussion took place withing the hallowed walls of Canterbury. This episode may – and that's a *big* if – have been a preparatory step in what happened. The implication is, that Warwick and York needed Henry's support, or at least acquiesce, to bring about dynastic and governmental revolution.

One of the first acts following Warwick's coup was the king granted the controversial manor of Wressle back to the Nevilles. As could have been predicted – it perhaps was – the Percy-Neville feud, now re-ignited contributed directly to the death of the duke of York. The Percy family wanted to resolve their long-harboured grudge against Salisbury and York.

Word reached Westminster in August that the earl of Northumberland refused to acknowledge the change in regime. Through Warwick's intercedence, Northumberland was charged with uttering 'false hoods arouse discords among the magnates of the realm'. The king – Warwick in essence – through letters patent issued arrest warrants for the apprehension of John Katryall of Selby, Richard Thirlwall of Wressle, Robert Tate of Wyggington, John Leigh of Skelton, John Quynsell, Robert Thomson *sic* Tomlynson clerk of Wressle, with others from York. Those authorised to apprehend these men included Sir Thomas Neville, Sir John Conyers, Sir James Pickering and others.[43] We will come to Thomson and Thirlwall again.

Northumberland was using Wressle to send out chevauchée into the Yorkshire and Lincolnshire countryside, spreading fear and causing as much destruction as possible. Warwick now used these disturbances, which he may have anticipated, by convincing the king to begin stage two of his plan.

Northumberland's raids gave Warwick the excuse to convince the king that the only way to prevent further disturbances was to allow York to return. How and when Warwick broached this with the king is not known, but the king must have agreed to Warwick's pleas. A council was held on 23 August. Attending was the Archbishop of Canterbury, the bishop of Exeter, the earls of March, Salisbury, Bourchier, the prior of St John's Wenlock, Say and the dean of St Severins. This was a Neville gathering, with some key allies. The new regime needed money to fight what seemed to be a costly war with the Scotland and France. Without money, the long-term outlook was very uncertain. The queen and her son were still at large. Action had to be taken.[44]

The Yorkist revolution destabilised the country: well, Yorkshire, the Marches and the West Country. On 28 July, Warwick via Henry issued a warrant to arrest people 'spoiling, beating, maiming and slaying' in the counties of Devon, Herefordshire and Yorkshire. Also in Bristol, Sussex and Shropshire. In Yorkshire Sir Thomas Neville, son of the earl of Salisbury, Sir John Neville (either Thomas's brother or the other Sir John Neville, of Woodhall near Pontefract), Sir Thomas Harrington were named as commissioners to arrest and 'commit the guilty to prison'. Also named were John Thwaytes, Henry Sotehill, Robert Nevill (of Liversedge, Bristall, West Yorkshire) and Thurston Banastre.[45] Henry Sotehill, owner of the Manor of Soothill near Batley, purchased in 1457 the Manors of Wrenthorpe (Wakefield) and Ardsley for £300. Henry, sergeant-at-law, was a member of Richard, duke of Gloucester's household prior to his death in 1479. He had been attorney for Edward IV and is named in the Plumpton correspondence. His son, also Henry, founded the Sotehill Chantry at Wakefield Parish Church, 12 November 1495.

Thurston Bannister was also local to Wakefield. Born in Ouchthorpe, Stanley in 1411, son of Roger and Isabel Bannaster who also held the manor of Clifton near Brighouse. Thurston was grave of Stanley in 1434 and 1458, and was described in a legal case as gentleman in 1471. In 1474 and 1746 he signed over to his cousin Roger Nowell land in Stanley and om the Great Oldfield at Sandal to found a chantry, Henry Sotehill being an executor under his will of 1474, proved 1478. His chantry was founded 24 September 1478, but not executed till 5 June 1480. Sir John Pilkington also founded a chantry in Wakefield Parish Church in 1475, to prayer for the soul of Richard duke of York, and his sons Edward and Richard. That local men to Wakefield were named as commissioners implies a degree of local disturbance and unease with the Yorkist revolution. The West Country and Bristol were no doubt influenced by Exeter and the Courtney's to start 'troublemaking'. In Yorkshire, John Talbot had taken the key officers in the Manor of Wakefield, which seems to have been opposed locally.

On 24 August 1460 the king through letters patent, commissioned York and Edward, earl of March as well as the earls of Warwick and Salisbury to travel north to Wressle and to arrest Richard Thirlwall then holding Wressle for 'uttering falsehoods to arouse discord amongst the magnates of the relm'.[46] The king composed a letter to the earl of Northumberland ordering him to explain why he was garrisoning Wressle against the crown.[47] The Calendar of Patent Rolls tells us that when the order to return lands to Salisbury was sent to Northumberland, the earl's servants 'murdered the king's messenger John Drayton' on 24 August.[48] Parliament ordered that the earl was to appear before the king in person to answer for his disobedience and contempt. If he refused to comply, Northumberland was forfeit all his lands.[49] Henry himself, when asked to support action against, Northumberland replied:

> The kyng agreeth to this acte provided alweys that notwithstondyng this act he be not put fro his libertee in usyng of his prerogatif to eny persone or persones comprised in the said acte or to eny othir that to whom the seid acte may extende.[50]

Northumberland was exploiting the situation to 'feather his own nest' and escalate his own sense of grievance. War was not yet a forgone conclusion, at least in 1460. It is also undeniable that Warwick had used the situation with Northumberland to secure the return of York from Ireland, no doubt flattering the king that York was the only man who could resolve the situation.

# Chapter 19

# YORK'S RETURN

The events following Northampton had exposed the weakness in the machine of government. Queen Margaret – despite being constitutionally invisible – had been able to restore royal authority following the Loveday, but she was unable to overcome the central problem that had beset the regime since 1450, if not earlier: Henry's presence did not convey authority on those who ruled around him.[1] Warwick now found himself in the position that the queen had been. With Henry unable to rule, factionalism and governance by hesitant committee was almost unworkable as the last 15 years had showed. The solution to return trust in royal authority was to replace Henry with York. In acting in this way, the queen was able to show that the Neville earls were destroyers of the realm, complicit in bad governance, by levelling the same charges the Yorkists had against her husband.

Moreover, John Watts suggests that Richard may not have been acting out of dynastic self-interest when he challenged Henry VI, and that his attempts to paint his treason as loyalty throughout the early stages of the clash of clans between York and Lancaster were not hypocrisy. Instead, he argues, they were the sincere actions of a loyal knight who was only too well aware that for the long-term security of the country a new king was needed. Moreover, he contends it was Henry's court who sought as early as his landing in Wales to infer he had a dynastic interest in the crown in an effort to undermine his platform.[2]

The duke's reiteration of these concepts suggests claiming to be a loyal servant, seeking to save the imperilled crown, was a purposeful distancing of himself from his father's treason. Yet challenging this, we see usurpation had been York's goal at Ludford in declaring Henry dead. Perhaps since 1455, the best way to save the commonweal, restore justice and good governance was for a loyal subject to replace

Henry. Richard believed Henry VI was failing in his duty to protect his own servants, i.e. himself as Lieutenant of Ireland, and the national interest. Perhaps in his own mind, it was not treason, but the ultimate act of loyalty. He alone could provide the leadership needed. This is not how contemporaries viewed his actions. York's motivation for usurpation was certainly complex, and not framed around a single issue. Ego, yes, was one component, and it is that which has come to dominate the discussion of the events.

## Dublin to London

Having been attained by Parliament, it was impossible for York to land in England without the fear of arrest or being assassinated by his opponents. The Tudors in the Marches were causing unrest, and if York advanced to Ludlow without promise of safe passage, no doubt they would have taken advantage of the situation. It was up to Warwick and the Calais earls to convince the king to call the duke back and allow him safe passage. The queen must have realised the threat York posed: it was common knowledge in Rome, Bruges and the streets of London that Henry was to be removed. The queen knew Warwick's coup relied on York returning from Ireland. She therefore sought to kill or apprehend York once more in Ireland.

On 22 July, York's adherents, who included a contingent of men from Dublin, seized two more ships in Bristol harbour to help convey him and his men to England. Aware of York's imminent departure, James Butler now became centre stage in preventing York leaving Ireland. During the summer of 1460, at the behest of the earl of Ormand, Conn O'Connor Faly of Offaly invaded County Meath, where York's main possessions lay, defeating the English levies that York had sent against him. Shortly afterwards, Sean O'Reilly launched a raid into County Lough, but was killed by the mayor, James Dokeray, and citizens of Drogheda at Corbollis by Mapastown Bridge on 3 September 1460. This victory cemented Yorkist control of Ireland, and allowed York to leave knowing he had a secure base to fall back upon if the next stage of the coup failed.[3] The queen was now powerless to stop his return. No doubt she had been as busy as Warwick in building alliances.

We are not sure when the messenger from Warwick arrived in Dublin. But it did so with promptitude. The Abott of St Albans tells us that York had been summoned by an amiable letter from Henry.[4] To get word from London to Dublin and for York to set sail and land in a little over two weeks is remarkable. I suspect York had already made preparations to leave Ireland – he must have chartered ships and crews, as well as gathered men and provisions, long before August, and just needed to be told to put the next stage of the plan into action. His return had been predicted two months earlier.

London, perhaps the richest city in the world at the time, was key to what happened next. Many merchants in the City of London were reliant upon international trade, particularly of wool. This trade with the continent was primarily through Calais and ports in Burgundy. The political turmoil of 1459 and 1460 saw the trade drop to roughly one-third of its earlier amount. This had a large economic impact upon London: blame was laid squarely with the ineffective Lancastrian administration. The Yorkists were able to recruit the merchant class to their cause, particularly Italian and Burgundian merchants, and cemented their power base in London and the weald. York returning to power offered economic stability. Indeed, the Doge in Venice ordered 'By letters and other statements has heard of the discord and war in England' and continued his letter that he had concern 'for the safety of the merchants of the galleys, and of the property of his subjects' in London. War meant destabilisation of trade.[5]

With parts of the country falling into anarchy, and Henry seemingly incapable of calling his allies to heel and 'playing nicely' with the new Yorkist regime, direct action was needed.

## Usurpation

Preparing the way for York's return and the planned coup, Bishop Thomas Basin noted that:

> the aforesaid Duke of York, the earl of Warwick, and their parties, eager to seduce the people . . . presented Henry as a traitor to the Kingdom rather than as a legitimate king. With these suggestions, the aforesaid duke and earl incited large crowds of the English people throughout the kingdom of England into a most dangerous sedition against Henry.[6]

York now openly challenged Henry to be king by right. Henry was incapable of saving his people: war with France and Scotland loomed, and Henry was the wrong man to be able to face these threats and to resolve the turmoil facing the country. Effective and stable governance was needed and York (and Warwick) believed that only they could save the country. York perhaps reckoned that he could obtain the throne though legal means – unlike Henry Bolingbroke through usurpation and force of arms – or at least become Protector once more, and establish some semblance of order out of the increasing tide of chaos.

York arrived in England 'about the feast of the Nativity of the blessed virgin' according to Benet, which would be 8 September.[7] He landed at Redband on the northern tip of the Wirral. He was dressed we are told in white and blue clothing, embroidered with falcons and fetterlocks, his personal badge.[8] He headed to Chester, which was held by the Stanley and Savage families.[9] With York once more in England, Warwick could think about implementing the next part of his ambitious plan to remove Henry, which he had already revealed to his Burgundian allies. On 15 September, March gave orders for Sir John Fastolf's house in Southwark to be prepared for York's arrival. The hastily assembled household included John Clay who had been York's household treasurer in Normandy. Duchess Cecily and her young sons George and Richard took up residence soon after. York himself was at Ludlow, where according to Waurin, he was acclaimed as the true and rightful heir to Richard II.[10] It was here at Ludlow, or Shrewsbury according to Wavrin where Warwick and yet met in conference for four days.[11] Wavrin was largely describing this episode from Warwick's 'Apology', prepared in the first half of 1469, where Warwick deliberately exonerated himself and Edward, earl of March from the taint of usurpation and York's bid for the crown. Warwick's argument, made after he events, has largely been followed by historians: we must always question our sources, ask when they were written and above all else why. Warwick was careful to stress in the news sheet that he was a peacemaker, a reconciler of the two factions and that York had made his bid for the throne without his support or blessing.[12] This was demonstrably false, as York had made a bid a year earlier in Warwick's presence.

About the meeting, Antonio de la Torre, a Milanese mercenary man-at-arms in the pay of Warwick,[13] reports a great gathering of the Yorkist elite took place (my translation from the Latin):

> I inform your Serenity that my most illustrious lord the King is doing well, and also the illustrious princes and lords Richard Duke of York, Edward his eldest son Earl of March, Richard Earl of Salisbury, Richard Earl of Warwick, and the said William Lord of Fauconberg.
>
> The Earl of Salisbury received his brother into his favour with the great applause and the highest congratulations of his people and subjects, by which matter that Kingdom to do and pursue all those things which concern its rights, state and honour, it seemed to the wise to be restored, composed and reintegrated, and there is indeed hope They are preparing to move their arms against their enemies next summer.[14]

The 'brother', we assume, was John Neville, Baron Neville, or perhaps his older Ralph Neville, earl of Westmorland, as it would be unlikely to be Salisbury's brother George Latimer who needed to be reconciled but his half-brothers and their heirs. This reconciliation between the two factions of the house of Neville was perhaps nothing more meaningful than the events of the Loveday in 1458. It does help explain the presence of Baron Neville in the retinue of York and his commission to raise arms: if York and Salisbury believed the Neville feud was over, they were being hopelessly naïve. Neville was playing a double game.

The meeting in mid-September, I believe, had one objective: to stage-manage the next phase of the coup. Warwick and his inner circle agreed that with their 'trump card' in place with York's return, they could act: how willing York was in this we know not. He either drove the events forward with a desire for retribution, and an insatiable lust for power – the traditional view of these events which downplays Warwick's involvement – or York was acting the part assigned by Warwick. As with any coup leader, Warwick, like Abbe Sieyès in 1799, needed 'a sword', a charismatic man, a man of proven track record and ability for the nation to rally around. York had the track record, but like his son Richard, lacked 'people skills'.

York summoned Cecily to him on 23 September, to meet him at Hereford. At Shrewsbury, Warwick and countess Anne left return to London, to stage manage what happened next. Warwick denied any knowledge.[15] Yet it is undeniable that Warwick in his letter to his European allies' months earlier shows, he had planned and orchestrated what happened next since the beginning of the year.[16] Usurpation of the crown had been York's goal since 1458 and of his closest allies, if not since 1455. York's pronouncement that the king was dead, long live King Richard, at Ludford shows his intent. Usurpation was the goal of Warwick, and how far the duke was circumstances victim is harder to gauge. For fact, Warwick knew about the taking of the crown and he planned it, despite his vocal denials once York was dead.

To put the next part of the plan into action, York arrived at Abingdon, 'there he sende for trompeters' to herald his arrival in London.[17] He entered London on 10 October under the royal standard 'with the pomp of a great following, arrived in no small exultation of spirit for he came with horns and trumpets and men-at-arms', according to Abott Wethemstede who may have been present.[18] Another tells us that his sword was born upright and bore the arms of England.[19] As could be expected for an event stage-managed by Warwick, who had travelled ahead to welcome him to the city, the timing was perfect: Parliament had already begun, and it was their support Warwick and York needed for the next stage of the coup to succeed.[20] An eyewitness noted:

Ther cam my lorde of York with viij horses and men harneysed atte X of the clock and entred the paleis with his swerde born uppe right by for him thorow the halle and Parliament chamber. And ther under the cloth of etstate stondyng he gave them knowlich that he purposed nat to ley daune his swerde but to challenge his right.[21]

The Crowland Chronicler tells us what York appears to have done next:

he approached the royal throne and claimed the sole right of sitting on it, he then put forward a genealogy tracing his lineal descent from Lionel Duke of Clarence, to whose successors, he asserted, the kingdom of England rightly belonged, since he was the elder [son of King Edward III], rather than to the descendants of John Duke of Lancaster, the younger brother from whom Henry was descended; he also protested that he would no longer endure the injustices which the three Henry's, who were usurpers, had for so long inflicted upon his line. Thereafter, he immediately entered the inner rooms of the palace, compelled King henry to remove to the queen's apartments, and took over the king's apartments himself. This disturbance continued, albeit without bloodshed or killing, for about three weeks, during which time the whole Parliament was occupied with discussion of the duke's lineage and rights.

This scene is remarkably similar to that presented by Warwick in his 'Apology'. Indeed it may be based on it.

The Pope commented, based largely on Warwick's version of events from early 1461, that:

the prelates and peer of the realm (an assembly which they call Parliament) convened in London to discuss matters of state. First, they voted to rescind the acts of the Parliament of the preceding year; for by that the Duke of York, the Earl of Salisbury, and the Earl of Warwick had been declared enemies of the realm. When these had been rescinded, the Duke of York said the throne was his since he was most closely related to the murdered King Richard, it was intolerable that the heirs of a murderer should reign.[22]

The Pope adds Warwick forcibly opposed York.[23] The Pope writing in 1461 and other documents from 1460 prove the lie to Warwick's 'Apology' from 1469 where he downplays his involvement in events. Warwick's 'Apology' is a carefully crafted piece of propaganda written at a time when he needed to win over French allies and Queen Margaret. It is not reliable history.

If York was to take the crown, he needed to stage a coup, he needed 'shock and awe': he got the shock, with the House stunned into silence. York and Warwick had hoped for Parliament to agree York should be king there and then. The plan relied on Parliament acquiescing to York's demand, and a prompt coronation, but they had misjudged the situation: York had lost. The way for usurpation had been prepared since Northampton. York the 'conquering hero' could not win 'hearts and minds' to his cause. Abbot Whethamstede acidly remarked 'the duke's high-handedness' as well as his 'ill-considered presumption' cost his cause support, particularly amongst those peers who were politically undecided in their loyalty. York also lost support among the merchant class, for whom further political turmoil would be economically disastrous. The Lords vetoed the coronation on 13 October.[24] Unlike 1399 when Henry Bolingbroke had almost universal support and military superiority, the duke of York led a faction against a universally acclaimed king. York and Warwick did not act in his name, or have control over the whole political elite. The process of usurpation could not be as carefully orchestrated as Warwick and York hoped. It remains possible that usurpation was York's extemporization of the events to suit his own ends, rather than waiting until he had full military and political control, hence Warwick's reported anger.[25] We noted earlier, in July it was 'common knowledge' that goal of Warwick was to make Edward, earl of March successor to Henry rather than make York king. Had plans changed? York knew that even if he took control of the king, his position was not secure as he had learned to his cost. York's only chance of security for him, Warwick, Salisbury and his family was to remove Henry. Whatever Warwick had hoped to achieve, the Neville regime quickly found that for the majority of their supporters, usurpation was not acceptable.[26] Christine Carpenter comments:

> The resistance of the assembled lords, possibly even of York's closest allies, tells its own story of the power that monarchy still held after so many years of misgovernance and of the risks of cutting off the vital support of the nobles that York was running. It is noticeable how few major lords fought for the king at Northampton, before York claimed the throne, and how many more fought at Wakefield and St Albans, after he had done so.[27]

To resolve the matter, a council was established at Black Friars on the following day, 11 October to debate the right of York to the throne.[28] As important as those who attended were those who were absent: Henry

Percy, earl of Northumberland, Ralph Neville, earl of Westmorland, Henry Holland, duke of Exeter and George Neville, Baron Latimer.[29] After deliberation and much argument, on 16 October, the claim was presented to the house of Lords: Henry did not concede, but asked the Lords to find fault with York's argument. The Lords passed it to the judges and sergeants-at-law.[30] About this process, the Pope comments:

> Henry VI heir to a wicked and violent king. A Parliament which had been bullied and intimidated into passing its measures was not valid. The kingdom rightfully belonged to York, for if the murderous line was were excluded, he stood first in the order of succession, and thus he demanded the crown. Henry was to live thenceforth as a private citizen.
>
> These demands seemed just. But weighing against them were the oaths they had taken to King Henry, the length of his reign and his fathers' victories over the French, the ancient enemies of the English nation. When York pressed his more strongly, they nearly resorted to arms.[31]

It is undeniable that York did have a claim to the throne, and one that was stronger than one might initially think. Henry VI's grandfather, Henry IV, had usurped the throne from his cousin Richard II. Henry IV was the son of John of Gaunt, Edward III's fourth son, and it was this lineage that provided Henry VI's claim to the throne. York was descended from Edward III's third son, and so from a dynastic perspective, he could be seen to have the stronger claim.

This situation was not as easily resolved as York hoped it would be: Parliament was caught in the middle. They could side with Henry, but York's army was an immediate and present threat in the city. Alternatively, they could side with York and risk a prolonged period of civil unrest by deposing an anointed king. After two weeks of judgement, Parliament decided on a compromise. By 22 October the king requested them to discuss the matter: on 25 October the Lords arrived at the compromise that Henry should remain king but that York and his heirs should succeed him and echoed the treat of Troyes. Henry would remain king for the duration of his life, York and his heirs were named as Henry's heirs in a document known as the Act of Accord agreed six days later. A writer close to Warwick comments that he:

> already knew that the people of London were ill-satisfied with it. If the Count summoned the Archbishop of Canterbury to come quickly, and he told him that, in order to do all good, he would go to the Duke of Yorc,

and remonstrate with him the great evil he had done, and that he should look carefully at the great promises made by him to the king and other lords of the country.

The latter sentence is perhaps correct at 'reading the room'. This piece of text from Warwick's 'Apology' is an expert piece of writing to place the blame on York for the usurpation of the crown. The writer carefully distances Thomas Neville – Warwick's brother – as well as Edward, earl of March from the coup. The young earl of Rutland is placed centre stage. The scene is set for the death of York and Rutland, and Warwick and March to be divinely ordained to take the crown. The 'Apology' has been taken as literal truth for 565 years, when it is a carefully crafted literary device by Warwick or someone very close to him.[32]

Rather than putting the duke of York on the throne, the Act merely recognised the validity of the Yorkist title. It was ultimately an act of realpolitik, and an outcome neither Warwick nor York were satisfied with: Chronicler Gregory was at pains to point out the duke of York kept the king under house arrest with 'force and strength until, at last, the king, for fear of death, granted him the crown: for a man who has little wit will soon be afraid of death. I trust and believe there was no man that would have done him bodily harm.'[33]

It is undeniable that the solution which Parliament ultimately came to, was almost worthless as it contradicted the very basis on which it was made. The Lords were accepting the duke's claim that he was the true king and in making provision for York's accession in the event of Henry's abdication: the Act in its simplest form postponed Richard's accession to a moment more politically propitious. Either the duke was the rightful king or he was not. If York was king by right, then Henry VI had no right to rule until his death or abdication: as John Watts says 'what true king would agree to be subject to a usurper?'[34] York was now a proven perjurer: had his concern for the commonweal and just government, merely been a persona behind which York could hide his ruthless ambition? His contemporaries felt sure of this, and it is certainly a reasonable conclusion to draw from the facts as they exist.

The Act of Accord in essence supported the status quo engineered by Warwick with the first coup in July: the continuation of Henry VI's kingship under Yorkist control was the safest means of proceeding for the time being. No contemporary would have accepted the notion that a King could be made by Parliament, for the king's right to rule depended on hereditary right, or force of arms, not by judgement of Parliament: thus, usurpation drew allies to the queen. In acting as he did, York probably had in mind the events of January 1327 when Parliament, the Church and the *communitas* had moved aside Edward II in favour of his son. Parliament had also laid aside the king's heir: in theory York was on strong ground with precedent on his side. Yet unlike in 1327 or 1399, Parliament simply could not simply push Henry aside: If Henry was not king, and neither had been his father or grandfather, then what was the legality of all oaths, offices of state, gifts, pardons etc issues in the name of the King? If Henry was not king by right, then the previous 60 years was legally 'null and void'. Parliament, Lords and the judges had no option other than to keep Henry, and move aside Edward prince of Wales in the manner of 1399, otherwise they too would be perjurers and oath breakers.

Furthermore, it is undeniable that the whole proceeding relied on the compliance and assent of Henry VI, who probably failed to understand what was being asked of him. If Henry had not agreed to what was being asked of him, then no discussion could have taken place: we are left to wonder as to king's grasp of the political events and their implications as they unfolded. It must have also been obvious that this was also Henry's death sentence. How long would York keep 'the puppet' alive before he assumed the crown? In this regard the queen and her allies had to act quickly, like the leaders of the 1400 Epiphany Rising.

Despite constitutional irregularities, Warwick's stage-managed second coup had proceeded almost exactly as he anticipated it would. York was technically Prince of Wales.[35] The duke of Burgundy heard this directly from Warwick on 10 November. Warwick had kept his uncle, Fauconberg, who had gone back to Calais, 'up to speed' with news. He acted as a conduit to the duke.[36]

Usurpation of the crown had been York's goal since 1458 – perhaps not him, but his closest allies the Nevilles – if not since 1455. Did usurpation lay behind his actions over the previous decade? P.A. Johnson and Matthew Lewis would suggest not, but both writers only place usurpation as considered from September 1460, which as we have seen was already being discussed as a *fait accompli* in June and July 1460. York's pronouncement that the king was dead, long live King Richard at Ludford shows his intent. usurpation was the goal of Warwick, and how far the duke was circumstances victim is harder to gauge. For fact, Warwick knew about the taking of the crown and he planned it, despite his own vocal denials. York and Warwick owed their success through the support and intervention of the papacy as well as the

Italian League and the duke of Burgundy. Usurpation could not have occurred without strong alliances against France. Margaret of Anjou and her father Rene held influence over Charles VII: without Medici money, Burgundian troops, Papal blessing and Milanese influence, Usurpation was simply not possible. Indeed, Coppini acknowledged his and inter alia the role the Papacy played in removing Henry VI in August, writing to Sforza that 'the lords here, the kinsmen of the king, who through my hands have won back the state'. This power grab by Warwick, gave Burgundy and Milan new allies again France, and Warwick Coppini told Sforza 'if they had some incitement they would go to France with a considerable force to vindicate the claims of this kingdom'.[37] Indeed, the duke of Milan instructed his ambassador Prospero Camulio to draw the duke of York tighter into the Italian League alliance with Burgundy.[38]

Chapter 20

# PROTECTOR YORK

Whichever way we look at it, York's bid for power had failed. He was back where he had been in late spring 1459, yet in 1460 he had lost any credibility to govern, and moreover his actions had further destabilised an already volatile situation.

York, as de facto Protector, was as vulnerable to the problems of authority as he had been during two previous terms in office. The Yorkists' claim that they were acting not against the king, but against 'evil councillors' simply did not hold true in October 1460: Prince Edward in a letter to the City of London, gave thanks to God that York had showed himself as a 'fals traitour' driven by selfish motivation, and could no longer blind the people with his lies.[1] The queen made much of York's action and branded him a traitor who claimed the throne through 'an untrewe pretense feyned a tytle to my lordis coronne and roiall estate and preminencne contrary to his lieguance and solempne othes of his own offer'.[2] The royalist response demanded the magnates, nobles and communities to ask themselves where government lay. Was it with York and the puppet Henry or with Margaret and her son, Edward prince of Wales? That the queen was acting in the name of her son, and not her husband, shows clearly that Henry was already sidelined by both factions: what was needed was a strong king and not a return to government by committee in the name of the king. With York as king in waiting, it was probably already a foregone conclusion that Henry would mysteriously die like Richard II or Edward before him. Yet, with two contesting factions both claiming royal authority, who were subjects obliged to obey?

Without the guarantee of obedience, the task of governance was much harder: it meant the creation of an absolute power. It meant elimination of the opposition, and extermination of counter claimants: it is why Henry VIII had the de la Poles executed, why Elizabeth I had Mary Stuart executed in 1588 and why, as a Milanese observer commented in 1496, 'King Richard . . . put to death his nephews, to whom the kingdom belonged'.[3] Even if true that the duke of York's grandsons were alive into the 1490s as many supporters of Richard III believe, sufficient men of influence – the duke of Britanny who released Henry Tudor from captivity, the king of France who helped fund Tudor's invasion and the Italian League who helped bankroll Tudor – believed he had murdered them, along with men of influence in England to precipitate a revolution. Richard III never publicly declared the boys alive, nor Henry Tudor: even if – and that's a BIG if – the boys were alive, the rumour of their deaths and Richard's failure to quash this rumour, lost him his throne. Yet being named king by choice did not always mean security – Edward IV learned this to his cost: kings were disposable at the whim of great magnates. It was a lesson Henry VII had to learn. About Henry one period writer noted, 'the king is rather feared than loved . . . but if fortune allowed some lord of the blood royal to rise and he had to take the field, he would fare badly owing to his avarice; his people would abandon him'.[4]

Elimination of opposition, and centralisation of power back into an absolute monarch, was Yorkist policy from 1455, and a necessity if any sense of stability was to be created in government: king by choice was rather different from king by right. It was a policy that found its fulfilment in Henry VIII, the duke of York's great-grandson. As a policy it invited further instability and criticism as Henry VIII found when faced with the Pilgrimage of Grace and the Wakefield rebellion of 1541; just two of the direct challenges to the absolutist necessity of Henry VIII's reign. York's actions paved the way ultimately to civil war from 1639. York, at first, articulated failings in medieval governance that had been exposed with the rebellion let by Wat Tyler and John Ball. Government was 'playing catch up' to a changing world and the changed status and influence of the *communitas*. This tension was not fully resolved until the Glorious Revolution of 1688 or perhaps 1832.

On the world stage, York's coup had weakened his position with some. On French observer writes at the time:

> the duke of Yorck made an overture to the king, your said father, by means of those of Scotland and others, that he should be pleased to give him favour and aid in his quarrel with king Henry, and made great offers in the case to the king, your said father, would have liked to accept it; and was the issue was much debated in the Council . . . and it was the

opinion of all that ... the king ought not to hear it, that the duke of Yorck was subject to the said king Henry, and had paid homage and oath of fealty to him as to his sovereign, and that no quarrels of subjects wishing to undertake them against their sovereign ... were not just.[5]

York the oath breaker was isolated internationally. Warwick and the earl of March were considered traitors.[6] We also need to remember, it was Warwick who had brokered deals with the Papacy, the court of Milan and the duke of Burgundy, not York. Warwick had more influence and patronage than he did.

For those willing to trust York, he seemed sufficiently secure on the world stage that foreign policy negotiations restarted. That York had allies and he could reward them, is shown by the arrival of the Burgundian ambassadors on 1 October to negotiate the existing truce into a lasting peace.[7] On 6 October a treaty between the Dauphin and Milan was agreed, and extended to York and Warwick in December. York (we assume Warwick), according to an ambassador at the Court of Savoy writing to the Dauphin informed him that 'the cavalry and archers of England in march will cross into France'.[8] Clearly, York had agreed to invade France in new year 1461: for him to agree to this speaks either of his over confidence he felt in his position, OR he was prepared to say anything to keep alliances (men and money) operating. In either case, York believed his position was safe. But again, we are guilty of hindsight revisionism. For fact, York controlled Henry and government; Queen Margaret and the duke of Exeter were without allies, without substantial finances and were negotiating to find asylum in France. York controlled the mechanisms and finances of state. He was protected by the law of treason. Only the Courtenays in the West Country and the Percy family seemed to be holding out against the Yorkist revolution. On paper at least, York had won: all he had to do was to 'knock a few heads together' as he had done in the past, and the revolution was secure, hence he could offer military aide with a degree of confidence to his allies.

## Confrontation
In the midst of deliberations about York's foreign policy, the thorny issue of Northumberland's recalcitrance was discussed. Northumberland rejected any calls to appear before Henry and deliberately escalated the situation. On 8 October Parliament wrote again to Northumberland, believing he was behind the trouble in the North or would have influence over Thirlwall and others, ordered the earl to 'cause to be removed from Wreshill castle all the evil doers who hold the same'

who were 'lying in wait, beating, maiming plundering and slaying.' John, Lord Clifford was likewise so ordered to surrender Penrith to Salisbury and remove the garrison which was causing trouble.[9] Presented to the Court of King's Bench during Hilary term 1462 was an indictment against Thirlwall, which had previously been taken at Caister in October 1461. The indictment records that Robert Warter during October 1460 had arrived at South Kelsey in Lincolnshire. The village was ransacked and looted, along with the manor house which belonged to Richard Haundsard esq. The village and manor house were again raided in January 1461, led by Richard Thirlwall of Wressle, servant to the earl of Northumberland. Thirlwall took away £40 in money and charters and obligations worth £100, as well as pieces of armour, a white warhorse valued at £4 and 100 marks in money from Haunsard's brother.[10] Thirlwall was clearly a dangerous man along with his associate Warters: West Yorkshire and North Lincolnshire was slipping into anarchy orchestrated by Northumberland. The Haunsard's were prominent supporters of the duke of York, who owned land in Lincolnshire, as well as Thornton and Blacktoft in Yorkshire. The elder Richard Haunsard would be found a place in the duke's retinue.

Northumberland was raiding into York's Manor of Wakefield: 'The earl of Northumbria, the lords of Clyfford, and Dakyrs, and Nevylle, held a council at York, and destroyed the tenants of the duke of York and the earl of Salisbury.'[11] Probably evidencing this, William Wodehouse the Grave of Sandal reported:

He does not answer for any profit coming from the winter and summer agistment of Sandal Park, because no men wanted to agist their beasts in it on account of rebels attacking day after day and driving the tenants' cattle to Pontefract; Nor does he answer for any profit from herons within the said park, because nothing was possible this year; Nor does he answer for the grazing of the lord's park called Thrustonhawe, because it lies open in common and not enclosed and no profit could be taken from it this year by oath of the accountant.
    Total nothing.[12]

He adds that grange farm attached to the castle was vacant 'for want of lessees on account of the insurrection of various rebels of the king at Pontefract'.[13] Appendix 1 and 2 present the impact of Lancastrian raids in the manor, most of the damage seemingly occurring once the duke was dead. Northumberland's chevauchée across the North became so infamous, that the news was reported in France and

Burgundy. One chronicler noted that in London 'lords of the country and the ladies complained to him [Warwick] of the great maulz and damages which had been received by the duke of Sombresset' and adds that when Warwick went on pilgrimage to Walsingham, 'the earl of Northumberland . . . made a great mass of men-at-arms and . . . assembled ten thousand men' to attack him. Warwick, learning of the intended attack, had found safety in Ely. As a chronicler noted 'it was lawful at the beginning of the war'.[14]

On 14 October, Parliament had had enough of Northumberland and Clifford's defiance: Ralph Lord Greystoke (1406–87), Henry Lord Fitzhugh (1429–72) and Sir Thomas Lumley, Sir John Neville, John Harrington, John Hastings, William Scargill and Sir John Saville, amongst others, were charged with the task of taking Pontefract, Penrith and Wressle. They were empowered to carry with them a siege train and to recruit men from Yorkshire and neighbouring counties to lay siege to the castles if necessary. The Sheriffs of London issued proclamations against Northumberland in the name of the Lords and Bishops assembled in Parliament, explaining Northumberland had occupied Pontefract and Wressle with 'great strength and might' and was in effect a traitor for disobeying royal demands. If Northumberland would not remove his garrison in 20 days, his lands would be forfeit.[15]

Fitzhugh and Greystoke were long-term members of the retinue of the earl of Salisbury. As Michael Hicks has put it, Salisbury attempted to extend the power and influence of his family, not just through the traditional route of marrying his children into local gentry families, but also using contracts and retaining 'to bind to him important individuals of rank or domicile naturally beyond his ambit'. Retainers were themselves then able – and expected – to raise their own tenants when required for a lord's service; Salisbury relied on this in 1459 when those he summoned who could themselves 'call on tenants and friends in times of trouble'.[16] He did so again in 1460. Hicks identifies different degrees of proximity to the earl through his retaining. Men such James Strangways, William Fitzhugh and Greystoke would often join Salisbury on royal commissions.[17] Salisbury's retainers were themselves interconnected, especially in Yorkshire. James Strangways married into the Darcy family; Sir John Saville constable of Sandal married Salisbury's retainer Sir Thomas Harrington's daughter; William Fitzhugh's son and heir married Salisbury's daughter Alice.

The central elite of Salisbury's power base would be at Wakefield in December 1460: Thomas Colt, Sir Thomas and Sir John Harrington, Sir Thomas Parr, and Sir James Pickering. The earl had the backing of an impressive line-up of experienced northern magnates.[18] Despite statements by Keith Dockray that Greystoke and Fitzhugh fought at Wakefield and St Albans, and were 'playing a double game'.[19] IF they were it comes as a remarkable turn for events for Greystoke to be with Edward IV in Hull after easter 1461, along with Warwick, Fauconberg, Lord Say. Moreover we read '26s 10d for the expenses of Lord Greystoke giving the town counsel'.[20] Dockray is reliant on unreliable sources such as Gregory's chronicle in writing 'reliable' history and misses the point of what these sources actually are compared to more reliable empirical sources.

On 31 October, York and the Lords Temporal and Spiritual swore on oath to uphold the provisions of the agreement. Those who broke the agreement were considered traitors and their lands would be forfeit. An account of the Accord and swearing of oaths was sent to every sheriff for proclamation, and a writ from Parliament ordered the Accord to the generally published.[21]

The Act of Accord was, in its simplest form, a dynastic revolution and made armed conflict inevitable. It went beyond what York's opponents were willing to accept. Jean du Clercq across the Channel knew some of this:

> the duke of Yorck, proposed in Parliament that the crown of England should belong to him and should be king, and that the said Parliament agreed the said duke of Yorck be granted the kingdom and the crown . . . after his death [Henry VI], the said crown belonged to the duke of Yorck and his heirs; and by this agreement the king would pay each year, during his life, to the duke of Yorck or his children, twenty thousand escus or florins of England . . . After which the king begged the duke of Yorck to make peace between the queen and country, who was then at Yorck and had twenty thousand combatants assembled, and sent word to the king that she wished to come to London . . . would not in any way hold or obey the said appointment.[22]

If York and Parliament hoped that the general proclamation and threat of attainder was sufficient to call Northumberland to heel they were badly mistaken. Ignoring the legalities of the situation, the chevauchée from Pontefract and Wressle continued. Chaos was slowly engulfing the North Midlands and the West Riding. York had to act if he was to stem the disaffection being sewn by Northumberland, and knew that the only way to combat Northumberland was in direct confrontation. By the end of November, nothing had been heard of Northumberland or Clifford: they had not acceded to Parliament's wishes. the Percy-Neville feud was accelerating to a climax: refusing to compromise, Northumberland disobeyed King and Parliament. Perhaps seeing

Salisbury in the ascendant and raising troops, Northumberland perhaps felt he had no option open to him other than to act in a way to safeguard his own position and possessions: if the duke of York cemented himself in power, then both he, Somerset, Clifford and all those engulfed in the northern dispute would find themselves outside of power, and perhaps even attained in direct retaliation for the events of 1459. Revenge and fear were at the heart of the events as they unfolded.

From being a loyal subject, Northumberland now refused to obey the king, and became a traitor. In his own mind, he was supporting the queen and the heir apparent, Prince Edward, and was operating to wrest the king back from the influence and custody of York, Salisbury and Warwick in a replay of the politics of the previous decade: Henry VI was incapable of governing, and others ruled in his place: for now, York held the king and therefore power. The 'trump card' the Yorkists held was if the king broke the agreement, York or his heir would be king.[23]

York may have won power, but he did not control the nation: the initiative now passed to the queen and her supporters. York had no real power or control outside of London as the actions of the queen and her allies cruelly exposed. Warwick bargained on being able to contain Lancastrian dissent over the winter until the next campaigning season. If in re-igniting the Percy-Neville feud over Wressle, Warwick and his allies had hoped it would 'be all over by Christmas' they were badly mistaken. As in 1453–5, the events at Wressle, a long festering grudge between two major families, was destabilising not only the North, but the nation as a whole. York's usurpation spiralled events out of control, handing the initiative to the queen, and her allies in France and Scotland. In playing his 'game of thrones' with Milan and Burgundy, Warwick perhaps underestimated the skill of their opponents.

# Chapter 21

# MARGARET'S FLIGHT

'Gregory's Chronicle' (one of a number of London-based vernacular chronicles written in the late 1460s and ascribed, probably wrongly, by its first editor James Gairdner to the mayor and alderman William Gregory) claims that Queen Margaret called for Somerset, Devon, Roos, Neville, Clifford and Latimer to assemble with the duke of Exeter at Hull. It is accepted without question by many historians. Yet history tells us the queen was in Wales; moreover, no Lancastrian faction existed, yet. The great army which marched to Wakefield existed only in the minds of chroniclers and later historians. The facts are, the queen was in Wales, with the duke of Exeter, the Prince of Wales and a handful of others.[1] These included the bishop of Lichfield and Coventry and one of his clerks, John Whelpdale. He was a canon at Lichfield Cathedral, resident from 1454 until he died in 1490, having attended Cambridge, and was the holder of a benefice outside the diocese, a canonry in Lincoln from 1470 to 1483.[2] From here, the queen, the prince and Exeter headed to Scotland.

None of the events in England went unnoticed amongst European princes. The new Yorkist regime seemed secure, and negotiations began with France and Burgundy. At the start of September, one of the Dauphin Louis' emissaries, the Seigneur de la Barde, was invited to London and resided at Grey Friars in London, Warwick's headquarters.[3] De la Barde was given safe conduct by Henry VI on 15 September and travelled back to Burgundy within a few days, having met the earl of Warwick who had gave him a courtly welcome, providing him with a safe conduct to travel at will for the next three months between Burgundy and England. Warwick was hoping for military aid from Burgundy and the Dauphin to use against Margaret before landing in France to attack Charles VII. De la Barde was back in England on 23 January.

In France, Somerset was at Guines: as it was impossible for Warwick to evict him due to the strong defences, Somerset was 'biding his time'. Always cautious, not a soldier, but a diplomat and ambassador, Somerset has been maligned by Yorkist propaganda. He had been allowed safe conduct to France dated 16 July 1460. The queen had asked for his release and other prisoners, if we believe the Prince de Narbonne, it was not possible to release them.[4] I believe – and may be wrong – this includes Trollop and others from Hammes and Guines.[5] Somerset – like his father and uncle – and Trollop for Ludford Bridge became the 'bogeymen' of the Yorkist propaganda machine. All 'bad things' were ascribed to them, regardless of guilt.[6] On being released, Somerset wrote to Pierre de Brezé, Seneschal of Normandy. Trollop may have remained in Guines. Despite being named by Yorkist sources as present in coming battles, the Pastons infer he was not back in England until mid to late January 1461. De Brezé was the king's principal agent in all that concerned relations with England. He was in constant communication with Margaret of Anjou and kept Charles VII informed of all the news that reached him. Jean Doucereau, a faithful and intelligent servant, was his constant intermediary. De Brezé informed Charles on 26 July that:

> He has written to me as great seneschal and as far as I can know, he is not considering leaving the said place of Guines until he has news from a man whom he has sent from there, for whom he is waiting for day by day, so he knows for certain what intentions the queen is and of the fate of the Kingdom.[7]

Who the agent was, we do not know. Certainly, he would have learned of the queen's flight to Wales and her appeal for sanctuary. De Brezé was better informed that Somerset, as he already knew that the queen was fleeing to Wales, and thence to France.[8] Warwick had travelled to Calais to witness the oath-taking personally, prior to Somerset being released, before returning to London with Earl Rivers, and his son Anthony, via Sandwich and Greenwich. These men, we suspect, were hostages to ensure Somerset's good behaviour.[9] However, this could all be 'fake news' from Warwick to show Somerset as a perjurer and oath breaker. Wavrin via Warwick goes out of his way to make Warwick 'saintly' and Somerset an untrustworthy megalomaniac: he goes on to describe Warwick defeating Somerset in 1464. Somerset becomes Warwick's main protagonist, ergo his reputation had to be blackened to set the scene for the later story, which Wavrin may have learned directly from Warwick in July 1469 when the two met.

We cannot be sure when Somerset landed back in England, presumably at Corfe in Devon.[10] We know nothing of his whereabouts till he appears in Exeter in early November. He is then in Bridgewater on 10 November with the earl of Devon gathering troops. With memories of the father of earl of Devon's sacking of the city, and fearful of a similar episode, the anxious citizens of Exeter sent a gift of £5 to Somerset as a sign of their goodwill, and simultaneously dispatched a servant of John, Lord Dynham to London to warn York of his activities. York assumed Devon and Somerset would attempt to attack Bristol, and warned the mayor and council of the city to place the castle in readiness for defence.[11] Remember the concern in late July about Exeter and Devon causing trouble in the West Country? Warwick was right to be worried that the Neville coup would ignite simmering tensions.

Whatever was being planned by Devon and Exeter may not have been in response to the Act of Accord. It was perhaps a re-run of earlier grievances. On 31 October, the king, York, March and Rutland swore public oaths to keep the peace and uphold the agreement; it was not made public till 9 November. Any attack against York was now treason.[12] The earl of Devon was perhaps promulgating his own vendetta once more: we noted earlier the Exeter had been the focus of such depredations, so the request for help from York and 'paying off' the earl may have been part of assuaging the earl of Devon before York could send troops. In the south-west the Courtenay feud was ready to boil over, in the North, the Neville feud was in full swing. Local grievances, as much as the Act of Accord, drove events forward. The Act of Accord did not prevent conflict, it was one factor in an escalation of grievances and the inability of York to govern that led to armed confrontation. The Act of Accord gave the differing warring clans and factions a sense of purpose and unity that they had lacked until now. IF they were to retain their position, influence and wealth (many Lancastrian magnates had profited handsomely from the dismemberment of York, Salisbury and Warwick's estates, they were prepared to fight for it. Greed and ego drove events forward. York headed a weak, minority faction. He did not have the loyalty of a majority of the lay peers. For the peasant in his field, or the rich burgess, who the king was did or did not really matter: what mattered was loyalty to their lord and acting on his will. The king or protector York did not command, they co-ordinated. That the king had absolute power is true, but he did not wield it at local level. If your lord said take up arms, you did. The King was distant, a concept for the majority of people. The Tudors were to change this.

## Scotland

There is no doubt that as summer wore on the Yorkist lords became more concerned about the activities of Margaret and Exeter. On 9

August they instructed, in the king's name, 'our right trusty and entirely welbeloved brother Therl of Pembroke' to deliver Denbigh castle to his deputy and 'accept our right trusty and entirely welbeloved cousyn the Duc of York our approved and true liege man and noo traytour, our true subget and noo rebell, our right faithful frende and no one ennemye'. The reception of this command in Wales was predictable enough, and eight days later William Herbert, Walter Devereux and Roger Vaughan, the new Master of the Ordnance, were dispatched to Wales to subdue the rebels.[13] Just as concerning as events in Wales was the news that the Scottish king, James II, had crossed the border and was laying siege to Roxburgh castle. Plans were made for the earl of Salisbury to go north, and northern lords were commissioned to raise men to resist the invaders.

When Parliament made its judgement, naming Edward, earl of March heir, Margaret was in north Wales with the duke of Exeter.[14] Believing that the Yorkist revolution was complete, Queen Margaret wrote to her uncle, Charles VII seeking asylum for herself and her son. She believed the Yorkists had won, and unless her uncle sent a significant army to England, the Yorkist revolution would be complete. The letter was carried to Paris by her chaplain who landed in Britanny. The king put the matter under discussion in his Council. After much deliberation:

> and that it pleased him [Charles VII] to have pity on her and her said son, and to send someone to escort them into this kingdom, and to give them safe conduct to be there three or four years until they can recover; and the matter was much debated in the king's council, your said father, in the presence of all the lords and people of his council, and after several altercations it was concluded, in the presence of the king, your said father, that they were to send beyond the Sieur de Genlis, messire Jehan Carbonnel, and a secretary, and letters and instructions were given to them for them to show the said queen.[15]

Charles transmitted his reply on 20 October 1460 in a letter written by Master Bertrand Briçonnet, one of his secretaries.[16] Jehan Carbonnel accompanied by M. de Genly was in England by 13 December, but by the time they had arrived, Margaret was travelling to Scotland. They took with them 'some brigandines, that the king our lord has written to us and charged to male'.[17] Presumably this was a token gesture of helping Margaret militarily. That no Lancastrian faction existed is shown by her desperation to escape and of Charles to raise finances and secure allies. On her behalf, Charles VII attempted to broker some form of agreement for Scotland to come to the military aid of Margaret. One eyewitness at the French court tells us that Charles sent word:

> to Scotland, for this matter, and to beg the king, his mother, and the people of the three states of the said country, that they would give to the said king of England and to the prince her son, all assistance, aid, and comfort that could be done, and wrote in the same way to the said king of England what he had made known in Scotland in favour of her.[18]

Had Charles sent Margaret to Scotland? We can find no archive documents that support this, but we believe that Charles was the 'power behind the throne' of Margaret at this stage. Mary recognised Queen Margaret as holding legitimate power, in response, the Scottish regency government gave priority to the queen's offer to hand over Berwick in return for military aid.[19] In the war for 'hearts and minds' it allowed Warwick to charge the queen and her allies with collusion with the enemy.[20]

For Margaret to seek asylum clearly shows she believed she was backed into a corner. At this stage she lacked allies. She had travelled to Scotland in the company of the duke of Exeter, as well as William Percy (1428–62), bishop of Carlisle, brother of the earl of Northumberland, and John Hales (1400–90), bishop of Coventry and Lichfield. The queen on her journey to Wales after Northampton had lodged at Malpas with the bishop. He was appointed by Margaret and would serve during the Readeption as keeper of the privy seal.[21] The bishop was accompanied by his clerk John Whelpdale, who suffered attainder for this.[22] It was near Malpas, according to Gregory's chronicle, that the queen was robbed of her jewels and goods worth some 10,000 marks (£6,666 13s 4d), either by retainers of the Stanleys or by one of her own servants. Soon afterwards, Margaret arrived at Harlech, where she was greeted warmly, before travelling onto Denbigh and Pembroke's protection.

The Yorkists had another queen to worry about. Since late autumn the duke of Burgundy had sent a mission to Scotland to uphold the existing treaty. To this end Henry had given safe passage to Burgundian ambassadors and George Abernathy on 25 October 1460: they travelled north to meet the queen regent at the college of Dumbarton.[23] The head of the mission, Louis de Bruges, lord of Gruuthuse (1422–92) and his co-ambassador Josse de Halewijn were hoping to reconcile her with her uncle, the duke.[24] We note that during October and November the duke of York worked hard to dissuade the regency government from alliance with Queen Margaret.[25] Presumably York's delegation was in consort with that from Burgundy. The embassy returned to Burgundy on 13 February 1461.[26] The Scottish delegation was matched by the arrival in London of Jean de Lannoy, the Marshal of Burgundy Thibaut de Neufchâtel and others. They were still in London on 30 December.[27]

Before she headed to Scotland, in November Margaret had written to the mayor, aldermen and common council of London. Her letter decried the 'verray pure malice' of York in seeking to destroy the king, herself and their son. She then explained how the duke of York had through 'untrewe pretense feyned a tytle to my lordis coronne and roiall estate'. She denied Yorkist propaganda that an 'unsen power of straungeres' had been assembled to rob the citizens of their goods, promising that should the Lancastrians come to London, 'ye nor noon of you shalbe robbed, dispoiled nor wronged by any personne' in her company. The appeal, and a similar one in the name of the Prince of Wales, fell on deaf ears and does not appear to have been answered.[28]

As January 1461 dawned, the queen was isolated: she lacked formal allies and had precious few armed men with her. Despite her representations, Margaret, it appears, received nothing concrete in support from her uncle the King of France or the Scots, who were beset by their own internal problems after the king's death. Moreover, the court was caught up in the diplomatic wranglings between the French king and the duke of Burgundy, save a vague promise to cease their attacks on the border. It had become overwhelmingly clear to Margaret that the only way to restore her son's rights was to rely on her Lancastrian supporters in England centred on those lords who had sworn to defend her son and husband at the Coventry Parliament

With the queen in Scotland, it is hard to say what lines of communication they were between her and the Lancastrian magnates who were loyal to her. Jasper Tudor was with James Butler in Pembroke, Devon and his Champernowne allies were causing trouble in the west country. In the north Henry Percy took centre stage. Aware that if he was to maintain his hold on Wressle and Pontefract, in all eventualities he would have to fight to do so. The Act of Accord transformed his struggle against the Nevilles into a national cause. There is nothing to suggest that their assembling of men predated the end of October, which Yorkist chroniclers tell us the queen masterminded, yet the reality was probably more a piecemeal and ad-hoc reaction to events. Northumberland, John, Lord Neville and others who all harboured grudges against York and Salisbury used the opportunity to solve both their own points of contention, and at the same time and 'get back the king into power, as they had him before'.[29] The mustering of men in the North may have been in direct response to Margaret's letter to the

City of London. In this process Northumberland took the lead across the North of England.

Hicks states that Somerset's return to England gave the queen the military leadership she was looking for.[30] I am not so sure. Firstly, Somerset was, undeniably, no great military leader and in no way gave a new aggressive and imaginative style of warfare. Secondly Hicks – as do others – assumes Somerset was in England. French historian, Gaston Du Fresne de Beaucourt argues persuasively, Somerset was in France, heading to join Margaret in winter 1460. He believed this from three points of evidence. Firstly, Charles VII, aware that Briçonnet's letter, which we mentioned earlier, had gone unanswered, another letter was sent to Margaret on or after 6 December. This was carried by Somerset who was given free passage on that date.[31] In his letter, Charles assured his niece he would help her cause militarily, and sent an ambassador to Mary of Guelders.[32] That Somerset had crossed to England and then returned is confirmed by Gaston come de Foix who was present in France at the court of Charles VII. He tells us Somerset left France, took information to the queen, and then returned to France to meet with Charles:                    ·

> and was afterwards sent back to the queen of England, to tell her that the king was willing to help and assist her and those of his party in the quarrel she had with king Edward, and that he had made known to the kings of Spain and Scotland, his allies, so that they might do the same on their part.[33]

It is hard to disprove our contemporary writer, whose letter was completed on 6 August 1461. Therefore Somerset was, it seems, travelling on or shortly after 6 December to join Margaret. In an undated letter, Charles VII wrote to:

> To Monseigneur the Duke of Sommerset, the sum of fourteen hundred livres tournois, who the King our sire ordered him to be bailed, by way of gift, both to defray his costs whilst he remained at Monstiervilliers, awaiting his passage, and for the supplies of the ship on which he is to pass from the said place of Monstiervilliers to England.[34]

The account was audited on 19 January 1461 which may date his sailing from France. Certainly, de Beaucourt believed Somerset remained in France until he had heard about events in England. Winter storms no doubt also delayed his sailing.[35] Somerset with the queen was in York on 20 January 1461.[36] We know Charles's letter had arrived with the queen, as in reply Margaret wrote imploring money and military aid.[37] The Dauphin, as shown in a letter of 9 February to the duke of Burgundy who received it on the 16th, knew some of this.[38] Therefore, a strong argument can be made – and one I believe, as did Beaucourt – that Somerset was not present at the Battle of Wakefield, his attainder no doubt referring to his actions in the West Country, in consort with the earl of Devon, Thomas Courtenay.

As the Prince de Narbonne stated, whatever Parliament had decreed, peers bound by their oath to Henry, and fearing to commit perjury, rallied to the queen as Archbishop Basin noted: 'a prudent and courageous woman, with several princes of the kingdom sought to end the perilous state and danger of their affairs . . . of the nobility of the kingdom, by far the greater part favoured King Henry'.[39]

The Act of Accord gave the queen and her supporters had a simple cause to fight for: to uphold the universally recognised king against a usurper.[40] That few rallied to the cause – at least initially – comes as no surprise. Her request for sanctuary in France was probably well known and if the queen was not prepared to stand and fight, why should others? Rouge Croix Pursuivant, serving the duke of Burgundy, made at least two trips from England to Scotland (one in October, the other November) to prevent an alliance between Scotland and Margaret with France.[41] Whatever faction emerged, it was not led by the queen, and may not have been of any national sense. Local grievances lay behind what happened, and not who or who would not be the next king. In the North, the earl of Northumberland drove events forward. He was in Beverley during December, raising troops:

> ther was a commission directed to ye inhabitants of the said Beverley from the Erle of Northumberland and the Lord Nevell chargyng every man that was betwyx lx and xvj yeres shuld there in the most sensabyll Aray awaytt uppon the sayd lordys to the entent to bring henry att that tyme beyng kyng of this lond outt off prison and owt of hys enemyes hondys uppon payn of forfeiture of lyffe and lyme.[42]

Northumberland and Lord Neville, in the name of the king, ordered every man between the ages of 16 and 60 to gather at Beverley. Before the northern lords could act offensively against York, they had to secure their local positions.

We met Neville earlier: he was the brother of the feeble-minded earl of Westmorland, head of the senior branch of the Neville family, an implacable enemy of Salisbury and his son Warwick. Neville had been first summoned to Parliament as Lord Neville in November 1459, and he had received numerous rewards from Salisbury's forfeited estates. He was again rewarded by Henry VI in March 1460 for his efforts against Yorkist rebels in the North and had raised men for the Lancastrians at Northampton. Northumberland, was joined by the earl of Westmoreland on 12 December. Lord John Neville, then at Raby, was party to Northumberland's activities thanks to mounted messengers.[43] Neville was using his commissions signed into law by York in the name of Henry to raise men around Beverley for the Lancastrian cause to fight to free Henry.[44] It his supposed treason that makes its way into the *English Chronicle*, 'a carefully constructed piece of Yorkist propaganda or, more accurately, myth making'.[45] Lord Neville himself did not leave Raby, and wrote from there on 28 December 1460 to the corporation of Hull asking them to accept him as Exeter's deputy admiral in the town, asking them to 'certifie to me of what that I can doo to your hertes ease & wele of your towne & the cominaltie of the same'.[46] Securing the port of Kingston-upon-Hull was crucial to Lancastrian ambitions. Its mercantile community, alongside those of York and Beverley, provided the Lancastrians with the only realistic prospect of keeping any sort of army in the field in the middle of winter if the northern lords were to take the war to York. The loyalty of the port was uncertain: a chain was put across the haven, barring its entrance but also preventing wheat and other foodstuff from being exported. On 12 November, when the towns Yorkist-supporting mayor was attending Parliament, the magistrates agreed that no victuals should leave the town, but if this was due to pressure by the Lancastrian lords is unclear.[47]

It is absolutely incredible that York trusted Neville – as he did Fitzhugh and Greystoke – to raise men on his behalf: clearly York believed the reconciliation between Neville and Salisbury was real. It also speaks of York's hubris: was he trying to let 'bygones be bygones' and rule from the centre? He had been capable of this a few years earlier, but his own actions had changed everything. Rather than antipathy to him, many nobles now simply wanted him dead: did he not realise this? It is perhaps understandable that York had no option but to trust men who had historically been opponents of him and his Neville allies. In trying to govern from the centre, the duke had to win 'hearts and minds', which would ultimately cost him his life. His son Edward's own magnanimity to the earl of Northumberland resulted in more rebellions after Towton. The future Richard III learnt from this: be ruthless, exterminate opponents, and leave no heirs to challenge your position. Trying to 'build bridges' and win 'hearts and minds' however laudable, was never going to win over the most truculent Lancastrians, who exploited the situation to their own ends. The three Yorkist kings, like their Tudor successors, never wholly ruled an acquiescing nation. Henry VII faced rebellion for much of his reign, and his son faced open civil war in 1539 to 1541, based in part on grudges and memories of the events the tumultuous 1460s.

Returning to Neville and why he chose to remain in the North, the duke of Exeter, still nominally admiral of England in December 1460, had appointed Neville as his deputy in Yorkshire following Egremont's death. The magistrates and urges of the strategically and economically important port of Kingston-upon-Hull had spent much of the 1450s fiercely resisting Lord Egremont's claim to exercise that office.[48] Neville remained in the north as gaining admittance to Hull was more important than facing York. Despite the prominence given to Neville by some writers, he was not at the coming clash. Neville had more pressing local demands to contend with that a recalcitrant York. Nor was James Butler, earl of Wiltshire. In October he was in Utrecht. From Utrecht, Wiltshire was busy raising men in Ireland for the Lancastrian cause and travelled to Wales at the end of the year to help Jasper Tudor, earl of Pembroke. Wiltshire was back in Burgundy in the first weeks of 1461. He carried with him £1,900 in silver, which he offered to Philippe le Bon, duke of Burgundy for mercenaries. Castigated by Dan Jones as 'perhaps the greatest coward of his generation' he was with all probability in Zeeland when Mortimer's Cross was fought, despite assertion by Jones 'he ran away'. Where did Wiltshire get such a huge sum from and in ready cash? Wiltshire had already lost 2,000 marks and 300 sarples of wool in Calais which Warwick had – and let's be blunt – stolen to fund his invasion, which Wiltshire claimed was valued at £24,000. As with Neville, he took no part in the events of December 1460.[49]

What happened next was designed and instigated by John, Lord Clifford, Sir Ralph Percy (1425–64) and his older brother Henry the earl of Northumberland.

## York's reply

Despite their coup, the new regime's hold beyond the south-east and Home Counties was slipping, thanks to the efforts of the Courtenay earls of Devon once more.[50] Wales and vast tracts of Yorkshire and Northumberland were beyond the control of London. Yet we accept, recalcitrance is not war: no military action was launched between June and December. The Act of Accord was a cause for war not a declaration of war. York, with allies on the world stage, and knowing full well that he faced local mobs just as he had done half a decade earlier, believed all he had to do was to 'knock a few heads together': he was confident of repeating his earlier success. He probably did not feel he needed a huge army; one had not been necessary before, and York gambled that he did not need one again. It was winter after all, not the season for fighting battles, more so as he had a campaign to organise in France in the near future. All that was needed was to arrest the ringleaders and leave the rest to his lawyers and deputies.

Rightly or wrongly, York gambled everything and decided to lead an army north to defeat the recalcitrant northern earls. If he won, God had ordained him to be king, if he lost, he would be killed and God had ordained it for his treason. York must have been acutely aware that if he lost, he would lose everything. But what choice did he have? As the Lancastrian threat grew, York approached the Londoners for loans, but only half of the requested amount of a thousand marks was received as Duke Richard refused to guarantee repayment of previous loans made to the Lancastrian earl of Wiltshire.[51] It is unlikely large sums of money were available to fund his armed retinue.[52]

In the coming game of chance, York had to consecutively 'roll 6s' which was exceptionally unlikely: his namesake son would be in the same predicament in 1483 against Buckingham and again in 1485 against Henry Tudor supported by disillusioned Yorkists. The career and personality of father and son are incredibly striking in their similarity and ultimate fate. Unlike 1455 or 1459, where York was not protected by the law of treason, he had been declared heir to the throne, to be a sacred person and protected by the law of treason. Resistance to him was treason. If York bargained this would protect him, as it had done Henry at Dartford and Ludford, he was wrong.

The duke had spent much of November raising money and recruiting troops. Both the Scots and the queen posed a threat. Certainly, with the city of York and much of the North opposed to the new regime, having a strong military presence in the North over the winter of 1460 made sound strategic thinking. It would allow a consolidation of power. Edward was sent to Shrewsbury to contain the Tudor threat. Salisbury was commissioned to confront the Scots and the duke himself would lead an army north to confront the queen.[53]

Parliament was prorogued on 29 November. York met, we assume, several times with Warwick, Salisbury and others. Through letters patent the king commissioned York on 8 December:

In the counties of Northampton, Leicester, Warwick, Lincoln, Nottingham, Derby, York and Lincoln and in the towns of Kyngston upon Hull, Nottingham and Newcastle Upon Tyne, touching on treasons, insurrections, rebellions.[54]

York's immediate retinue was to include:

> Ralph Earl of Westmoreland, William Viscount Beaumont, Henry Grey, Sir Leo de Wellys, Sir Richard Wellys, Sir Henry Fitzhugh, Sir Ralph Greystoke, Sir John Neville, Sir John Prysot, Sir Peter Ardern, William Yelverton, John Markham, Richard Byngham, Niocholas Ayssheton, Robert Danvers, Robert Danby, Walter Moyle, John Nedeham, Sir Thomas Harrington, Sir William Eure, Sir James Strangeways, Sir William Gascoigne, Sir William Rither.

The list was largely theoretical, and many of course were Lancastrian devotees and never served with York. His retinue was composed of knights at the head of retinues, and men of the legal profession. As Hicks makes clear, lawyers were particularly useful to a lord, and York clearly recruited among them heavily; they had a duty to attend his council meetings as well as represent him in court.[55] York would have need of lawyers and clerks if he was to issue acts of attainder or other legal forfeits to ensure the king's peace and enforce the king's laws. Magnanimity may have been the 'name of the game' played, but York was naïve to trust most of these men, as we shall see.

## A date with destiny

If York was to have any semblance of authority, he had to secure the North, and *inter alia* control Queen Margaret. His revolution stated that he was to provide law and order: if we are to judge from the chaos engulfing the North, his actions had precipitated a climatic breakdown in governance.

Perhaps knowing full well that his power base rested with the Nevilles, York, through the king, made sure that Salisbury was appointed on 10 December 'to aid the duke and to arrest and commit to prison all persons guilty of unlawful gatherings' and to recruit men with the assistance of the sheriffs of Nottingham, Derby, Lincoln, Cumberland, Northumberland, York, Cambridge and Huntingdon.[56]

Parliament wrote York's commission into law:

> The king, understanding and hearing that great rebellions, murders, riots, unlawful and felonious looting of his subjects, heinous extortion and oppression are daily practised, attempted and committed in various regions of his realm of England and Wales, contrary to the public good and common weal; so that it is probable that not only the overthrow of the good and peaceful governance of the said realm, but also the outrageous and immeasurable disturbance and violation of its peace and tranquillity will result and ensue; in consequence of which his enemies and adversaries of Scotland and France may be encouraged, to our danger

and peril, to advance and hasten to put into practice the unyielding and insatiable malice which they have schemed and plotted against his said realm and its subjects, who have recently borne and suffered, and daily bear and suffer, the too great, too lamentable and too grievous assaults and injuries of the said enemies; has, by the advice of the lords spiritual and temporal, and the commons assembled in this present Parliament, and by its authority, ordained and decreed that his dearest cousin Richard, true and rightful heir of the realms of England and France, and of the lordship and land of Ireland, the duke of York, shall have and take upon himself the charge and task of riding into the regions of the said realm of England and Wales where the said rebellions, murders, riots, looting, extortion and oppression are practised, committed and attempted, to repress, subdue and pacify them, and also to resist his said enemies of France and Scotland within his said realm or which the support of the said subjects is necessarily required; and therefore grants, ordains and decrees, by the said advice and authority, that every sheriff, with the power and might of his shrievalty, and every mayor, bailiff, officer, official and subject of his said realm of England and of Wales, shall support his said cousin in the said purpose, as the case requires, and for the same purpose shall be ready at the command of his said cousin, to obey him and perform his command as they would obey the king's command, according to due legal process in England, and in Wales according to the customs there.[57]

No doubt aware of how vulnerable his position really was, York had inserted directly into law a clause protecting him from attack. The king:

... grants and decrees, by the said advice and authority, that any rebellion, insurrection, disobedience or offence done to or against his said cousin, in executing the said charge under the king's authority or doing anything associated with it, by any person or persons of whatever estate or condition he or they may be, shall be taken, deemed, considered, held and accepted, as if it had been done to or against the king's person and command. And furthermore, he ordains, grants and decrees, by the said advice and authority, that his said cousin, whenever he takes it upon himself to ride against any of the said rebellions or riots, shall have such adequate, suitable and acceptable reward for his costs and expenses, as shall be thought reasonable by the king and his council, and shall have sure and adequate payment of it. And the king ordains, by the said advice and authority, that all such persons thus repressed, subdued and pacified, shall afterwards be dealt with according to the said laws and customs.[58]

The obvious issue was putting theory into practice in a real-world scenario, as Matthew Lewis pithily comments.[59] On 8 December, the officers of the exchequer gave from the king £1,000 and a further sum of £118 13s 4d 'for artillery, gun powder and other habillements of war'. The same document gave to the earl of March 650 marks.[60] After receiving his commission, York and his son Edmund, fully confident they were acting in the name of the king against traitors, probably left London on 11 December, taking with them only a small force drawn from Londoners and the Weald of Kent. His ally Richard Neville, earl of Salisbury rode through London with 100 men from Cheapside.[61] Warwick remained in London and the earl of March was dispatched to Wales to confront Jasper Tudor. The Yorkists were confident of success, borne out by a letter to the duke of Milan dated 10 December: 'I have strong hopes if God gives victory to our affairs, as seems likely, and the heavens also render aid . . . Do not fear, my lord, because God and Justice are for us.'[62] The earl of Warwick remained in London to guard the capital, but evidently the Yorkists feared attack by the French as on 17 December Warwick was appointed to take a fleet to sea.[63]

### The duke's retinue

York's immediate entourage included his nephew Edward Bourchier (1442–60) – York's sister Isabel was Edward's mother – and his older brother Humphrey Bourchier, Lord Cromwell (1436–71) (not Ralph de Cromwell, 3rd Baron Cromwell [1393–1456] who we mentioned earlier), Salisbury's younger son Sir Thomas Neville and his son in law William Bonville, Lord Harrington and Bonville's father, also called William Bonville. Expecting to confront the invading Scots he carried with him an artillery train.[64] York's retinue was drawn from Kent and London. We are told by chroniclers that a man called Lovelace led the Kentish contingent who had aided Warwick's invasion earlier in the year.[65] Richard Lovelace (c.1393–1466) appears to have been a participant of Cade's Rebellion in 1450, in which members of the family, possibly brothers, were involved. As a youth he was apprenticed to William Foucher. He was later admitted as a freeman of the Mercers Company, London in 1415.[66] Either through business, or marriage he acquired considerable fortune. In his will he bequeathed various manors to son John and a 'manor called Heuer' to daughter Katherine, perhaps as a dower for her marriage to William Founteyne. His son, Sir Richard Lovelace (c.1440–1501), became marshal of Calais under Henry VII and was knighted after the Battle of Blackheath.[67] We cannot be certain which Richard Lovelace was present at Wakefield or the Second Battle of St Albans.[68] However, as Richard senior was 67 years old in 1460, we suspect it was his son, aged approximately 20. According to both the *Registrum Monasterii Sancti Albani* and the *Annales Rerum Anglicarum*, Lovelace was captured at Wakefield, but released on the understanding he would betray the Yorkists, which he did at the Second Battle of

St Albans resulting in a Lancastrian victory. Waurin repeats the same story. The latter two sources may simply be repeating the Abbot of St Albans, which seems to be the earliest account: but he was physically present during the battle. It is through the Mercers Company that Lovelace no doubt came into the sphere of John Harrow.[69]

Captain John Harrow was a prominent London mercer. As he was serving his apprenticeship by 1422–3, he would have been born about 1406. He owned land in Kent – which may link him to Lovelace – in Tenterden, Cranebroke and Halden.[70] He was Warden of the Mercers' Company in 1443 and 1449. At times, he fell afoul of the wardens; he was fined 'for words spoken in court' and 'for lying and uncourteous language'. Although a common councilman by 1444, he never attained the rank of alderman. He was three times Member of Parliament. in the city, and the chroniclers indicate that he was more markedly active in the Yorkist cause than most of his contemporaries in London.[71] Harrow had besieged the Tower of London earlier in 1460, and was clearly a wanted man.[72]

Bale gives York 300 men and Salisbury 100,[73] with an unknown number of guns.[74] We cannot state with any degree of confidence about the size and nature of this army. One of the best funded and equipped armies of the era was that sent to France in 1441 commanded by York. He had with him two earls, six knights banneret, 30 knights, 657 men-at-arms, and 2,100 archers. York's personal retinue for the Poitiers campaign mustered 107 knights and bannerettes, and 472 archers: 579 all told.[75] It is unreasonable to assume that the force he gathered in winter 1460 was much more, and was probably substantially less, perhaps half that number.[76] The sole indication of the size of the Yorkist army is hinted at by the quantities of weapons stolen by the Lancastrians in the aftermath of the Battle of Wakefield: 24 guns, 200 lances, 600 bows and 500 sheaves of arrows.[77] This does not speak of a vast army.

We do not know York's line of march to Sandal, but he seems to have travelled to the Midlands.[78] The shortage of horse feed, food for the soldiers and billets may have forced the Yorkists to split their forces, marching north via Watling Street and Nottingham, as well as taking the Great North Road through Stamford. John Benet's chronicle is alone in telling us that York stopped at Nottingham before heading to Yorkshire, suggesting the duke himself may have taken the former route, Salisbury the other. We do know York was joined by men from Nottinghamshire, and also Shrewsbury which had sent forty men to join the duke in the North.[79] As several contemporary writers observed, the weather had been terrible throughout 1460, and heavy rain had flooded the countryside, destroyed crops and turned the roads into quagmires.[80]

Perhaps in preparation for crossing the River Ryton or to visit the town's fair held annually on 17 December to obtain victuals, a party of York's army were surprised and routed by Somerset's men. Our sole source of this is Pseudo-William of Worcester writing his *Annales rerum Anglicarum*.[81] In most modern accounts, we are told that it was York's vanguard which was destroyed: but our sole source for the incident describes them as *praeeuntes* (literally 'goers before'), while the part of the manuscript that enumerates what occurred is damaged. 'Scouts' is a better understanding than vanguard.

Historian Anthony Goodman states that the loss of the vanguard contributed directly to the defeat at Wakefield, as it robbed the duke of his 'eyes and ears' for reconnaissance, to protect foraging parties, and was a result of complacency.[82] Assuming this event happened, it did not materially affect the Yorkist march north.[83] If York's men were attacked it was, as Parliament had made clear, an act of treason which as David Grummitt comments 'can only have stiffened the duke's resolve'.

If the clash took place – and that is a big if as we have just one source about the battle, and a not very reliable one at that – the probable explanation for York heading to Worksop is that Yorkist forces had come to raid the market which was held every Wednesday since 1275. This dates the event to 16/17 December. Coming into the town the day before the market would have provided the Yorkists with a good opportunity for obtaining provisions from farmers and labourers as they were coming into town. How many were killed or wounded is not known, and we are not certain the event took place: it seems a 'convenient' explanation for the defeat of the duke at Wakefield weeks later.[84] Again, if a Lancastrian force attacked York at Worksop, as we noted above, the Act of Accord was broken, thus the crown was forfeit: it may simply be a device by Pseudo-Worcester and also Warwick in his 'Apology' to present the Lancastrians, and Somerset in particular, as untrustworthy, and un-able to act within the law. All rather too convenient, especially as the events at Worksop cannot be corroborated.

Indeed, such are the vagaries of history that we cannot place York securely between London and Wakefield. It is possible the duke arrived at Conisbrough in December, as the Constable[85] of the castle records hay being taken from a barn 'for use of the lord's horses and his office holders there'.[86] Conisbrough would be a logical stopping point on the duke's journey north, especially as it was held by his retainer Edmund Fitzwilliam. Conisbrough was well-stocked with artillery taken from the Lancastrian earl of Shrewsbury's castle at Sheffield after the Battle of Northampton the previous July.[87] The guns captured at Wakefield may be guns from Conisbrough as much as those dragged from Kent.

# Chapter 22

# WAKEFIELD

When York left London, winter had already arrived: the temperature was probably below zero and remained so into the new year. On St Martins Day 1460 (11 November) the vast mill ponds at Newmiller Dam and Wakefield bridge had frozen.[1] It was also very wet: one source tells us rain in November had inundated large parts of East Anglia and Kent. No doubt this was true of Yorkshire. Abbot Whethamstede thought that due to the torrential rain that had fallen all summer and into early autumn, God had 'decided to send a new flood upon the earth'.[2] Wet and cold weather would have delayed the duke's march from London, and would also have reduced the opportunity to obtain forage for horses and food to feed the army with.

York is said have arrived in Wakefield 'shortly before Christmas'.[3] The date has traditionally been given as Sunday, 21 December.[4] The real date was Christmas Day, as we shall see. Abbot Whethamstede states that when the Yorkists arrived they erected their tents not far from the town of Wakefield.[5] Presumably this was in the Burghmantofts, the enclosed fields south of the town, but off the flooded Ings and within the town's bank and ditch. Wakefield was the most populous town in the West Riding, was a centre for cloth finishing and had both a market and faire. It was wealthy from the finishing and dyeing of cloth, as the magnificent tower and spire at the parish church completed by 1420 attest to. The town was the administrative centre of the vast Manor of Wakefield. The *caput* was at Sandal, but since the twelfth century the town and its Borough and Soke had been administered from the Manor House which stood by the parish church, referred to in 1308 as the Earl's Hall. This was a large high-status residence, fit for an earl, in this case of Warenne. Under Henry VIII, this building became the *caput* in 1539 when Sandal was decommissioned: the castle was a court house and office space for the peripatetic Manorial court, as well

213

as the steward of the Manor. It had little or no military or residential function. The Moot Hall and Manor House, where York spent his last days, were swept away during slum clearances in the 1930s.

Wakefield was – and is – situated on a prominent hill in the Calder Valley, protected by rivers on three sides (Chald, Ings and Skitterick) which were crossed by narrow bridges. The town itself, despite lacking walls, was defended by a bank, ditch, fence and hedge which formed the terminus to the narrow burgage plots which radiated off the four principal streets. Access to the town was through four gatehouses, known as Bars. Ostensibly to collect tolls for those attending the weekly market and the two annual fairs, the gates were closed at night and guarded by watchmen. The Westgate Bar was the largest and grandest of these: of two or three floors, with a basement, built from stone. A second was on Kirkgate, and a third on Northgate. North of the town stretched the large Outwood and the outfields of the town, relatively flat farming country. Access from the 'other side' of town was altogether different.

Approach from the south was across the narrow chantry bridge which was very easily defended, and formed a constriction point for any attacking force. Wakefield bridge with its chantry was very easily defended with a barricade and virtually cut Wakefield off Sandal castle to the south. The east side of Kirkgate, which led from the bridge to the parish church, was bounded for most of its length by the river Skitterick, and where the York Road crossed it was via a little drawbridge. The river bounded the back of the burgage plots, making assault from this side almost impossible.

South of the town was the earl's Ings, and then enclosed fields by a stock-proof fence.[6] To the north, south and west were the infields of the demesne, defended by ditches and stock-proof hedges since the 1260s.[7] Many fields had already been enclosed by this date.[8] Almost certainly there was no dense woodland or forest of any kind near the castle or Wakefield for that matter. Despite archive evidence to the contrary, we read in a number of modern works that discuss the battle about 'woods as black as crows' wings' around the castle at Sandal, from which the Lancastrians ambushed York. The writers fail to inform the reader that this is fiction. Indeed, the battle of Wakefield is one of the most written-about encounters of the Wars of the Roses and the least researched.[9] The park enclosing the castle to the north and west had sparse planting: eighty-nine trees in 40 acres is not dense woodland.[10] The idea that there were 'dense woods black as crows', out of which the Lancastrians ambushed York, is wrong.[11]

Following the route at Ludford and York's attainder, since 14 October 1459, the manor, graveship and borough (*vill*) of Wakefield had been under the control of Lancastrians. Sir Richard Welles, Lord Wiloughby, whose father Lionel owned land in the Manor of Wakefield in the Graveship of Stanley was placed as overseer.[12]

At the Great Court on 16 November 1459, under the stewardship of Welles, elected as bailiff for Wakefield vill, we note 'Thomas Turton stat in officio prepositi ibidem ut in anno precedente qui receptus est et iuratus'. The bailiff of the manor was William Turton. Appointed to be bailiff in Thornes was John Gargrave of Snapethorpe, son of York's tutor William Gargrave. Gargrave's son in law, John Bunny of Bunny Hall, was bailiff of Alverthorpe.[13] Since 1307 according to the court rolls, John de Gargrave had occupied a house that stood directly alongside the Earl's Hall in Kirkgate which he enlarged in 1311, the land costing 12d. He was forester and park keeper of Wakefield and Outwood. This John's four times great-grandson, Sir John Gargrave, was Master of the Ordnance under Henry V and a Governor in France, whose son Thomas was likewise Master of the Ordnance and Marshal of the English army of Henry VI in France and was killed during the Siege of Orléans along with the Earl of Salisbury in 1428. The remaining son, William, was the aforementioned tutor to Richard, duke of York.[14] John Bunny, son of William Bunny grave of Wakefield in 1411, was himself grave in 1474.[15] The Bunny family, related by marriage to the Haselden and Gargrave families, came to national prominence under Elizabeth I. Following York's attainder, in December John Vincent was named as receiver: he had held the post previously under York and had – we assume – recanted of his loyalty. William Stoke, king's servant and sergeant of the porter within the gate, replaced Vincent on 1 February 1460.[16] Stoke never took the job, as he died on 3 February, and in his place Joly Gilys, described as king's servant, was named receiver of the Manor of Wakefield.[17] On 4 April 1460 Johnn Vincent re-appointed as receiver. He had been granted the position on 10 December 1459, but lost it to Stoke. Vincent was granted the fee farm of Kirkstall, pasture in Cottingham and rents from Allerton and Sherwood in Nottinghamshire.[18]

Two of the Lancastrian administrators were Gawain Lamplewe and Robert Tomlynson. The latter was indicted earlier in the year for the murder of a King's Messenger and attacking the Manor of the Hansard family.[19] A warrant for his arrest was issued.[20] Robert Thomson (*sic*, Tomlynson), clerk of Healhaugh, clerk of Wressle and servant of Henry Percy, earl of Northumberland, had been charged as part of the 1453 Percy-Neville feud.[21] Robert Tomlynson, esquire, 'for good service against the rebellion' was made master and surveyor of the king's mines in the New Forest, Yorkshire on 13 January 1460.[22] Now king's sergeant, he was further rewarded with a grant for life of the magistracy of lead mines in the New Forest, formerly held by the earl of Salisbury, on 29 March.[23] He was also charged with the murder of Richard Neville, earl of Salisbury, along with Lamplewe.[24] Clearly, Tomlynson was a violent, and supremely loyal, member of Northumberland's retinue.

The constableship of Sandal, as well the offices of Steward and Forester of Wakefield and Sowerby passed to John Talbot, the earl of Shrewsbury, replacing Sir John Saville, the Yorkist incumbent.[25] John Talbot was granted 100 marks a year from the Manor of Wakefield on 19 December 1459.[26] The New Park was occupied by Shrewsbury up to July 1460. It had been in his possession since summer 1459, the tenure returning to York on his death at the Battle of Northampton.[27] Talbot does not seem to have acted as steward of the Manor according to the court rolls or occupied Sandal. He is not so named at the Great Court (Magna Curia) held there on 2 May 38 Henry VI (1460).[28] The town was Lancastrian in feeling, as the parish priest suffered attainder probably for preaching against the Yorkists and we note John Amyas, gentleman of Wakefield, refused to take the oath of allegiance to Edward IV. Another amongst the dukes' tenants who did not approve of the turn of events was Richard Lyster, who suffered attainder.[29]

For whatever reason – and one we shall never know – the duke chose not to use Sandal as his base, but the town of Wakefield. With the town held – we assume physically – by Lancastrians, it seems unlikely that York simply 'walked' into the town.[30] The town was too valuable to be handed over without a fight. Whatever fighting occurred, if any, we know the duke was victorious. It is perfectly possible that this 'battle' south of the town has been conflated with events that took place later, and is that recorded by Leland.

Thirlwall, Lamplewe and Tomlynson knew that if they were captured, they would be summarily executed: they also knew that capturing or killing the duke was essential. Closing the town gates against the duke perhaps precipitated a skirmish between Chantry Bridge and the gates. That the Yorkists won this encounter we are sure and York was in the town on Christmas Day 1460 and ejected the Lancastrians, assuming they had not 'scarpered'. York appointed loyalists to manorial offices.[31] That the duke of York was not accompanied by a large and well-equipped retinue or large household comes from the manor records. The bailiff of Alverthorpe, William Burton, provided an ox valued at 10s for the 'use of the household of the lord lately Duke at Wakefield in the month of December and in January in the aforesaid period by the oath of various tenants at this audit'.[32] York's household had also been provided with a single ox in 1459. Clearly the numbers present in the duke's retinue in winter 1460 and summer 1459 was broadly similar, and indicates the lack of a strong armed retinue with the duke.

There is unquestionable proof York was in Wakefield with his household. Fresh fish was supplied from the 'fishery of the eastern section of the Calder, that is to say from Wakefield milldam to Yar Well Gate in Stanley . . . reserved for the lord, lately for the Lord's men coming there' again to the household in Wakefield.[33] We also find in the Manor Accounts of 29 September 1460 to 29 September 1461 that the earl of Northumberland paid 26s 8d, and his bailiff, Gawain Lamplewe paid 30s to the Lord's account for costs incurred in the town. Quite what these sums represent we can only guess at: damages and losses of goods, one assumes. York's newly appointed officers, John Clapham and Henry Burwell, under-bailiff of the town of Wakefield, reimbursed the manor 40s 1d for hay, 16s 8d for 6 quarters of beans, and £10 2s 8d for 5 quarters of oats: this is all horse feed.[34] Were these the costs for sustaining the Yorkist army?[35] The very small expenses specifically for the duke's household does not speak of a large and magnificent armed retinue.[36] Mythos implies York lost the ensuing battle because his men were out foraging.[37] If the Yorkists requisitioned food and issued IOUs then the Receiver of the Manor would have noted this. If the Yorkists looted for supplies, the Manor records would also record this. The accounts are silent.[38] On the evidence available to us, therefore, York had with him a few hundred men, perhaps a lot less. Any suggestion of foraging parties depleting his forces seems, therefore, a deliberate obscuring of the facts. However, their maybe some truth in this. The small size of York's retinue may have led the earliest writers to believe it was nothing more than a foraging party.

Chapter 23

# THE BATTLE THAT NEVER WAS

The Lancastrian – or at least Percy – retinue having been ejected from Wakefield, news travelled no doubt to Henry Percy himself who was perhaps by now behind the walls of Pontefract Castle. That the news was transmitted by runners and messengers is recorded in the town book for Beverley which records in late November 'paid to one labourer walking to Leconfield to hear the rumours. 4d'.[1] This was perhaps news of York heading north, or other local disturbances. York, it seems, had planned to march to York directly along the Great North Road, but it would have taken him past Pontefract Castle, held by Northumberland's men. York had to detour to Wakefield to cross the Calder and Aire rivers. Before Northumberland had left Beverley he had met with Ralph, 2nd earl of Westmoreland, and had conversations with John, Lord Neville, via letter, who as we noted earlier, remained steadfastly at Raby. Westmoreland, Pollard implies, headed back to county Durham. Westmoreland seems, however, to have left armed men in York to form part of Percy's retinue: Richard and Thomas Tunstall of Thurland in the county of Lancaster, Henry and Robert Bellingham of Burneside in the county of Westmorland, Roger Wharton of Brough in Cumbria, and Richard Kirkby of Kirkby Ireleth. As Beverley is 40 miles from Pontefract, and with short winter days, the journey would have taken perhaps three days.[2] At Pontefract, Percy was joined men who had been recruited in the York area by other lords who were loyal to the queen. These men included Thomas Barton, of Helmsley, and his lord, Thomas Roos. As Percy's column marched via Market Weighton across the Wolds, his forces were swelled by men from Selby which included John Caterall late of Brayton, William Fyppes of South Duffield, as well as Anthony Nuthill from Hedon near Hull. One of the

Beverley contingent was Henry Cliff from Lockington. It is possible Percy's retinue included Thomas, James and George Dalton, all of Lilburn in the county of Northumberland, gentlemen.

Northumberland was also joined by a number of prominent Lancastrians from further afield who now lent their weight in opposition to York: from the South-West, servants of Exeter and Devon such as Sir Baldwin Fulford, Alexander Hody, Thomas Philip Dartington, Nicholas Latimer and James Luttrell. Despite not being present physically himself, some of the retinue of Somerset probably were, which included Sir Thomas Fynderne.[3] Others who joined the earl at Pontefract included Gervais Clifton and men from London. Clifton, the Treasurer of Calais, had been sheriff of Kent since November 1458 and remained executing commissions in the county until the Yorkist lords landed at Sandwich in June 1460. By this time, he was treasurer of the king's household, a position he held until was dismissed by York in September. In his retinue were – perhaps – John Nayler, Giles St Lo, William Joseph and no doubt others all described as being of Calais or its immediate environs.[4] Alongside Northumberland's retainers Sir John Heron of Ford, Henry Bellingham and Sir Richard Tunstall were and men associated with the royal household such as Sir Edmund Mountfort, Robert Whittingham and William Grimsby.[5]

Also en route to Pontefract were Lord Clifford and his brother. For the queen and her supporters, it was their moral duty to sweep away York and to restore her son to the line of inheritance.[6] The assembled Lancastrian army probably mustered no more than 2,000, and perhaps less.

## The battle?

After the celebration of the feast of St Thomas Beckett on 29 December 1460, what happened next is shrouded in mystery.[7] The events of the Battle of Wakefield are confused when we look at contemporary writings, and because of this, have become elaborately embroidered in myth.[8] Previous accounts of the battle are described from chronicles, largely written by persons unknown and at times and places unknown, or letters from men who were not present. In both cases what is presented is gossip, rumour, hearsay and propaganda. We rely for our narrative on legal depositions as well as the records of the Manor of Wakefield written down soon after the events took place. We also noted that drawing a conclusion on historical matter such as the Battle of Wakefield is perhaps pointless. In merely attempting to impose order on something that is inherently and irremediably chaotic – we do not have all the facts at our disposal.

First and foremost, we need to acknowledge there is no such thing as a battlefield – the word assumes a special area was kept apart purposefully for fighting, which is a nonsense: there is a field in which a battle takes place. For Wakefield, we can be certain that no such battlefield exists where the Victorian memorial cross states the conflict took place.[9] Why the duke lodged in Wakefield is lost to history. Sandal offered far greater security: for whatever reason, the duke chose to lodge himself in the Earls' Hall in Wakefield. Perhaps he left a garrison at Sandal as Davies' *English Chronicle* suggests. York could easily have outpaced Salisbury who, it seems, had the artillery and infantry with him. He could have gone ahead, and lodged in Wakefield with his household, leaving Sandal available for Salisbury.[10] But we don't know this. We know nothing about where Salisbury actually was between Cheapside and his death. That Salisbury had few men with him, comes from the fact that in the 1640s the castle could accommodate barely 150 men, slightly more than the chronicles say he had with him.[11] This is speculation of course: all we know is York and his household were in Wakefield from Christmas Day to 29 December. If the army was encamped in the fields close to the town, these would have been the Burghmantofts on the southern side of the town. Comprising 6 acres of meadow, bounded by the town bank and ditch, and importantly above the flooded Ings through which the River Chald passes.

What happened next is obscured by mythos mixed with fiction. Indeed, the accounts of nineteenth-century historians like Richard Brooke, Alex Leadman and Clements Markham, who relied heavily on a single text by Chronicler Hall, which appeared 100 years after the battle based on the memories of a man who did not exist, have to be considered as pure fiction.[12] No contemporary described the composition of the opposing armies, how command was apportioned between the lords present, where the battle was, or the course of the battle itself in any meaningful way.

The 'official line' propagated by Edward IV was of his father being ambushed and killed:

> Richard late Duke of Yorke hadde more right and more title vnto the Crowne of England than the saide Harry, he innocent goyng towarde Yorke at Wakefeld sette vpon hym oute of array and kelled hym and his sonne the Erle of Routeland, the Erle of Salusbury and Lord Harington with othir diuers gentills and comoners.[13]

Not a battle, more an unfortunate chain of events led to the duke's death: opportunism by the Lancastrians. What seems to have happened, is that when York left London his plan was to establish himself in York over the winter, and had no plans to remain in Wakefield longer than necessary. Salisbury also came north, with his son, and the victorious soldiers led by Harrow who had taken the Tower of London. That his journey was slowed by mud and ice is a given.

Some time on the morning of 29 December, York, his household, servants, retainers and baggage train left Wakefield. En route to York, by planning or happenstance they blundered into the men of Lord Clifford. One participant in the ensuing skirmish believed it to be a deliberate in a written statement of March 1462.[14] In a second deposition, they add more detail:

> on the 29 December in the 39th year of the reign of King Henry VI . . . with force and arms, that it to say, with swords, staves, bows, arrows, spears and langue de boeufs,[15] having gathered to him many malefactors and disturbers of the said late king's peace . . . equipped in manner of war, that is to say, with jacks, sallets, corslets, brigandines and doublets of defence, who lay in wait to kill and murder.[16]

Whatever happened, it was unexpected. York with his retinue, servants and baggage on the march was exceptionally vulnerable, assuming he had not ridden forward with a handful of retainers. That York had left Wakefield, without a well-armed retinue was foolhardy and speaks of his belief that no one would dare attack him, as he was protected by the Law of Treason. In his defence, he had expected to receive reinforcements: but Neville, Greystoke and others were playing a double game. York realised he had no option but to get to York as quickly as possible to find safety behind the City's walls Salisbury was perhaps with a rearguard – assuming he was in Wakefield. We know nothing about his movements or Rutland's, till both are killed in Pontefract on 31 December. Arrogant, entitled and undeniably a narcissist, York's supreme act of hubris led to his downfall. Our writer, Thomas Colt, was writing within weeks of the battle, so he can be considered fairly reliable, given he was physically present at the battle. In the fighting, Richard Anson was killed.[17] Sir Thomas Harrington (1403–60) was mortally wounded and died the following day.[18] His son John was killed, executed along with other prisoners the same day it seems.[19] Thomas's death, alongside that of his immediate heir, led directly to his children's feud with Lord Stanley during the early years of the next reign.[20]

In whatever fighting that took place, York and senior Yorkists were captured, one of whom was Sir Thomas Ferrers (c.1425–98), who was later ransomed for 300 marks.[21] For whatever reason, York was not killed at this point. The prisoners were then taken back to Wakefield as records of the Manor of Wakefield attest to:

> And to the same accountant for Oliver Hancok' 14 s. for the cost of 12 ells of woollen cloth bought by him from Robert Kente by order of John Vyncent' late receiver there for bandages for various people being with the lord late duke of York at Wakefield for the months of December and January in the 39th year [December 1460–January 1461], to be paid before the next account, until when the warrant for having allowance for it is deferred.[22]

Were the bandages to bind wounds or to bind hands? Perhaps both, but it shows prisoners were taken and housed in Wakefield, no doubt at the Moot Hall. The battle is called the Battle of Wakefield because it ended in Wakefield. It was not fought in Wakefield or its immediate environs. That the bandages came from the township of Stanley, north east of Wakefield, on the York road, rather implies that the fighting took place away from the town. IF the fighting was in Wakefield, why bring bandages from two miles away when the merchants' shops would have had ample local supply? The battle is not in Wakefield nor was ever at Sandal. No documents from the Manor of Wakefield, or the earliest chronicles, ever mention York being at Sandal Castle. The battle demonstrably did not take place on the fields below the castle. The memorial cross to the duke at Manygates is arguably 'fake news'. That a sword and supposed human remains were found is not proof of the battle here. One sword an army does not make. We know the Lancastrians 'trashed' the area around the castle and could have easily been dropped by a Lancastrian during the ransacking of the castle and Wakefield area. We do not have the reported human bones to assess if they are actually human. There is no evidence whatsoever of any battle at the traditional battlefield of Manygates. This is a piece of fiction invented by Edward Hall, embroidered by Shakespeare and embedded into history by Victorian and later writers who believed Hall had access to lost sources. Using Hall's chronicle, and that of Wethamstede, the Crowland continuator etc, to write objective history is akin using the adventures of Biggles to write about the air war 14/18: yes, Sopwith Camels are real enough, but little else. Hall, like Wethamstede, was more interested in telling morality stories embroidered with fiction, than reporting objective history. This is why we must go back to primary documentation such as legal cases, wills, and local-level sources, such as those of the Manor of Wakefield which have been revelatory in unlocking the narrative of events as they happened rather than imagined. A number of modern historians have added substantially to the narrative of Hall, but do not make it clear that what they are writing is yet more fiction. Arguably, York was making for Methley to cross the river Aire at Woodlesford, and whatever fighting took place in the Graveship of Stanley which adjoins the Manor of Methley. The accounts of the Manor are silent on major damage to the town, which riles out any fighting in the town. The accounts tell us manor bake house needed repairs, but we cannot be certain of this was as a result of 'the battle'.[23] The majority landowner in the graveship of Stanley was Lionel, 6th baron Welles (1406–61). He certainly had a grudge against the Yorkists, having been taken prisoner at Blore Heath. His son had participated at Ludford. Lionel had been named as part of York's retinue, but clearly was 'playing his own game' and that he was a supporter of Margaret is evidenced by his death at Towton. Welles had married into the Lancastrian Waterton family of Methley, and lies buried in Methley church. Welles' son-in-law and neighbour, Sir Thomas Dymock, was killed in Lancastrian service in 1469, and his son Richard, was killed in 1470 leading the Welles rebellion. Dymock, as lord of the Manor of Newland – which directly abutted Methley and Welles manor of New Hall – now Hatfield Hall – in Stanley is suggested by one of his tenants being accused of the murder of the earl of Salisbury.[24] How much of the ambush was owed to Welles? It would be easy enough for a Lancastrian loyalist in Wakefield to inform Welles of York's itinerary, and also Henry Percy, and make plans accordingly to intercept him. We suppose that from Pontefract, Northumberland Clifford had to head north-west to Castleford, cross the river Aire on the stone bridge, and then sweep head to join the York Road at Woodlesford an Swillington. An idea of the wounds suffered by the injured from a second document written at the time, which tells us John Sclatter, who had fought at both Blore Heath and Ludford Bridge, suffered:

> great injuries and mutilations suffered in the wars of our noble father at Wakefield, where he lost his right hand and badly injured the other, so that he may neither clothe nor feed himself, as it evidently appears, to be taken yearly during his life from the issues and profits of our mill situated on our water of Lune in our parish of Lancaster, called Lune Mill, with the appurtenances belonging to our duchy of Lancaster.

Sclatter was awarded 4 marks compensation per annum for the remainder of his life.[25] These injuries are consistent with two scenarios, a man fighting for his life defensively, using his hands and lower arms to protect his head, having lost his weapon; or a man raising his hands to heaven in supplication to his captor to spare his life, and having his pleading hands mutilated by an axe or sword.

That none of the sources give us an accurate idea of what happened where or give any geographical locations beyond Wakefield, tells me that the writers did not actually know what occurred. Gregory for example merely states 'met with the Duke of Yorke at Wakefylde, and there they made a grete jorney apon the Lorde and Duke of Yorke'.[26] Bale adds nothing more substantive.[27] Benet merely says York was killed.[28] None of these accounts are at odds with York being ambushed. That this event occurred in mid- to late afternoon is given by some chronicles.[29]

The duke and his household, accompanied by his baggage, was incredibly vulnerable. York perhaps expected men like Fitzhugh and Greystoke to join him, along with Welles who had a commission to raise troops we remember. That the former 'sat on the sidelines' may be inferred by their reported treason. As we mentioned before, that he was heading to York to establish sessions, with little or no armed retinue and never expecting to be attacked, speaks of his naiveite and moreover of hubris. It is almost incredible that York felt himself immune: the treason laws said yes, attacking him was treason, but what penalty would the attackers face? With York dead, it was easy enough to reassert royalist cum Lancastrian authority, and no one would face any charges. That York trusted due legal process was madness. He had tested the limits of the law since 1450: he must have been only too aware of the level of hate and animosity towards him, and his own fate if things went wrong. And yet his own arrogance, and belief in the law overrode any common sense or logic – if any – he possessed. York had committed treason and gotten away with it several times, bolstering his own sense of invulnerability and importance. We get a hint of this in contemporary texts. The papal legate, Coppini, wrote on 9 January 1461 urging his correspondent, Lorenzo de Florencia, then with Queen Margaret, to counsel Somerset to 'not be arrogant because of the trifling victory they have won, owing to the rash advance of their opponents'. This is hinted at by the Crowland Chronicle continuator writing around 1471: York 'incautiously engaged the northern army at Wakefield . . . without waiting to bring up the whole of his forces'.[30] From there it was bound into Vergil's and Hall's account and featured prominently in the accounts of later historians.

The only 'soldiers' we can place in Wakefield are men loyal to John, Lord Clifford and possibly Henry Percy.[31] Certainly neither side numbered into the thousands. The 6,000 to 8,000 Yorkists and 20,000 Lancastrians present reported by chroniclers is fiction. Again, the discussion of the force with York as a foraging party, implies the small size of the retinue with York. Despite this, the fighting was deadly as David Grummitt comments:

What I think we have at Towton and Wakefield is a veritable bloodbath among the men-at-arms – the lords, knights and esquires and men-at-arms (not all were armigerous by any means) especially those linked to noble households, and even more so the Lancastrians – and perhaps also the archers attached to lords' households. That is why, for example, we see such high losses among the knights and esquires retained by the earl of Northumberland at Towton, but not among the tenants and others men from his estates . . . The longbow is deadly in the hands of a trained archer – such as the 300 men in the royal household from 1455 – but at much shorter ranges than we imagine and fired at a flat trajectory. The advances in armour technology by the 1450s mean battles are decided up close.

Statistically, perhaps most of York's retinue were killed: because these men were lower status, we lack their names, they left no wills and certainly they had no assets of sufficient value for court claims to be made. Perhaps 150 men were left dead.

The figures given in chronicles for the number of soldiers present, the numbers killed are hugely exaggerated as Dr Tim Sutherland makes clear, by at least a factor of ten.[32] We can also be certain that the men named at Wakefield like Devon, Exeter, Lord Neville, Somerset in chronicle accounts were almost certainly elsewhere when the battle took place. Possibly confirming the relatively small size of the Lancastrian army, the accounts of the Honour of Pontefract are totally silent on conflict, rebels, raids and disturbance. They are silent also on the need to feed an army: whatever force was present was contained and fed in the castle. These accounts therefore overwhelming evidence of the localised nature of the damage carried out in Wakefield described in Appendix 1 and 2.[33] The garrison who held the castle in the English Civil War was no more than 200: another strong indication that whatever body of troops was at Pontefract which attacked the duke of York at Wakefield, was not into the thousands of men.

The truth probably is that the duke of York's last battle was a total fiasco. It is not impossible Clifford was tipped off about York's movements. That the Lancastrians had sympathisers in Wakefield who could keep Northumberland informed is a reasonable conclusion. [34] Perhaps beginning with a hail of arrows from concealed archers to kill men and horses, as well as cause panic, a few hundred men-at-arms and others rushed the column, killing and wounding. Once the duke was captured, all was over. The humiliated duke was dragged back to Wakefield under guard as night fell on a freezing December evening. It is reasonable therefore that both sides needed to invent ''a battle' for propagandist reasons. York HAD to be killed in a climatic showdown to show the power of the queen, and because for the Yorkists any other conclusion would be a PR disaster. That the Yorkists quickly invented the myth of foraging parties and ill-discipline to explain the inexplicable is part of this almost immediate mythologisation of the Battle of Wakefield from a street brawl to a climatic show down. A newssheet was hastily written in January to March 1461 which is now housed in the Bibliothèque Nationales de France.[35] It alludes to the treason of Somerset, Trollop and others.[36] That this account was promulgated across Europe, and adapted by English writers, implies it was believed to have a degree of truth about it. It is this text that was the basis for English chronicle accounts, centred on John, Lord Neville.[37] That York was killed at Wakefield led to the natural assumption that this was where the battle was. The 'angry young men of St Albans' and Northampton wanted revenge, and revenge they took. The confusion about what happened at Wakefield and the duke of York's death presented in the contemporary sources only make sense if the official version of events has been manipulated from a very early stage following Edward's coronation, or sooner. Later information was obviously biased in favour of the new king Edward IV. At the same time, the lack of stability and the continuation of fighting meant that the Lancastrian position was not yet eliminated, which means chronicles from the 1460s will be biased and reflect current societal thoughts about the queen, Northumberland and others. From 1471, certainty of total victory again makes its way into the written record. We also admit that the newssheets which passed back and forth around Europe over the subsequent days and weeks referred to a battle at Wakefield, the details of which are so scarce in the vast majority of cases, it shows that no one really knew what happened. Edward would not have wanted his father to have been simply murdered at a re-run of Ludford. State manipulation of the events into a battle were, as we said, an exercise in propaganda: the treason of Neville and Trollop were an artifice generated by Warwick and Edward to explain the inexplainable, based on facts that Neville had betrayed York, as had Trollop. The victors write the history: when Edward came to write about Towton into the Rolls of Parliament, he deliberately ignored the defeat at Ferrybridge. The battle and losses never happened. History is what Edward said it was. Given that both Wavrin and the anonymous writer of *An English Chronicle* used narratives that prepare the ground for Edward IV's accession in March by highlighting the faithlessness of the Lancastrians by portraying the Battle of Towton as an act of vengeance for the deaths of York and Salisbury. The similarities between *An English Chronicle* and the continental accounts associated with the Monstrelet Continuator (BnF MS Fr 88) and Wavrin moreover suggest that both may have drawn upon similar newsletter sources to describe the events of 1459 to 1461. Both texts, for example, described the detailed negotiations that preceded the Battle of Northampton in July 1460, and both attributed the Yorkist victory there to the treachery of Edmund, Lord Grey de Ruthin.[38] Both writers relied on the same newssheet which been circulated on the continent, it is tempting to identify their common features with such documents associated with the earl of Warwick.[39] It is important to note that Wavrin knew Warwick and was a friend of owner of BnF MS Fr 88, Louis of Bruges, Lord of Gruuthuse, who was in England at the time of the duke's death. Indeed, de Gruuthuse hosted Edward IV and his brother, Richard, duke of Gloucester, in Bruges in January 1471. It was now that Wavrin met the two Yorkist princes in person. Perhaps it was this meeting that inspired Wavrin to use the manuscript in Gruuthuse's possession to compose an account of Wakefield which presented the duke of York in more favourable terms than the original 'official' Yorkist narrative developed in the early 1460s presented in the Chronicle *From Rollo to Edward IV*.[40] That Warwick was at sea when Wakefield was fought, perhaps even in Calais, meant he was able to distance himself from the debacle, and begin to craft his 'Apology' to blame anyone except himself. As David Grummitt comments:

> Whatever the origins of the stories, the differing accounts of Wakefield should remind us that the chronicle accounts of the Wars of the Roses were not simple retellings of recent events from hearsay or the testimony of eyewitnesses, but complex, politically charged narratives designed to alter perceptions of the past and guide their readers' actions in the future.

We must always challenge our sources: if by questioning Yorkist propaganda, we are castigated as Tudor supporters and biased, so be it. Objectivity was not at the fore front of the message that Edward, or Warwick for that matter with his 'Apology', where concerned by. It is undeniable however, that as we are still talking about the Battle of Wakefield 500 years later, as public relations exercises go, it has been quite successful. What ever happened, we cannot prove Northumberland or Clifford had any direct planning in the event planning. Plumpton and Rigby's presence may indicate this. It was a local grievance 'gone bad', the outcome being inevitable due to York's naiveté. Did he honestly think no one would try and kill him whilst protected by the law of treason? His hubris knew no bounds.

Chapter 24

# THE AFTERMATH

Whatever happened at Wakefield it was not a battle or anything coming close to one. The facts that we have imply what happened was an opportunist event. York blundered into the Lancastrian army. It was probably not planned, and we can be sure the queen probably knew nothing about it. As Richard Knowles FSA commented over 30 years ago, the fighting was 'in all probability . . . more of a brutal skirmish than a set piece battle'.

On Tuesday, 30 December, the Lancastrians started to kill their prisoners. Clifford was probably behind this. Why do I think this? A petition to the chancellor in about 1462 relating to a dispute between two Northamptonshire gentry records that, on 1 May 1461, Robert Tanfeld of Cransley sent his servants to abduct his rival, Robert Isham, from his house at nearby Pytchley. When Isham was brought to Cransley, Tanfeld issued an ominous threat: if Isham refused to release him from the surety of the peace he had been required to find, on Isham's complaint, he 'shulde be seruyd with a blocke and a axe aftir the lord Clifford lawez'. Clifford was dead in March 1461, but it is clear that he had a reputation being violent in a manner that went beyond the accepted limits of contemporary norms.[1]

The Lancastrians' treatment of the Yorkist lords captured at Wakefield witnessed the suspension of the accepted laws of war, which already had been brutally broken at St Albans in 1455. Executed in the market place of Wakefield where the town's gallows and maiden stood were Sir Edward Bourchier (1422–60) and William Bonville, 6th Baron Harington (1442–60) who in 1458 had married Lady Katherine Neville, a daughter of the earl of Salisbury. Another was Richard Haunsart or Hansard, who held manors in Kelsey and Thornton in Lincolnshire and Blacktoft Yorkshire. He is recorded as having 'been slain at Wakefield'.[2]

Another victim was Sir James Pickering (1396–1460), the oldest son of Sir James Pickering, of Ellerton, Yorkshire and Killington, Westmorland, and his wife Mary Lowther. He married Margaret Lascelles of Escrick, Yorkshire, and they had at least seven children, although the names of only two are known: James (1419–77) and John.[3] A subsequent document from the Court of Common Pleas tells us 'Sir James Pykering [sic]' was killed 'on 30 December at Wakefield in Yorkshire'.[4]

Present at the battle in the retinue of the duke was sergeant-at-arms Geoffrey Southworth. A court case by his widow, Dame Elizabeth Bold, tells us he was 'slain at Wakefield in the service of the duke of York'. His estates were seized, as were goods from the household and tenants in Carleton, Yorkshire in retribution by the Lancastrians. She claimed to have been imprisoned in the days following and held to ransom by the Lancashire esquire William Syngulton. Soon after her release, she married one of Edward IV's sergeants-at-arms John Conyers and together the two pursued her captor at law for redress.[5]

Two others may also have been executed or killed in battle. John Bere, from Berwick-upon-Tweed, sat as an MP for Carlisle from November 1449 with another Neville man, Thomas Derwent alias Derwentwater. A close associate of Thomas Neville, son of the earl of Salisbury, he may have been killed at Wakefield, or equally Towton.[6] We cannot be sure he was actually killed in either conflict. The bodies were probably dumped in a mass grave close to the Church of All Saints, Wakefield. Sir Henry Retford is noted by chroniclers as killed at Wakefield.[7] We cannot prove this. He was certainly a Yorkist as he was attained after Ludford Bridge. His forfeited lands included the manors of Broughton, Castlethorpe in Irby, Worlaby by Saxby, Carlton Kyme, Killingholme, Caythorpe, Carlton Paynell, Burton and Rothwell in Lincolnshire.[8] From a document dated 11 February 1462 we learn that John Shirwood was granted the position as clerk to the Sherriff of Yorkshire, in recognition of his service to Richard, duke of York and to the earl of Salisbury. This was to enable him to support his three widowed daughters: their husbands John Bolton, William Goldesburgh and William Wardop, had all been 'unlawfully executed', presumably at Wakefield.[9]

We cannot state any man was actually killed in battle beyond Anson. That men were wounded is a given, but whatever occurred was extremely unusual as Dr David Grummitt remarks. The number of later court cases, and granting compensation is atypical and unheard of for any other battle of the period: it further underlines that what happened was outside of the accepted normality of how men were killed in battle, and that we are not dealing with a 'battle' in any traditional sense.[10]

## Pillage and plunder

During 30 and 31 December, the Lancastrians remained in the Wakefield area, and carried out an 'orgy' of destruction 'for days one end'.[11] The Bailiff of Wakefield reports that John, lord Clifford replenished his retinue's supplies from the town:

> For the expenses of 6 [illegible] of various chariots captured by Lord de Clyfford at Wakefield and staying with them 5 weeks 3 days, that is for 20 quarts of beans which they supplied to them £6 13s 4d and 44s for 6 mules, 6 blankets, 6 linen cloths for the aforesaid lord, in total £19 6s 8d.
>
> Likewise, he showed a certain writ for various sums paid by him for guarding the town of Wakefield amounting to £7 19s.[12]

The town was thus protected from the worst excesses of the violence conducted by a Lancastrian mob from Pontefract who occupied Sandal Castle, burning parts of it to the ground.[13] The theft of cattle – and what else? – from Sandal and surrounding villages provided the Lancastrian army with supplies for the next week or more.

Leaving Wakefield on the afternoon of the 30th, York and Rutland were still alive. En route to Pontefract, Salisbury were captured, one chronicler says by servants of Andrew Trollop.[14] All three were killed in Pontefract, and as a contemporary writer comments: 'And the Earl of Salisbury, John Harowe the captain of foot, and other prisoners [my emphasis], were beheaded at Pountfret at the end of December.'[15] My emphasis on other prisoners. How and where Salisbury was captured we shall probably never know. He perhaps came north on the Great North Road, with the artillery and slower moving foot soldiers, perhaps to siege Pontefract, allowing York to head directly to York. Salisbury never seems to have been with York in Wakefield or Conisbrough. The artillery captured at Wakefield could easily have been with Salisbury. The events of 29 to 31 December in Wakefield, Pontefract and elsewhere have become combined as a single event fixed in time and place at Wakefield on 30 December, which does not relfect the reality of what happened. We know guns, bow staves and arrows were captured, but not where, when or if with York or Salisbury. What occurred at Pontefract was an extreme example of aristocratic violence. For discussion of the sources about the prisoner's fate and the killings of Rutland and others, see Appendices 3, 4 and 5. The date and place are confirmed by Milanese mercenary de la Torre writing from London and presenting Warwick's version of events.[16]

## The duke's execution

Clifford and Northumberland now reaped their revenge for events at St. Albans five years earlier. Hall's account of Clifford's merciless execution of Edmund, earl of Rutland on Wakefield Bridge is apocryphal, but it captures something of the Lancastrians lords' bloodthirsty orgy of violence in the wake of the Battle of Wakefield. Their bloodlust was fuelled by their personal hatred of York and Salisbury. The pairs treatment of their enemies was reflected in the behaviour of their retainers and servants towards York's men, the suspension of the accepted laws of war, and the destruction and theft of Yorkist property. Despite being a prisoner, Clifford and Northumberland wanted York dead.

How was York killed? One modern writer, with no shred of evidence whatsoever, claims that the duke was wounded to the knee, captured and executed.[17] This is the view taken in 2022 by French historian Georges Minois.[18] Beyond reasonable doubt, York, as we have said, was not killed at Wakefield, but was, as Parliament recorded correctly, killed alongside his son and Salisbury. Dr Livia Visser Fuchs believes that almost as soon as York was dead, Warwick issued his famous – infamous? – 'Apology' and perhaps shortly before a newssheet which neatly explained the events away, document Bnf MS Fr 88 for the French edition, and *An English Chronicle*, published by Davies for the English edition.[19] Warwick's 'Apology' is not reliable history, dating I believe not to 1461 but to 1469. Also unreliable is the Warwick version of events of Northampton, Wakefield, St Albans etc which were passed to Wavrin.[20] Therefore we have to look beyond the 'traditional' source material to find answers. Andriaan de But (1437–88), was a Cistercian monk at Ter Duinen in Flanders, which he entered in 1457 before moving to Paris in the following year (the translation is my own):

> In the year of the Lord 1461 in England, after various conflicts by the Dukes of York, King Henry had defeated the duke of York and whom he had taken prisoner, the same Duke of York was captured by Andréa Trolot and by the same hand he cut this throat with his sword.[21]

Elsewhere, on two occasions de But says Rutland was killed side by side with his father at prayer in a monastery along with Salisbury.[22] On bended knee, in prayer, the duke would have been incredibly vulnerable to attack from behind. Such a violent death does correlate rather well with accounts of Salisbury's death: we read he was to be ransomed, but hatred overcame his captors who killed him. Why York was not killed in Wakefield, we know not: I do accept that he may have been killed in Wakefield, but my reading of the various sources

implies he died side by side with Salisbury in Pontefract. I am happy
to be proven wrong! Our monk had been in Paris from 1458–60, and
was with the Burgundian court in 1460, and was present with Louis
XI in Paris in 1463. He was in the right place, at the right time, to read
and hear first-hand accounts of what happened. The duke had been
stripped of his armour and Roger Thorpe was accused and convicted
of the theft of 'certain armour and other equipment of war belonging
to the duke'.[23] Parliament recorded the duke was:

> traitorously, horribly, cruelly and tyrannously murdered . . . and
> also the worthy and good lords Edmund, earl of Rutland, brother
> of our said sovereign lord, and Richard, earl of Salisbury; and not
> content with this, they had them beheaded after they were dead with
> abominable cruelty and spite, out of their insatiable malice, contrary
> to all humanity and nobility.[24]

As the Yorkists controlled Parliament, the Roll said what the Yorkists
wanted to be said, in this case a statement that was not fundamentally
true but reflected something of the truth. The reliability of the
document is therefore suspect: moreover, it directly names Somerset
for planning the crime, which is rather challenging as Somerset was
either in Scotland or France at the time. Yet despite what Parliament
said, the earliest accounts of the event do not mention post mortem
decapitation. London chroniclers when mentioning this event state
'ut dictur' (as it is said) which rather suggests that the event was
questioned at the time. That this story travelled into Europe and was
believed, even if never happened, is supported by Burgundian[25] and
French[26] sources.[27]

The documents are almost universal in stating the duke was
captured alive and then beheaded after death.[28] Jean de Roye
(c.1425–c.1490) who was chamberlain and counsellor to Louis XI, and
secretary to the duke Jean II of Bourbon from 1465 tells us what he
thought happened next:

> And after he was dead they chopped off his head, which they put at the
> end of a spear; and around his head they placed a crown of fur in the
> form of a royal crown, in mockery of the fact that he wanted to make
> himself king of the said kingdom.[29]

In this, the Abbot of St Albans agrees,[30] as does the chronicler Tanner.[31]
It is also suggested in a letter to the duke of Milan written from Ghent
on 1 February 1461.[32] The writer of a *Short Latin Chronicle* implies
post-mortem decapitation and notes 'the heads of the slain lords of

which, as it is said, are above the gates of the city of York and were scandalously and discordantly [?] exposed'.[33] Again Pseudo-William of Worcester records 'a paper crown[34] was placed in derision on the head of the Duke of York'.[35] Andriaan de Butt also reports this identical event, adding the epithet was 'this is he who wanted to be king of England'.[36] The brief notes of historical events during the reigns of Henry VI and Edward IV compiled in the 1460s catalogued today as Lambeth Ms 448 state that the severed heads were placed on the walls of Pontefract castle and not York. Yet none of these accounts are by eyewitnesses: they merely reported London gossip in the months after the duke's death. The problem with de But and Whethamstede is they are writing is to suit a definite agenda. The Pope had sanctified the Yorkist cause, ergo what they composed was designed to stress its divine favour, whilst simultaneously damning the Lancastrians. In the Catholic year, 30 December had its own religious meanings, which will influence their discussion of events.[37] It is unclear how any of the chroniclers actually received their information; perhaps they read a copy of the newsletter that circulated among the Pastons or even a similar letter like Bnf Fr 88. Therefore, our writers are not presenting history, but morality lessons. Indeed, the words de But uses, *rex Anglorum* instead of *rex Angliae*, was no doubt his conscious imitation of the biblical *rex Iudaeorum*. The duke became a Holy Martyr rewarded with his unfading crown of martyrdom.[38] This understanding of divine favour, intermixed with classical references, by both writers, has, alas, been misunderstood by most historians: de But and our abbot are not writing reliable history. That no crowns or heads on spikes are mentioned in BnF 88 is significant. Nor does Wavrin mention this. If this event at happened, the Yorkists would have used the event as a piece of propaganda to show the 'bloodthirsty' nature of the Lancastrians. It is probably not true that York's severed head was placed on Micklegate Bar, despite it being believed in Europe.

Contrary to the story propagated in Europe, the man who killed the duke seems to have been James Luttrell and not Andrew Trollop:

> It was ordained that the said James for his murder of the King's father Richard, late duke or York, be attained of high treason and forfeit to the king all his possessions which he had on 30 December, 39 Henry VI in England, Ireland, Calais or the marches.[39]

Almost the first action of Edward IV within hours of being formally declared king on 4 March 1461 was to order post mortem inquisition into the lands of James Luttrell.[40] Two days later, Edward issued a proclamation that offered £100 to any man who put to death Andrew Trollop, William Grimsby, formerly treasurer of Henry VI's chamber, and the 'two bastards of Exeter'.[41] The latter were certainly not involved at Wakefield, and most certainly had nothing to do with Salisbury's death despite chronicle evidence.[42] Whatever crime they were guilty of, it was for St Albans and not Wakefield. Trollop being names is understandable: was a wanted man by the Yorkists for Ludford Bridge and his actions at St Albans. We are sure he was not at Wakefield, still being in France at this time despite what chroniclers say and only left France in late January 1461, some of his men being captured on landing in Norfolk, recorded by Clement Paston, as they sought to join the queen.[43] Within a week of his accession to the throne, Edward IV ordered the sheriff and escheator in Somerset and Dorset to seize all the possessions of the dukes of Exeter and Somerset, the earls of Devon, Wiltshire and Northumberland, and Sir James Luttrell on 10 March 1461.[44] Was Luttrell at Wakefield? I believe so: Devon was certainly with the queen in January, but son and heir was certainly present and no doubt had Luttrell with him, so yes, guilty.

The victory at Towton may explain the lack of detail in the contemporary accounts of the duke's burial: the drama of his death and filial piety of his son were of more interest, thus absolute facts about the date of death are confused: no one source tells the same story about how the duke died.

We can be absolutely certain that once York was dead his mortal remains, rather than being buried at Wakefield, were taken to Pontefract for burial at St Richard's Friary.[45] The reason for mutilation of the dead can be found in Papal Bulls of the time which imply that disfigurement would put the soul in danger of not being resurrected as the soul could not identify its body and thus could not be resurrected on the day of judgement.[46] Indeed, whilst working for York Archaeology excavating a cemetery of decapitated Roman gladiators in York, Dr Patrick Ottaway commented that post-mortem decapitation was a ritual act, to prevent the dead from coming back as ghosts to haunt the living. The Romans firmly believed that the dead could rise from the grave to wreak harm on the living, removal of the head made the cadaver unrecognisable to the soul, therefore could not rise from the grave.[47] Death and brutalisation of the dead were used as 'terror weapons' in an age of devout faith.[48] It went 'way beyond killing': decapitation meant the soul was condemned to purgatory, any chance of a heavenly after life destroyed and the body could never be resurrected.

Not all the prisoners were killed, as Appendix 3 shows. If we believe Wavrin, Lovelace and his gunners were bound over, and were to serve in the Lancastrian army. Certainly twenty-four guns/cannon were captured in the wake of the battle, and certainly formed part of the array at St Albans.[49]

## Victory

In the aftermath of York's death, the Lancastrians celebrated their victory. According to a document in the British Library compiled in the nineteenth century compiled from numerous, and perhaps unreliable, heraldic and genealogical sources, twenty men were knighted by Northumberland, Devon, Roos and Clifford. Some of those mentioned include Alexander Hody, Robert Whittingham and Henry Bellingham, but also family members like Devon's brother John and Roger Clifford, Lord Clifford's brother.[50] The accuracy of this list may be questioned, but as David Grummitt comments, 'dubbing knights would have given the victory a military and chivalric symbolism it otherwise lacked'.[51] From Pontefract the Lancastrian host split: some headed to Beverley: William Gascoigne and Richard Aldborough, the later indicted for the murder of the earl of Salisbury, were in Beverley by 12 January. So too – presumably from the Lancastrian army at Wakefield – were two knights, John and William Normavill,[52] and another veteran of the battle was rewarded with 'one lagan of red winc' which was 'given to master Haines the foot captain 12d'. No doubt these men were in 'the camp' somewhere close to the town. Clifford, established himself in Kingston-upon-Hull.[53] Also in Hull was Thomas Roos of Helmsley. Somerset, or at least one his servants was in Beverley by March.[54] The burgess of Hull gave gifts to Sir Ralph Percy and Lord Clifford, the victors of Wakefield.[55]

York's death transformed the political landscape. News of his death enabled the queen to come to a settlement with Mary of Guelders on 5 January. Having secured military aide, in defiance of embassies from Burgundy and the now dead York, she travelled south to York. It was here on 20 January that she met with the dukes of Somerset and Devon, the earls of Northumberland and Westmoreland, Ralph Neville, his brother John, Lord Neville, Henry, Lord Fitzhugh, Thomas Roos of Helmsley, Lord Dacre[56] and Thomas Scrope. The peers ratified a treaty that perhaps marked an end to Scottish raids over the border and a marriage between Prince Edward and the daughter of Mary of Guelders.[57] A definite Lancastrian faction emerged headed by the queen. Also, with Margaret, since October 1460 it seems, was James Butler, earl of Wiltshire. He sought mercenaries from Burgundy,

offering £1,900 in silver.[58] Margaret lost no time in transmitting the
news of her triumph to friend and foe alike. Her letter to the duke of
Burgundy arrived moments before Warwick's did.[59]

Victory at Wakefield meant that two conflicting governments
continued to co-exist. Warwick and Edward, held the king and
governed the Home Counties and south-east, Queen Margaret and her
allies held sway over the south-west, most of Wales and the North. Both
believed they were the sole ruler, and sought the total extermination
of the other. Wakefield changed the political landscape dramatically.
It was the tipping point for cementing an alliance between Margaret
and Mary, in defiance of the Burgundian ambassadors' appeals. It
allowed Margaret to assemble a large armed retinue in East Yorkshire,
once the key port of Kingston-upon-Hull had opened the gates to
her. On 22 January the queen issued a proclamation to 'be made
throughout my lords countre of York' continuing that 'false malicious
meanes' had been employed to keep her from the kings presence. She
used this a rallying call 'that every man that tendreth and loveth the
kynges welfare, the queenes and my lord princes be redy in his best
araye to awite upon thaim'.[60] At Hull she began to form an army. The
accounts of the burgess record a payment for a horse that the late
queen had, gunpowder and 7s 2d for men that rode to the St. Albans
with the queen.[61]

As Richard Knowles observed over 30 years ago, the Battle of
Wakefield was 'in all probability . . . more of a brutal skirmish than
a set piece battle'.[62] Rather than heroically – or foolishly – leaving
the safety of Sandal Castle to engage a larger Lancastrian force, the
duke and a few dozen companions were probably surprised by a
larger Lancastrian force on 29 December, led by Lord Clifford. York
and Salisbury's deaths were a major, but far from fatal, blow to the
Yorkist cause. London and many in the surrounding counties now
rallied behind the earl of Warwick. Warwick still had Henry VI in
his custody in London: Warwick represented legitimate government
and Yorkist propaganda now worked overtime to present the
conflict in terms of North versus South, rather than Lancastrian
versus Yorkist.

Wakefield shifted the political landscape drastically: it witnessed
an arms race between York and Lancaster. There could be no more
pretence of political compromise between the scions of the houses
of Lancaster and York. The armies that faced each other at St Albans
and Towton were hastily assembled now. So concerned by the
queen's preparations, Warwick attempted to prevent 'evil doers' from
supplying arms and victuals to the queen on 26 January. Two days

later Warwick sought to identify from which Norfolk port supplies and armed men were heading north. A commission was established in Cambridge on 7 February for a similar purpose.[63] The war was just beginning as the country tipped into the bloodiest and longest phase of sustained fighting of the Wars of the Roses. Conflict had become inevitable, and it is undeniable that by the end of the 1450s the gentry and squirearchy, as much as the nobility, were desperate for some way out of the impasse: many did not care whether it was a Lancastrian solution or a Yorkist one, as long as it meant that strong unitary rule was brought about. The 'clash of clans' represented the duality at is most basic, the nothingness of Henry: if Henry had been monarch, all powerful, then alternative sources of authority would not have existed. Unitary rule could only be achieved by the destruction of one side or the other. York's declaration that Henry was dead at Ludford meant that no longer were their two rival forms of authority acting in the name of an ineffective king, rather he initiated a war to the death between two equal factions about who would be king. As Christine Carpenter argues 'the need to go to war to decide the succession is partly explained by Henry's extreme limpness'.[64] Edward and Warwick now faced a bloody battle for the crown of England.

Chapter 25

# CONCLUSION

How do we draw all these strands together? What is the 'So What?' of this study.

As we have shown, the duke of York exposed and sought to exploit the nullity of Henry VI. He had no justification for what he did, other than naked opportunism by a narcissist with a sense of entitlement and victimhood; a man who held others to standards of behaviour he did not himself. No 'Golden Age' was lost with his death. He was more a follower than a leader once under the influence of the young earl of Warwick.

For York, the appeal from *communitas* during Cade's Rebellion – which he may have had a hand in creating – to take control of government in the wake of the foreign policy failure of Suffolk and Beaufort in France and Scotland, set his life on a trajectory that led to his death. The sole solution to the problem of Henry VI was his removal from power, like Edward II and Richard II. Unlike 1399 however, there was no single rival faction or claimant. Henry, like Edward II, had few of the qualities that made a successful medieval king. The factionalism that led to both monarchs' removal from power had remarkable similarities, in a long period of civil turmoil, backed by differing factions, one led by the queen. The parallels between Edward II and Henry VI are notable, and in this genre the fate of Thomas, duke of Lancaster (1278–1322), the most powerful noble in the land, who lost his bid for control. The ultimate destiny of both men, Thomas of Lancaster and Richard duke of York, has a degree of synchronicity that is hard to ignore. Both men gambled on a pitched battle and lost, both men lost their heads and were buried within a mile of each other at Pontefract. Both men failed to rally sufficient nobles and the gentry to their side to guarantee victory. Unlike Thomas of Lancaster, York was a follower and not a leader: Warwick was as much kingmaker from 1456 as 1470.

The cause for war in 1459, as we discussed, is complex. Economic instability, a weak king, demand for structural changes in governance – growing from the demands made during the peasant's revolt – all stimulated by 1450 rebellion, but armed conflict was not a foregone conclusion. The tipping points came in the relationship between the ruled and the ruler, exacerbating underlying tensions, the most important of which being economic decline. The bedrock of the kingdom's wealth, the wool trade into Europe, was disrupted, the economy faltered and the exchequer was reliant on loans from leading nobles. The Yorkist faction – the Nevilles led by Warwick – for personal and familial gain, sought to harness popular and gentry unrest: in this, Warwick succeeded magnificently, but at the cost of York's life. York was always going to be expendable: even in summer 1460 rumour said that Warwick was to make Edward, earl of March king. York was a useful figurehead, a sword to lead the coup as Napoleon had been for Cambercérès in November 1799, but ultimately a disposable asset. The Yorkists, with York as king in all but name, from 1458 never attempted anything approaching governance from the centre: it was a Neville power grab focused on Warwick. Warwick and inter alia York were never going to win over the most truculent Lancastrians, who exploited the situation to their own ends, especially so whilst a rival claimant existed. Whilst ever a king in waiting existed with an alternative government, the Act of Accord could never have been the beginning of a new era of peace and harmony. York had declared an all-out war of extermination between the two factions; a rift that would not be healed till 1746

The three Yorkist kings, like their Tudor, Stuart and Georgian successors, never wholly ruled an acquiescing nation. Henry VII faced rebellion for much of his reign, and his son faced open rebellion and perhaps the spectre of civil war in 1539 to 1541, based in part on grudges and memories of the events the tumultuous 1460s. Nor was Elizabeth secure in her position, with a string of rebellions and the threat of invasion to face, which she was not guaranteed to defeat. Richard III realised that government by committee, which what the rule of Edward V would have meant, was unworkable and moreover, understood that whilst ever a rival claimant existed to challenge his authority, he had to be ruthless, exterminate opponents, and to leave no rival claimants to challenge his position. That his own revolution was a failure, and his inability to govern from the centre as his brother had managed from 1471, demonstrates that the nobility, gentry and squirearchy were no longer willing to tolerate factionalism and partisan governance. That the nobility found a new inheritor of the crown after the death of the Prince of Wales, and were prepared to rise in rebellion, shows the existential weakness of Richard III's position.

Partisan government was never likely to garner wide support, but the fact the Yorkists were in power for 25 years, albeit intermittently, implies that a more pronounced sympathy for the Yorkists existed than for the royal government of Henry. This does not necessarily mean however, that the Yorkists represented the will of the people: it is perhaps truer to say that the promise of 'things can only get better' was more important than the messenger. It had been obvious by the mid-1440s to the nobility and gentry, as much as the *communitas*, that 'business as normal' since 1422 of the nullity of Henry by committee was not working nor could it work. The support York and Edward achieved is evidence enough that by the end of the 1450s the gentry and squirearchy, as much as the nobility, were desperate for some way out of the impasse: many did not care whether it was a Lancastrian solution or a Yorkist one, as long as it meant strong unitary rule was brought about. The 'clash of clans' between York and the crown represented the problem at the heart of government at its most basic, the nothingness of Henry: if Henry had been monarch, all powerful like his father, then alternative sources of authority would not have existed. The void which was Henry at the heart of government, was openly exploited by competing factions for personal gain; it meant unitary rule could only be achieved by the destruction of one side or the other. That two rival forms of authority acting in the name of an ineffective king, existed, as Christine Carpenter cogently argues 'is partly explained by Henry's extreme limpness'.[1] Partly: so, who else was to blame other than Henry? The economic conditions of the middle decades of the fifteenth century meant a huge reduction in incomes for magnates and nobles. The implications of this meant that the magnates were more prepared to contest inheritances. Perhaps more importantly, the collapse in tax revenue meant the Crown had less money to fight wars and to distribute in patronage. A stressed and deflating economy, with less money around, combined with a vacuum at the heart of government exploited by factionalism, perhaps made conflict inevitable.

If Henry had been monarch, king in more than name, then no one would have dared criticise his ordinances and royal will. That they were, and a war to the death between two equal factions, about who would be king and more over about the relationship between the ruler and the ruled, broke out can be blamed on Henry and partisan government. We do not deny, however, that the events of 1459 accelerated as they did through paranoia, largely driven by Warwick, was symptomatic of the lack of governance and trust from the centre. The paranoid delusions about loss of power, status and wealth by one faction, who sought to eliminate its rival, despite royal assurances, showed starkly the nothingness of Henry and all edicts in his name. That the Yorkists in 1460 then endeavoured to harness the nothingness of Henry and his largely meaningless royal cypher to validate their government, reinforces the point, that no one believed Henry was actually king in more than name. Yet that York conceded his claim to be king in October 1460, showed the unwillingness of 'vested interest groups' to replace Henry with a king that they may not be able to exploit for their own gains. How much of this was brokered by Warwick we shall never know. The *English Chronicle*, Wavrin and allied texts are all from Warwick's viewpoint, so too Parliament. What we have are not Yorkist chronicles, but Warwick's versions of events. When it comes to the all-important Parliament of 1460, we have Warwick's voice loud and clear and almost no others. The Pope, the Milanese, the French were all reporting what Warwick said. Warwick needed not York as king but for Edward to be heir: once this had been agreed, York was dispensable. Ultimately, as we said earlier, both sides needed a monarch that was exploitable/malleable to legitimise their faction. Margaret had legitimacy through her husband, Warwick through the new Prince of Wales, Edward, earl of March. That York met his death demonstrates the inherent weakness of his position, both in terms of support from Warwick, and the opportunism of the Percy faction, as much as a 'political game changer' for both sides to create new, stronger alliances. York, as much as Henry VI and Richard II, was disposable.

Indeed, a direct consequence of the Yorkist revolution, and the factionalism which Henry Percy or Warwick led and exploited, was that kings became, as we said earlier, disposable assets: whilst ever a rival claimant could be found, who was more acceptable to the *communitas*, nobility or squirearchy, then the king could be changed as needed. The myth of absolute monarchy was broken and placed power not with the king, but with those around him or her, especially 'overmighty subjects' like Warwick. The Readeption of 1469–71 is ample evidence of this. The creation of a many-headed hydrae of the 'will of the people' lead to the English Civil Wars – a war between the governed and the government at is most basic. Disposable monarchy and this tension led to two further revolutions, that of 1688 and 1714: the 1745 was perhaps the last expiring gasp of the many-headed hydra.

\*\*\*

I hope this book has presented new facts to the reader and placed the duke's life and death once more in the world context. I owe my late mother a debt of gratitude for instilling a love of history and I hope this text does justice to her original scheme of research to examine the politics leading to the duke's death. Did the country miss out on a golden age with his death? No, absolutely not. York and the Nevilles' revolution would never have been accepted by all the nobles and magnates until Edward Prince of Wales was dead. History would have panned out as it did in the 1460s with York as king facing down rebellion after rebellion. York offered 'more of the same' and not structural change that had been demanded since 1450, or even the 1380s and would take the Civil Wars of the 1640s and 1650s to resolve. York's hubris, sense of entitlement lead to his death, driven to ever more extreme positions by Warwick, the man who was the third king to quote Andriaan de But in the 1460s. Whosoever Warwick chose to be king, would be king be that York, Edward or Henry. It was Warwick who brokered the Yorkist alliances. York and Warwick owed their success through the support and intervention of the papacy as well as the Italian League and the duke of Burgundy. Usurpation could not have occurred without strong alliances against France. Margaret of Anjou and her father Rene, held influence over Charles VII: without Medici money, Burgundian troops, Papal blessing and Milanese influence, usurpation was simply not possible without the threat of French invasion. Indeed, Coppini acknowledged his and inter alia the role the Papacy played in removing Henry VI in August, writing to Sforza that 'the lords here, the kinsmen of the king, who through my hands have won back the state'. This power grab by Warwick gave Burgundy and Milan new allies again France, and Coppini told Sforza 'if they had some incitement they would go to France with a considerable force to vindicate the claims of this kingdom'.[2] Indeed, the duke of Milan instructed his ambassador Prospero Camulio to draw the duke of York tighter into the Italian League alliance with Burgundy: 'To the Duke of York you will say practically the same as we told you to say to the Duke of Burgundy about remembering the ancient friendship and our disposition. To the Earl of Warwick, you will commend his worth and valour and say that it will always gratify us to do his pleasure.'[3] The Battle of Wakefield and the duke's death could have ended the Yorkist power struggle; that it did not owes largely to Warwick and his European allies.

Yet the geopolitical unrest in Europe into which Edward came to power, would witness the last successful invasion of England by the French when Henry Tudor backed by his French allies defeated Richard III at Bosworth. The duke of York and his son, backed Burgundy in the battle for superiority between France and Burgundy. France ultimately won this conflict, and France became the super power of Europe. Warwick had seen the way the wind was blowing and had come to conflict with Edward over French policy, leading to the Readeption of 1470–1 and Warwick's death. The Battle of Wakefield was a turning point in world history. The death of the duke of York heralded the Yorkist age which witnessed the birth of the Renaissance in England.

That the duke spent the last week of his life as a free man in Wakefield and not Sandal Castle is a given, and was brutally murdered in Pontefract. Why York did not occupy Sandal is lost to history. We have no clear facts about the Battle of Wakefield – but this has not stopped 500 years of writers carefully crafting a myth that is on very shaky foundations; indeed, it was likely not a battle at all. The suggestion from French and English writers that there was an appointed day of battle, that the Lancastrian army was led by the queen herself, and that York was killed in the fighting all found their way into Vergil's and Hall's account and may point to an earlier 'Lancastrian' origin for the early Tudor narratives. Yet they are not reliable accounts in themselves.

The prominence given by recent historians to the accounts of Wakefield contained in Wavrin and *An English Chronicle* is understandable. We like to find easy solutions, and these accounts are the fullest and, in terms of their narrative logic, the most coherent contemporary accounts we have. Yet the qualities that enable them to fulfil the historian's desire to explain the past are precisely those that should give us pause in accepting their veracity.

Is this the final word on the duke? No. Give two historians the same data, and they will come to two different conclusions depending on personal bias. I come at the duke of York as a specialist in the armies of Napoleon 1er. I have less 'baggage' than most Wars of the Roses researchers, which as I said in my introduction lays be open to accusations of anti-Yorkist bias, for endeavouring to be objective in looking behind the very effective Yorkist PR. The victors write the history is often quoted, and in the case of the events of the 1450s and 1460s is objectively true. The Yorkists sought to control the narrative, to justify their treason and usurpation. Is this the final word on how the duke died? No. There may be lost Lancastrian accounts of Wakefield to be found. Certainly, such texts were in circulation on the continent in the early 1460s. Writing before 1467, the Burgundian chronicler, Jacques du Clercq who was one of the secretaries to Philip the Good, duke of Burgundy, and showed a particular interest in English affairs. He seems to have had access to now-lost newsletters: they could lie in an archive room in the Netherlands or France. Burgundian courtier,

George Chastellain, also seems to have had access to contemporary material. Time will tell. But will these accounts change the interpretation of the events? I don't think so. My friend and research colleague Dr David Grummitt came to broadly similar conclusions working totally independantly that there was no battle at Wakefield in the traditional sense. Whatever the origins of the stories recorded by the chroniclers, the differing accounts of the Battle of Wakefield should serve as a stark reminder to us that the chronicle accounts of the Wars of the Roses were not simple retellings of recent events. They are not eyewitness accounts and are drawn from hearsay or the later testimony of eyewitnesses. Rather than seeking to tell the story of the events as they happened, these sources are complex, politically charged narratives designed to alter perceptions of the past and guide their readers' actions in the future. They contain a different concept of truth to the Manor of Wakefield Court Rolls and ancillary documents. Because historians routinely use these chronicle accounts – and other items of Yorkist propaganda – as though they were categorical truth rather than a 'version of the truth'; we have to test what is said with other sources of information, other 'truths.' As is so often the case with battles from the period, to build a theory of what happened based on one or even a few stated sources often result in an incorrect narrative. Other examples abound and it is essential that, to fully understand the events, it is necessary to cross-reference the chronicles and to re-interpret rather than to accept their rather romanticised and editorialised content as being correct. This is not to say that the chronicles are valueless or wrong, but a more careful analysis needs to be undertaken. If anything, this book is a call to arms to look at the fifteenth century not from chronicles but local-level archives: what was the impact at local level? What can manorial records say that is new on the period? As this book shows, legal documents and manorial records are an untapped resource to study the events of the period. If we are to understand the events of the period, we have to look beyond the propaganda disseminated by both factions to more reliable empirical data, captured in the mundane administration of the country.

This is my attempt to make an attempt to impose a narrative on source material which, as my friend Dr Livia Visser Fuchs adroitly comments, is grossly incomplete, and more over inherently and irremediably chaotic. It may be wrong to try and impose a specious conclusion on such material. More archive documents await discovery which will shed more light on the duke and his life, and indeed I accept I am guilty as charged of not exhaustively examining all the sources that have been printed or recorded in archive indexes. But I hope I have added to the discussion about the duke's life and opened up new avenues of research.

# APPENDIX 1: MANORIAL ACCOUNTS OF THE BATTLE OF WAKEFIELD 1460–1461

**TNA DL29/560/8899 Manor of Wakefield Receiver's Accounts 29th September 1460–29th September 1461.**

[Sandal]

Account of William Wodehous grave from St. Michael's Day 39 Henry VI [29 Sep 1460] /................/ king of England to the same day /1/ Edward IV [29 Sep 1461].

[Farm of the demesne with farm of the mills]

For £4 in farm of demesne lands with appurtenances attached leased to various tenants he does not answer for the said period of account because it is vacant in the lord's hand and not let for want of lessees on account of the insurrection of various rebels of the king at Pontefract and residing for days on end in Sandal castle, for which reason the said demesne lands were not leased and there was nobody wanting to hire or occupy them at that time, by witness of various men and of the said accountant at this account/audit; But he does answer for 2s in grazing of various pieces of the said demesne land sold to John Hopkynson this year; And for 116s 8d for the farm of the water mill called Newmylles leased to John Netilton' this

[for next year]

year then are leased in respect of next year to the said John for £6; For the farm of the fulling mill there below the castle for the said period he does not answer because it was destroyed in the time of Edward lately Duke of York; Nor does he answer for 66s 8d for the farm of the meadow called Erlesyng' for the said period, because it is in the lord's hand for want of letting and it is mown and included within the lord's grange/barn, and the hay from it is to be accounted for next year; Nor does he answer for 13s 4d for the farm of the fishery in le

Newmyldame, because it is reserved to the lord for his men coming to fish there; Nor does he answer for 3s 4d in the farm of one piece of meadow called Damstede and the said piece of meadow [is?] between the mill pond there and the castle, because it is mown and kept within the lord's grange; But he answers for 3s 4d for the farm of a piece of land on the lord's waste in Thrustonhawe leased to John Sripinell' and John Passelowe for a iron bloomery to be built on it.

Total 112s

[Proceeds of pigs in Sandal and Thrustonhawe]

He does not answer for any profit coming from the winter and summer agistment of Sandal Park, because no men wanted to agist their beasts in it on account of rebels attacking day after day and driving the tenants' cattle to Pontefract; Nor does he answer for any profit from herons within the said park, because nothing was possible this year; Nor does he answer for the grazing of the lord's park called Thrustonhawe, because it lies open in common and not enclosed and no profit could be taken from it this year by oath of the accountant.

Total nothing

[Perquisites of the court]

But he does answer for 11s in perquisites of 4 tourns and 14 courts there in the immediately preceding year held as appears in their rolls delivered and examined at this audit, [but] at first not charged for want of the rolls being returned; And for 10d in perquisites of 8 courts held there this year as appears by their rolls delivered and examined at this audit.

Total 11s 10d

Sum total of receipts with arrears £57 6s 2½d half farthing.

**From which**:

[Costs of hay]

And 18d paid for mowing spreading gathering and making hay from a meadow of the lord called Damstede with carriage of it, lately mown for feeding the animals within the lord's park in winter, and now put into the barn there because there are no animals within the park.

Total 18d

[Costs or repairs]

And 15s paid for a pair of mill stones, 4s 2d for boards, 8d for nails and other things bought for repair of various defects and breaches of the lord's mills standing damaged with wages of various carpenters and others from the castle with 6s 8d allowed for the milldam of the said mills at the time of their repair as appears by a writ for 38s 8d by William Hyncheclyff; And for 10s 11d paid to various people repairing various defects in various buildings within the castle <7s 4d> and the park pale <3s 7d> as appears by another writ.

Total 49s 7d

[Monies paid to J Vyncent]

And for 11s for monies paid to John Vyncent former receiver by John Sprigonell' grave there in the 38th year the oaths and witness of various men at this account; And £11 for monies paid to John Woderove Esquire by the said accountant from the proceeds of his office this year by a writ given on the 16th July 1 Edward IV and 20s by John Norton' farmer of the agistment in the park there in the year immediately preceding by acknowledgment/approval of the said receiver and so in total £12.

Total £12 11s

Sum total of allowances and payments £16 11s 7d. And he owes £40 14s 7½d half farthing.

**From which**

10s are allowed to him for the benefit of John Sprigonell' grave of Sandal in the 38th year (paid for the price of one bull for the household of the late Duke by Thomas Gayton' clerk of the said household And 20d are allowed to him for the benefit of John Erle grave there in the immediately preceding year for amercements not levied from various people amerced in certain cases in the court roll of that year because none have goods and chattels within the jurisdiction from which the amercements or any part of them could be raised as he says on oath. And he owes £40 2s 11½d half farthing.

**From which**

7s 11d paid to William Turton' for carrying hay from Erlesyng' to the barn of the castle by acknowledgment of the said William; And 4s allowed him paid to a man for breaking ice on the millpond of the lord's new mill there in winter; And 12d annually for the better preservation of the fishery in the millpond there by the contract made with him by the lord, that is to say for this year and 3 years preceding not allowed before; And he owes £39 11s ½d half farthing {{Which are charged in the account of the next year}} **From which**

[Charged]

£4 15s 1½d half farthing on John Sprigonell' grave there in the 38th year for his arrears.

£10 8s 4d on John Erle grave there in the immediately preceding year with 9s 4d for perquisites of the court for the same year charged above.

112s 3d on the lord's accountant this year from which ..................... paid

to John Clapham in the castle there in various .......... 74s 9½d
which he says he himself paid for various reasons and ......................
..................................................................................................etc.

m1 dorse
  Wakefield fee[1]
  Farm of mills with fisheries and strays:
  And [he answers/renders account] for 20s the issue of fulling mills
there[2] taken by John Walker at various times in the aforesaid period and
not more because the said mills stood vacant both because of repairs
and because of various rebels coming continually from Pontefract castle
attacking the lord's tenants there, and unsettling and driving them
from their farms[3] and lands, so that they did not dare to be occupiers
of these farms for fear of death, by the oath of the accountant and of
various witnesses at this audit.<formerly at £4>. And for 3s from the
farm of the fishery of Newmylbroke as far as the Calder formerly in
the tenure of John Norton' for 20d leased to John Woderove this year.[4]

Fee of the bailiff
  Money payments:
  Sum of allowances and payments £29 5s 9d. And he owes £85 11s
8½d. Afterwards he is charged with 7s 11d received from William
Wodehouse the grave of Sandal for carriage of hay from the lord's
meadow called Erlesyng' by acknowledgement of the said William.
Sum of debts together £ £85 19s 7½d. From which are allowed him 28s
8d. paid for works of mowing <19s 8d>, spreading, lifting and gathering
and for the future grazing of the meadow there called Erlesynges and
further for carriage of 22 <9s 4d> cartloads of hay arising from there to
the lord's barn/grange <19 7s 11d> next to (iuxta) the castle and town
<3 12d> of Wakefield and le Helme <j 5d> in the park there as appears
by a certain writ deposited at this audit. And he is exonerated of 66s 8d
charged above between the arrears and the farm of fulling mills there
in the year immediately preceding charged on the farmers, because
the said mills stood vacant and not let for want of repairs for the whole
year by the oath of the tenants at this audit. And so he owes £62 4s 3½d

(membrane 4)
  Wakefield Town
  Farm of mills:
  And (he answers for) 100s issue and profits of the mills there, that
is to say from St. Michael's Day at the beginning of this account until
Christmas day next following exploited by the said accountants for

the same period by writ deposited with this audit. And for £6 13s 4d from the issue and profits of the said mill from Christmas Day until the following Easter charged on Henry Burwell' and Robert Barr' occupiers of the office of bailiff there for the same period by the said writ. And for £8 16s 6½d issue and profits of the said mills from that Easter until the following St. Michael's Day thus held by the said writ for the said period. He does not answer for any profit arising from le Samondehekkes there for the aforesaid period because no profit was or could be taken from them for that period as they say on their oath. Formerly £4.

Proceeds of the court and farm of partidges and baking:
..... Nor does he answer for the proceeds of the court there for the aforesaid 3 quarters of the year. He does not answer because no courts were held there. For the other proceeds of the court for the aforesaid quarter of the year he does not answer because no court was held there in the said period . Sum nothing.

(m4 dorse)
    Stanley
    Farm of the agistment of the old park:
    He does not answer for 20s in farm of 2 coal pits there in Stonhawe in the aforesaid wood during the aforesaid period because there was a lack of lessees. But he does answer for 30s for farm of 2 other pits in the said wood let to John Lewyse this year. And for 12d in farm of 2 Cokeshottes in the said outwood (bosco forinseco) let this year.
    Sum 31s

Sum of all allowances:
    ......... For the farm of coal pits there because nobody dared to occupy the said pits on account of various rebellions in northern parts by the witness and oath of various tenents at this audit.

membrane 5
    Wakefield Graveship
    Sale of croppings:
    And for 5s 2d for sale of croppings of trees of the old park for repairing the pale this year sold to various persons within the said period.

membrane 5 dorse
    Salary of the accountant:

And he is allowed 4s to be paid for a close of the lord's meadow called Falbanke lying open because nobody else wanted to take the said meadow to farm.

Extra:
Memorandum that the accountant showed a certain writ for various sums in order to have allowance for them, that is 146s 8d.
Received from the Earl of Northumberland 26s 8d.
Received through Gawan Lamplewe 30s.
Received through John Clapham and Henry Burwell' 40s 1d.
Through the said John and Henry as in the price of 6 quarters of beans 16s 8d.
Received through the sam John and Henry as in the price of 5 quarters of oats £10 2s 8d.
For the expenses of 6 /............./ of various chariots captured by Lord de Clyfford' at Wakefield and staying with them 5 weeks 3 days, that is for 20 quarts of beans which they supplied to them £6 13s 4d and 44s for 6 mules, 6 blankets, 6 linen cloths by? for? (per?) the aforesaid lord, in total £19 6s 8d.
Likewise he showed a certain writ for various sums paid by him for guarding the town of Wakefield amounting to £7 19s

membrane 6
Stanley
Sale of croppings with the farm of coal pits:
He does not answer for sale of fallen croppings without browse because nothing of the sort had been sold there this year. Nor does he answer for 30s in the farm of 2 coal pits there in Stonehawe within the aforesaid wood that is to say during the aforesaid period. He does not answer because they lay in the lord's hand for want of lessees. But he does answer for 30s in the farm of 2 other coal pits in the said wood leased to John Lewes this year.
And for 12d for the farm of 2 cokeshotes in the said outwood this leased this year.

Sum of allowances and payments:
............ From which 10s are allowed him for the benefit of Oliver Hancocke the grave their in the preceeding year for the farm of coal pits there, because nobody dared to occupy the said pits on account of various rebels at Pontefract and elsewhere and moreover daily fled from them, by the oath and witness of various tenents at this audit.

Alverthorpe

Receiver:

From which are allowed [for the benefit of William Turton?] 10s paid to Richard Kynnesley for 1 ox bought from him for use of the household of the lord (pro expens' hospitii domini) lately Duke at Wakefield in the month of December and in January in the aforesaid period by the oath of various tenents at this audit.

membrane 11?

Conisbrough Graveship

Farm of demesne land:

He does not answer for 30s in farm of that demesne meadow there dualcalled Cutyng lately leased to various tennants of the lord there during the aforesaid period because it was enclosed within the park for feeding the lord's game during the winter. Nor does he answer for 11s. in farm of a demesne meadow there called Erlesyng because it is mown and stored within the grange there both for use of the lord's horses and his office holders there coming from time to time as well as for feeding the game in the park there in time of winter.

Farm of the fishery:

He does not answer for 2s in farm of the fishery of the river Don lately in the tenure of John Clerkson' that is during the said period, because it was appropriated by the lord lately of Egremont and his servants during the same period by oath of the accountant and witness of others at this audit.

# APPENDIX 2: MANORIAL ACCOUNTS OF THE BATTLE OF WAKEFIELD 1461–1462

**TNA DL29/560/8900 Manor of Wakefield Receiver's Accounts 29th September 1461–29th September 1462.**

membrane 1
    Sandal
Farms of demesne lands with farms of mills: And he does not answer for the fulling mill there below the castle that is to say for the aforesad period because it had been destroyed in the time of Edward late Duke of York.

He answers for 13s. 4d. for the farm of the fishery of the water of the Newemyldame for the aforesaid period because it is reserved for the lord for his men coming to fish in the same. Nor does he answere for 3s. 4d. for the farm of a piece of land on the lord's waste in Thrustonhawe leased to John Sprigonell' and John Passelowe for building a bloomery on it.

Profit from pigs at Sandal and Thurstonhalgh:
    Nor does he answer for any profit arising from the pannage of pigs in the aforesaid park [Sandal Park] because there was no master there this year by oath of the accountant.

Membrane 2
    Osset
    Amongst components of monies owing to the Lord:
    On the Earl of Shrewsbury for the agistment of the park there [Wakefield New Park] occupied by him from the feast of St. Michael in the 38th year [29th Sep 1459].

252

until the feast of the Nativity of St. John the Baptist next following from then [24 June 1460], 106 s. 8 d.

Membrane 4 Wakefield Vill

Gawain Lamplewe, Robert Tomlynson' sergeants of the Earl of Northumberland
    occupying the office and receiving the yield and profit of the aforesaid demesne [the Vill of Wakefield as opposed to the graveship or the fee/soke] from the feast of Saint Michael
    in the 39th year [29 Sep 1460] until the feast of Christmas next following from then [25 Dec 1460] by the information and advice of William Gargrave Esquire as well as on Richard Lyster' occupying the office and receiving the yield and profit of the aforesaid demesne from the said feast of Christmas until the 11th day of July next following from then.

# APPENDIX 3: PRISONERS

The 'Battle' of Wakefield is remarkable for the number of petitions and other legal documents generated by participants who were captured and made prisoner. We can be certain most of the senior Yorkists were captured, held in Wakefield under guard by Lord Clifford, and were so ill-treated that they later made complaints about their treatment through legal process. About these legal documents, leading historian of the Wars of the Roses Dr David Grummitt comments:

> these complaints are a key piece of evidence that Wakefield was different. We do not get so nearly so many such suits for any of the other battles; something different is going on at the 'battle' of Wakefield.[1]

We quite agree: these documents, I believe, reinforce the argument made by Thomas Colt that the duke was ambushed, and we are not dealing with a battle as we understand it. None of these documents mention any other Lancastrians other than Northumberland and Clifford. These sources, independent of the Manor of Wakefield accounts, seemingly confirm no other Lancastrian troops were present other than those of these men. No mention is made of Somerset, Devon or other notable leaders. What happened at Wakefield was between York, Clifford and Northumberland.

A legal case made its way to the Court of Chancery in 1466: Robert Percy of Scotton near Knaresborough, who had fought for Richard Neville, earl of Salisbury, at the Battle of Blore Heath on 23 September 1459, claimed that Plumpton had despatched his men to raid his property in the immediate aftermath of the rout of the Yorkists at Ludford Bridge three weeks later, which he described as the Battle of Ludlow. The Chancery papers furthermore tell us Percy was abused and robbed of his goods and property 'at the field of Wakefield' by William Plumpton. Percy adds that having been made a prisoner following the Battle of Wakefield, Plumpton laboured to have 'his hede stryken of' in revenge for his participation at Blore Heath in

1459: all very reminiscent of the fate of Salisbury and his son Thomas. Furthermore, Percy tells us in a sworn legal statement that in retaliation for his treason against Henry VI, in order to provide food and supplies for the Lancastrian army, Plumpton plundered his lands of livestock and goods worth in excess of 100 marks.[2] This confirms Plumpton's rather 'bloodthirsty' streak, and shows to emphasis the extreme violence which the Lancastrians metered out to prisoners. Plumpton, like others in Northumberland's service, were violent men who used murder as a tool to redress their grievances.

Another example of the use of violence and intimidation comes in a petition presented to Edward IV in 1467 by a former Carlisle MP, the elderly Thomas Derwent. He had been porter at Pontefract Castle from 9 February 1440, till 1447 or thereabouts.[3] In the petition, Derwent requested the confirmation of his office of king's serjeant and fee of 12d. a day, and recounted his 'long service to the king's family and followers in the wars'. A long-standing servant of 'the right noble and good earl of Salisbury' and a veteran of earlier battles, notably Blore Heath and Ludford. Derwent adds he was 'the said earl of Salisbury at male iournay of Wakefield, and theyr taken prisoner and taken Skypton' when 'he again suffered as he had after Ludford'. Skipton was the stronghold of another notoriously violent Lancastrian, John, Lord Clifford. Unlike his master, he was ransomed for £20, a heavy sum for a man of his modest rank, but his troubles were not over. Having raised the ransom, whilst travelling north to his home in Carlisle he was captured by another leading Lancastrian, Humphrey Dacre, and taken to the Dacre castle of Kirkoswald (near Penrith). Dacre, younger brother to Ranaluf sometime MP for Cumbria, grandson to the 1st earl of Westmoreland, reacted unfavourably to the discovery in his captive's possession of a pedigree justifying the Yorkist title to the throne. Fortunately for Derwent, however, Dacre did not make good his threats to kill him and contented himself with depriving him of his remaining £22.[4] Dacre married Mable Parr, daughter of Sir Thomas Parr whom we mentioned earlier.

We find again in the Court of Chancery another case of violence towards prisoners. Edward Routhe, clerk, brother and administrator of John Routhe, deceased, quitclaimed against John Redsham for mistreatment, goods and ransom exacted from complainant after the Battle of Wakefield. After the battle his legal process tells us he was made a prisoner and taken to Hull – in the custody of John, Lord Clifford no doubt – having fought for 'the most famous prince, the duke of York' in the retinue of the earl of Salisbury. He reports that his lands were broken into, cattle and other goods removed and family abused by Redsham and other servants of the earl of Northumberland.[5]

A similar story emerges from another case taken to Chancery in a claim made by John Barowe, brother of Richard Barowe, servant to Thomas Neville. Sir Thomas Neville (c. 1429–60) was the second son of the earl of Salisbury. Richard Barowe, we are told by his brother, fought with the retinue of Sir Thomas Neville at Wakefield. He tells us Sir Thomas was killed, after which he was 'made prisoner at the field of Wakefield.' He goes onto recount he was ransomed – *'finance'* – with goods and other money being extorted whilst held captive by a squire 'sometime servant with the Earl of Northumberland.' Northumberland's servants were charged with committing trespass and 'breaking and entry' in forcible removing livestock and other possessions to provision the queen's army.[6]

Similar details emerge in a court case presented by John Romney. He tells us he 'fought under Lord Cromwell at Northampton, Wakefield, St Albans' and in the wake of the battle was taken prisoner and ransomed. In the case he brought, however, he was acting for another member of the retinue, whose lands in London had been attained by the vicar of Croydon, following his death at Wakefield. The document presented to George Neville as Chancellor is damaged and extremely difficult to read.[7] Romney was in the retinue of Sir Humphrey Bourchier, was heir to Ralph Cromwell, 4th Baron Cromwell (1393–1456) the progenitor of the crisis over Wressle as we discussed earlier. Cromwell had married, before 1433, Margaret, daughter of John, Baron Deyncourt. She was 17 years of age at her marriage, and died on 15 September 1454, leaving no issue. The barony on Cromwell's death fell into abeyance between his two nieces, daughters of his only sister Maud, who was second wife of Sir Richard Stanhope (d. 1436) of Rampston. The elder was Maud, who married Robert, Baron Willoughby de Eresby, and died on 30 August 1497; the younger, Joan, married, firstly, Sir Humphrey Bourchier (son of Henry Bourchier, first Earl of Essex), who was summoned to Parliament from 1461 to 1471 as Lord Cromwell or Lord Bourchier de Cromwell. His brother Sir Edward Bourchier was killed at Wakefield, for no other reason than he was Duke Richard's nephew.[8] Somehow, Sir Humphrey, it seems, escaped being made prisoner.[9] Rather than a battle, the Yorkist elite and leaders were rounded up and some killed. Fighting men lived to fight another day.

What these cases we mentioned show, is that extreme acts of violence were meted out by the earl of Northumberland and his retinue to captives taken at Wakefield. Furthermore, the court cases evidence that the earl of Northumberland, as well as Clifford, sought to extract retribution against Yorkists and plundered the lands of Yorkists to provision the army. Moreover, these cases confirm the presence of retinues headed by Clifford and Northumberland. We have no evidence from court cases or the Manor of Wakefield to place Exeter, Devon or any other leading Lancastrians at Wakefield. Reasonably we conclude, they were not present.

At the First Battle of St Albans and Northampton, the Yorkists exterminated their enemies: sham trials and judicial murder were the standard operating procedures of the duke of York, Warwick and Salisbury. Wakefield marked a significant turning point in the code of chivalry: at subsequent actions, both sides now sought to eliminate their opponents: any leader from the opposing camp that was captured was killed: it ensured *they* would never fight again. This elimination of rivals made the outcome of battles more decisive, but sowed further bitterness and desire for revenge. The Lancastrians learned the lessons taught them by the duke of York and deployed them to devastating effect at Wakefield and the second St Albans.[10]

Confirming the reference to systematic destruction of the duke's property mentioned by the steward of the manor, we know from legal documents presented to the Court of King's Bench by Thomas Colt in February 1462 that Roger Thorpe, Nicholas Rigby and other servants of the earl of Northumberland had plundered from lands of the duke of York goods worth £5,000, removed hard cash to the value of £1,000, and valuable war horses' worth £200. The case continues:

> Thomas Colt, gentleman, makes complaint against Roger Thorpe . . . having gathered to him many malefactors and disturbers of the said late king's peace, unknown to the same Thomas, to the number of 20,000 persons, equipped in manner of war, that is to say, with jacks, sallets, corslets, brigandines and doublets of defence, who lay in wait to kill and murder the same Thomas at Wakefield in the county of York, and then and there assaulted the same Thomas, and beat, wounded and maltreated him, so that his life was despaired of, and inflicted other enormities on him, to the damage of £2,000 to the same Thomas, and contrary to the late lord king's peace etc.

Colt claimed he was made prisoner and was subsequently beaten by Roger Thorpe 'and wounded him with intent to murder him by striking off his head'.[11] The malefactors are no doubt the Lancastrian forces. Roger Thorpe was the son of Thomas Thorpe we mentioned earlier, and clearly harboured a grudge against York. We can be certain that Thorpe was of a very violent tendency as he is mentioned in another contemporary source. In this document he is described as 'of London, esquire' and was among those appealed by Alice, dowager countess of Salisbury, as accessories to her husband's murder following the battle.[12] By the time of his death on 22 August 1467, Colt had become one of the most important and best-rewarded royal servants of gentry rank by the new king Edward IV. William Plumpton was charged in March 1462 for the theft of livestock worth a massive £560 from Middleham and elsewhere.[13] This later no doubt refers to the plundering of the Neville estates before the Battle of Towton to provision the Lancastrian army. After their victory at Wakefield, Plumpton joined Margaret on her march south and according to a later indictment, on 8 February 1461 at Stamford Plumpton plundered the property of two local merchants. No doubt he was also at the Second Battle of St Albans nine days later and returned north with the Lancastrian army after their failure to gain entry into London.[14]

As Jane Dawson noted in 1997, not all the prisoners were killed: of those who lived, she notes Sir John Saville, the steward of the manor and former Constable of Sandal, as well as the receiver of the graveship of Sandal, John Woodruff/Woderove. Sometime before the Second Battle of St Albans, the prisoners from Wakefield and that battle were taken to York.[15] Quite when or how they were captured we cannot say. We do know, Sandal was occupied by the Lancastrians, so they were presumably taken when the castle fell. How this occurred we do not know. Whilst in Wakefield, they were guarded by men from Lord Clifford's retinue.[16] Jane Dawson evidences these men's capture this with a surviving deed of enfeoffment dated 29 March 1461 and witnessed by John Neville (the Marquis of Montague), Sir John Saville and John Woodruff.[17] John Neville had been captured after the Second Battle of St. Albans and held prisoner in York until his release on 30 March. For all three men to witness the deed the conclusion must be that as Neville was in York, so too were Saville and Woodruff. Others mentioned in this deed were tenants in the Wakefield area. Two days after the ascendancy of Edward IV, Sir John Saville retained his offices in the Duchy of York and was appointed Sheriff of Yorkshire immediately after. To be selected and confirmed in these offices it is evident that Saville enjoyed crown favour and retained the trust of the king.[18] Sir James Strangeways (1410–1516) and Sir Thomas Pickering are named as prisoners in a letter to John Paston of 23 January 1461 Pastons. We cannot prove this.

We know of no Lancastrians killed or wounded specifically at Wakefield. A possible casualty was John Catterall. His son Alan, in the first year of the reign of Henry VII, sought to overturn the Act of Attainder against his father who had been 'killed in the service of Henry VI', but does not say which battle. Catterall senior had suffered attainder for participation in the Battle of Wakefield and had been charged with the murder of the earl of Salisbury: this rather supposes he was not killed. A writ of *diem clausit extremum* was issued on 17 October 1464, which implies he died somewhat after Wakefield or Towton. The writ was issued with inquisitions being undertaken by the escheator of Yorkshire concerning property forfeited under the November 1461 Act of Attainder. The inquisitions were held by the escheator were an essential process in establishing who owned what before the forfeited land could be transferred to new ownership. No escheator was appointed until November 1463, and records of the Duchy of Lancaster show that the bailiffs in the West Riding had been unable to collect rents due to disturbances in the county.[19] Catterall's lands were handed to Sir John Pilkington, of Snapethorpe, Wakefield. John Catterall's father-in-law, William Flemming of Wath upon Dearne, who made his will in September 1460, and was proved 7 May 1461 may have been killed at Wakefield or, indeed, Towton. Catterall himself was something of a trouble maker, he had been ordered to be arrested in August for spreading discord between the magnates: a time when the Nevilles held power.[20] We stress that neither man's deaths can be linked directly to Wakefield which makes for a distinctly one-sided encounter.

As we noted, not all the prisoners were killed, and not all of York's retinue was made a prisoner. Sir John Conyers, who brought the case of Dame Bold we mentioned earlier, was certainly at Wakefield, but lived to tell the tale.[21] He was married to Alice Neville. Rewarded for his fidelity to the house of Neville, he was a retainer of the Earl of Salisbury in the 1450s. He had fought at the battles of Blore Heath and Ludford in 1459, and suffered attainder and confiscation of his estates by the temporarily victorious Lancastrians in consequence. He transferred his allegiance to Salisbury's son Warwick after his execution and perhaps fought at Towton in March 1461, and certainly entered Edward IV's service.

That we can't confirm any men killed in combat does reinforce the suggestion made by Thomas Colt that we are dealing with an ambush that rapidly overwhelmed the Yorkists within minutes. What happens at Wakefield is unusual, and perhaps exceptional in the course of the Wars of the Roses. It is not a battle in any traditional sense, of that we are sure.

# APPENDIX 4: THE EARL OF RUTLAND

Legend implies the earl of Rutland was killed in flight heading across Chantry Bridge. Seeking sanctuary in the chantry on the bridge, he was dragged to his death in a scene made famous by Shakespeare. Pseudo-William of Worcester reports:

> On December 29 at Wakefield when the Duke of York's men were roaming through the countryside for victuals, a horrible battle took place between them and the Duke of Somerset, Earl of Northumberland and Lord Neville with a great army; and there were killed in the field the Duke of York, Thomas Neville, son of the Earl of Salisbury, Thomas Haryngtone, Thomas Parre, Edward Boucher and many other knights, squires and common soldiers to the number of 2000. After the battle Lord de Clyfforde slew Lord Edmund, the Earl of Rutland, son of the Duke of York, as he was fleeing on the bridge at Wakefield.[1]

Other than Hall writing in the 1540s – and he cannot have met any survivors of the battle – this is the only source to mention this event. The source is clearly some fact and some fiction: again, it is written from gossip and hearsay, 10 or even 20 years later. The fact that the gossip the writer wrote down is partly wrong is easily demonstrated by the fact that Thomas Parre was not killed at Wakefield, but died four years after the battle.[2] This error is repeated by other writers. We know the Yorkist army was not out foraging either: if they had been the records of the Manor of Wakefield would record this, and they do not. One of the earliest reports of Rutland's death written in 1461, the *Chronicle from Rollo to Edward IV* reports Rutland was killed in the fighting.[3] The *Brut Chronicle* tells us that Rutland fell in battle along with Sir Thomas Neville and others.[4]

Other contemporary sources say Rutland was captured, put to death and then beheaded: Andriaan de But believed this to be the case,[5] as did Jacques du Clercq secretary to the duke of Burgundy, writing before his death in October 1467.[6] A third writer comments:

> On the first day of January, in this year, the battle took place, which was very bloody, and hardly contested; but this time, fortune turned against the duke, who was made prisoner, together with his second son and the earl of Salisbury. Shortly after, the queen had them beheaded.[7]

A fourth, this time English, writer contends:

> the forsaid duc of Yorke and therle of Rutland his sonne and therle of Salisbury were afrosaide takern at Wakefelde and then beheded. And the twoo lorids of Hartingtonys the older and the Yonge slayne in batell the same day.[8]

For this writer, all three were made prisoners and then executed. With such contrasting statements made by contemporary writers, it is impossible to draw a conclusion. That Rutland is not even mentioned in the two eyewitness accounts rather implies he was not with his father, and likely therefore to have been with Salisbury. We cannot place Rutland, or Salisbury at Wakefield. We simply do not know where these men were between leaving London, and the latter being killed in Pontefract. We cannot say where Rutland died, but we can be certain it was not on Chantry Bridge.

Myth implies John, Lord Clifford killed Rutland. Yes, extremely likely, but at Pontefract with his father and uncle. If Rutland's death had been more macabre than the others, the 'official line' would have made much of this. Therefore, we can be sure Rutland's death was no more tragic than of his father: indeed, the Roll of Parliament does not distinguish Edmund's death as being more shocking than of his immediate family.[9] Written by the Yorkists to present the history they wanted to present, if Clifford had butchered Rutland in the manner popular myth suggests, you can be sure they would have made much of it. Alas, they do not, therefore Rutland's death, was not sensational in the manner many believe it to have been. However, unless other documentation written within days of the battle emerges in archives, that places other Lancastrians in Wakefield, Clifford is guilty as charged. Yet, history is never so simple.

The 'official line' propagated by the Roll of Parliament has Edmund, like his father and uncle, killed and then his dead body mutilated. My feeling is he, like Salisbury, was butchered at Pontefract in the Dominican Priory. Nor was Rutland alone in being killed before the age of 20. William Bonville, Lord Harrington, was 18 years old when he was killed alongside his father, leaving his widow Katheryn Nevill, to whom he had been married for two years, and his six-month-old daughter, Cecily. Bonville's death is never transmuted into child killing: clearly Rutland's transfiguration into a 'holy innocent' was pure propaganda by Pseudo-William of Worcester. It is supremely unlikely Rutland and his tutor were spectators to the battle as Hall describes. Yet, Shakespeare's account has been the most influential account of the Battle of Wakefield ever written, and has prejudicially affected all later narratives of the battle.

# APPENDIX 5: THE EARL
# OF SALISBURY

The chronicle evidence implies that Salisbury was captured on the night of the battle, i.e. the night of 30 December, and taken to Pontefract: how and where he was captured is not known. Nor do we know he was taken by men in the service of his former ally, Andrew Trollop.[1]

The *English Chronicle* records, 'The Earl of Salisbury was taken alive, and led by the said Duke of Somerset to the castle of Pomfret, and for a great sum of money that he should have paid for grant of his life' but before he could be ransomed, he was killed by townsfolk.[2] This is exceptionally unlikely: Pontefract was one of the strongest castles in the country, and it is inconceivable the townsfolk simply walked in and killed the earl. However, the story has some truth about it as a Pontefract man, John Smith, was charged with attempted murder of the earl in 1454.[3] Men from Pontefract were also charged with the murder of the earl by his widow Alice. It seems reasonable to support the suggestion made by Thomas Basin that 'the duke of York and the father of the count of Warwick, who were captured in the conflict and immediately beheaded'.[4] Salisbury's fate is also recorded by Pseudo-William of Worcester:

> beheaded at Pontefract by the Bastard of Exeter . . . where at the same time the bodies of York, Rutland and others of note who fell in the battle, we decapitated, and their heads affixed in various parts of York, whilst a paper crown was placed in derision on the head of the Duke of York.[5]

The *Brut Chronicle* confirms it was not just Salisbury who was executed after the battle:

> John Harrow of London, Capitayn of Ye foot-men & Hanson of Hull, which were brought to Pountfret & after Per beheded, & per hedes sent to York, & per sett upon ye statkes &c.[6]

Richard Anson, MP for Hull, was killed two days earlier and not at Pontefract.[7] Confirming the date of execution as 31 December, Antonio de la Torre merely says Salisbury was killed 'on the last day of December near a castle called Pontefract'.[8] He also confirms York, Salisbury and Rutland were all killed side by side in Pontefract in what is surely one of the earliest accounts of the event dating to 9 January 1461. A Calais newssheet[9] reports (my translation):

> the count of York died their along with Roteland his son, the count of Salsebery and messire Thomas his son with several other noble men of their company. Which battle was fought in front of the town of Wacquefild on the penultimate day of December, in the year one thousand four hundred and sixty. Of which the queen Margueritte was very joyful, so were all those who held her party: and on the other hand were the counts of La Marche and Warrewic, who had lost their fathers there, but for the time being could not amend it.[10]

The truth probably is that Salisbury, his son, and retinue were amongst prisoners in the custody of Lord Clifford.[11] Where and when they were captured is not known. That Sandal was ransacked and set on fire may hint that the earl was lodged in the castle: if so, how did Clifford gain entry? That Clifford would have passed through Pontefract on his way to Hull, is a given.[12] We know the earl was killed at Pontefract from a legal case brought by his widow, Alice. To this end the duchess sued a common-law appeal of murder against forty-eight Lancastrians she believed guilty. The instigators of the crime had planned and 'deliberately lain in wait to murder her husband at Pontefract in County York' by 'traitorously striking off his head'. The duchess demanded justice to be done against those still alive.[13] Such acts of extreme violence were 'standing operating procedure' for the earl of Northumberland.

# APPENDIX 6: SOURCE COMMENTARY ON THE BATTLE OF WAKEFIELD

In order to understand the changing perception of the Battle of Wakefield before and after the Readeption, we need to go back to our source material. The first account is dated 9 January 1461:

> Some of the lords of the queen's party, rendered desperate by the victory of the lords here and especially the Earl of Warwick, assembled a force in the northern parts, eighty miles from London, to come and attack their opponents here who are with the king, and get back the king into power, as they had him before. Accordingly, the duke of York with two of his sons, and Warwick's father, the Earl of Salisbury, went out to meet them. And it came to pass, that although they were three times stronger, yet from lack of discipline because they allowed a large part of their force to go pillaging and searching for victuals, their adversaries who are desperate, attacked the duke and his followers. Ultimately, they routed them, slaying the duke and his younger son, the Earl of Rutland, Warwick's father and many others. This news caused great alarm in these parts, although it seems Warwick was not there . . . this engagement took place on the last day of December near a castle called Pontefract.

Found in BnF MS Italian 2132, we note Prospero de Camulio, Milanese Ambassador to the French Court, writes to the Secretary of the Duke of Milan from Ghent on 1 February:

> The news from England is that the Queen has recently fought with the Duke of York and taken York, which is a fine city. The king and the Earl of Warwick thought that the forces of the duke and of the earl's father and brothers were sufficiently strong, but they were defeated, and they were slain the duke, his son, the Earl of Warwick's father and his two sons, and 12,000 to 16,000 men. Many others, were slain in other battles

subsequently; the numbers it is said to amount to thousands. When the king heard this, he was much moved, although the Duke of York seems rather to have been slain out of hatred for having claimed the kingdom more than anything else. It was decided that the Earl of Warwick should go avenge the affront and he has gone with 60,000 combatants, some say more. Things remain in the balance, and so the dauphin considers that I must not at present think of going to do anything in England, and just same with the Burgundians.

He implies that the duke of York was drawn into a battle, which provided the Lancastrians with the opportunity to defeat the duke that they were looking for, which is ostensibly the narration given by the *Chronicle from Rollo to Edward*.

The earliest and fullest account we have is by Jacques du Clercq who was secretary to the duke of Burgundy (1448–67). It was written before his death in October 1467 (age 43 years) as part of a history of Burgundy. The duke of Burgundy was an ally of the duke of York. Indeed, in winter 1460 the young dukes of Clarence and Gloucester were in his keeping. Philip sent troops to Edward's aid, fighting at Towton. What gives this account a degree of reliability is that Edward and Warwick must have transmitted news to Philip in Dijon: this would have almost certainly included news about the death of the duke of York. Our writer, at the heart of Philip's court, we suspect, is merely reporting what was gossip and news in the court in spring 1461, the translation is my own from BnF MS 5054 reserve:

The Queen of England, who was displeased and angry at the agreement that her husband had made to the Duke of York, to the detriment of her son Edward, assembled as many men-at-arms as she could; and with her was the duke of Somerset and several other dukes and counts; and came before the said town of the duke of York [Wakefield]; and ill was the day of battle assigned between the people of the king and the duke of York; and the day, which was approximately the first day of the year above said, the two parties appeared; and there was with the said Duke of York, his second son, the earl of Rutland, the earl of Salisbury, and several other lords, and on the side of the king were the lords above named and a captain named Treslot, and there was a big battle; but the hand of fate was against the said Duke of York; for he was discomfited and suffered many losses; the said Duke of York, his second son, and the earl of Salisbury, Lord Neville, Lord Haringeois [William Bonville], Lord Thomas de Hermant [Sir Thomas Harrington] and Lord Jehan Harintoy [John Harrington] all died there; but the Duke of York and the earl of Rutland his second son, and the earl of Salisbury were made prisoners;

and that very day all three were beheaded and killed. And because the said Duke of York had wanted to be king of England, after the said duke was beheaded, on the advice of the said captain Adrien Treslot, a paper crown was placed on his head in derision and their heads were placed on lances on the gates of the said city of York.

Published sometime before 1467, this account is presumably, like du Clercq's account of Towton, based on a newssheet issued by Warwick via Calais. Robert Bale, working at the same time as Du Clercq, mentions Trollop aka Treslot. A version of the Monstrelet Continuator dated 29 May 1471 in the Bibliothèque Nationales de France which was present to Edward IV writes about Wakefield as follows:

On the first day of January of this year then commenced a battle which was fought with great ferocity, so deadly it was a horror of murder of one party against the other. However, discomfort fell on the duke of York and this prince, his second son and the conte of Salisbury were decapitated and his head was placed on lance surmounted with a paper crown as he had wanted to be king.

This document can be found at BnF MS Fr 20354 folio 117. The same story is also found in BnF 2679 folio 407 verso which is another edition of Monstrelet which concludes in 1467. This text is ostensibly the same as the Tanner MS. Gregroy BL SM Edgerton 1995, the Short English Chronicle, and the chronicle of John Benet are all variations of the du Clercq text. Benet uniquely before 1490 mentions Sandal Castle which is not mentioned in any other account till Virgil. Despite this, the earliest accounts written before 1470 – as the final edition of BnF 20534 appeared in May 1471, we assume its contents existed before the final production volume appeared, presumably in 1470 – fail to describe where the battle was, cannot agree on the date, or the names of the dead or participants.

Indeed, the text by Jean de Roye (c.1425–c.1490), who was chamberlain and counsellor to Louis XI and secretary to the duke Jean II of Bourbon from 1465, is rather confused. His chronicle begins with the Battle of Northampton, copied from the work of Jean Chartier (potentially) and his account of Wakefield is clearly based on the earlier du Clercq narrative, the translation being my own from BnF MS Fr 5062 folio 2-3:

At this time, in the said kingdom of England there once again happened the same discomfiture as before dictated and thus was made by the said earl of Warwyk, the duke of Sommerset, cousin of the said king Henry of England, accompanied by several other young lords, relatives and heirs of the other princes and lords who had been killed defending the throne of the said King Henry of Lancaster, formed large masses of men-at-arms and came to hold the country against the said Duke of York. And so, they came to find him and his company, and in a battle, all of which were killed. And in this field, called the field of Saint-Albons, the said Duke of York was killed; and, after he was killed, they chopped off his head, which they put at the end of a spear; and around his head they placed a crown of fur in the form of a royal crown, in mockery of the fact that he wanted to make himself king of the said kingdom. And with them died in this field six barons, knights, squires and people of name of the said kingdom and a large number of other men of war, who were estimated from 60 to 100,000.

Jean du Roye is confused over Wakefield and St Albans. Presumably this is from the same broad period of production as du Clercq, i.e. before 1467. Again, David, bishop of Utrecht, in the Kattendijke chronicle, confused Wakefield and Saint Albans:

In the twelfth month before the end of the Year 1460 there was a fortification in England which was fought over at Saint Albans, where the King and the Duke of Somerset with their supporters maintained the upper hand against the duke of York and the count of Warwick, where many people fell on both sides. But the duke of York's father was spared along with many lords. Then afterwards in an act of severe revenge their heads were hacked off.

The repeated use of the same two or three newssheets by French writers demonstrates news was transmitted rapidly into Europe in the wake of the battle. This should not be surprising as Warwick wrote his 'Apology' in New Year 1461 to exonerate himself to his allies of the defeat at Wakefield and the death of the duke of York.

The French sources are almost universal in stating the duke was captured alive and then beheaded after death. The death of the duke is ascribed to Andrew Trollop who had brought about the duke's downfall at Ludford Bridge. The sources are transmitting facts as the writers believed them to be. They may not necessarily be true in themselves.

Drawing a conclusion on historical matter such as the reliability of these sources, is somewhat speculative and perhaps pointless. Indeed, such a conclusion is merely attempting to impose order on something that is inherently and irremediably chaotic – we do not have all the facts at our disposal.

The account in du Clercq, and variations of it, was the most popular of Wakefield, and continued to be so until the 1540s. Both Wavrin and Hall chose to ignore this account. Wavrin when writing his own chronicle chose to use a document in the possession of Louis de Gruuthuse, sometime earl of Winchester. Wavrin, as we said was writing at the time of the Readeption, and met Edward, and his Wydeville in-laws in person in winter 1470–1. Perhaps to flatter his host, and to write more floridly about his patron (Edward), he chose to use a remarkable text about Wakefield:

> Andrew Trollop, who was a very subtle man of war, told the Duke of Somerset that they would not be able to get the Duke of York outside the town without consequent human loss. They therefore prepared 400 of the most courageous men, well indoctrinated for what they had to do – i.e. they were to go into the town and tell the duke that they were coming from Lancashire to rescue him. When the Duke of York, who never suspected such betrayal, saw all those people coming to him, he was so happy that he let them in straight away.
>
> The same night the Duke of York organised for somebody to be on the watch in order to watch for the Duke of Somerset who was in the field and to observe the extent of his power. But at dawn of the day, Andrew Trollop accompanied by other warriors, informed the Duke of York, without introducing themselves, that they were coming to rescue him, which made the duke of joyful that he went outside the town to fight his enemies.
>
> It was then that Andrew Trollop betrayed him, knowing the Duke of Somerset to be nearby, he started to skirmish and the Duke of Somerset who was ready, charged viciously the Duke of York and his allies against him whom Andrew Trollop and his troops turned swiftly and so did the people sent by him the night before to the town.

BnF MS Francais 88 Chronique des guerres advenues en France, en Angleterre et en Bourgogne depuis l'année 1444 jusqu'en 1471 dates to the 1470s as a finished volume, but that does not mean its contents were not written before the finished volume was created. This book was never widely distributed as a popular edition: the edited version by Wavrin was distributed not in the same way or as a popular edition as du Clercq or other Monstrelet Continuations. What it says is unique. The majority of the text is more or less the same as the du Clercq Monstrelet Continuation. Where it differs is in the treatment of English history 1459–61, which may well be Warwick's 'Apology'. This text was used by Wavrin, as he met the document's owner, Louis of Bruges in the first months of 1471. This story given in BnF 88 is ostensibly the same story as the later *English Chronicle 1377-1461* and is repeated by Gregory's Chronicle, the Chronicle of London, or MS Edgerton 1995. Dr Livia Visser Fuchs believes the 'Apology' which includes this story of Wakefield was created in 1461 and passed to Wavrin when Warwick met the former in Calais in 1469: however, the document may have been created in 1469 to support his own political manoeuvring to remove Edward. We cannot be certain when the 'Apology' was created as historians are divided on the date for this document. The 'Apology' itself can also be found in BnF MS Fr 20358, which may be slightly later version of BnF MS Fr 88, considered a draft copy of Wavrin's work found at BnF MS Fr 84.

BnF MS Francais 15491 folio 87 is closely related to this text, but has Trollop's men wearing the livery of Warwick: 'Andrieu Trolot, qui estoit ung tres soubtil homme de guerre, dist au duc de Sombresset quil scavoit bien que sans grant perte de gens on ne povoit avoir de duc d'Yorc hors de la ville, si triouva manière de toute la nuit faire a ses gens palletos ou estoit le ravestocq, livree au comte de Warewic.' It is also found in BnF MS Fr 84 folio 153 recto, the copy of Wavrin offered to Edward IV: this French edition, as far as we can tell the only complete set of Wavrin's study held in France, was owned by Louis of Bruges. Again, seemingly significant is that Wavrin chose BnF 88 as the basis for his text on Wakefield and not the copy of the Monstrelet Continuator he actually owned which merely says:

> On the first day of January of this year then commenced a battle which was fought with great ferocity, so deadly it was a horror of murder of one party against the other. However, discomfort fell on the duke of York and this prince, his second son and the conte of Salisbury were decapitated and his head was placed on a lance surmounted with a paper crown as he had wanted to be king.

This document, Lille BM E20 folio 147, is identical to BnF Fr 20354 folio 117. Wavrin clearly chose to use the Louis of Bruges' text over earlier texts. He probably did so, to present a more chivalric death for Edward's father.

This statement about Warwick's livery, led some writers to think Warwick was present and escaped after the battle in a little boat BnF MS Francais 20354 Chroniques de Saint-Denis, folio 117 for example, presented to Edward in early 1471. British Library, Harleian MS 4424 offers a text which is an abridged copy of BnF 88, published in Ghent in 1483. Folio 157 also mentions the escape. This story appears in Warwick's 'Apology', placed after Ludford. Adding that they were in his livery was a device to cast aspersions on Warwick's loyalty: once a traitor, always a traitor, clearly a device of the 1470s added to the earlier text.

Clearly the compiler of the source confused Ludford and Wakefield and inexpertly edited the two texts together at this stage. That the events of Ludford, Blore Heath and Wakefield are 'garbled' is not surprising. BL Harl. 4424, folio 157, and BnF Fr 88, folio 138 verso both write confusingly and contradictorily on the events, amalgamating Blore Heath and Ludford and ending with Loveday of 1458. This confusion is partly due to the insertion of Warwick's 'Apology' which ends with a reconciliation between the Yorkists and Henry, allowing Richard, duke of York to be heir. Warwick then distances himself from what happened next, the 'Apology'. We come back to this again. The escape on the boat is garbled from BnF MS 20358 which correctly relates John Dynham in the flight of Warwick and the earl of March after Ludford. In the accounts of the Battles of Blore Heath, Ludlow and Northampton found in BnF MS Fr 15491, folio 90v-91v, the text is clumsily edited into the text in the wrong place chronologically in the text. Clearly the fact that BnF Fr 20358, Nor BL Harley 4424 or BnF Fr. 88 mention these battles may argue that they were either so little known in France, or when they occurred so obscure the compilers simply omitted them. BnF Fr 15491 was put together in a workshop that had access to an abbreviation of the Monstrelet Continuator and to a version of Wavrin's Recueil. The composer was content to rely wholly at first on the Monstrelet abbreviation, but at some point he decided more was needed and started to 'mix' the text with a Recueil version. It is related to BnF Fr 20358, which we assume is earlier than BnF 15491, and come after BnF Fr 88, owned by Louis de Gruuthuse and has unique accounts of Wakefield and the events of Palm Sunday that Wavrin chose to use over the Monstrelet text. Indeed, the BnF MS Fr 88 can be considered a 'third book' of Monstrelet, the second of the continuation, that does not exist in any other copy. Moreover, our chronicle reports the splendour and ceremonies of the court in which Louis of Bruges participated, such as the treaty with Scotland over Berwick, the Pheasant banquet in Lille, the funeral of Philip the Good and the wedding of Charles the Bold with Margaret of York in Bruges. Some final chapters, devoted to the English civil war, concern him even more personally. The defeat of Edward IV and his flight to Holland, his stay in Bruges and then his departure from Zeeland to reconquer England all depict the context in which Louis of Bruges welcomed the deposed king into exile. It is understandable that he was the one who commissioned the manuscript. This volume is also complementary to the Chroniques de Monstrelet in his possession BnF MS Fr 2680, but constituted a separate narrative.

What is important, is that the various French texts as well as the earliest English texts like Benet, all place the battle in or around the town of Wakefield and not at Sandal Castle.

The King's Antiquary, Leland, like Virgil, records popular public perception of the events in the mid to late 1530s, 70 years after the Battle of Wakefield had taken place. Popular perception/public opinion is very different to fact:

> The main points of interest which I noted in Wakefield were these: There is a fine stone bridge of nine arches, under which flows the River Calder. On the east side of this Bridge is an excellent chapel of Our Lady, with a foundation for two chantry priests attached to it. Some claim it was the townspeople who founded this chantry, although it is also attributed to the Dukes of York, since the obtained the licence of mortmain. I also head a report that one of the instigators was a servant either of Edward IV's father or of his brother, the Earl of Rutland. A fearful battle was fought in the fields south of this bridge. When the Duke of York's men turned to fight, either the duke himself, or his son the Earl of Rutland, was killed just up from the bars beyond the bridge leading up the slope to the town of Wakefield, which is built in a very fine position at the top. A cross to commemorate this event has been erected on the spot. The popular version of the story in Wakefield is that the Earl was trying to take refuge in the house of a poor woman, but in fright she shut her door, and immediately the earl was killed. Because of the slaughter of men which occurred in this battle, Lord Clifford was dubbed 'the butcher'.

Leland does report some fact. Firstly, the cross is mentioned in the will of Joan de Thorpe from 1420. Clearly the cross had no relevant to the events of 1460. It stood at the junction of Kirkgate and Warrengate. The Bar or Gate stood where the West Yorkshire History Centre stands in 2025. The area in the Middle Ages to the late eighteenth century was known as the 'softs'. It was bisected by the Chald and Skitterick rivers. In the very wet year of 1460, the area other than the road would have been almost impassable. North of the Bar were tenter grounds for cloth, tanning pits and industrial use, as well as fields as far almost as to the cross. The area had been abandoned since the Black Death was not re-occupied till the 1580s. Leland's conversations with – we assume educated – burgers contain a marked degree of truth. The dukes of York had the right of advowson for the Chantry since 1397. Moreover, it was re-founded on 31 May 1463 by two of York's servants, Thomas Colt and the lawyer Henry Soothill. They appointed William Kyngrave as priest.

When it comes to the Battle of Wakefield, what Leland had read or was told, it seems, was merely a re-telling of the narrative in Davies' *English Chronicle*, which appeared in popular editions in the early sixteenth century. The degree of relationship between the *English Chronicle*, and these texts needs much scholarly attention. One is copied from the other and therefore they are not independent points of correlation as heretofore considered.

The killing of Rutland by Clifford which Leland mentions, and calls 'the butcher' is in part inspired by *The Annales of William of Worcester* from the later 1470s, if not the 1480s. Copies of the Monstrelet Continuator were made and circulated in England by 1483. Clearly it seems, the persons Leland spoke to were retelling the stories they had been told by parents or grandparents, or indeed they may have indeed read, the various texts which became embedded in folk memory. That local tradition placed the battle in Wakefield – some remembrance of York being in the town probably did exist – and not Sandal is hugely important. All bar Benet, English and continental sources prior to Virgil are all consistent in placing the battle in Wakefield and not Sandal Castle.

Ironically, the fields that Leland mention were in 1460 known as 'Le Grete Old Field' was in the Graveship of Sandal. The field was ditched, paled and hedged around. We only find reference to Sandal Castle once the battle is lodged in distant memory. An Italian pseudo-historian, Polydore Virgil, ordained a priest in 1496, we think had access to oral histories from those who had been part of the court of Edward IV, Richard III and Henry VII: his work is at its most valuable for the period after 1485, and its value for the years 1461–85 lies in its presentation of popular opinion 50 years after the events he writes about took place. He mentions 'a castle adjoyning, which towne is called Wakefielde'. From here it becomes the key location for Hall. The battle of Wakefield could easily be used as propaganda to 'prop up' the ailing regime of Henry VIII. His unpopular marriage to Anne Boleyn, the break with the Papacy and consequential religious changes (the Pilgrimage of Grace of 1536–7 being in direct response, centred in Pontefract), the enclosure of common land sparking rioting in 1535, all marked a rising tide of tension in Henry's reign, as he increasingly became a despotic tyrant. Indeed, the abortive Wakefield Plot of March 1541 against Henry VIII was followed by a massive – and armed – royal progress to the North that summer, although historians have tended to see the progress as being more concerned with a projected meeting between Henry and James V of Scotland at York than pacifying the North. Thus, in the aftermath of these events, we see print culture promoting the

Tudor – and therefore Lancastrian – side of history, so that reminding the country as a whole of the fate of those who opposed the Crown was 'no bad thing' in propping up Henry. Accordingly, accounts after 1485 may be more fiction than fact. The story by Edward Hall published in 1548, after his death, is fiction. No man called David Hall existed in the retinue of the duke of York, yet it is the most believed version of the battle. It has no basis in fact. Sandal Castle had nothing do with the battle. Yet the 'man in the street' of Wakefield in 2025 will tell you the battle of Wakefield was at Sandal Castle. In both Leland's time and our own, False Memory is at work.

# NOTES

## Introduction

1 P.A. Johnson, *Duke Richard of York 1411-1460*, Oxford: The Clarendon Press, 1988.

2 Matthew Lewis, *Richard Duke of York: King by Right*, Stroud: Amberley, 2017.

3 For an example of such rhetoric see https://awhistory.co.uk/files/ module_document_pdfs/king_edward_iv_-_traitor_war_criminal_ murderer_and_thief_-_fact_sheet.pdf

4 Livia Visser-Fuchs, *History as Pastime: Jean de Wavrin and His Collection of Chronicles of England*, Donnington: Shaun Tyas, 2018.

5 Anthony James Pollard, 'Introduction' in Anthony Pollard (ed.), *Problems in Focus: The Wars of the Roses*, London: Macmillan, 1995, pp. 1–19, p. 2.

6 Paul Fussell, *The Great War and Modern Memory*, Oxford: Oxford University Press, 1975, p. 311.

7 John Coates, *The Hour Between Dog and Wolf*, London: Fourth Estate, 2012.

8 Aron Guverich, 'The French Historical Revolution: The Annales School', in Hodder et al., *Interpreting Archaeology*, London and New York: Routledge, 1995, pp. 158–61. This short paper offers a good introduction to the notion and concept of the Annales school for those unfamiliar with its theory of history.

## Chapter 1: Beginnings

1 D.C. Coleman, *The Economy of England 1450-1750*, Oxford: Oxford University Press, 1977, pp. 48–50.

2 Anthony Steel, 'The Financial Background of the Wars of the Roses', *History*, Vol. 40, no. 138/139 (1955), pp. 18–30.

3 John Watts, *Henry VI and the Politics of Kingship*, Cambridge: Cambridge University Press, 1996, pp. 363–6.

4 Carpenter's views echo her former student John Watts as well as Quentin Skinner. Professor Michael Hicks, Ralph A. Griffiths and

Bertram P. Wolffe, however, take the view that Henry VI was an active monarch before 1453, very much involved in government; moreover, the bad decisions were Henry's alone and no one else's. This book is not the place to discuss Henry and the divergent historiography of the man. In following Watts and Carpenter, I open myself up to harsh criticism from those who support the conventional view of Henry, most latterly expounded by Hicks. Moreover, supporting the Hickian judgement on Henry would likewise leave me open to critique of bias. In either paradigm, depending on the reader's bias, I can be judged of fitting the evidence to a pre-existing hypothesis. Yet, it will be my treatment of Somerset and York that will draw the ire of Ricardians: daring to look behind Yorkist propaganda, suggesting the Yorkists had no right to rule, had no right to instigate a revolution, and moreover Somerset, that Yorkist nemesis, is more sinned against than sinning. Wherever history becomes devolved in such a manner, where a man dead over 500 years can be the object of 'love', we have progressed from the study of history to the study of psychology, opinion, and wishful thinking.

5   Christine Carpenter, *The Wars of the Roses: Politics and the Constitution in England, c.1437–1509*, Cambridge: Cambridge University Press, 1997, p. 93. See also ibid., pp. 115 and 128.

6   David Grummitt, *A Short History of the Wars of the Roses*, London: I B Tauris, 2013.

7   Pollard (1995), p. 56.

8   D. McCulloch and E. D. Jones, 'Lancastrian Politics, the French War, and the Rise of the Popular Element', *Speculum*, Vol. 58, no. 1 (1983), pp. 95–138.

9   This was the title for an exhibition at the Musee de l'Armée in Paris concerning the French Wars of Religion; a war dominated by family feuds, religion, politics enabled by a succession of weak kings. Sound familiar?

10   David Grummitt pers comm 07/01/2025.

## Chapter 2: Richard Duke of York: the Man Who Would Be King

1   T.B. Pugh, *Henry V and the Southampton Plot of 1415*, Gloucester: Alan Sutton, 1989, p. 145.

2   Ralph A. Griffiths, *The Reign of Henry VI*, University of California Press, 1981, p. 666.

3   The National Archives [TNA hereafter] E101/410/6, fol. 40.

4   Janes Dawson, *Richard Duke of York and the Politics which led to the Battle of Wakefield* (B.Ed. thesis), Bretton Hall, 1997, p. 12.

5   Dawson, p. 17.

6    TNA E404/56/154.

7    Dawson, p. 18.

8    BnF MS Français 26066, pièce 3832.

9    Ibid. Piece 3838.

10   British Library [BL hereafter], Additional Manuscripts [AD MS hereafter] 11542, ff. 81-81v.

11   TNA E404/56/155.

12   Ibid., E 403/736/13.

13   Bibliothèque Nationales de France [BnF hereafter] MS Français 26066, Notes, pièces et recueils divers (Quittances). Charles VII, roi de France, pièce 3938.

14   Dawson, p. 25.

15   BnF MS Français 25775. Montres de gens de guerre, pièce 1480.

16   TNA E404/57/130.

17   BnF MS Français 25776. Montres des gens de guerre, folio 1528. See also ibid., folio 1529.

18   TNA E101/54/9.

19   BnF MS Français 26068. Quittance et pièce divers, Charles VII, roi de France no. 4339, dated 3 August.

20   Ibid., folio 4340. Despite water damage, rendering the document partly illegible, it is confirmation by Talbot that one Laurens Philippe of Mantes had served in York's army with his cart and four horses, which had been used to carry boats and *besognes* to *faire le passage de la riviere d'Oise*, for a period of 12 days which ended on 27 July.

21   Ibid., folio 4343 a report of victualing Pontoise dated 5 August 1441. Also Ibid., folio 4344 dated 6 August. Both are in the name of Talbot and not York.

22   Dawson, p. 21.

23   Ibid., pp. 21–2.

24   Carpenter, p. 98.

25   Ibid.

26   BnF MS Français 23189. Recueil de pièces originales, en français et en anglais, plus particulièrement relatives à la Normandie sous la domination anglaise (1410-1448), pièce 17.

27   Dawson, p. 21.

28   Carpenter, p. 99.

29   Ibid. p. 100.

30   BnF MS Français 25776, piece 1531. See also ibid., piece 1532.

31  J.L. Laynesmith, *Cecily Duchess of York*, London: Bloomsbury Academic, 2019, p. 44.

32  Ibid., p. 41.

33  Ibid., p. 45.

34  BL Harley Manuscript 116.

35  Carpenter, p. 101.

36  Laynesmith, p. 41.

37  Ibid., pp. 45–7.

38  BnF MS Français 4054. Recueil de lettres et pièces originales, et de copies de pièces indiquées comme telles dans le dépouillement qui suit, piece 35 escript à Rouen, Avril 1445.

39  Laynesmith, p. 41.

40  Dawson, p. 23.

41  BnF MS Français 4054, pièce 35 escript à Rouen, Avril 1445.

42  BnF MS Français 15537. Recueil de pièces originales relatives principalement aux différends entre Louis XI, alors dauphin, et Charles VII (1420-1500), piece 5 Lettre du duc d'York au roy de France.

43  BnF MS Français 4054, pièce 34, Escrpit de Honnefleu, 21 Septembre 1455.

44  BnF MS Français 26067 Quittances et pièces divers, Charles VII, roi de France, pièce 4134.

45  Archives Nationales de France [AN hereafter], Collection Dom Lenoir, 4, pièce 207.

46  BnF MS Français 26067, pièce 4116.

47  Ibid., pièce 99, Ruchard duc de York à Charles VII, Londres, 23 Décembre 1448.

48  Dawson, pp. 23–4.

49  Carpenter, p. 101.

50  BnF Français 26075, pièce 5486.

51  Archives Communales de Mantes, BB4, folio 107.

52  Laynesmith, p. 49.

53  Dawson, p. 24.

54  TNA E28/76/26.

55  Johnson, p. 65.

56  TNA E28/77.

57  Carpenter, p. 98.

58  TNA E159/220. See also ibid., E202/126.

59  Ibid. E199/50/48. See also ibid., E364/79.

60  AN K68/19 pièces 1-2.

61  AN Collection Dom Lenoir, piece 286.

62  Op cit.

63  Margaret Lucille Kekewich et al. (ed.), *The Politics of Fifteenth-Century England. John Vale's Book*, Stroud: Sutton, 1995, p. 183.

64  Bertram Wolffe, 'The personal rule of Henry VI' in B. Chrimes, C.D, Ross and R.A. Griffiths (eds), *Fifteenth Century England 1399-1509*, Manchester: Manchester University Press. 1972, pp. 29–48, p. 42.

65  Kekewich (1995), pp. 40–2.

## Chapter 3: Chaos and Confusion

1   Bertram Wolffe, *Henry VI*, Yale: Yale University Press, 2001, p. 195.

2   TNA E404/63/11.

3   TNA C81/1546/18.

4   Carpenter, p. 102.

5   Griffiths (1981), p. 496.

6   Ibid. p. 497.

7   TNA CPR 1446-52, p. 43.

8   Johnson, p. 65.

9   Carpenter, p. 97.

10  BnF Français 4054, folio 74, lettre adressée au roi d'Angleterre Henri VI, Fevrier 1447.

11  Davies (1856), p. 88.

12  Ibid., folio 73, lettres du roi d'Angleterre concernant la restitution du Mans et des autres places occupées par les Anglais au pays du Maine 23 octobre 1447.

13  Ibid., E403/765.

14  Bnf Nouvel Acquisition Français 3642, pièce 804.

15  Archives Département de l'Orne. A416. See also Archives Département de la Sarthe H305.

16  BL Add MSS 11542 folio 90.

17  Thomas Basin, *Histoire des règnes de Charles VII et Louis XI*, Paris: J. Renouard, 1855, tome 1, pp. 191–2.

18  Kekewich, pp. 38–9.

19  Dawson, p. 35.

20  BnF Français 26075 Charles VII, roi de France. Notes, pièces et recueils divers (Quittances), pièce 5486.

21   Carpenter, p. 97.

22   BnF Chappée 89, Guerre de Cent ans. Folio 148. Commission, Rouen 12 Mai 1447.

23   BnF Français 4054, pièce 13 Escript à Chierburt, la veille de Marie Magdelaine.

24   Laynesmith, p. 50.

25   Carpenter, p. 102.

26   Johnson, p. 67.

27   Ibid., p. 69.

28   Johnson, pp. 56–66 gives an excellent summary of York's financial dealings, which need not be reproduced here.

29   Ibid., p. 70.

30   Carpenter, p. 102.

## Chapter 4: Somerset's Failure?

1    Archives Département de la Seine Maritime, G2133, 17 Aout 1448.

2    BnF Nouvelles acquisitions françaises, 7629, Charles VII Roy de Franc 1443-1448, folio 410. Quittance, 24 Novembre 1447.

3    Johnson, pp. 70–1.

4    Stevenson, Vol. 2, part ii, p. 702.

5    BnF Français 26077 Charles VII, roi de France. Notes, pièces et recueils divers (Quittances), pièce 5834.

6    BL Add MS 11509, folio 114 verso.

7    Norman Davies, *Paston Letters and Papers of the Fifteenth Century*, 2 volumes, Oxford: Clarendon Press, 1971, Vol. 1, p. 108.

8    BnF Nouvelle Acquisitions Français 7629, pièce 411.

9    BnF Français 4054, pièce 63.

10   TNA E404/64/117.

11   BnF Francais 26076, Charles VII, roi de France. Notes, pièces et recueils divers (Quittances), pièce 5729.

12   Ibid., pièce 5722. See also ibid., pièce 5744.

13   Johnson. pp. 70–1.

14   TNA E404/64/137.

15   BnF Français 4054 folio 82, Adam, Bishop of Chichester, Robert Roos ambassadeurs du roi d'Angleterre, Henri VI, déclarent les treves generalles établies entre leur souverain et le roi de France, du 15 mars 1448 au 1er avril 1450.

16   BL Add MS 11509 folio 37.

17   Ibid., folio 30 verso.

18   Davies, (1971), Vol. 1, p. 104.

19   BnF MS Français 24112, Grand coutumier de Normandie – Miscellanées pièce 97.

20   Op cit, p. 104.

21   BnF Français 4054, pièce 86. Mémoire récapitulant les entreprises faites contre la trêve, sous le gouvernement du duc de Sommerset, en Normandie. 1448.

22   Is this Andrew Trollop?

23   Op cit, pièce 92 instructions données par le roi Charles. 22 Aout 1448.

24   Ibid.

25   Carpenter, p. 103.

26   Basin, Vol.1, p. 194.

27   Cardinal Beaufort died in April 1447: François de Surienne (c. 1398–8 April 1462) who led the attack states the plan was developed in early 1447. This explains Somerset's unwillingness to accept Suffolk's policy of withdrawal, if a 'double game' was being played out around Henry over policy and influence.

28   Dawson, p. 41.

29   Carpenter, p. 105.

30   Davies (1971), Vol. 1, p. 108.

31   Dawson, pp. 38–43.

32   Joseph Marie Bruno Constantin Kervyn de Lettenhove, *Chroniques relatives à l'histoire de la Belgique sous la domination des ducs de Bourgogne*, Bruxelles: F Hayez, 1870, pp. 304–05.

33   Dawson, pp. 38–43.

34   'Henry VI: February 1449', in Parliament Rolls of Medieval England (Woodbridge, 2005) British History Online https://www.british-history.ac.uk/no-series/Parliament-rolls-medieval/february-1449 [accessed 25 March 2024].

35   BnF Française 4045, pièce 93, Henry à Charles, Beverley, 9 Octobre 1448.

36   Watts (1996), p. 364.

37   Michael Hicks, *Warwick the Kingmaker*, Oxford: Blackwell Publishing, 2002, p. 66.

38   BnF Française 4045, pièce 83, Escript à Rouen, ce vendredi derrenier jour de fevrier 1449.

39   Ibid. pièce 84, Escript à Rouen, le IXe jour de mars 1449.

40   Amedée Hellot, *Les Chroniques de Normandie 1223-1453*, Rouen: Chez l'éditeur, 1881, p. 82.

41   Davis (1971), Vol. 1, p. 87.

42   Basin, Vol. 1, p. 192.

43   Archives département de la Seine-Maritime, Echiquier de 1448. Registres Manuel, folio 81. See also Ibid. Registre des appointements, folios 20–21.

44   BL Add MSS 11509 folio 130.

45   Griffiths (1981), p. 684.

46   Carpenter, pp. 107–10.

47   Ibid., p. 112.

## Chapter 5: Defeat

1    Basin, Vol. 1, pp. 338–41.

2    A.J. Pollard, *John and the War in France, 1427-1453*, London, Royal Historical Society, New Jersey, Humanities Press, 1983, p. 64.

3    M.H. Keen and M.J. Daniel, 'English diplomacy and the sack of Fougères in 1449', *History*, 49 (1974), pp. 375–91.

4    Basin, Vol. 1, p. 19.

5    C.D. Taylor, 'Brittany and the French Crown: the Legacy of the English Attack on Fougères (1449)', in J. R. Maddicott and D. M. Palliser (eds), *The Medieval State: Essays Presented to James Campbell*, London and Rio Grande, 2000, pp. 252–3.

6    Ibid., p. 196.

7    BnF Francais 4054 Folio 149 Résumé des violations commises par les Anglais contre la trêve conclue entre Henri VI et Charles VII.

8    Arthur Bourdeaut, 'Gilles de Bretagne entre la France et l'Angleterre', *Mémoires de la Société d'Histoire et d'Archéologie de Bretagne* volume 1 (1920), p. 107.

9    Op cit.

10   Henry VI: February 1449', in Parliament Rolls of Medieval England, (Woodbridge, 2005) British History Online https://www.british-history.ac.uk/no-series/Parliament-rolls-medieval/february-1449 [accessed 25 March 2024].

11   BnF Français 26078, pièce 6035.

12   Ibid., Français 26078, pièce 5997.

13   Ibid., Français 26247 Quittances, et pièces diverses (1267-1783), pièce 206.

14   Archives Communales de Mantes, BB5 folios 21-22.

15   Hicks (2002), p. 68.

16   TNA E101/71/4/923.

17   Ibid., E101/54/11.

18   Ibid., E403/777.

19   Ibid., KB9/109 membrane 25.

20   Ibid., E101/53/33.

21   Ibid., E28/80/15.

22   Ralph Griffiths, 'The Winchester Session of the 1449 Parliament: A Further Comment', *Huntington Library Quarterly*, 42 (1979), pp. 189–91.

23   Stevenson, Vol. 2, p. 256.

24   Basin, Vol. 2, pp. 76–8.

25   BnF Francais 2701 Recueil d'épîtres, discours, harangues et sermons, pièce 92.

26   BnF Francaise 4054 Folio 153 Procès-verbal du conseil tenu par le roi Charles VII touchant les violations commises par les Anglais contre le Treve, 31 Juillet 1449.

27   Archives Communales de Liseux, CC25.

28   Archives Communales de Mantes, BB5, folio 27-28.

29   Ibid., folio 29.

30   Philippe Contamine, 'Chapitre VIII. Les trois temps de la reconquête finale (1449-1453)', in Phillipe Contamine (ed.), *Charles VII. Une vie, une politique*, Perrin, 2017, pp. 293–312.

31   Davies (1971), Vol. 1, p. 105.

32   BnF Francaise 4054 Folio 158 Acte par lequel le roi Charles VII, 29 octobre 1449.

33   Op cit.

34   BnF Francais 18930, Chronique de Rouen, des origines à 1492. Pièces 107.

35   Flenley, p. 134.

36   TNA CPR 1447-1451.

37   Lewis (2017) p. 140.

38   Johnson, pp. 74–5.

39   Laynesmith, pp. 50–1.

40   Op cit, p. 76.

41   Laynesmith, p. 56.

## Chapter 6: Into Opposition

1    Johnson, p. 79.

2    John Beaumont (1409–60) was killed at Northampton and was one of those singled out for bad governance by the Yorkists in 1460. Beaumont not only supported Suffolk's policy but backed him during his impeachment, so it comes as a surprise he was not punished by the mob

in 1450. This was perhaps because he had jumped ship to support the duke of York. Indeed, he joined York on the king's council during the former's first Protectorate (March 1453–January 1454). Switching sides again, his new loyalty was demonstrated when the queen on 28 January 1457 appointed Beaumont to the council of the young Prince of Wales.

3    Carpenter, p. 94.

4    Ibid., p. 114.

5    Michael Hicks, 'From megaphone to microscope. The correspondence of Richard, duke of York with Henry VI in 1450 revisited', *Journal of Medieval History*, Vol. 25, no. 3 (1999), pp. 243–6.

6    F.J. Furnivall, *Hoccleve's Works III: The Regement of Princes*, London, 1876, st. 695, lines 4859-65.

7    Watts (1996), p. 39.

8    Hicks (2010), pp. 66–8.

9    Davies (1971), Vol. 3, p. 83.

10   Carpenter, p. 115.

11   Ibid., p. 80.

12   Hicks (2010) p. 79.

13   Watts (1996) p. 269.

14   Hicks (1999), p 250.

15   Ralph Alan Griffiths, 'Richard, duke of York, and the crisis of Henry VI's household in 1450-1: some further evidence', *Journal of Medieval History*, Vol. 38, no. 2 (2012), pp. 244–56.

16   Carpenter, p. 117.

17   Ibid., p. 119.

18   Griffiths (2012), pp. 244–56.

19   Hicks (1999), pp. 250–1.

20   TNA KB9/271/117.

21   Ibid.

22   Ibid.

23   Hicks (2002), p. 71.

24   Carpenter, pp. 120–1.

25   Grummitt, p. xxxii.

26   Jack Robert Lander, *Government and Community: England, 1450–1509*, Cambridge, MA.: Harvard University Press, 1980, p. 2.

27   Kekewich, pp. 13–14.

28   Hicks (2002), p. 71.

29  Carpenter, pp. 120–1.

30  Johnson, p. 83.

31  Ralph Alan Griffiths, 'Duke Richard of York's intentions in 1450 and the origins of the Wars of the Roses', *Journal of Medieval History*, Vol. 1, no. 2 (1975), pp. 187–209, pp. 204–05.

32  Carpenter, p. 123.

33  Griffiths (1975), p. 204. See also ibid., pp. 205–06.

34  Kekewich, p. 15.

35  Hicks (2002), p. 72.

36  Kekewich, p. 188.

37  Carpenter, p. 123.

## Chapter 7: The Road to Rebellion

1   Davis (1971), Vol. 2, p. 55.

2   TNA KB9/64A/26.

3   Ibid., KB9118/1/16.

4   Ibid., C1/1/66.

5   Stevenson, Vol 2, part ii, pp. 718–22.

6   TNA E404/67/38.

7   Johnson, p. 86.

8   Thomas Courtenay (1414–58).

9   Henry Holland, earl of Exeter (1430–75).

10  William Fitzalan, 9th earl of Arundel, 6th baron Maltravers (1417–87), married Joan Neville, eldest daughter of Richard Neville, 5th earl of Salisbury, and Alice Montagu. He fought at Ludford Bridge in 1459 for the king, but backed his father and brother-in-law Warwick in 1460, fighting at the Second Battle of St Albans.

11  Henry Percy, 2nd earl of Northumberland (1393–1455).

12  Goswin Frhr von der Ropp (ed.), *Hanserecesse Zweite Abtheilung Herausgeben Vereine fur Hansiche Gedichte*, Volume 3, Verlung von Duncker & Humbolt, 1881, p. 507.

13  Griffiths (1981), p. 647.

14  Ropp, pp. 507–08.

15  Ibid., p. 511.

16  Griffiths (1981), p. 565.

17  Flenley, p. 137.

18  Johnson, p. 89.

19  Hicks (2002), p. 73.

20  Hicks (1999), p. 255.

21  Griffiths (1981), p. 648.

22  Hicks (2002), p. 73.

23  Hanham, pp. 30–1.

24  Hicks (2002), p. 74.

25  TNA KB9/270A/42.

26  Johnson, pp. 90–1.

27  TNA SC 8/29/1409.

28  Johnson, pp. 95–100.

29  Carpenter, p. 125.

30  Ibid., p. 124.

31  Watts, p. 278.

32  Johnson, pp. 99–101.

33  Charles Lethbridge Kingsford, *English Historical Literature In The Fifteenth Century*, New York: Burt Franklin, 1913, p. 372.

34  Hanham, p. 32.

35  Carpenter, pp. 126–7.

36  TNA KB27/77 Rex membrane 106 verso.

37  Johnson, p. 103.

38  Ibid., p. 101.

39  TNA SC 8/29/1409.

40  Hanham, p. 32.

41  Carpenter, p. 124.

## Chapter 8: Dartford

1   Carpenter, p. 121.

2   John Stow, *Annales of England to 1603*, p. 649.

3   Kekewich, p. 19.

4   Davies (1971), Vol. 1, pp. 97–8.

5   Lewis (2017), p. 158.

6   Stow, pp. 648–9.

7   Hicks (2010), p. 102.

8   Johnson, p. 109.

9   Kekewich, p. 19.

10  Hicks (2010), pp. 101–03.

11   Johnson, pp. 108–15.

12   Hicks (2010), p. 104.

13   Ibid., p. 103.

14   Johnson, pp. 321–2.

15   Carpenter, p. 128.

16   Johnson, p. 119.

17   Laynesmith, p. 60.

## Chapter 9: The King's Madness

1    Carpenter, pp. 126–8.

2    Sally Fairweather pers comm, 17/06/2024. She is a mental health nurse working on an acute assessment unit with the NHS with over a decade of experience working with in this genre of mental health, assessing capability, treatment etc.

3    TNA CPR 1452-1461, p. 584.

4    TNA KB 27/775 Rex m 90v.

5    Ibid KB 149 membrane 8.

6    Ralph Griffiths, 'Local Rivalries and National Politics: the Percys, the Nevilles and the Duke of Exeter, 1452–55', *King and Country: England and Wales in the Fifteenth Century*, London: Hambledon, 1991, p. 322.

7    Michael Hicks, *English Political Culture in the Fifteenth Century*, London: Routledge, 2002, p. 105. Hereafter Hicks (2002).

8    Ibid., p. 88.

9    Ibid., p. 87.

10   Griffiths (1991) p. 322.

11   TNA KB 149/9/11, membrane 16.

12   TNA KB 27/804, rot. 65. Named from the West Riding gentry were: Thomas Percy, Lord Egremont; Richard Tempest of Bracewell; John Stapleton of Wighill; Sir William Rither; John Caterall; Thomas Clapham of Beamsley; Thomas Frost of Featherstone (his granddaughter Margaret married Josceline, younger brother to Henry Percy 'the magnificent fifth earl of Northumberland'. Choir stalls exist in Wakefield and Sandal churches erected to their memory c.1510); James Hamerton; Stephen Hamerton; John Pudsey; Henry Vavasour of Hazelwood; William Fairfax of Selby; Robert Hopperton; John Leventhorpe of Womersley near Pontefract (Baron John Neville, son of Ralph, earl of Westmoreland held the moated manor at Wood Hall, a mile north of the village. It passed to his daughter Joan, and to her husband Sir William Gascoigne.); and Oliver Pickburn of Doncaster.

13   Hicks (2002), p. 89.

## Chapter 10: The First Protectorate

1    Carpenter, p. 129.

2    Wolffe (2001), p. 275.

3    Watts (1996), p. 302.

4    Ralph Griffiths, 'King's council and the first protectorate', *The English Historical Review*, Volume XCIX, Issue CCCXC, January 1984, pp. 67–82, p. 79.

5    TNA C 49/53/13.

6    Hanham, p. 36.

7    Hicks (2010), p. 106.

8    Carpenter, p. 130.

9    Kekewich, p. 20.

10    Davis, (1971), Vol. 2, pp. 295–9.

11    Griffiths (1981), p. 724.

12    Johnson, p. 134.

13    Carpenter, p. 130.

14    Griffiths (1981), p. 725.

15    BnF Français 5051. Chronique de Charles VII, roi de France, par Jean Chartier.

16    Op cit, p. 721.

17    Hicks (2010), pp. 106–07.

18    Ralph Alan Griffiths, 'Local rivalries and national politics: the Percys, Nevilles, and the Duke of Exeter', *Speculum*, volume 43 (1968), pp. 589–632.

19    Johnson, p. 133.

20    Hicks (2010), p. 107.

21    Carpenter, p. 132.

22    Johnson, pp. 139–40.

23    Ibid., p. 133.

24    Ibid. pp. 133–4.

25    Dawson, p. 45.

26    TNA Calendar of Close Rolls, Hen IV, Vol. II, 1402-1405, p. 432.

27    TNA SC 8/231/11516.

28    TNA CPR 1413-16, p. 65.

29    W.P. Baildon (ed.), *Inquisitions Post Mortem relating to Yorkshire during the Reigns of Henry IV and Henry*, Yorkshire Archaeological Society Record Series, 59, Leeds 1918, pp. 116–17.

30  West Yorkshire Archive Service Leeds: WYL160/205/520 *Compotus Rolls of the lordship of Wakefield and Hatfield, with Sandal Castle, 1270-7.*

31  TNA DL/43/11/17.

32  Ibid., DL 44/151.

33  Johnson, pp. 144–6.

34  TNA KB 149/9/7 The document is badly water-damaged and partly unreadable.

35  Johnson, pp. 142–6.

36  BL Harley MS 50 folio 49 verso states: 'Anno domini m.ccccmo LiiiJo Kalends Novembr commissum bellum grande inter filios comitis Sarum dictur Nevyl dominum Thomas et dominum Johannem milites et dominum Thomas Percy dominum Egremundus at Ricardus Percy filios comitis Northumbirea in argo quaddam ixutra Catton ubu capti sun predicti Thomas et Ricardus frater eius gravitier vulnerate et multi ex parte eorum occusu, sunt inter qous strenus miles Johannes Salvin occubuit. Aliqui eciam alterius oartus vulnerate peruerunt.'

37  Hanham, p. 32.

38  Hicks (2010), p. 115.

39  Carpenter, p. 133.

## Chapter 11: Countdown to Conflict

1   Carpenter, p. 134.

2   Dawson, pp. 46–8.

3   Carpenter, p. 134.

4   James Ross, *Henry VI. A Good, Simple and Innocent Man*, London: Penguin, 2016.

5   Lauren Johnson, *Shadow King. The Life and Death of Henry VI*, London: Head of Zeus, 2019, pp. 555–7.

6   Griffiths (1981), p. 254.

7   K.B. McFarlane, *The Nobility of Later Medieval England*, Oxford: The Clarendon Press, 1973, p. 284.

8   Carpenter, p. 134.

9   Johnson, pp. 154–5.

10  Carpenter, pp. 134–5.

11  'Henry VI: July 1455', in Parliament Rolls of Medieval England (Woodbridge, 2005) British History Online https://www.british-history.ac.uk/no-series/Parliament-rolls-medieval/july-1455 [accessed 24 March 2024].

12  Ibid.

13    Hicks (2010), p. 108.

14    Johnson, pp. 154–5.

15    Anthony James Pollard, *Warwick The Kingmaker: Politics, Power, Fame*, London: Hambledon Continuum, 2007, p. 29.

16    Lewis (2017), p. 247.

17    Ibid., p. 239.

18    Carpenter, p. 135.

19    Hicks (2010), p. 109.

20    Lander (1990), p. 51.

21    Johnson, p. 156.

22    Pollard (2007), p. 29.

23    Lewis (2015), p. 62.

24    Dawson, pp. 51–3.

25    Visser-Fuchs (2018), pp. 381–2.

26    Archivio di Stato di Milano [hereafter ASM] Sforza Correspondence – Foreign Powers [hereafter SCFP] Bishop of Novara to Francesco Sforza, 4 July 1455.

27    Archives de la Cote d'Or, Dijon, B.11942, no. 258 relation Bataille de Saint Albans.

28    ASM SCFP 566 Bishop of Novara to Francesco Sforza, 4 July 1455.

29    TNA MS C 47/37/3/4-11.

30    Ibid.

31    Archives de la Cote d'Or, Dijon, B.11942, no. 258 relation Bataille de Saint Albans.

32    BnF Français 5051.

33    ASM SCFP 566 Bishop of Novara to Francesco Sforza, 4 July 1455.

34    Archives de la Cote d'Or, Dijon, B.11942, no. 258 relation Bataille de Saint Albans.

35    ASM SCFP 566 Bishop of Novara to Francesco Sforza, 4 July 1455.

36    Visser-Fuchs (2018), p. 398.

37    Archives de la Cote d'Or, Dijon, B.11942, no. 258 relation Bataille de Saint Albans.

38    Stowe, pp. 660–1.

39    BnF Français 2860. La Chronique de BERRY.

40    ASM SCFP 566 Bishop of Novara to Francesco Sforza, 4 July 1455.

41    Ibid., p. 661.

42  Archives de la Côte d'Or, Dijon, B.11942, no. 258 relation Bataille de Saint Albans.

43  Carpenter, p. 135.

## Chapter 12: The Second Protectorate

1   Griffiths (1984), p. 81.

2   TNA KB69/16 membrane 88. See also KB 27/780 Rex membrane 40 recto. CPR 1452-61, p. 305.

3   H.C. Maxwell-Lyte, *A history of Dunster and of the families of Mohun & Luttrell, Part I*, St Catherine Press, 1909, pp. 118–29.

4   TNA KB69/16; RP, v. 282-3, 285, 332.

5   Hicks (2010), p. 116.

6   TNA KB 27/782 Rex membrane 165.

7   Carpenter, p. 139.

8   Ibid., p. 137.

9   Dawson, pp. 49–53.

10  Op cit.

11  Hicks (2010), p. 118.

12  Herbert Heaton, *The Yorkshire Woollen and Worsted Industries from the Earliest Times up to the Industrial Revolution*, Oxford: Clarendon Press 1920, p. 47.

13  Ibid. p. 60.

14  Hicks (2010), p. 119.

15  Archives Nationales de France K 69, folio 13.

16  BnF MS Fr 26082 folio 6721.

17  Archives Nationales de France K 69 folios 151-153.

18  TNA, E101/54/16.

19  BnF Français 18441 Dépositions de onze témoins dans le procès Jean II, duc d'Alençon, en 1456.

20  Ibid., folio 58-61.

21  Ibid., folio 42.

22  Ibid., folio 45.

23  Ibid., folio 63.

24  Ibid., folio 48.

25  Ibid., folio 104.

26  Ibid., folio 105.

27  BnF MS Latin 10187, folio 31.

## Chapter 13: York Ascendant

1    Carpenter, p. 140.

2    Hicks (2010), p. 120.

3    BnF Fr 5044 folio 167.

4    Hanham, p. 39.

5    Hicks (2010), p. 120.

6    BnF Français 18441 Dépositions de onze témoins dans le procès Jean II, duc d'Alençon, en 1456, folio 109.

7    Paston Letters, Vol 1, pp. 377–8, 386–7, 392.

8    Carpenter, p. 140.

9    BnF MS Latin 1081 folio 45. See Also Stevenson, Vol. 1, p. 330.

10   Laynesmith, p. 66.

11   Ibid., pp. 66–7.

12   AND Lille, B 2030, folio 175.

13   Hicks (2002), p. 128.

14   TNA KB9/35 membrane 40. See also ibid., membranes 32 and 115.

15   Johnson, p. 176.

16   Carpenter, p. 141.

17   Ibid., pp. 141–2.

18   Layensmith, p. 67.

19   Hicks (2010), p. 133.

20   Ibid., p. 134.

21   Archives Departement du Nord [hereafter ADN] Lille B 2034 folio 162. See Also ibid, folio 193.

22   BnF MS Fr 15537, Recueil de pièces originales relatives principalement aux différends entre Louis XI, alors dauphin, et Charles VII (1420-1500), folio 215-16.

23   ADN Lille, B2026 folio 275 verso.

24   Paston Letters, Vol. 1, p. 416.

25   Hicks (2002), p. 132.

26   Johnson, pp. 180–1.

27   Ibid. p. 181.

28   Ibid. p. 183.

29   Hicks (2010), p. 139.

30   Ibid. p. 140.

31   Hicks (2002), p. 135.

32  Carpenter, p. 143.

33  Johnson, p. 184.

34  TNA Calendar Patent Rolls [hereafter CPR] 1452-61, p. 428.

35  Griffiths (1981), p. 699.

36  W. Wheater, *Knaresburgh and its Rulers*, Leeds, 1907, p. 187.

37  Carpenter, p. 144.

38  ADN Lille B 2030 folio 191 verso.

39  TNA CPR 1452-1461, pp. 436–7.

40  Schofield, Vol. 1, p. 28.

41  ADN Lille, B 2034 folio 183.

42  Hicks (2002), p. 147.

43  TNA, E159/233, Recorda, Easter 35 Hen VI, rots. 12-13.

44  ADN Lille B 2034 folio 183.

45  Ibid., B 2030 folio 210.

46  Dawson, p. 68.

47  BnF MS Fr 15537 Folio 165.

48  Penny Tucker, 'The Earl of Warwick's use of sea-power in the late 1450s', *Southern History* Vol. 42 (2020) pp. 1–20.

49  Rymer's Foedera with Syllabus: 1459, p. 410.

50  Ibid., p. 80.

51  ADN Lille B 2030 folio 235 verso.

52  Ibid., folio 245.

53  Léopold Delisle, *Histoire du chateau et des Sires de Saint-Sauveur-le-Vicomte*, Paris: Valonges, 1863, p. 345.

54  Charles Pinot-Duclos, *Œuvres complètes de Duclos*, Paris: Chez Belin, 1820, Vol. 2, p. 509.

55  Gaston Du Fresne de Beaucourt, *Historie de Charles VIII*, Paris: A Picard, 1891, Vol IV, p. 262.

56  ADN B2030 folio 247, 264, 267. See also TNA C76/140 membrane 3 20 July 1458, C76/140 membrane 8, 20 August 1458.

## Chapter 14: Beginning of the End?

1  ASM SCFP 566 Raffaelo De Negra to Bianca Maria Visconti, Duchess of Milan 24 October 1458.

2  Tucker, p. 20.

3  Hicks (2002), p. 152.

4  Pollard (2007), p. 37.

5    Carpenter, p. 143.

6    Stevenson, Vol. 1, pp. 370–7.

7    BnF MS Fr 27169 (Pièces originales 685) Pièces originales du Cabinet des Titres. Folio 212 verso.

8    Stevenson, Vol. 1, pp. 370–7.

9    Ibid., Vol. 1, p. 358.

10   BnF MS Fr 15537 Recueil de pièces originales relatives principalement aux différends entre Louis XI, alors dauphin, et Charles VII (1420-1500). Folio 215-16.

11   ADN B2034 folio 233. Somerset was directly involved in the peace negotiations and paid handsomely by Philippe on 13 November 1458.

12   Gilles-André de La Roque, *Histoire généalogique de la maison de Harcourt*, Paris: S Cramoisy, 1662, Vol. 3, p. 525. See also BnF MS Fr 4054 Recueil de pièces relatives principalement aux rapports de la France et de la Bourgogne sous les règnes de Charles VII et de Louis folio 170.

13   ADD B2034, folio 53.

14   Trinity College Dubin MS. E. 5. 10.

15   BnF MS Fr 26085 Folio 7193.

16   Stevenson, Vol. 1, p. 358.

17   Dawson, p. 56.

18   Tucker, p. 20.

19   BnF MS Fr 15537 Recueil de pièces originales relatives principalement aux différends entre Louis XI, alors dauphin, et Charles VII (1420-1500). Folio 215-16.

20   Stevenson, Vol. 1, p. 363.

21   BnF MS Fr 26085. Folio 7193.

22   Op cit.

23   BnF MS Fr 4054 Folio 170.

24   BnF MS Fr 28170 Cabinet des Titres, folio 127.

25   BnF MS Fr 1474 Quittances, et pièces originales, folio 2517.

26   BnF MS Fr 26889 Pièces originales du Cabinet des Titres, Dossier Bonnaire, folio 13.

27   BnF MS Fr 15537 Folio 215-16.

28   ADN B 2034 Folios 103 to 123.

29   Kervyn de Lettenhove, *Œuvres de Georges Chastellain*, Brussels: F. Heussner, 1866, Vol. 3, pp. 427–8.

30   BnF MS Fr 5044, Recueil de pièces relatives principalement à la Bourgogne, au Portugal et à l'Allemagne de 1343 à 1575. Folio 34. This

is written by a spy at the court of Burgundy to Charles VII, it implies insincerity on the duke's part.

31  Kervyn de Lettenhove, *Œuvres de Georges Chastellain*, pp. 428–9.

32  BnF MS Fr 17517 Propositions et discours relatifs à la réconciliation du roi Charles VII avec le Dauphin, plus tard Louis XI. (1458-1459), folio 13-18.

33  ADN B 2034 Folio 104 verso.

34  TNA C76/141 membrane 18 dated 10 April 1459.

35  ADN B 2034 Folio 124 verso, 21 Mai 1459. See also ibid., folio 127 verso 22 Mai 1459.

36  BnF MS Fr 26085 Quittances, et pièces diverses. Folio 1277.

37  BnF MS Fr 27169, folio 212.

38  Op cit.

39  Stevenson, Vol. 1, p. 367.

40  1 sheave = 24 arrows.

41  Hicks (2002), p. 156.

42  Dawson, p. 56.

43  Pollard (2007), p. 205 states 1457, Hicks (2002), p. 156 gives 1459.

44  Stevenson, Vol. 1, p. 369.

45  Hicks (2002), p. 156.

46  BnF MS Fr 15491, folio 88v-90v.

47  Tucker, pp. 16–20.

## Chapter 15: Oblivion

1  TNA E 403/819, membrane 4.

2  Hanham, p. 44.

3  Hicks (2002), p. 158.

4  De Beaucourt, Vol. IV, p. 262.

5  Ibid., pp. 275–81.

6  ADN B2034 Folio 133 verso.

7  ADN B2058 Folio 159 verso.

8  CPR 1452-1461, p. 504.

9  On 29 August 1459 six local justices of the peace were appointed to investigate the bailiff and his 'opprobrious words' against Henry VI. Bawtry belonged to Richard Neville, earl of Warwick. KB27/800, Rex membrane. 11d.

10  James Butler, earl of Winchester.

11  Thomas Courtney, earl of Devon.

12   BnF MS Fr 15491, folio 90v-91v.

13   BL MS Harley 543, folio 16.

14   Hicks (2010), pp. 141–2.

15   Jessie Hatch Flemming, *England under the Lancastrians*, London: Longmans, 1921, pp. 138–9.

16   Hicks (2010), pp. 141–2.

17   TNA DL 29/560/8899 membrane 2 verso.

18   Johnson, pp. 186–7.

19   TNA CPR 1452-1461, p. 636.

20   Ibid., p. 451.

21   Ibid., p. 561.

22   Ibid., p. 591.

23   Ibid., p. 571.

24   Ibid., p. 637.

25   Ibid., p. 568.

26   Simon Payling pers comm 17/11/2023.

27   TNA CPR 1452-61, p. 553.

28   Ibid., pp. 531, 538.

29   Ibid., pp. 527, 530, 532, 539.

30   https://www.british-history.ac.uk/no-series/Parliament-rolls-medieval/november-1459 [accessed 29 February 2024].

31   Ibid.

32   The events here appear in some French chronicles for example BnF MS Fr 15491, if. 90v-91v: 'APREZ ce que le duc dYorc eut prins ladministracion du royaulme dAngleterre, aulcuns seigneurs nen furent A fuller pas contentz, et par especial ceulz quy plus prez se account of disoient apartenir audit roy Henry par proximite de the battle sang, telz que le duc dExcestre, les enfans de feu le Heath, and duc de Sombresset, le seigneur de Beaumont et autres, events lesquelz de Beaumont et Excestre firent grant armee; which avec lesquelz se joignirent le comte de Willechier, le preceded comte dEnchier, monseigneur Fidelan, le seigneur de Welles et autres tous lesquelz seigneurs povoient avoir en leur compaignie environ de quinze a seize mille hommes de deffence, tous a cheval. De laquele assamblee les nouvelles venues au duc dYore, il fist prestement assambler ce qui polt de gens pour resister a lentreprinse du duc d'Excestre et ses alyez, donnant la charge et conduite de ses gens feablement aux comtes de Salsbery et de Warewic. Lequel comte de Warewic avoit grant voix du peuple pour ce qui le scavoit entretenir par belles doulces parolles, en soy moustrant famillier et communicatif avec eulz comme soubtil pour parvenir a ses fins, en

leur donnant a entendre que de toute sa puissance il tenroit la main a
laugmentacion et utillite de la chose publicque du royaulme, et que toute
sa vye ne serroit autre, parquoy il acquist la bienvoeillance du peuple
dAngleterre, telement quil estoit le prince duquel ilz faisoient la plus
grant exstime et a qui ilz adjoustoient plus grant foy et credence lequel
lors favorisoit le duc dYorc et sa bende, quy ayant comme dit est la
charge de son armee, adcompaignie de environ vingt chincq chevalliers
et de six a sept mille hommes deffensables, entre lesquelz navoit pas
quarante hommes darmes, vint a deux compaignies a Elouher prez
dune forest entre la ducie d Yorc et la comte Derby. Quant le comte de
Salsbery, le comte de Warewic et leurs gens aparcheurent droit a ung
point de jour larmee d'Excestre et du seigneur de Beaumont derriere
une grant forest haye, dont on ne veoit que les boutz des penons, ilz se
misrent a pie a larriere dune forest qui leur faisoit cloture a ung coste, et
de lautre avoient mis leur charroy et leurs chevaulz lyez les ungz auz
autres, et par derriere eulz avoient fait ung bon trenchis pour sceurete,
et devant eulz avoient fichie leurs peux a la fachon dAngleterre; et
lorsquilz se furent mis en ordonnance de bataille, se vindrent rengier
devant eulz larmee dExcestre tous a cheval, et faisoient bien leur conte
datraper Warewic et avoir sa compaignie a grant marchie, a pou de
traveil et dangier. Lesquelz de Warewic et sa routte, aprez eulz estre
confessez et mis en estat de morir, baiserent tous la terre sur quoy
ilz marchoient, de laquele ilz mengerent, concluant que sur ycelle
ilz morroient et viveroient: et quant lesdis seigneurs dExcestre et de
Beaumont se veyrent si prez de leurs annemis quilz peuvent employer
leur trait ilz se prindrent si onniement a tyrer que cestoit horreur,
et si radement que partout ou il ataindoit satachoit telement quilz
tuerent moult de chevaulz et environ vingt ou vingt deux hommes
de la compaignie dudit Warewic, et de la compaignie dExcestre bien
de chincq a six cens. Pourquoy ledis dExcestre desmarcherent en
recullant environ le trait dun archier, mais pou aprez renchargerent
impetueusement sur ledit de Warewic, a laquele rencharge morurent,
de ceulz dExcestre environ cent, et des Warewic dix. Alors le seigneur
de Beaumont et sa compaignie, considerans que peu a leur honneur
et ancores moins a leur prouffit exploitoient a cheval, se misrent a pie
environ quatre mille hommes qui sen vindrent joindre a la bataille
de Warewic ou ilz combatirent main a main comfortez de leurs gens
a cheval, lesquelz advisans la resistence quon faisoit a leurs gens de
pie prindrent le large des champz, si laisserent ceulz de pie convenir
a leur entreprinse, parquoy ung chevallier de la routte du seigneur de
Beaumont, quy avoit desoubz lui environ cinq cens hommes, se prinst
a cryer avec les siens: 'Warewic, Warewic!' et fraper sur la compaignie
dudit de Beaumont, pourquoy ilz desmarcherent ancores en recullant:
et lors Warewic parchevant ceste chose crya quon marchast avant, ce
qui fut fait, et finablement, furent le comte de Beaumont et les siens
descomfis, si en morut a ceste besongne par le raport des heraulz
environ deux mille hommes et de ceulz de Warewic chincquante six, et
y furent prins ledit comte de Beaumont, le seigneur de Welles et douze

autres chevalliers, et le demourant sen fuyrent; laquele bataille fut ou mois de Septembre trois ou quatre jours avant la feste de Saint Michiel.'

33   TNA CPR 1452-1461, p. 546.

34   Tim Thornton, 'The Battle of Blore Heath: Sources, Historiography and Implications for the Outbreak of Conflict, 1459-60', *Midland History* 49:1 (2024), pp. 33–52.

35   TNA CPR 1452-1461, p. 547.

36   Ibid., p. 546.

37   Ibid., p. 551.

38   Keith Dockray, *Henry VI, Margaret of Anjou and the Wars of the Roses: From Contemporary Letters and Records*, Stroud: Fonthill Media, 2016, p. 98.

39   Carpenter, p. 145.

40   John Watts, 'Ideas, Principles and Politics', in Pollard (ed.) (1995), pp. 110–34, p. 129.

41   Dockray (2016), p. 98.

42   Hicks (2010), p. 144.

43   Stowe, pp. 81–3.

44   Carpenter, p. 154.

45   Ibid., pp. 152–3.

46   Ibid.

47   Ibid., pp. 149–52.

48   Kekewich, pp. 27–8.

49   Anthony James Pollard, *North-Eastern England during the Wars of the Roses: Lay Society, War, and Politics 1450-1500*, Oxford: Clarendon Press, 1990, p. 269. See also Pollard (2007), p. 41.

50   https://www.british-history.ac.uk/no-series/Parliament-rolls-medieval/november-1459 [accessed 29 February 2024].

51   BL Egerton MS 1995, folio 490.

52   Hicks (2010), p. 164.

53   Carpenter, p. 146.

54   BnF MS Fr 15491, folio 88v-90v.

55   Dawson, p. 72.

56   An almost contemporary French account reports: 'LA besongne de Blouher [Blore Heath] conduite comme dit est au A fuller prouffit du duc dYorc et du comte de Warewic fut account of cause pour ung tempz de refréner le corage des tenans less battle la querelle du roy Henry, mais ce non obstant tantost aprez se resveilla le comtent par le fait du duc Henry de Sombresset, lequel practiqua a layde des grans seigneurs de sa bende de rentrer ou gouvernement du roy Anglois, si fut pour

une espace eslongie le roy Henry du duc dYorc, lequel avec le comte de Warewic et leurs aidans assamblerent ung grant peuple jusques a lexstimation de bien cent mille hommes, pareillement en firent le roy et le duc de Sombresset, le duc d'Excestre, le duc de Boukingham, le comte de Pennebrocq [Pembroke], frere au roy de par mere, le comte de Richemont, le comte de Willechier, le comte de Beaumont, le comte de Chirosbury [Shrewsbury] et autres qui assamblerent aussi environ cent mille hommes; lesqueles deux grosses compaignies sentrecontrerent a Ludelo [Ludlow] prez de Galles, dedens laquele ville estoient le roy et les seigneurs de sa compaignie. A lencontre, du roy, avec le duc dYorc et le comte de Warewic, estoient Monseigneur Edouard comte de La Marche, fils audit duc dYorc, le comte de Salsebery pere de Warewic, et entre les autres Andrieu Trolot, lequel avoit entreprins de livrer lesdis seigneurs au roy, lesquelz de ce advertis se partirent droit a mienuit laissant leurs gens sans conduite, lesquels eulz voians en ce party se rendirent a leurs ennemis et furent tous despouillies, mais toutesfois en y eut chincq des principaulz a qui on trencha les testes, et tous ceulz de la garnison de Callaix, quy povoient estre environ six cens, y furent despouillies en chemise. Ainsi comme Vous oez se departy ceste assemblée; si alla le roy a Londres, le duc dYorc en Yrlande et Warewic a Callaix: et fut ceste assemblée entre Toussains et le Noel.' BnF MS Fr 15491, folio. 90v-91v.

57  Jack Robert Lander, *The Wars of the Roses*, Stroud: Sutton, 1990, p. 67.

58  Hicks (2010), p. 147.

59  Carpenter, p. 145.

60  https://www.british-history.ac.uk/no-series/Parliament-rolls-medieval/november-1459 [accessed 29 February 2024].

61  J.P. Gilson, 'A Defence of the Proscription of the Yorkists in 1459', *The English Historical Review*, 26 (1911), pp. 512–25, pp. 517–8.

62  Dawson, p. 87. Gascoigne was related to the earl of Salisbury: his wife Joan was daughter of Baron John Neville, son of Ralph, earl of Westmoreland, and was father-in-law to the 4th earl of Northumberland. Son, William, marriage Margaret Percy, daughter of Henry Percy, 3rd earl of Northumberland, killed at Towton.

63  Reginald Sharpe, *Calendar of Letter-Books of the City of London: K. Henry VI* Volume 10, London: His Majesty's Stationery Office, 1911, p. 403.

64  'Rymer's Foedera with Syllabus: 1459', in Rymer's *Foedera* Volume 11, London: 1739-1745, pp. 419–37.

## Chapter 16: Warwick the Kingmaker

1  Livia Visser-Fuchs, '"Warwick, by himself": Richard Neville, Earl of Warwick, "the Kingmaker"', in *Receuil des Croniques D'Engleterre of Jean de Wavrin*, Publication du Centre Européen d'études Bourguignonnes (XIVe-XVIes), 41 (2001), p. 151.

2    BnF MS Fr 88 folio 139.

3    BL Harley 4424, folio 259 verso.

4    ADN B 2040 Folio 165 verso.

5    Hicks (2010), pp. 149–51.

6    ADN B 2034 Folio 193.

7    Ibid. B 2040 Folio 165 verso. See also TNA C76/142 membrane 22.

8    Johnson, p. 199. He lists Strangeways, James Dockray, John Bolyngton, Thoms Colt, Sir John Wenclock, John Cornwalsh, John Gogh, Thomas Newbury, William Grifftitz, John Bourchier, Sir James Pickering, Roger Eyton, Thomas Browe, William Whelpdale, Nicholas Harpisfield, maser Thomas St Just. However, Dockray was James Dokeray, mayor of Drogheda, and Cornwalsh was an Irish judge and MP opposed to York.

9    Berry, Statute Rolls, Henry VI, p. 741 (38 Hen VI, ca. 37).

10   Dawson, p. 73.

11   Johnson, p. 199.

12   Dawson references *La Historia delle cose facte dallo invictissimo duca Francesco Sforza, scripta in latino da Giovanni Simoneta et tradocta in lingua fiorentina da Christophoro Landino*. This text was published in Milan in 1490.

13   BnF Fr 20358 folio 201, 'il sen alla a Londres, si flit grant merveilles des seigneurs et du peuple quy vindrent audevant de luy hors de la ville, et mesmement les enfans portoient grans estandars et alloient chantant comme sil eust este Dieu. Ainsi comme vous oez a grant sollempnite et joye flit le comte de Warewic recheu en Ia cite de Londres et menez ou conduis jusques a son logis, ouquel, lui descendu, vindrent tantost devers luy le maisre de Londres, les bourgeois et marchans pour Ic remercyer des grans biens que ja piecha avoit fais et pourchassies au pays et ancores faisoit journelement; si lui presenterent de grans dons, et auz dames pareillement, sy en fist on grant feste parmy Ia ville.'

14   Friederich Brie, *The Brut of England or The Chronicles of England*, London: Kegan Paul, 1906, p. 528.

15   Ibid.

16   Davies (1971), Vol. 1, p. 123.

17   Margaret Meserve and Marcello Simonette, *Pius II Commentaries*, Massachusetts: Harvard University Press, 2007, Volume 2, pp. 177–9.

18   Dawson, p. 24.

19   Hicks (2010), p. 175.

20   BL Egerton MS 1995 Folio 203 recto.

21   'Rymer's Foedera with Syllabus: 1459', in Rymer's *Foedera* Volume 11, London: 1739-1745, pp. 419–37.

22   Op cit.

23   BnF MS Fr 304 folio 15. Piere de Breze wrote to Charles on 24 February 1460 that Margaret had written him to him demanding aid to contain Warwick's fleet at Calais, and seemingly acceded to her demands: 'Ausy elle m'a mandé que je mette toutte la paine que je pourray à guaingner le navire du conte de Warvich, et que en touttez fasons que je pourray le grever et fere dommage, que je le face, car, ainsy qu'il luy semble, cela servira beaucoup à son fait et à la matère pourquoy elle antant anvoyer les gens de par de sà; et pour ce j'ay commancé à faire abiller le navire, et me semble que, cy c'est vostre plesir, que ledit Warvich s'au santira et est nécessité qu'il se face. Ausy je vous vouloye dire les segrettez chozes qu'elle m'a mandé, par quoy eusiez couneu le bon vouloir qu'elle a eu et a anvers vous, yui n'est pas peu de chosze.'

24   Dawson, p. 77.

25   De Beaucourt, pp. 277–81.

26   Foedera, pp. 430–7.

27   Lander (1990), p. 72.

28   However, these disturbances were noted in a French text, described as a rebellion of York's loyal dependents who want to keep their 'money' for their lord and refuse to give it to the king's agents. BnF Fr. 20358.

## Chapter 17: Warwick's Revenge

1   Lander, pp. 72–3.

2   Hicks (2010), p. 174.

3   ASM SCFO 566. Francesco Coppini to Sforza, 22 March 1460.

4   Brie, pp. 528–9.

5   Cora Schofield, *The Life and Reign of Edward the Fourth, King of England and France and Lord of Ireland*, London: Longman, Greens & Co, 1923, Vol 1, p. 59.

6   Lambeth Palace Library, MS 632. Folio 255.

7   BnF MS Fr 15491, folio 89v-91v.

8   TNA C 1/27/471.

9   Ibid C 1/27/383.

10   George Burnett, *Rotuli scaccarii regum Scotorum. The Exchequer rolls of Scotland*, Edinburgh: H.M. General Register House, 1878, Vol. 7, p. 33.

11   Anthony James Pollard, *The North of England in the Age of Richard III*, Stroud: Alan Sutton, 1996, p. 194.

12   Flemming, pp. 133–4.

13   ASM SCFP 566 James II., King of Scotland to Francesco Sforza, Duke of Milan. 28 Juni 1460.

14   BL Harley 4424, folio 259 verso.

15   ASM SCFP 566 Otto de Carreto, Milanese Ambassador at the Papal Court, to Francesco Sforza, 6 Mai 1460.

16   Constance Head, 'Pope Pius II and the Wars of the Roses', *Archivum Historiae Pontificiae*, Vol. 8, 1970, pp. 139–78, p. 152.

17   Commenteries book 3, p. 268.

18   Alison Hanham, *John Benet's Chronicle, 1399-1462*, London: Palgrave Macmillan, 2016, p. 46.

19   Hicks (2010), p. 149.

20   Brie, p. 529.

21   Hicks (2010), p. 175.

22   TNA SP 63/114 folio 278, piece no. 331.

## Chapter 18: Warwick's Victory

1    Feodera, pp. 438–9.

2    E159/236, recorda Mich. rot. 79.

3    Ibid., pp. 450–6.

4    Small seagoing vessel, being able to sailed and rowed.

5    TNA SC 1/60/48 Simon de L. to Thomas Thorpe: account of a sea battle. Dated at Calais. Penny Tucker notes the writer was probably Simon Lawless dit Sijmon Lauwels had been released from prison by Warwick for 'piracy' and was in his pay in 1463. Tucker, p. 14.

6    Dawson, p. 83.

7    Johnson, pp. 200–03.

8    Dawson, pp. 84–6.

9    Mesevre, p. 179.

10   ASM SCFP 566 Francesco Coppini, Bishop of Teramo, the Papal Legate, to King Henry VI, 4 July 1460.

11   Brie, p. 529.

12   Lander (1990), pp. 73–4.

13   William George Searle, *Christ Church, Canterbury. I. The chronicle of John Stone, monk of Christ Church 1415-1471*, Cambridge: Deighton, Bell & co, 1902, pp. 79–80.

14   Dawson, pp. 53–4.

15   Carpenter, p. 146.

16   Lander, p. 74.

17   Hicks (2010), p. 148.

18   Head, p. 155.

19  Ibid., p. 156.

20  Carpenter, p. 146.

21  Hicks (2010), p. 153.

22  BnF MS Fr 15491, if. 90v-91v reports 'Edouard comte de La Marche, filz dudit duc dYore, en sa compaignie le comte de Warewic, le comte de Kent, le comte dArondel, le marquis de Montagu et son frere messire Thomas de Neufville et autres. Et dautre part le roy Henry avoit le duc de Sombresset, le duc dExcestre, le duc de Boucqinghuem, le comte de Northumbeland et autres qui aussi estoient assamblez a Northantone, a la garde de laquele ville estoit commis de par le roy le seigneur de Greriffin avec de treize a quatorze cens hommes, et le roy et son ost estoient en ung parcq oultre la ville sur une petite riviere.

Lors les comtes de La Marche et de Warewic tyrerent vers la ville de Northantonne, venans de Callaix ou ilz avoient fait leur assamblee; laquele ville de Northantonne qui est une des fortes villes dAngleterre, qui, ce non obstant, fut emportee dassault aprez que le capitaine les eut escarmuchies lespace de heure et demie, sy dura lassault environ demye heure depuis que ledit seigneur de Greriffin se fut retrait a la porte, avec lequel entrerent par force ses annemis, quy pillerent la ville en passant oultre et aprochant lost du roy prochain de la, qui la sestoient fortiffiez sur ladite riviere merveilleusement et fait ung tres fort parcq,lequel incontinent ilz assaillirent tres asprement. Si dura peu ledit assault, car it avoit en la compaignie due roy dedens le parcq plusieurs quy estoient Warewics en corage, et mesmes les canonniers, quy par laschete maulvaise navoient mis nulles pierres en leurs engiens, parquoy quant ilz bouterent le feu dedens nen saillirent que les tampons, laquele chose parchevant les seigneurs quy dedens le parcq estoient, par maniere subitte rompirent ung quartier dudit parcq pour issir et sen fuyrent en Northumbelland. Si furent illec prins le roy, le duc de Boucquinghuem le seigneur de Beaumont, le seigneur de Greriffin et autres, lesquelz tost aprez furrent decapittez.' The text then jumps from Northampton to the Battle of Wakefield. The compiler clearly had no access to Warwick's 'Apology' which may not have been widely circulated according to Visser-Fuchs. This therefore means that Warwick's own version of events, the story HE wanted to be told, was not common knowledge. Therefore, we urge greater caution about the use of the 'Apology' without its context being made clear.

23  The Latin states 'tam de machinis suis bellicis, et fortitudine castrametationis'.

24  Lander, p. 75.

25  Wavrin writes: 'And to him who says that those who reckon without one's host customarily reckons twice over; I say to him that it is very difficult to guard against a traitor, as you can hear, because before going into battle the Earl of Warwick had ordered his war chiefs to warn their men that all who bore the ravestoc noue [the black ragged staff – the

badge of Grey of Ruthin] were to be saved, for it was they who were to give them entry to the park. After the Earl of Warwick had had his men instructed in what they must do, he sent forward the advance guard, commanded by Lord Fauconberg, which descended to the bottom of the valley; and the earls of March and Warwick led the [main] battle, which pushed so far forward that they came to fight hand to hand in a great struggle which lasted three hours and would have lasted much longer had Sir Ralph Grey not betrayed the Duke of Buckingham by allowing the Earl of March inside the camp on his side, as a result of which there was much killing. King Henry was captured by an archer called Henry Montfort.' BnF MS Francais 20354.

26  H.T. Riley, *Registra quorundam Abbatum Monasterii S Albani*, London: Longman and Co, 1872, pp. 372–4. Wavrin and Whethamstede's account are not greatly at variance with what we have learnt about the battle from other sources. The treachery of Lord Grey is given due prominence and confirmation is provided that it had been raining heavily.

27  Bale believes the casualties to have been light, fewer than sixty killed. Flenley, pp. 150–1.

28  R.I. Jack, 'A Quincentenary; the Battle of Northampton, July 10th 1460', *Northamptonshire Past and Present*, Vol. 3 (1960), pp. 21–5.

29  Duclos, p. 510.

30  Jean Alexandre Buchon, *Chroniques d'Enguerrand de Monstrelet, nouvelle édition entièrement refondue sur les manuscrits, avec notes et éclaircissements tome XIV*, Paris: Verdière & Co, 1826, p. 43.

31  Hanham, pp. 46–7.

32  Dawson, p. 71.

33  Presumably, Mary Stewart, Countess of Arran (13 May 1453–May 1488), eldest daughter of James II.

34  Dawson, p. 27.

35  BnF Bréquigny 83, Mémoires de Bréquigny sur l'histoire de Calais sous la domination anglaise. Folio 58.

36  BnF M. Fr. 20487, Lettres de Louis XI, folio 64.

37  TNA KB 9/75.

38  BnF Ms. fr. 20428, Lettres de Louis XI folio. 17 bis.

39  Duclos, p. 509.

40  Dawson, p. 38.

41  Ibid., p. 25.

42  Searle, p. 81.

43  TNA CPR 1452-1461, p. 608.

44  Johnson, p. 210.

45   TNA CPR 1452-1461, p. 607.

46   TNA CPR 1452-1461, p. 608.

47   TNA CPR 1452-1461, p. 610.

48   CPR 1452-61 p. 610 (24 August 1460).

49   TNA C49/32/8.

50   TNA C49/32/7.

## Chapter 19: York's Return

1    Kekewich, pp. 30–1.

2    Ibid., p. 22.

3    Dawson, p. 93.

4    Wethamstede I, p. 368.

5    Calendar of State Papers Relating To English Affairs in the Archives
     of Venice, Volume 1, 1202-1509. Originally published by Her Majesty's
     Stationery Office, London, 1864. Letter No. 366.

6    Basin, p. 297.

7    Hanham, p. 48.

8    BL Egerton MS 1995 Folio 201 verso.

9    BNF Français 20136 Recueil de pièces relatives à l'Angleterre et à
     l'Écosse. (XVe-XVIIe siècle). Folio 75.

10   Laynesmith, pp. 76–7.

11   Johnson, p. 211.

12   Visser-Fuchs (2018), p. 414.

13   Malcom Mercer, *The Medieval Gentry: Power, Leadership and Choice During
     the Wars of the Roses*, London: Continuum, 2010, p. 56. De la Torre had
     joined the Calais garrison in early 1460 through Coppini's efforts. In
     1466 de la Torre mustered as one of Warwick's retinue, and held the
     recordership of Calais. David Grummitt, *The Calais Garrison: War and
     Military Service in England, 1436-1558*, Woodbridge: The Boydell Press,
     2008, p. 106.

14   ASM SCFP 566 Antonio de la Torre to Francesco Sforza, Duke of Milan.
     5 Septembris 1460.

15   Hicks (2010), p. 156.

16   Laynesmith, p. 77.

17   BL Egerton MS 1995 Folio 202 recto.

18   Lander, p. 78.

19   Laynesmith, p. 77.

20   Johnson, p. 212 note 91.

21   BnF MS Français 20136 Recueil de pièces relatives à l'Angleterre et à l'Écosse. (XVe-XVIIe siècle). Folio 65.

22   Meserve, p. 181.

23   Warwick wrote his own version of events, known as the 'Apology' in early 1469. The 'Apology' has been reconstructed by Dr Livia Visser-Fuchs. That the Pope should align with Warwick's version of events is exactly why Warwick wrote this 'Apology' In it he places the blame on what happens next 100 per cent on to York, Rutland and Edward. Warwick writes: 'ains entra dans La chambre du duc, quil trouva apuye a ung dreschoir, et quant le duc le parcheut il marcha avant, si saluerent Inn lautre, et Ia y eut grosses parolles entreulz deux, car Ic comte remoustra au duc comment les seigneurs et le peuple estoient mal contentz contre lui de cc quil voulloit ainsi deboutter Ic roy de Ia couronne. Enire lesquelles parolles vint le comte de Rotelland frere au comte de La Marche, si dist an comte de Warewic: 'Beau cousin, ne vous courouchies pan, car vous savez que cest nostre droit davoir Ia couronne, et quelle apartient a monseigneur mon pere qui cy est, et laura quiconque le voeille veoir'. A laquele parolle respondy le comte de La Marche illec present et dist au comte de Rotelland: 'Mon frere, ne despitez nulluy, (car) tout ce fera bien'. Aprez ces parolles dites et que le comte de Warewic eut bien entendu Ia voullente du duc dYorc, Il se party de Ia tres mal content sans prendre ongie a personne, sinon au comte de La Marche auquel ii prya tres affectueusement que le lendemain II se volsist trouver a Londres auz Jacopins ou se tendroit ung consesl, lequel respondy quil ny fauldroit pan.' BnF Fr. 20358, folio 204. The episode very likely never happened as it is not mentioned in BnF Fr 88, BnF MS Francais 20354 Chroniques de Saint-Denis nor BL Harley 4424 or anywhere else in Burgundian, French or English sources. The 'Apology' is the only reference to this, and this text was not in wide circulation. It must be considered suspect history at best. As we have seen Warwick drove events forward for his own personal benefit. It is exceptionally unlikely that he got 'cold feet'. This would be against the personality and temperament of the man. As Dr Livia Visser-Fuchs notes 'Warwick comes across as virtuous and politically blameless; sensitive to the situation, loyal to Henry and prepared to tell York exactly what he thinks about his plans; he also has a particularly good relationship with young Edward of March, who is himself sensible and conciliating . . . I suggest it was the earl himself who desired to create this moderate image and impress people with his loyalty to the reigning king . . . been made to exonerate him of disloyalty to his anointed king after York's attempted coup and before Edward realised the claims of his house at the Battle of Towton, i.e. between October 1460 and the end of March 1461. It is even more probable, however, that it was composed after York's death on 30 December 1460: when York was alive foreign observers identified Warwick with the Yorkist cause and saw him as its main support, but it was York who gave the Yorkists their legitimacy and his death weakened Warwick's position for a while, making him

very aware of opinions and doubts abroad.' I would add the text also is applicable to the events of the Readeption, from 1469 to Warwick's death at Barnet. Dr Graeme Callister, Dr David Grummitt and I are all of the opinion that the 'Apology' reasonably dates from 1469. The three battle accounts could date from lost newsletters issues in 1461 given the similarity of the account by Jacques du Clercq who died in October 1467 account of Towton with that given by George Neville and presented by someone close to Warwick in Bnf MS Fr 88 and allied texts. Two separate and lost texts could have been edited together.

24  Dawson, p. 68.

25  Lander, p. 79. Lander here is reliant on Wavrin, and in turn is reliant on Warwick's 'Apology' so may not be reliable. BnF MS Francais 88 Chronique des guerres advenues en France, en Angleterre et en Bourgogne depuis l'année 1444 jusqu'en 1471 folio 150-155 does not mention Warwick's anger, which is also not to be found in BnF MS Francais 20358 Chroniques d'Angleterre. These two writers are working for a lost document that ends with the coronation of Edward IV. Both were used by Wavrin, who added in Warwick's 'Apology' rather imprecisely. We note that 20358 includes the 'Apology' but omits the three battles of Ludlow, Blore Heath and Northampton which were, presumably, a stand alone document that the writer did not have access to. Indeed BnF Fr. 88 as well as BL Harley 4424 contain two redactions of the work of the self-styled Monstrelet-continuator, as well as another closely related text, Jacques Du Clercq's Chronique. By comparing these texts Dr Livia Visser-Fuchs was the first scholar to 'isolate' Warwick's 'Apology', and secondly to analyse as far as possible Wavrin's own image of the Kingmaker. Lander was unaware of Warwick's 'Apology'.

26  Hicks (2010), p. 156.

27  Carpenter, p. 147.

28  BnF MS Francais 20136 folio 65.

29  Laynesmith, p. 79.

30  Hicks (2010), p. 157.

31  Meserve, p. 181.

32  BnF MS Fr 15491, folio 90v-91v.

33  BL Egerton MS 1995 Folio 202 recto.

34  Kekewich, p. 34.

35  TNA C 49/32/3 Act granting the principality of Wales to Richard, duke of York.

36  Archives Département du Nord, Lille [hereafter ADN] 2040 Recette générale des finances. Comptes et pièces comptables de Robert de Le Bouvcrie, receveur général de Philippe le Bon (1459-1464). 2e compte (1460, 1er oct.-30 sept. 1461) Folio 163.

37 ASM SCFP 566 Francesco Coppini to Francesco Sforza, Duke of Milan. Written at Canterbury, 6 August 1460.

38 Ibid. Instructions of Prospero Camulio, 24 December 1460.

## Chapter 20: Protector York

1 Kekewich, p. 143.

2 Ibid., p. 142. By describing the duke as 'Late' does not mean that this was written after 30 December 1460. York had lost his title in 1459, and the queen no doubt refused to accept his resumption of it, so it very likely dates from late 1460 rather than into 1461. We do accept that writing such a letter would fit with the queen's hope to take London in February 1461, and hoping the city would abandon the Yorkist cause. In both scenarios, the contents importance doesn't materially change in their significance. The unusually well-informed writer of BnF MS Francais 88 Chronique des guerres advenues en France, en Angleterre et en Bourgogne depuis l'année 1444 jusqu'en 1471 folio 150-155 mentions letters from Henry to Margaret and return in late October or early November 1460. The same story can be found copied at BnF MS Francais 20358 Chroniques d'Angleterre, folio 205. These two writers are working for a lost document that ends with the coronation of Edward IV. BnF Fr 88 is therefore a foundational document in any narrative of the events of 1460, and has been almost totally ignored for studying the Battle of Wakefield. That the writer of BnF MS Fr 88 and Fr 20358 state Margaret sent word to London following the king writing to her about the Act of Accord, may offer secure dating to early November 1460.

3 ASM SCFP 567 Giovanni de Bebulcho to Messer Bartolomeo Chalco, Secretary to the Duke of Milan.

4 Ibid.

5 Duclos, p. 512.

6 Ibid., p. 511.

7 BnF Bréquigny 83, folio 58. du Clercq book IV, chapter XIV also discusses much of this.

8 De Beaucourt, p. 305.

9 TNA CPR 1452-1461, p. 649.

10 TNA KB 9/928 m28. See also ibid., m29.

11 Dawson, p. 58.

12 TNA DL 29/560/8899 membrane 1. The accounting period of the Manor of Wakefield since 1309 for rents was Michaelmas, 29 September, the Feast of the Purification of the Blessed Virgin, 2 February and Whitsun, 20 June. At the start of winter, on St Martin's Day, 11 November, a pig rent was paid by free tenants as income for the lord as payments for the grazing of pigs in his demesne or private woodland. The accounts of

the Manor, Appendix 2 and 3, has very few empirical dates. This event, like all those mentioned in the accounts, could all be related to the battle, rather than occurring over a period of months. The fixed point for this excerpt is it occur after 11 November and before 2 February.

13   TNA DL 29/560/8899.

14   BnF MS Fr 88 folio.147, BnF MS Fr 15491,folio.238v; fr.20358, folio.235.

15   TNA CPR 1452-1461. p. 651.

16   Michaels Hicks, *Bastard Feudalism*, London: Routledge, 1995, p. 36. See also ibid., pp. 38 and 50.

17   M.J. Devine (2006) (PhD thesis). University of Teesside.p. 176.

18   Keith Dockray, 'Contemporary and Near-Contemporary Chroniclers: The North of England and the Wars of the Roses, c. 1450—1471', in L. Clark, and P. Fleming (eds), *The Fifteenth Century XVIII: Rulers, Regions and Retinues, Essays Presented to A. J. Pollard*, Woodbridge: Boydell & Brewer, 2020, pp. 65–80.

19   Dockray, Keith (2004). 'Greystoke'. Oxford Dictionary of National Biography (online ed.). Oxford University Press. Accessed 19 January 2025 @ 11.03.

20   David Grummitt pers comm 21 January 2025 citing Hull City Archives BRL 4.

21   BL Additional MS 38690 item 6.

22   Du Clercq, Vol. 1, p. 447. Du Clercq correctly reports the information that the queen had written to London – the letter exists – and she was now de facto leader of the opposition. Du Clercq is writing verifiable history from a now lost newssheet, independent of Warwick's 'Apology'. He had access to a detailed account of Ludford Bridge, which is also covered by Warwick's 'Apology' but is clearly a different source as it lacks the story about Warwick's escape in a little boat after the battle to Calais. The same news sheet contains details on Blore Heath, which were used by Wavrin. Visser-Fuchs (2018), p. 475.

23   Brie, p. 530.

## Chapter 21: Margaret's Flight

1   BnF M. Fr. 20487, Lettres de Louis XI, folio 64.

2   https://etheses.bham.ac.uk/id/eprint/3571/1/Southworth_MPhil_12.pdf.

3   Dawson, p. 93.

4   Duclos, p. 511.

5   Somerset/Trollop had recruited Thomas Brampton late of Guisnes, esquire, Thomas Crawford late of Calais, esquire, John Aldeley late of Guisnes, esquire. Others included Sir Thomas Fyndern, who had been

a member of the Calais garrison under Andrew Trollop, and likely therefore a professional solider who switched sides at Ludford. From – we assume – the Hammes garrison was Sir Simon Hammes. He had held a large retinue under the duke of Somerset in France in 1443, and led a larger retinue during the ill-fated 1450 campaign in Normandy. TNA C 65/106 rot. 19

6    Trollop was a wanted man long before the events of December 1460. A master porter of Calais, in August 1454 he was charged with the commandeering of a Portuguese ship, the owner being reimbursed by the crown for the theft. In March 1457 Trollop, John Stafford and John Clifton seized three ships in the channel carrying £4,000 of wool exports. For this the men were arrested. Griffiths calls Trollop a 'free booter' who seized and stole from 'the ships of allies and subjects alike'. A gifted military strategist, skilled in land warfare he was undoubtedly not. Despite the act of attainder, Edward IV treated Somerset with a marked degree of leniency: archive documents show Somerset is happy on embassy between Margaret and the continent in December/ January, and again in the summer. As David Grummitt argues, another good indicator Somerset wasn't implicated in the murder of Duke Richard, despite the act of attainder, is the leniency he is shown. That the attainder was a catchall device for misdemeanours committed between Ludford Bridge Wakefield, and the second attainder covers St Albans as much as Towton, has to be the correct understanding of these documents.

7    BnF MS Fr 20487 Papiers de Jean BOURRÉ, secrétaire et trésorier royal. Folio 64.

8    Ibid.

9    BL Harl.4424, folio.259v; also reported in BnF MS Fr 88 folio.145, BnF MS Fr 15491, folio.236v; fr.20358, folio.233. These texts all form part of Warwick's 'Apology'.

10    Schoefield, Vol. 1, p. 114 states Somerset landed at Corfe Castle about St Matthew's Day, 21 September drawn from chronicles..

11    David Grummitt pers comm 7 January 2025 citing Devon Record Office, Exeter Receivers Roll 38-39 Hen. VI, 1459-1460 ECA/3/1/1/1/114.

12    Anthony Goodman, *The Wars of the Roses: Military Activity and English Society, 1452-97*, London: Routledge, 1991, pp. 114–15.

13    *POPC*, vi. 302-5.

14    BnF MS Fr 20487 Papiers de Jean BOURRÉ, secrétaire et trésorier royal. Folio 64.

15    Duclos, p. 510.

16    BnF Ms Fr. 20417, folio 23.

17    Ibid. Français 26997 (Pièces originales 513) Briconnet. See also Duclos, p. 510.

18   Duclos, p. 510.

19   BnF Ms Fr 20488, folio 23.

20   Hicks (2010), p. 159.

21   BnF Ms Fr 20488 folio 23.

22   TNA C 65/106 rot. 19.

23   TNA C76/143 membrane 11, 12, 14.

24   ADN B 2040 Folio 154 to 155. See also ibid., folio 175.

25   BnF MS Fr 20136 Recueil de pièces relatives à l'Angleterre et à l'Écosse. (XVe-XVIIe siècle). Folio 68.

26   TNA C76/143 membrane 6.

27   ADN B 2040 Folio 229 verso.

28   *Letters of Margaret of Anjou*, pp. 225–6; *John Vale's Book*, ed. Kekewich et al, pp. 142–3.

29   ASM SCFP 566 Antonio de la Torre to Francesco Sforza Duke of Milan, 9 January 1461.

30   Michael Hicks, *Who's Who in Late Medieval England*, London: Shepheard-Walwyn, 1991, pp. 313–15.

31   Beaucourt, pp. 296–7.

32   BnF MS Fr. 20404, Recueil de pièces originales provenant de la Chambre des comptes, de copies, d'extraits et de dessins formé par Gaignières et concernant les maisons royales de France, les princes du sang, etc. folio 13.

33   Duclos, p. 509.

34   BnF MS. Fr. 20683, Comptes originaux, provenant de la Chambre des comptes (1287-1489), folio 51.

35   De Beaucourt, p. 297.

36   BnF Ms Fr 20488 folio 23.

37   De Beaucourt, pp. 327–8.

38   ADN Lille B 2040 folios 171-172.

39   Basin, Vol. 1, p. 298.

40   Hicks (2010), p. 159.

41   Scofield, Vol. 1, p. 116.

42   TNA C 1/27/435.

43   George Poulson, *Beverlac: or the History and Antiquities of the Town of Beverley*, Beverley, 1829,Vol. 2, pp. 232–3.

44   TNA, C1/27/435.

45   David Grummitt pers comm 21 January 2025.

46    Hull City Archives, BRL 4, BRB 1, ff. 73-4; Poulson, *Beverlac*, pp. 227–30, 232–4.

47    Hull City Archives, BRB3A, ff. 72-4; *House of Commons 1422-1461*, ii, pp. 664–7.

48    David Grummitt pers comm 21 January 2025

49    Cox, *Wakefield*, pp. 86, 88. For Wiltshire's landing in Wales at the end of December see H.T. Evans, *Wales in the Wars of the Roses* (Cambridge: Cambridge University Press, 1915), pp. 124–5. For Wiltshire in Zeeland in either late 1460 or the first weeks of 1461 see ADN B 2040 folio 64

50    BnF MS Fr 15491, folio 92 reports 'Le Duc si chevaulcherent tous ensamble trois ou quatre jours jusques a une ville appelee Wilquefild. Quant le duc dYorc fut illec arrive, pour obtemperer a la pryere du roy, il assambla jusques au nombre de dix mille combatans, puis envoia par devers la royne lui faire scavoir que la voullente du roy si estoit quelle venist a Londres; et quant la royne fut advertie de ces nouvelles, et avec ce que le roy Henry son mary hearing of avoit resigne sa couronne et son royaulme aprez rangement son trespas au duc dYorc et a ses hoirs, elle en fut moult troublee pour amour dun seul filz quelle avoit defies him. du roy de le veoir estre ainsi deboute de son patrimoine, sicque elle envoia deffier le duc dYorc, lequel oyant la voullente de la royne et que nullement elle ne vouloit consentir cel apointement, il commenca de aprochier la royne, de quoy la royne fut tost advertie, pourquoy elle envoia querir le duc de Sombresset auquel elle manda le lieu ou ledit duc dYore et ses gens estoient logies. Ces nouvelles furent portees devers le roy Henry que tout le pays de West et de Cornuaille se mettoient sus, ou estoit la royne Marguerite sa femme en personne, adfin de obvier au and the deshirtement de son filz. Quant le jeune duc de Sombresset eut oy le mandement de la royne il of the assambla grans gens pour venir combatre le duc dYorc et ses aydans, et adont monseigneur de Sombresset demanda de ce conseil a Andrieu Trolot quy estoit avec luy, lequel luy dist que tantost len responderoit.'

51    TNA, E404/72/1/23; Scofield, *Edward IV*, i, p. 118.

52    Johnson, pp. 220–1.

53    Ibid., pp. 219–21.

54    CPR 1452-1461 pp. 652–3.

55    Hicks (1991), pp. 1–40.

56    CPR 1452-1461. pp. 653–4.

57    TNA C49/63/6.

58    Ibid.

59    Matthew Lewis, *The Wars of the Roses. The key players in the struggle for supremacy*, Stroud: Amberley, 2016, p. 115.

60    Schofield, Vol. 1, p. 118.

61  Ralph Flenley, *Six Town Chronicles of England*, Oxford: Clarendon Press, 1911, p. 152.

62  ASM SCFP 566 Francesco Coppino, Bishop of Terni, Papal Legate, to Francesco Sforza, Duke of Milan.

63  CPR 1452-61, pp. 642–3. Antonio de la Torre on 9 January 1461 seems to think Warwick was not in London. ASM SCFP 566 Antonio de la Torre to Francesco Sforza Duke of Milan, 9 January 1461. BnF MS Francais 20354 Chroniques de Saint-Denis, folio 117 tells us Warwick escaped the carnage of the battle to come in a little boat and headed to Flanders. Is this a garbled version of the truth? BL Harley MS 4424 offers a text which is an abridged copy of BnF 88, published in Ghent in 1483. Folio 157 but adds 'Le conte de Warvich eschappa de celle bataile et lrouva son moyen dissir du rayaume et de venir a Callaiz en ung petit batel a pou de gens moult adventureusement.' My translation: The earl of Warwick escaped from this battle and found his way out of the kingdom and went to Calais in a small boat with many adventurous people.'

64  Flenley, pp. 152–3.

65  Ibid., p. 152.

66  Lovelace, Richard. New Apprentice, Mercers' Company 1415. Records of London's Livery Companies Online. Apprentices and Freemen 1400-1900.

67  A.J. Pearman, 'Kentish Family of Lovelace, No. I', *Archaeologia Cantiana*, Volume 10, 1876, pp. 177–84. See also Rev. A.J. Pearman, 'The Kentish Family of Lovelace, No. II', *Archaeologia Cantiana*, Volume 20, 1893, pp. 54–63.

68  Malcolm Mercer, 'The Strength of Lancastrian Loyalism during the readeption', *The Journal of Medieval Military History*, Volume 5, 2007, pp. 84–98.

69  Dawson, p. 102.

70  TNA C 1/103/41 Short title: Newbery v Bygge.

71  Josiah Clement Wedgwood, *The History of Parliament: Biographies of the Members of the Common House 1439–1509*, London; H.M.S.O. 1936, volume 1, pp. 429–30.

72  Desmond Seward, *A Brief History of the Wars of the Roses*, London: Constable and Robin, 2007 p. 80.

73  Flenley, p. 152.

74  TNA E404/71.

75  TNA E101/54/9

76  York potentially had no more than twelve knights and knights bannerettes with him. This was not a large army. The contemporary figure of 300 men seems very reasonable.

77  TNA, KB27/803, rot. 16d.

78 Hanham, p. 49.

79 D.R. Walker, 'An Urban Community in the Welsh Borderland: Shrewsbury in the Fifteenth Century' (University of Wales, PhD, 1981), pp. 391-2; TNA, E159/238, *brevia directa baronibus*, Mich 1 Edw IV, rot. 43d.

80 Gardiner, pp. 153–4.

81 Dawson, p. 58.

82 Goodman, p. 42. See also ibid., pp. 177–80.

83 *Letters and Papers*, ii. (2), 775; Helen Cox, *The Battle of Wakefield Revisited*, York, 2010, pp. 48–52.

84 Dawson, p. 100.

85 The constableship of Conisbrough had been handed to Lord Egremont in December 1459 CPR 1452-61 p. 534 This is confirmed by the accounts of Lordship which state Egremont was in possession September 1460 to September 1461 TNA DL 29/560/8899, membrane 11. However, the previous constable, Nicholas Fitzwilliam was included in the Lancastrian commission of array for the West Riding issued on 21 December 1459: CPR 1452-61, pp. 559–60. In November 1460, he certainly held Conisbrough Castle for the duke, equipping it with artillery seized from the earl of Shrewsbury's lordship of Sheffield: CPR 1461-7, pp. 14, 479, see also Johnson, p. 223.

86 TNA DL 26/590/8899, membrane 11.

87 Ibid.

## Chapter 22: Wakefield

1 TNA DL 26/560/8899 membrane 1: '7s 11d paid to William Turton for carrying hay from Erlesyng to the barn of the castle by acknowledgment of the said William; And 4s allowed him paid to a man for breaking ice on the millpond.'

2 David Grummitt pers comm, citing 'Brief Notes' now Lambeth MS. 448.

3 Davies (1856), pp. 106–07.

4 Dawson, p. 68. This date is confirmed by the Short Latin Chronicle which states 'whence they came to the town of Wakefield on Sunday in the holy week of Christmas.' 'A brief Latin chronicle', in John Stowe, *Three Fifteenth-Century Chronicles with Historical Memoranda*, ed. James Gairdner, London, 1880, pp. 164–85.

5 The chroniclers are precise about this, the first reference to Sandal comes in the 1480s. Accounts written 1461–80 tell us the battle was at Wakefield. Bale reports the battle was 'in the north beside pountfreite in a feld called wakefield'. Chronicle from Rollo to Edward IV states 'goyng towarde Yorke at Wakefeld sette vpon hym'. Whethamsted tells us 'the town of Wakefield, which is on the fringes of the County

of York'. A Short English Chronicle says 'rode northewarde to kepe her Crystmas. And there lay in her wey at Wakefelde to stope hem.' Gregory's Chronicle reports 'the Quenys party, met with the Duke of Yorke at Wakefylde.' A Short Latin Chronicle gives us a date of arrival: 'whence they came to the town of Wakefield on Sunday in the holy week of Christmas'. Antonio de la Torre in dated letter 9 January 1461 tells us 'this engagement took place on the last day of December near a castle called Pontefract'. In fact, we only find a reference to Sandal is in *An English Chronicle*. Charles Ross judges this text to be 'more a scrap book than a deliberately composed piece of work', and compiled by a writer at work in 1491. Wiliam of Worcester gives us a date of 21 December and a place at Sandal. An Italian pseudo-historian, Polydore Virgil, ordained a priest in 1496, we think had access to oral histories from those who had been part of the court of Edward IV, Richard III and Henry VII: his work is at its most valuable for the period after 1485, and is value for the years 1461–85 lies in its presentation of popular opinion 50 years after the events he writes about took place. He mentions 'a castle adjoyning, which towne is called Wakefielde'. Stowe, Ranin and Hall are all writing after 1536. As could be easily understood, the Battle of Wakefield became a key piece of propaganda to 'prop up' the ailing regime of Henry VIII. His unpopular marriage to Anne Boleyn, the break with the Papacy and consequential religious changes – the Pilgrimage of Grace of 1536–7, centred in Pontefract, being in direct response – the enclosure of common land sparked rioting in 1535, all marked a rising tide of tensions to Henry, as he increasingly became a despotic tyrant. Indeed, the abortive Wakefield Plot of March 1541 against Henry VIII was followed by a massive – and armed – royal progress to the North that summer. Historians have, however, tended to see the progress as being more concerned with a projected meeting between Henry and James V of Scotland at York than pacifying the North. Thus, in the aftermath of these events we see print culture promoting the Tudor and therefore Lancastrian side of history, reminding the country as a whole of the fate of those who opposed the Crown was 'no bad thing' in propping up Henry. Therefore, accounts after 1485 may be more fiction than fact. The truth is, we cannot prove York was at Sandal. The Manor of Wakefield accounts report the 'household of the lord (pro expens' hospitii domini) lately Duke at Wakefield in the month of December and in January', TNA DL 29/560/8899. No proof he was in Sandal. The editor of the Manor of Wakefield Court Rolls for publication by the Yorkshire Archaeological Society, Christopher Watson, a leading expert on Medieval Manorial documents, tells me 'I can't see why the place would be recorded as Wakefield if Sandal were intended. The distinction is always upheld in the court rolls for obvious reasons. Wakefield, the vill, graveship and borough, are not Sandal. The vill of Sandal is an entirely separate place lending its name to the graveship.' The duke of York was emphatically not at Sandal.

6    TNA MFC 1/199.

7     TNA DL/43/11/17.

8     Thomas Taylor, *The Rectory Manor of Wakefield*, Wakefield: W.H. Milnes, 1886, p. 310. See also ibid., pp. 312–13. See also C.M. Frazer, *The Court Rolls of the Manor of Wakefield from October 1433 to September 1436*, Leeds: Yorkshire Archaeological Society, 2011. We know some fields were enclosed as early as circa 1415: a document in the John Goodchild collection reports Castlefield as a land unit. The field(s) were bounded by ditches – referenced as Fossati – and presumably hedges. This land unit is identifiable on the tythe aware of 1844: Castlefield is a central block of two narrow fields running east to west between the Calder and Cock & Bottle Lane. It is extremely unlikely that just this block of land was enclosed by 1415. Presumably, the field system in which Castlefield forms a land unit, was laid formally laid out by the steward from the demesne of the Graveship. This is confirmed by a rental agreement of 1554, when Isabella Cockhill paid 2d for half an acre rent of land at Castlefield. Roger Agland also rented half an acre in Castlefield for the same sum to the Rectory Manor. Castlefield may have been the name for a larger land unit that was later subdivided into smaller units. This land unit can be traced from the Tithe award. Sadly, the Saville survey is missing at this most important of areas. In the Manor Court Rolls, we find in 1434 OldField, in reference to an enclosed field: John Turnour on his death surrendered to the Lord 1 ½ acres in Le Oldfeld within the Graveship of Sandal. This is likely the same parcel of land known as 'ye grete Oldfied' in later documents. This land unit was north of the castle, bounded on its south side by the Agbrigg brook, and is occupied today by much of modern-day Belle Vue and Sugar Lane Cemetery. The receivers accounts of 1460 also clearly mentioned enclosed fields around the castle. DL 29/560/8899 membrane 1 verso.

9     TNA DL 39/4/15 Roll of account of the trees felled within the lordship of Wakefield. No large stands of woods existed to be felled in 1485, nor 1460. The Manor Court Rolls of Wakefield in 1317 allude to the presence of timber and herbage within the manor, but give no specific locations. Timber, that is, fully-matured wood, was very expensive, valued at 4s.–5s. per trunk for oak and slightly less for other species, and was sold only sparingly. One of the few geographic locations we have for wood outside the Parks and Forest of Wakefield, is from April 1307 when a small stand at the Westwood in Crigglestone was sold in gross to four residents of that township for 25 marks (£16 13s. 4d.), though with clear instructions that the wood was to be coppiced. Moving on into the fifteenth century, woodland and timber management outside of the parks of Wakefield and Sandal, is notably missing in the published rolls 1439–41. It is exceptionally unlikely that a forest appeared in the intervening two decades. Woodland existed at Newmiller Dam, an unclosed park, with woodland for pannage. This we note, is 2.2 miles south east of the castle, and importantly below the horizon view the castle commands. It would be impossible to ambush the castle from woods 2 miles away as nay attacking troops would be clearly visible

from the castle. Any modern-day visitor to the castle can verify this observation. The castle keep was on the highest point in the landscape for a very good reason; it offered exceptional visibility for several miles. It was important to keep these site lines free from obstructions i.e. woodland. Such timber would have been used for firewood, and to construct the town and castle itself in the period 1100–20. We know the timber in the parks of the manor was managed for charcoal for iron smelting in 1460.

10 TNA SC 11/991 Wakefield [Yorkshire]: Valor of the lordship, with a survey of Sandal Castle and Wakefield Park. 5 membranes. 37 Hen VIII. See also TNA SP 15/9/1 folio 67 Note by Hen. Saville, surveyor, 'that the farm of the old park of Wakefield, part of the Queen's duchy of York, granted to John Paston by Henry VIII., is now in tenure of Sir Thos. Gargrave, 1 November 1569'.

11 John Sadler, *Towton: The Battle on Palm Sunday Field 1461*, Barnsley: Pen and Sword, 2011. See also John Sadler, *The Red Rose and the White: The Wars of the Roses, 1453-1487*, London: Routledge, 2013, pp. 93–7; David Cooke, *Battlefield Yorkshire: From the Romans to the English Civil Wars*, Barnsley: Pen & Sword Military, 2006, pp. 106–10; Paul Kendall, *Wars of the Roses: The people, places and battlefields of the Yorkists and Lancastrians*, Barnsley: Frontline, 2023; Anthony W. Boardman, *Towton 1461: The Anatomy of a Battle*, Gloucester: The History Press, 2022. All these sources mention woods that never existed.

12 TNA CPR 1452-1461, p. 561.

13 University of Leeds. Yorkshire Archaeological Society [hereafter YAS] / MD225/1/185 (1459) membrane 1 dorse.

14 John William Walker, *Wakefield, its history and its people*, Wakefield, 1939, Vol. 2, pp. 659–60.

15 Ibid., pp. 667–9.

16 TNA CPR 1452-1461, p. 550. See also TNA SC 6/1083/24, and TNA DL 29/560/8899 membrane 1.

17 Ibid.

18 Ibid., pp. 531, 567.

19 TNA KB 9/928 m28. See also ibid., m29.

20 TNA CPR 1452-1461, p. 608.

21 Ibid., KB9/149/11, membrane 6.

22 Ibid., p. 535.

23 Ibid., p. 577.

24 TNA KB9 149/9, membrane 8. The forty-eight men so indicted are likely to represent the leadership and 'rank and file' of the Lancastrian army present at Wakefield who were then thought to be living in 1462–3.

25 TNA CPR 1452-1461, p. 532. See also ibid., pp. 570–1.

26    Ibid., p. 533.

27    TNA DL 29/560/8899 membrane 4 verso.

28    YAS/MD225/1/185 (1459) membrane 5 dorse.

29    Dawson, p. 92.

30    Likely to include Thomas Dalton late of Lilburn in the county of Northumberland gentleman, James Dalton late of the same, gentleman, George Dalton late of the same, gentleman. Also likely to be part of this group was Sir John Heron, born in 1418, was appointed as constable of Bamburgh Castle on 7 February 1438, he and his son jointly holding the office from July 1459. He was escheator in Northumberland in 1439–40, sheriff of Northumberland in 1440–1, 1451–2, and 1456–7 and sat as MP for Northumberland in 1442, 1447 and 1449. He was killed at Towton. Others were likely to be Walter Nuthill late of Ryston in Holderness in the county of York, esquire. TNA C 65/106 rot. 19.

31    TNA DL 29/560/8900 membrane 4. The bailiff was Willim Gargrave, son of Sir John Gargrave and Margaret Scargill, daughter of William Scargill of Lead. Gargrave senior was Master of the Ordnance under Henry V 1415–22, and retained a position in France under Bedford. He had been tutor to Richard duke of York. Sir John Gargrave is buried at Bayonne, in France. William Gargrave was dead by 1474, when the villa (house), along with 11 messuages and 11 bovates of land at Snapethorpe was handed to Sir John Pilkington. Pilkington obtained a licence to crenelate in 1477. William Gargrave's brother-in-law, William Scargill jnr, was drawn into the service of Richard Neville earl of Salisbury, and was named a jurer in 1454 to try those indicted for the attempted murder of the earl. Scargill was also involved in legal matters for the earl. Pilkington was a member of Edward IV's household. Under bailiff was Richard Lyster the elder. John Vincent was re-appointed Receiver in the place of William Stoke from the royal household

32    TNA DL 29/560/8899 membrane 7 recto.

33    Ibid., membrane 1 verso.

34    Herny Burwell appointed Christmas Day 1460 TNA DL 29/560/8899 membrane 4.

35    TNA DL 29/560/8900 membrane 2 verso.

36    Based on the household accounts of George, duke of Clarence, the horse feed allocated would be a week's supply for 17 or 18 horses, double that if the duke was only present 25 to 29 December. An ox was reckoned to have 1,000 rations of meat: 200 men for 5 days 25 to 30 December? The retinue of Richard Wydeville, earl Rivers in 1441 comprised 39 knights and 119 archers or men-at-arms. The duke of York's retinue in 1460, although much smaller than we expect, is within 'normal' expectations. Hull raised thirteen men for the Battle of Northampton. The number of soldiers present in these 'armies' was much smaller than we think.

37  ASM SCFP 566 Antonio de la Torre to Francesco Sforza Duke of Milan, 9 January 1461.

38  However, as David Grummitt notes, absence of evidence, may not be evidence of absence. He notes: 'This is a common problem. Even where we know there are larg(ish) armies nearby (Coventry in 1470 for example) there is next to no evidence of supplying victuals. The Calais victualler is another example: he supplies the garrison with everything except personal armour and weapons (although they do occasionally buy it from him) and food.' Pers comm 01/01/2025.

## Chapter 23: The Battle That Never Was

1  Poulson, Vol. 2, p. 231.

2  We think this because the Lancastrian army contained men from York: Edmund Fish late of York, tailor, Thomas Frizell late of the same, smith, John Smothing late of the same, yeoman, Thomas Barton late of York, mason.

3  Charles Lethbridge Kingsford, *Prejudice and Promise in Fifteenth Century England: The Ford Lectures 1923–4*, Oxford: Clarendon Press, 1925. pp. 177–9.

4  TNA C 65/106 rot. 20. See also TNA KB 27/804, rot. 65.

5  *Parliament Rolls of Medieval England*, ed. Given-Wilson et al, 14: Parliament of 1461, items 13 and 19. For the biographies of Fulford, Fynderne, Grimsby, Heron, Hody and Mounfort see *The House of Commons, 1422-1461*, ed. Linda Clark, 7 vols, Cambridge: Cambridge University Press, 2020. For Henry Bellingham see Peter Booth, 'Landed Society in Cumberland and Westmorland c. 1440-1485: The Politics of the Wars of the Roses' (PhD thesis, University of Leicester, 1997), pp. 50–60. For Trollope see David Grummitt, *The Calais Garrison: War and Military Service in England, 1436-1558*, Woodbridge: Boydell and Brewer, 2007, pp. 78, 106–07.

6  Kekewich, p. 142.

7  Benet writes 'on the day after St Thomas the Martyr', Hanham, p. 49.

8  Lewis (2017), p. 306.

9  Since the 1850s, it has been assumed the battlefield location has been known and almost no detailed investigation of the landscape and battle has been undertaken. This lack of attention is in part because there is almost no geographic details in contemporary documentary evidence about the action and thus little can be said about the battle. Even its exact location and scale remain uncertain as the contemporary sources do not agree about its date or numbers involved. One of the problems facing a historian is that where evidence is missing to give hard facts about an event, subsequent generations of writers have often 'embroidered' on the truth to present 'fake news': the Battle of

Wakefield is one such case in point. None of the sources written in a period of 30 years after the duke of York was killed mentioned where the battle was. Since the 1850s Castle Grove Park has been identified as the battlefield. The recovery of a sword of mid-fifteenth century date close to the proposed battlefield, does not mean the battle was here, just that a sword was dropped here in the fifteenth century. The sword is 'supposed' to be from the battle because it was found on the 'supposed' battlefield. As with all battlefield finds, caution should be exercised in associating the sword with the battle in the absence of corroborative archaeological evidence, especially as the specific spot where it was found is totally unknown.

10    Davies (1856), pp. 106–07.

11    Ralph Flenley, *Six Town Chronicles of England*, Oxford: Clarendon Press, 1911, p. 152.

12    Clements Markham, 'The Battle of Wakefield', *Yorkshire Archæological and Topographical Journal* 9 (1886), pp. 105–23; A.D.H. Leadman, 'The Battle of Wakefield', *Yorkshire Archæological and Topographical Journal* 11 (1890), pp. 348–60; Richard Brook, *Visits to Fields of Battle in England in the Fifteenth Century* (London, 1857), pp. 53–66.

13    BL, Harley MS. 116, fol. 142-46 (ca 1505).

14    TNA E13/147 rot 18d.

15    A polearm with a blade very wide at the base and tapering sharply to a point.

16    TNA KB27/803, rot. 16d.

17    Richard Anson sat as MP for Hull from 1439 till his death. As MP and Lord Mayor of Hull, Anson was a man of local importance, rewarded by the Yorkists for his support. His town had sent thirteen men to fight for King Henry at Northampton. As David Grummitt makes clear, Anson was in Westminster for the 1460 Parliament and was briefly imprisoned during various pleadings for debt. He received wages for 75 days up to 25 December. After this he disappears, presumably having died. However, pleadings in the Exchequer of Pleas indicate that he fell during the battle on 29 December 1460, having taken up arms for the House of York. TNA E13/147, rots. 80-1; 148. 4 See also E13/167, rot. 10.

18    TNA, C1/1/138 Sotehill v Harrington. The case showed Sir Thomas Harrington, knight, held of the king in chief in the county of Lancaster, and when he died, and who were his heirs; when it was found that he died on 30 December (39 Henry VI) and that his heirs were Ann and Elizabeth, his granddaughters. Their father John was also killed. At the time of the inquest 1467/68, Ann was aged nine and Elizabeth eight. It was found also that the manors and lands of which Thomas and John, had been held since their deaths by sir James Harrington, the second son of Sir Thomas, without title or right.

19    *John Vale's Book*, p. 179.

20  A.J. Pollard, *North Eastern England During the Wars of the Roses: Lay Society, War, and Politics 1450–1500*, Oxford, 1990, p. 325.

21  TNA E 159/238 Brevia Mich 1 Edw IV rot. 29.

22  TNA DL 29/560/8899 membrane 5 recto.

23  Ibid.

24  TNA KB 27/804, rot. 65.

25  TNA C49/64/54.

26  BL Egerton MS 1995.

27  Flenley, pp. 114–53.

28  Hanham, p. 49.

29  Completed in 1471 and likely written soon after is an ecclesiastical chronicle, composed in Latin, about the authorship of which nothing is known. The text is as follows; the translation is my own: 'After the Parliament had been prorogued, this duke of York (with his son Edward), and the earl of Salisbury (with his son Thomas), set out with a strong force towards the northern parts to quell the tumults there and punish the malefactors; whence they came to the town of Wakefield on Sunday in the holy week of Christmas, and on the morrow of St. Thomas the Martyr they prepared for a fight. *But when the day was already declining* [my emphasis], either by their carelessness and neglect, or by treason, there was to put to flight of a great part of their army, they were slain with many valorous nobles.' Dawson, Appendix 3.

30  *Ingulph's Chronicle of the Abbey of Croyland*, ed. H. T. Riley, London: George Bell & Sons, 1895, p. 421.

31  Clifford's retinue included John Caterall, late of Brayton in the county of York, gentleman, Thomas Barton, late of Helmsley in the county of York, gentleman, William Fyppes, late of South Duffield in the county of York, yeoman, Henry Cliff the elder, late of Lockington in the county of York, Thomas Tunstall, late of Thurland in the county of Lancaster, and John Clapham, late of Skipton in Craven in Yorkshire, yeoman. Clapham we have already mentioned. TNA C 65/106 rot. 19 Thomas Tunstall (c.1430–99) was nephew of Henry, Lord Fitzhugh. His involvement at Wakefield was clearly familiar.

32  Tim Sutherland, *Killing Time: Challenging the common perceptions of three medieval conflicts – Ferrybridge, Dintingdale and Towton – the 'largest battle of on British soil*, Leiden, 2009.

33  TNA D/29/509/8247

34  Jane Dawson in 1997 pointed out that John Amyas, gentleman of Wakefield, refused to take the oath of allegiance to Edward IV. Another amongst the duke's tenants who did not approve of the turn of events was Richard Lyster, who suffered attainder. His woollen mill and dye works stood 250m from the town gate on Kirkgate on the north bank

of the Calder. Clearly, the population of the town were not all ardent Yorkists. Dawson, footnote 1, p. 92. Contrary to Dawson, the vicar of Wakefield, John Preston, who also suffered attainder, may have been so treated simply because he preached against the duke, which if the case, further strengthens ones suspicion that Lancastrian loyalists allowed Clifford et al to enter the town unopposed.

35    BnF MS Français 88 Chronique des guerres advenues en France, en Angleterre et en Bourgogne depuis l'année 1444 jusqu'en 1471 folio 144-146. 'Andrew Trollop, who was a very subtle man of war, told the Duke of Somerset that they would not be able to get the Duke of York outside the town without consequent human loss. They therefore prepared 400 of the most courageous men, well indoctrinated for what they had to do – i.e. they were to go into the town and tell the duke that they were coming from Lancashire to rescue him. When the Duke of York, who never suspected such betrayal, saw all those people coming to him, he was so happy that he let them in straight away. The same night the Duke of York organised for somebody to be on the watch in order to watch for the Duke of Somerset who was in the field and to observe the extent of his power. At dawn of the day, Andrew Trollop accompanied by other warriors, informed the Duke of York, without introducing themselves, that they were coming to rescue him, which made the duke of joyful that he went outside the town to fight his enemies. It was then that Andrew Trollop betrayed him, knowing the Duke of Somerset to be nearby, he started to skirmish and the Duke of Somerset who was ready, charged viciously the Duke of York and his allies against him whom Andrew Trollop and his troops turned swiftly and so did the people sent by him the night before to the town.' The same story can be found copied at BnF MS Francais 20358 Chroniques d'Angleterre, folio 205. This story was 'common currency' in Europe sometime before 1470. We cannot be sure it dates to much earlier. It COULD date from early 1461 as Dr Livia Viser Fuchs thinks, and is part of Warwick's 'Apolog'y. I am inclined to think it dates from the period of the readeption 1469-71.

36    BnF MS Francais 71 is closely related to this text, but places Trollop's men wearing the livery of Warwick: 'Andrieu Trolot, qui estoit ung tres soubtil homme de guerre, dist au duc de Sombresset quil scavoit bien que sans grant perte de gens on ne povoit avoir de duc d'Yorc hors de la ville, si triouva manière de toute la nuit faire a ses gens palletos ou estoit le ravestocq, livree au comte de Warewic.' This statement about Warwick's livery, led some writers to think Warwick was present and escaped after the battle in a little boat BnF MS Francais 20354 Chroniques de Saint-Denis, folio 117 for example. The ravestocq = ragged staff we met earlier at Northampton worn by Grey of Ruthin. It may be a confusion between Wakefield and Northampton, especially so as most accounts in French MS are confused about the events at Northampton, Wakefield and the second St Albans. The reference to Warwick is surely deliberate. The need to critique Warwick is obvious

when we consider this text was completed in 1471: Warwick was not long dead after Barnet. His treason had to be shown to be pre-meditated.

The chroniclers become confused about Warwick, and we find perhaps because of the lack of chronology and clarity of writing, that Warwick was felt to be present, which we note below, then escaped a on a little boat. Wavrin studiously notes Warwick's livery being used a 'Trojan Horse' and repeats this version of events. The account is designed to make Warwick look duplicitous and hints at treachery. The only time when Warwick's reputation needed to be 'damaged' was in January or February 1461 to show to European leaders that Warwick was not a trust worthy ally. Of course 'reputational damage' to show Warwick was not trustworthy, could also date from 1469–71, but it seems unlikely. Earlier in the text the writer mentioned Trollop and Warwick is studiously ignored, except for this reference, until the second St Albans.

The rumour of Warwick being present through this subterfuge may be partly why Antonio de la Torre sought to deny Warwick's presence, writing on 9 January 1461 'This news caused great alarm in these parts, although it seems Warwick was not there.' ASM SCFP 566 Antonio de la Torre to duke of Milan. This reference may in fact confirm Trollop's use of Warwick's livery: for a member of Warwick's household to be unaware of where Warwick was, or to downplay suggestions he was at Wakefield, implies that 'the rumour mill' implied the earl was, ergo does this admission by de la Torre further corroborate BnF Fr MS 71? Arguably yes, potentially dating this reference to very early in 1461 and confirming the outline of events in BnF Fr MS 88. However BnF Fr MS 88 and its allied texts dates in all probability from 1467-9. The manuscript was owned by Louis de Gruuthuse. He met Jean de Wavrin in Bruges in winter 1470/71. Wavrin chose to use this story of treason and treachery by Trollop and Somerset rather than earlier texts such as the *Chronicle of Rollo* to Edward IV to paint the death of his patron's - Edward's - father in more chivalric terms than heretofore commented. This text was the basis for the English Chronicle which appeared c.1471/74. The text by Wavrin is politically charged to praise Edward, and damn Warwick. Wavrin worked from preexisting documents, which he badly edited together.

37 Hanham, p. 49. Written sometime after summer 1462 is the chronicle thought to be by a priest, John Benet, who lists 'the Duke of Somerset, with the earl of Devonshire, the Earl of Northumberland, Lord Roose, Lord Cliffe, Lord Neville, [Henry] Lord Fitzhugh, [Richard West], Lord Warr, [Ralph Lord Greystoke].' Robert Bale, seems to have been writing in London within days of the Second Battle of St. Albans in February 1461 and records 'by the duk of Somerset the Erle Northumberland the Lorde Roos and the lord Clifford and the lorde Nevyll and andrewe trollop and ojers'. Flenley, p. 153. Naming these nobles does not necessarily mean they were physically present, just men in their pay. Moreover, the similarity in the names between the two writers makes

me suppose a degree of authenticity in what is being reported withing weeks of the event taking place.

38   *An English Chronicle*, ed. Marx, pp. 90–1; See also, Wavrin, vol. 5, pp. 297–300, 322–4; BnF, MS Français 15491, ff. 90v-91. Abbot Whethamstede's account of Northampton is very similar to that in *An English Chronicle* and the newsletters: *Registra Johannis Whethamstede*, pp. 372–4.

39   Warwick was probably also behind the circulation of newsletters in the wake of the Second Battle of St. Albans on 17 February 1461. These too stressed treachery as a reason for the Yorkist defeat and found their way into Wavrin's account and *An English Chronicle*. The treachery of Warwick's Kentish captain, Richard Lovelace, who had been captured and turned by the Lancastrians at Wakefield, provided a convenient link between the two events: Wavrin, 5, pp. 327–30; *An English Chronicle*, ed. Marx, p. 98. Visser-Fuchs, pp. 477, 483. One such newsletter was sent to the Dauphin Louis by 'one who was at the great battle on Shrove Tuesday' and reported to the duke of Milan by his ambassador at the French court.

40   Livia Visser-Fuchs, 'Richard in Holland, 1470-1', *The Ricardian* 6 (1983), pp. 220–8; See also Visser-Fuchs (2018), pp. 69–70.

## Chapter 24: The Aftermath

1    C 1/28/313.

2    TNA C 1/40/274.

3    TNA CPR 1461-1467: 3 December 1461 Grant, during the minority of the heir, to Margaret, late the wife of James Pikeryng esq, son and heir of James Pikeryng kt, deceased, for the relief of herself and her seven children of the custody of a messuage and 4 acres of land in Ellerton, co. York, in the king's hands by reason of the minority of James Pikeryng, kinsman and heir of the said knight, with the marriage of the heir.

4    TNA Court of Common Pleas (hereafter CP) 40/817, rot. 331.

5    TNA C 1/27/202.

6    Simon Payling pers comm 17/11/2023.

7    Davies (1856), pp. 106–07.

8    TNA CPR 1452-61, p. 551.

9    CPR 1461-1467, p. 107.

10   David Grummitt pers comm 12/01/2025.

11   See Appendix 1 and Appendix 2.

12   TNA DL 29/560/8899 membrane 5 verso.

13   The kitchen and bakehouse were of domestic scale when compared to neighbouring Pontefract, for example. It had no stables, no forge, no barns, and it was impossible to ride a horse or drive a cart through the gate passage. Archaeologically the bakehouse constructed c.1270–1400

was destroyed and out of use by c.1450 judging by recovered pottery which broadly fits the known documentary evidence for its destruction. Moreover, Sandal was in poor repair. The keep, erected on a manmade motte, was suffering severely from subsidence: so much so a new tower had to be built in 1483. These structural cracks are clearly seen on the drawing of the castle made in 1564. Indeed, a survey of 1538 the keep was not habitable, so too the great hall and others principal rooms which had been replaced with half-timbered buildings in 1483–4. TNA E 36/159. Showing the limited occupation of the castle from 1400 to 1484 is the fact that just four pottery groups can be dated to the period 1400–85. Occupation was liminal and limited – the duke of York used the castle perhaps three times between 1420 and 1460 based on documentary records – centred around the domestic buildings in the north eastern quadrant of the outer bailey. We are seeing a castle in decline and decay. Phil Mayes and Laurance Butler, *Sandal Castle Excavations 1964-1973*, Wakefield: Wakefield Historical Publications, 1983, pp 84–5. The Grave of Sandal reports 'the insurrection of various rebels of the king at Pontefract . . . residing for days on end in Sandal castle'. Later the same document he notes 'wages of various carpenters and others from the castle with 6s 8d allowed for the milldam of the said mills at the time of their repair as appears by a writ for 38s 8d by William Hyncheclyff; And for 10s 11d paid to various people repairing various defects in various buildings within the castle <7s 4d> and the park pale <3s 7d> as appears by another writ. Total 49s 7d' TNA DL 29/560/8899 membrane 1. It is probable the castle was damaged by the departing Lancastrians. David Grummitt argues all the damage noted in the Manorial Accounts was all in the immediate aftermath of the 'battle.' Christopher Watson argues the damage was carried out over a longer period. The documents – other than in exceptionally circumstances e.g. noting York in Wakefield December–January – cover the period 11 November to 2 February, therefore either conclusion fits the evidence. I err on the side of the damage being after the 'battle', but am not wholly convinced. The major unanswered question is, how did the Lancastrians get into the castle? The castle was easily defended by a handful of men. The locking bar of the gates could only be released by the garrison? What convinced them of the need to do so? OR had York left part of his force behind in the castle – in the English Civil War it could barely accommodate 150men with a dozen horses – and as Appendix 1 suggests, turned out to be Lancastrians? Very plausible that it was an 'inside job' as with whatever happened in the town of Wakefield itself.

14  Dawson Appendix 2, citing William of Worcester, and Davies *English Chronicle*.

15  Flenley (1911), pp. 166–7.

16  ASM SCFP 566 Antonio del la Torre to Francesco Sforza Duke of Milan, 9 January 1461. It is possible Salisbury was captured on the 29th and he and York were killed on the evening of 30 January in Pontefract. I am

not sure sufficient time existed to compress these events in 48 hours and short winter days.

17 John Sadler, *Towton: The Battle on Palm Sunday Field 1461*, Barnsley: Pen and Sword, 2011. See also John Sadler, *The Red Rose and the White: The Wars of the Roses, 1453-1487*, London: Routledge, 2013, pp. 93–7.

18 George Minois, *Richard III: le roi Maudit?*, Paris: Perrin, 2022.

19 Louis of Bruges, Lord of Gruuthuse who was in England when the battle took place, owned BnF MS Fr 88. Gruuthuse met Wavrin, Edward IV and Richard duke of Gloucester in Bruges in January 1471. As Livia Visser-Fuchs and David Grummitt, and I believe correctly think, Wavrin met the two Yorkist princes in person. Perhaps it was this meeting that inspired Wavrin to use the manuscript in Gruuthuse's possession to compose an account of Wakefield which presented the duke of York in more favourable terms than the original 'official' Yorkist narrative developed in the early 1460s present in *The Chronicle from Rollo*.

20 Visser-Fuchs (2018). Wavrin relied on the works of Enguerrand de Monstrelet and King of Arms of the Order of the Golden Fleece Jean Lefèvre de Saint-Rémy. He embellished their work. Beyond reasonable doubt, Wavrin seems to have had access to a number of newsletters covering the end of Henry VI's reign, the rise of Richard duke of York and his family, that are now lost. He also had direct access to Warwick. However, as Visser-Fuchs stresses, Wavrin was composing the part of the text concerning the rise of the duke of York and coronation of Edward IV when Warwick had abandoned Edward's cause and sought reconciliation with Henry VI and the French to restore the former to the English throne. Warwick's news letters on Northampton, Wakefield and St Albans, all copied down as part of BnF 88 and the English Chronicle and then embedded into Wavrin's own text, means that what we have therefore are not Yorkist accounts but those of Warwick. These sources therefore must be used with utmost caution.

21 Kervyn de Lettenhove, *Joseph Marie Bruno Constantin, Chroniques relatives à l'histoire de la Belgique sous la domination des ducs de Bourgogne*, Bruxelles: F Hayez, 1870 pp. 431–2. De But did use original sources when he could. For example, he quoted apparently verbatim the texts of the treaty of Péronne and of Mary of Burgundy's promises at the beginning of her reign, and many papal documents. At times, his account appears at first sight to be totally garbled rendering of the original; in some such cases a closer look at times reveals that he did have detailed information, but did not know enough of the background to make things clear either in his own mind or to his readers. In fact, it appears that de But received more information than he could cope with, too much conflicting detail to put into proper order. Sadly, has also been so little studied – least of all by English scholars. We must also note, that what de But wrote was not meant to be a chronicle account in any meaningful sense of the word. Yes, for want of a better word, he used primary sources to craft his story – emphasis on story – replete with Classical and Biblical references,

Either the source de But used, or he himself believed, that the Yorkists enjoyed divine favour thanks to the Pope's blessing, and thereby made the duke a holy martyr like Beckett. Again, English, Yorkist, writers like Benet stress this link with Beckett by mentioning the battle was the day after Becketts own death. De But also mentions the miraculous escape from Wakefield of Warwick: our monk is not inventing facts here, he is clearly working from a lost newsletter, as the same event is also presented in various texts of the Monstrelet continuator and other chronicles for example, BnF MS Francais 20354 Chroniques de Saint-Denis, folio 117 verso, noted earlier. Treslot/Trolot/Trollop appears again across chronicles, the writers again working from now lost sources. As we noted earlier, Warwick was at seat at the time. Had he actually landed in Flanders? Or is this a reference to taking the future Richard III and the duke of Clarence to Flanders, this giving an approximate date for when de But wrote this piece? Both are possible. Clearly our Monk was working with a lost newssheet. He had been in Paris from 1458–60, and was with the Burgundian court in 1460, and was present with Louis XI in Paris in 1463. He was in the right place, at the right time, to read and hear first-hand accounts of what happened. His work is appended to that of Giles de Roye, who died 1478. The writer of BnF 88 correctly presents Warwick's escape after Ludford and NOT Wakefield, clearly we are dealing with two conflicting lost documents prepared in 1460–3. Clearly, in the chaos between Wakefield and Towton, conflicting news was being generated and sent to Europe. These documents are now lost, but were studiously copied by French chroniclers, and then used as the basis for Wavrin's later account. We cannot simply discount French and Burgundian sources on grounds of chauvinism, when they were created in exactly the same manner as English chronicles and letters: hearsay and gossip. De But was an eyewitness to the events of 1469–71, and writes at his strongest for this period. He is fascinated by Warwick, both for his good and bad aspects of his personality. De But did use original sources when he could. For example, he quoted verbatim the texts of the treaty of Péronne and of Mary of Burgundy's promises at the beginning of her reign, and many papal documents. At times, his account appears at first sight to be totally garbled rendering of the original; in some such cases a closer look at times reveals that he did have detailed information, but did not know enough of the background to make things clear either in his own mind or to his readers. In fact, it appears that de But received more information than he could cope with, too much conflicting detail to put into proper order. Sadly, has also been so little studied – least of all by English scholars.

22  'In this year 1460 Margaret, Queen of England, the wife of the captive King Henry, with the help of some people, took prisoner the duke of York, when he with others, that is the duke of Warwick and the earls of Salisbury and Sufford, wanted to do his devotions in a monastery. This queen ordered the foresaid men to be beheaded, and also the first-born son of the duke of York, called Edmund, and Lord Rivers, [and she

had] this text set above [York's] head: This is he who wanted to be king of England [Hic est qul voluit esse rex Anglorum]. But Richard, Duke of Warwick, secretly escaped and soon joined the second son of the beheaded duke, scilicet domino Gilemer, otherwise named Edward, Earl of March, and started to act strongly against the party of the queen.' Lettenhove. p. 450.

23    TNA KB27/803, rot. 16d The duke would have had had more than one armour with him, which Thorpe looted, rather than taking the armour York was wearing. But to execute him, he would have had to be partially stripped of armour, assuming he was wearing it.

24    TNA C 65/106 rot 13.

25    BnF Ms-5084 réserve. La Cronicque Enguerran de Monstrelet states: 'fortune turned against the duke, who was made prisoner, together with his second son and the earl of Salisbury. Shortly after, the queen had them beheaded.' Again, we read from Le Cerq 'the Duke of York and the earl of Rutland his second son, and the earl of Salisbury were made prisoners' Buchon, p. 82.

26    Thomas Basin was also not aware of all the facts 'Ipse vero Henricus et ejus conjux, filia Renati, Siculorum regis, mulier prudens et animosa, cum pluribus regni principibus periculosum rerum suarum statum atque ancipitem iuspicientes, ex adverse contractis undique viribus et prsecipue nobilitatis regni, quae longe majore ex parte Henrico regi favebat exercitum validuAi coegerunt; cum quo adversarios prosequentes, prima vice in mense januario, secunda vice in mense februaria, contra ipsos seditiosos dimicarunt; in quibus duobus praeliis Henricus et sui potiti sunt victoria, fusis liostibus et multis millibus ex ipsis interemptts. Ceciderunt in hujusmodi djuobus praeliis pacefatus Eborraci dux et comes de Warvich senior', seu capti in conflictu statimque post capite plexi sunt'. Basin, Vol. 1, p. 298. The same confusion over Wakefield and St Albans is found in BnF Fr 2889 dated to 1483: 'At this time, in the said kingdom of England there once again happened the same discomfiture as before dictated and thus was made by the said earl of Warwyk, the duke of Sommerset, cousin of the said king Henry of England, accompanied by several other young lords, relatives and heirs of the other princes and lords who had been killed defending the throne of the said King Henry of Lancaster, formed large masses of men-at-arms and came to hold the country against the said Duke of York. And so, they came to find him and his company, and in a battle, all of which were killed. And in this field, called the field of Saint-Albons, the said Duke of York was killed; and, after he was killed, they chopped off his head, which they put at the end of a spear; and around his head they placed a crown of fur in the form of a royal crown, in mockery of the fact that he wanted to make himself king of the said kingdom. And with them died in this field six barons, knights, squires and people of name of the said kingdom and a large number of other men of war, who were estimated from 60 to 100,000.'

The lack of a clear and precise chronology of the events allows contestable chronologies to be created through bad editing and the attempt by the compiler to fit the facts as they have them from news sheets to what he thinks he knows from common gossip into a single narrative for both our French and Dutch writer. The confusion may be simply due to the chaotic nature of events between Wakefield and Towton and lack of sources. That BL Harl 4424 and BnF Fr. 88 are almost identical to Wavrin's 'Recueil' speaks of their better access to news sheets.

27  Kervyn de Lettenhove, *Joseph Marie Bruno Constantin, Chroniques relatives à l'histoire de la Belgique sous la domination des ducs de Bourgogne*, Bruxelles: F Hayez, 1870 pp. 431–2. De But did use original sources when he could. For example, he quoted apparently verbatim the texts of the treaty of Péronne and of Mary of Burgundy's promises at the beginning of her reign, and many papal documents. At times, his account appears at first sight to be totally garbled rendering of the original; in some such cases a closer look at times reveals that he did have detailed information, but did not know enough of the background to make things clear either in his own mind or to his readers. In fact, it appears that de But received more information than he could cope with, too much conflicting detail to put into proper order. Sadly, this has also been little studied – at least of all by English scholars. We must also note, that what de But wrote was not meant to be a chronicle account in any meaningful sense of the word. Yes, for want of a better word, he used primary sources to craft his story – emphasis again on story – replete with Classical and Biblical references, Either the source de But used, or he himself believed, that the Yorkists enjoyed divine favour thanks to the Popes blessing, and thereby made the duke a holy martyr like Beckett. Again, English, Yorkist, writers like Benet stress this link with Beckett by mentioning the battle was the day after Becketts own death.

28  For example, the Kattendijke chronicle was written by David of Burgundy (1426–94), illegitimate son of Philip the Good, and Bishop of Utrecht from 1456 reports Warwick's landing in the south of England (at Hamton) in 1460, and was also aware of the events of early 1461: 'Inter Jaer Heren M CCCC ende LXI was weder een opstal in Engelant, te weten coninc Heynric ende die coninginne, sijn wijft, mit horen hulperen an die een zijde, ende wert verdreven uut Enghelant ende toach in Scotlant. Ende due hartoech van Jorck wort tot London ontflangen voer coninck van Engeland. Ende in desen strijt bleven doot so men seide over XL man. 'Item tjaer daertevoren int jaer can LX was een opstal in Enghelant, sodatter gestreden wort omtrent Sinte-Albouts, daer coninic Heinric ende die hartoge can Sommerset mit horen hulperen due overhant behilden jegen den hartoghe can Jorck end de grave van Werwick, daer veel volcx bleef an beiden zijdfen mar daer wort onthoeft die hartoge can Jorcks vader mit veel heer. Dat dat na zwaerlicken ghewroecken wort, als verscreven is.' The key passage of the text states (my translation): 'But the duke of York's father was spared along with many lords. Then afterwards in an act of severe revenge their heads

were hacked off.' Livia Visser Fuchs pers comm 9 November 2024. Similarly, Archbishop Thomas Basin conflates Wakefield and St Albans in almost identical manner, the translation is my own ' Henry himself and his wife, the daughter of Rene, king of the Sicily, a prudent and courageous woman, with several princes of the kingdom they sought to end the perilous state and danger of their affairs, from the opposing forces which surrounded them on all sides, and with the nobility of the kingdom, who by far the greater part favoured King Henry's army they attacked them in force; with whom, pursuing their adversaries, the first time in the month of January, the second time in the month of February, they fought against the rebels themselves; in which two battles Henry and his men obtained a victory, and many thousands of them were slain. In two battles of this kind, the duke of York and the elder earl of Warwich fell, and were captured in the conflict and then beheaded' Basin, Vol. 1, p. 298

The same confusion over Wakefield and St Albans is found in BnF Fr 2889 dated to 1483: 'At this time, in the said kingdom of England there once again happened the same discomfiture as before dictated and thus was made by the said earl of Warwyk, the duke of Sommerset, cousin of the said king Henry of England, accompanied by several other young lords, relatives and heirs of the other princes and lords who had been killed defending the throne of the said King Henry of Lancaster, formed large masses of men-at-arms and came to hold the country against the said Duke of York. And so, they came to find him and his company, and in a battle, all of which were killed. And in this field, called the field of Saint-Albons, the said Duke of York was killed; and, after he was killed, they chopped off his head, which they put at the end of a spear; and around his head they placed a crown of fur in the form of a royal crown, in mockery of the fact that he wanted to make himself king of the said kingdom.'

The lack of a clear and precise chronology of the events allows contestable chronologies to be created through bad editing and the attempt by the compiler to fit the facts as they have them from news sheets to what he thinks he knows from common gossip into a single narrative for both our French and Dutch writer. The confusion may be simply due to the chaotic nature of events between Wakefield and Towton and lack of sources. That BL Harl 4424 and BnF Fr. 88 are almost identical to Wavrins 'Recueil' and has a clear chronology of event speaks of their better access to information.

29   BnF Fr2889.

30   The Abbot of St Albans tells us the duke was captured and then decapitated. He writes: 'They placed him on ant hill and placed on his head, as If a crown, a vile garland made of reeds, just as the Jews did to the Lord, and bent the knee to him, saying in Jest 'Hail King, without rule. Hail King, without lineage. Hail leader and prince, with almost no subjects or possessions.' And having said this and various other shameful and dishonourable things to him, at last they cut off his

head. The following day the Earl of Salisbury was taken to the castle of Pontefract and decapitated.' *Registrum Monasterii Sancti Albani*, p. 382. This hill could be Bitch Hill in Wakefield where the town's gallows were. We cannot be 100 per cent certain if the duke was killed and then decapitated later, or where. If we allow the abbott to be correct, the event took place in Wakefield market place, in the traditional place of execution in the town. However, and we cannot stress the importance of this, our Abbot's account of Wakefield is not a chronicle style account in any meaningful sense of the word, nor was it supposed to be. Replete with Classical and Biblical references, it was designed to stress the divine favour enjoyed by the Yorkists, while simultaneously damning the Lancastrians (or 'northerners' as the abbot calls them throughout his work). The hill he mentions is a direct allusion to Golgotha, and he is setting the duke up as a holy martyr like Beckett, replete with the crown of thorns. It is not reliable history, nor was it meant to be. Or should it be used as such.

31  Flenley, pp. 166–7.

32  'The news from England is that the Queen has recently fought with the Duke of York and taken York, which is a fine city. The king and the Earl of Warwick thought that the forces of the duke and of the earl's father and brothers were sufficiently strong, but they were defeated, and they were slain the duke, his son, the Earl of Warwick's father and his two sons, and 12,000 to 16,000 men. Many others, were slain in other battles subsequently; the numbers it is said to amount to thousands. When the king heard this, he was much moved, although the Duke of York seems rather to have been slain out of hatred for having claimed the kingdom more than anything else.' ASM SCFP 566 Prospero di Camulio, Milanese Ambassador to the Court of France, 1 February 1461.

33  'A brief Latin chronicle', in James Gairdner (ed.), *Three Fifteenth-Century Chronicles with Historical Memoranda by John Stowe*, London: 1880, pp. 164–85.

34  Jean du Roye BnF Fr 2889 states a fur crown: 'the said Duke of York was killed; and, after he was killed, they chopped off his head, which they put at the end of a spear; and around his head they placed a crown of fur in the form of a royal crown, in mockery of the fact that he wanted to make himself king of the said kingdom.'

35  Dawson, p. 78.

36  Lettenhove, p. 432. The Abbot of Saint Albans however has 'as If a crown, a vile garland made of reeds, just as the Jews did to the Lord', the duke was then mocked and executed. He adds 'The following day the Earl of Salisbury was taken to the castle of Pontefract and decapitated': *Registrum Monasterii Sancti Alban* p. 382

37  The date of 30 December was the feast day of Venustian and his sons, who were beheaded 30 December 303 along with Saint Sabinus of

Spoleto. Coincidence that York and his followers were killed this day in exactly the same manner in very similar circumstances?

38  Peter 5:4, 'When the Chief Shepherd appears, you will receive the crown of glory that will never fade away.' See also 1 Corinthians 9:24-27.

39  TNA CPR 1467-1477, pp. 522–3.

40  TNA C 140/5/43

41  Ross (1974), p. 35. The citation was as follows: 'to Henry Auger, John Copildike, Edmund Yns and John Maners, esquire, and to other the captains, masters, merchants, undermerchants, or quartermasters of ships of the fleet appointed to be sent to the northern parts of the realm. Order whensoever and wheresoever to make proclamation (as above): And that whatsoever person holding the party of the said adversary, that within ten days after this proclamation would depart from them, shall have grace and pardon of his life and goods, except Andrew Trollopp, William Grymsby, Everard Digby, William Feldyng, Thomas Fitzharry, Ellis Cornewayll, Doctor Moreton, Gerveys Clyfton, Thomas Tunstall, Henry Lowys knight, Thomas Parker of the Forthe, Thomas Everyngham, John Davet, both bastards of Exeter, Master Hugh Payn, Thomas Langton, Henry Beaumont, William Belynghams, Alexander Hody, Henry Tudnam, — Clapham the younger, and all other having lands etc. to the yearly value of 100 marks and over, and whatever persons shall effectually destroy and bring out of life Andrew Trollopp, the bastards of Exeter, William Grymsby, Robert Whityngham, Thomas Tresham, Thomas Fitzharry and Clapham the younger shall have for every one of them £100: and charging that no man rob, spoil, trouble or hurt any of the tenants of the lord Dacre of Gillesland, Sir Ralph Grey knight, or John Witherington squire, upon pain of death.' Calendar of Close Rolls Preserved in the Public Record Office. . . . Edward IV, 1461 – [1476] (London, 1949), pp. 55–6.

42  TNA KB 27/804, rot. 65.

43  'And my Lord Fitzwater is ryden northewards, and it is sayd in my Lord of Cawnterberys howse that he hethe takyn ijc. of Andrew Troloppys men. And as for Colt, and Sir Jamys Strangwysse and Sir Thomas Pykeryng, they be takyn or ellys dede. The comyn voysse is that they be de dede. Hopton and Hastyngs be with the Erle of Marche, and wer no at the fewlde. Wat word that ever he have fro my Lords that be here, it is well doo, and best for yow, to see that the contre be allweys redy to come bothe fote men and hors men.' Dawson Appendix 1. Given we know the Lancastrians based in East Yorkshire used a system of cabotage to transport wheat, barley, etc from Norfolk and Suffolk to Hull and perhaps Scarborough, it is a reasonable conclusion that Trollop had some degree of involvement, but only after Wakefield, when we know Charles VII was in the process of sending substantial military aid to Margaret, potential led by Comte de Charolais. BnF MS Fr 26087 folio 7503.

44  TNA CPR 1461-1467, p. 32.

45  Richard III paid for a perpetual mass for his father's soul at St Richards Friary, Pontefract. Rosemary Horrox, *Richard III*, Cambridge: Cambridge University Press, 1989, p. 148. Perhaps confirming this, a French source tells us that the duke was buried in the *hostel defreres mineurs*, but Pontefract lacked such a house of Franciscans. It could be conceivably be confused with the Dominican friary. Dawson, Appendix 2. The Crowland Continuation, the duke, Rutland and Salisbury were buried in a 'lowly burial place in the house mendicant friars'. Laynesmith, p. 209 gives both St Richard's Dominican Friary as the burial placed from the Crowland Continuation. Laynesmith also notes burial list for St Richard's compiled before 1504 which reports the burial of Richard and Edmund. Thirdly, a 1534 Herald's account of burials in the Dominican church in Pontefract reports the burials of the heart burials of York, Rutland, Salisbury and Neville. This would incidentally suggest that their bodies may have been embalmed in 1460.

46  Tim Sutherland pers comm. The author assisted Professor Sutherland whilst studying for his undergraduate degree in his geophysical and topographic survey of the battlefield, as well as post excavation analysis of the human skeletal material from Towton as well as metal detector survey recovered archaeological material, including early cannonballs.

47  Dr P Ottaway pers comm. 17/8/2004.

48  Yet we do note Saint Denis was beheaded, rose from the grave and carried his own head around, so clearly Catholic theology as not as 'clear cut' as we might think.

49  TNA, KB27/803, rot. 16d.

50  BL Add mss 46355, folio 2 verso.

Those dubbed by Somerset:

John, lord Clifford

James Luttrell

Robert Whittingham

Nicholas Latimer.

Dubbed by Northumberland:

Richard Percy, brother to the earl

William Gascoigne

Thomas Metham

William Bertram

Richard Aldborough

Thomas Elderton

John Mauleverer

Willaim Saint Quintin

Those dubbed by the earl of Devon:

John Coutenary, brother to the earl

Thomas Fulford

Alexander Hody

Richard Cary

Dubbed by lord Clifford were:

Roger Clifford, brother to the lord

Richard Tempest

Henry Bellingham

Thomas Babthorpe.

The list is compiled from familial geneologies and may be more fact than fiction

51   W.A. Shaw, *The Knights of England*, 2 vols, London: Sherratt and Hughes, 1906, Vol. 2, pp. 12–13.

52   William Normavill dit Normanvil of Topcliffe, made his will 24 March 1461, proved 20 January 1462. Presumably he was killed at Towton.

53   Poulson, Vol. 2, pp. 233–5.

54   Ibid. p,. 237.

55   Hull City Archives BRL 4 David Grummitt pers comm 01/01/2025.

56   Humphrey Dacre we mentioned earlier, or Ranulf Dacre (c.1412–61). His mother, Lady Philippe (born sometime before 20 July 1399 and death before 1458), was the daughter of the formidable Ralph Neville, 1st Earl of Westmorland (c.1364–1425) and his first wife Lady Margaret Stafford (c.1364–96). Ranulf married Eleanor FitzHugh, daughter of Henry FitzHugh, 5th Lord FitzHugh with their marriage appearing to have been childless.

57   BnF Ms Fr 20488, folio 23.

58   ADN B 2040, folio 34.

59   ADN B 2040, folio 169. The duke of Burgundy communicated news to the Dauphin on 9 February B 2040, folio 171. The duke sent news from Scotland to the Dauphin on 16 February. Ibid., folio 172.

60   BnF MS Latin 11892, folio 187.

61   David Grummitt pers comm.

62   Knowles, 'Wakefield', p. 264.

63   CPR 1452-1462, pp. 656, 658, 659.

64   Carpenter, pp. 154–5.

## Chapter 25: Conclusion

1    Carpenter, pp. 154–5.

2    ASM SCFP 566 Francesco Coppini to Francesco Sforza, Duke of Milan. Written at Canterbury, 6 August 1460.

3    Ibid. Instructions of Prospero Camulio, 24 December 1460.

## Appendix 1: Manorial Accounts of the Battle of Wakefield 1460–1461

1    In these accounts there are three returns for 'Wakefield'; Wakefield Fee, Wakefield Town (villa) and Wakefield Graveship (prepositura). I take the fee to be the farm of manorial assets, the town to be the borough and the graveship to be that part of the township not in the borough. This may not be correct.

2    At Wakefield

3    E.g. the fulling mills

4    One of the receivers, implying perhaps that another lessee/farmer could not be found.

## Appendix 3: Prisoners

1    David Grummitt pers comm, 01/01/2025.

2    TNA C 1/31/485.

3    TNA DL42/18, folio 135 verso; See also Ibid. DL37/26/15.

4    TNA SC8/107/5322.

5    TNA C 1/31/358 Redsham v Routhe. Plaintiffs.

6    TNA C 1/27/456 Barowe v Squyer.

7    TNA C 1/27/340 Romney V Croydon.

8    Anon, *Collectanea topographica et genealogica*, London: J B Nicholls, 1834, Volume 1, p. 394.

9    TNA C 140/8/36.

10    Hicks (2010), p. 160.

11    TNA KB27/803, rot. 16d.

12    TNA KB27/804, rot. 65.

13    TNA CP P40/802, rot. 441; See also Ibid. 804, rot. 237.

14    TNA: KB27/809, rot. 50. His victim on that occasion was George Chapman from whom he allegedly took goods worth £40.

15    Dawson, footnote 1, p. 92.

16    TNA DL29/560/8899 membrane 1, recto.

17    Yorkshire Archaeological Society DD 46/18/1.

18    Dawson, p. 98.

19    TNA DL/31/1.

20    Dawson, Appendix 10.

21    TNA C 1/27/202.

## Appendix 4: The Earl of Rutland

1    Dawson, Appendix 1. A very similar list is preserved in BnF Ms-5084 réserve but specifically states the battle was at Wakefield: 'the said Duke of York, his second son, and the earl of Salisbury, Lord Neville, Lord Haringeois, Lord Thomas de Hermant and Lord Jehan Harintoy all died there; but the Duke of York and the earl of Rutland his second son, and the earl of Salisbury were made prisoners; and that very day all three were beheaded and killed. And because the said Duke of York had wanted to be king of England, after the said duke was beheaded, on the advice of the said captain Adrien Treslot, a paper crown was placed on his head in derision and their heads were placed on lances on the gates of the said city of York.' In a later and different hand, Haringeois is noted as Hastings, Hermant as Aparre – presumably Parr. Clearly our source has been edited later, so presumably this annotation demonstrates our French source is earlier and may date from 1461–3, and has been amended when new information has to the attention of the writer, especially so as the writer, Jean du Clercq, who was secretary to the duke of Burgundy was dead in October 1467 aged 43. IF du Clerq is the author of the amendment, although the text has other edits noted at 1502, it could date the English Chronicle to be much earlier than 1470. We are at a loss as who Hermant could be. The note re Hastings is an error. Polydore Virgil names Sir Ralph Hastings as killed at Wakefield in his work *Anglica Historia* (drafted by 1513; printed in 1534). Sir Ralph Hastings died before 1 December 1495. Edward Hall names Sir Hugh Hastings as killed, in his book of c.1540. Again, an error, as Sir Hugh died in 1488. This rather supposes the editing was carried out later rather than earlier to BnF Ms-5084.

2    Sir Thomas Parr (1406–64) was Queen Catherine Parr's (1512–48) great grandfather. He was elected MP for Cumberland in 1429 and sat in the house till summer 1460. His grandfather, William Parr, made his career in the service of John of Gaunt, duke of Lancaster. Through that great retinue, he contracted a match far beyond the expectations of his modest birth. In about 1382 his friendship with another ducal retainer, Peter Roos, enabled him to marry Peter's niece, Elizabeth (b.c.1365), granddaughter and heiress-presumptive of Sir Thomas Roos of Kendal (the last male representative of a junior branch of the Lords Roos of Helmsley). Sir Thomas's death in 1390 brought Elizabeth a quarter of the valuable barony of Kendal, worth about 100 marks per annum, and the Parrs were immediately elevated to the forefront of the Westmorland gentry, a story partially preserved by Leland. He is linked

to another support of York at the Battle of Wakefield: 2 April 1444: he granted all his lands to (Sir) Thomas Harington, Robert Ingleton and others in the service of Sir Thomas Neville. British Library Additional Manuscripts. 38133, f. 151; By 1447 he was acting as steward of two north Westmorland manors for the earl of Salisbury's brother, Lord Latimer. Since Latimer was mentally incapacitated, it is likely that he was the earl's appointee. When the crisis came in 1459, Parr lost no time in declaring himself for the Nevilles. On about 2 September 1459 he was among those who left Middleham Castle in company with the earl of Salisbury, and he was present at both the Battle of Blore Heath on 23 September. and at the rout of the Yorkists at Ludford Bridge on 12 October. He was duly attainted with other leading Yorkists at the Coventry Parliament, and on 21 December 1459, it seems sought refuge in Calais with the earls of Salisbury and Warwick. If so, he must have been part of the Yorkist force which landed at Sandwich in June 1460, then either proceeding with Warwick to Northampton, where the Lancastrians were defeated on 10 July. On 12 November 1460 he and two of his sons, William and Thomas, were among those commissioned to arrest and imprison men guilty of unlawful assemblies in Cumberland and Westmorland. All three were present at Wakefield fighting with Sir Thomas Neville. All three survived the carnage and went on to fight at Towton. On 29 July, described as 'King's knight', he was given the wardship and marriage of the grandson and heir of Sir John Hotham of Scorborough (Yorkshire), who had been killed at Towton in the service of Percy. TNA CPR 1461-1467, p. 27. This was an extremely valuable grant: not only did the Hothams' hold several manors, including one at Staveley in Westmorland, but the heir was an infant. Sir Thomas died 24 November 1461: son William (1434–83) married the widow of Thomas Colt after his death in 1467, and brought some 600 men to Edward on the King's return from exile in 1471. Sir Thomas's younger brother Sir John Parr, was made Sherrif of Westmoreland in 1462, died in 1473. Reports of their death at Wakefield were clearly wrong.

3   BL, Harley MS 116, fol. 142-46 (ca 1505).

4   Brie, p. 531.

5   Lettenhove, p. 432.

6   BnF Ms-5084 réserve.

7   BL Harleian MS 4424 Folio 157. The date given, correlates with Archbishop Thomas Basin.

8   Kekewich, p. 179.

9   TNA C 65/106 rot. 19.

## Appendix 5: The Earl of Salisbury

1   Dawson, p. 80.

2   Davies (1856), pp. 106–07.

3    TNA KB9 149/9, membrane 8.

4    Basin, Vol. 1, p. 298.

5    Dawson, p. 28.

6    Brie, p. 531.

7    Richard Anson sat as MP for Hull from 1439 till his death. As MP and
     Lord Mayor of Hull, Anson was a man of local importance, rewarded by
     the Yorkists for his support. His town had sent thirteen men to fight for
     King Henry at Northampton. As David Grummitt makes clear, Anson
     is in Westminster for the 1460 Parliament and is briefly imprisoned
     during various pleadings for debt. He received wages for 75 days up to
     25 December. After this he disappears; presumably he died. However,
     pleadings in the Exchequer of pleas indicate that he fell during the battle,
     on 29 December 1460, having taken up arms for the House of York. TNA
     Exchequer Rolls [hereafter EC] EC13/167, rot. 10. 4.

8    ASM SCFP 566 England and Scotland. 566 Antonio de la Torre to
     Francesco Sforza Duke of Milan, 9 January 1461: 'Some of the lords of
     the queen's party, rendered desperate by the victory of the lords here
     and especially the Earl of Warwick, assembled a force in the northern
     parts, eighty miles from London, to come and attack their opponents
     here who are with the king, and get back the king into power, as they
     had him before. Accordingly, the duke of York with two of his sons, and
     Warwick's father, the Earl of Salisbury, went out to meet them. And it
     came to pass, that although they were three times stronger, yet from
     lack of discipline because they allowed a large part of their force to go
     pillaging and searching for victuals, their adversaries who are desperate,
     attacked the duke and his followers. Ultimately, they routed them,
     slaying the duke and his younger son, the Earl of Rutland, Warwick's
     father and many others. This news caused great alarm in these parts,
     although it seems Warwick was not there . . . this engagement took
     place on the last day of December near a castle called Pontefract.' Torre,
     writing from London, was passing on what he had been told – he was
     not an eyewitness. He implies the duke of York had the larger force, but
     it was compromised by the need to gather fodder and food. He then
     implies that the duke of York were drawn into a battle, and provided
     the Lancastrians the opportunity to defeat the duke. Much of the story
     is is propaganda to minimise the duke's death in terms of propaganda.
     BnF MS Francais 20358 Chroniques d'Angleterre, folio 205 reports are
     remarkably similar story: 'having fortified themselves in the town with
     all their power, but all this was of no use to them, for the fact that at the
     hour when they were invaded most of their people were going to forage.'

9    The document's emphasis on Andrew Trollop makes me suppose this is
     a Lancastrian document, potentially a text purely devoted to the martial
     exploits of Trollop, and like Warwick's 'Apology' the lost 'Trollop
     Chronical' was written into a larger text to make a fuller chronicle,
     across a broader time frame. Yet Trollop was very likely in Scotland.

10    BnF Fr 88 folio 146 the same story can be found copied at BnF MS
Francais 20358 Chroniques d'Angleterre, folio 205. The same story, but
abridged with a significant edit also appears in BnF MS Francais 20358.
These compilers are working from the same lost document(s) that ends
with the coronation of Edward IV in 1461. In these versions the story
moves back to Warwick's 'Apology'. BnF MS Francais 20354 Chroniques
de Saint-Denis, folio 117, completed by 1471. This text repeats the
same account of Wakefield and adds Warwick's escape to Calais in a
small boat. British Library, Harleian MS 4424 offers a text which is an
abridged copy of BnF 88, published in Ghent in 1483. Folio 157 adds:
'Le conte de Warvich eschappa de celle bataile et lrouva son moyen
dissir du rayaume et de venir a Callaiz en ung petit batel a pou de gens
moult adventureusement.' Therefore, English writers also believed the
outline of events presented in BnF 88. As we noted earlier, even those
in Warwick's household were unsure where Warwick was. Cistercian
Monk Andriaan De But repeats this story: as these writers are working
independently, we must conclude a lost newssheet existed presenting
this fact to non-eyewitnesses. This story of escape, correctly appears
in Warwick's 'Apology' placed after Ludford. Clearly the compiler
of the source confused Ludford and Wakefield and inexpertly edited
the two texts together at this stage. That the events of Ludford, Blore
Heath and Wakefield are 'garbled' is not surprising. BL Harl. 4424, f.
157, and BnF Fr 88, f. 138v both writing confusingly and contradictorily
on the events, amalgamating Blore Heath and Ludford and ending
with the Loveday of 1458. This confusion is partly due to the insertion
of Warwick's 'Apology' which ends with a reconciliation between the
Yorkists and Henry, allowing Richard duke of York to be heir. Warwick
then distances himself from what happened next, the 'Apology'. The
escape on the boat is garbled from BnF MS 20358 which correctly
relates John Dynham in the flight of Warwick and the earl of March
after Ludford. In the accounts of the battles of Blore Heath, Ludlow and
Northampton found in BnF MS Fr 15491, folio. 90v-91v an edition of
Wavrin's chronicle, the text is clumsily edited into the text in the wrong
place chronologically in the text. Clearly the fact that BnF Fr 20358, Nor
BL Harley 4424 or BnF Fr. 88 mention these battles may argue that they
were either so little known in France, or when they occurred so obscure
the compilers simply omitted them. The lack of a clear and precise
chronology allows contestable chronologies to be created through bad
editing and the attempt by the compiler to fit the facts as they have them
from newssheets to what he thinks he knows from common gossip.

11    TNA C 1/31/358 Redsham v Routhe. Plaintiffs.

12    Poulson, Vol. 2 p. 235.

13    The indicted men were:

John Sharp, late of Pontefract in the county of York, gentleman

Robert Tate, late of Wygginton in the country of York, gentleman

William Phippes late of South Duffield in the country of York, yeoman

Richard Ffilneby, late of Fluenby, in the county of Lincolnshire, esquire

Thomas Biride alias Thomas Brerewode, late of Derby in the county of Derbyshire, yeoman

John Morepath, late of Pontefract in the county of York's, souter

Ralph White of Pontefract in the county of York, mercer

John Whixley, late of Ripon, chaplain and

John Thomson, late of Ripon in the country of Yorkshire, webster, principals in the death of the late earl, and

Richard Tunstall, late of Thurland in the county of Lancaster, knight

Thomas Tunstall, late of Thurland in the county of Lancaster, esquire

Ralph Percy late of Bamburgh in county Northumberland, knight

William Plumpton, knight late of Plumpton in the country of York, knight

George Darell, late of Sesay, in the county of York knight

Gervais Clifton, late of London, knight

John Courteny late of Tiverton in the county of Devon, knight

John Pusday, late of Bolton in Bowelande in the county of York, knight

Roger Clyfford, late of Skipton in the county of York, knight

Henry Bellingham, late of Burnelshede in the county of Westmorland, knight

Henry Leventhorpe late of Pontefract in the county of York, chapman

William Everingham, late of Birkyn in the county of York, knight

John Everingham, late of Birkyn in the county of York, esquire

Richard Everingham, late of Birkyn, in the same county, esquire

Thomas Metham, late of Metham in the county of York, junior, knight

Ruchard Aldeborough late of Aldeborough by Burghlyng in the county of York, knight

Gawum Lampliewe, late of Pontefract in the county of York, esquire

Richard Thirlwalle, late of Wressle in the county of York, esquire

Christopher Radclyff late of York, gentleman

George Orell, late of York, gentleman

Cuthbert Colwell, late of Beverley in the county of York, gentleman

Richard Bellingham late of Bottesford in the county of Lincolnshire, gentleman

Nicholas Grene, late of Pontefract in the county of York, baker

John Caterall, late of Drayton in the county of York, gentleman

Thomas Barton, late of Helmsley in the county of York, gentleman

Thomas Helughby late of Tykill in the county of York, yeoman

Robert Thomlynson late of Healugh in the county of York, gentleman

Thomas Patchett, late of Beall in the county of York, gentleman

Robert Greenshawe late of Beverley in the county of York, tailor

Roger Thorpe, late of London, esquire

Dionysus Leventhorp late of Pontefract in the county of York, draper

Philip Billesdale, late of Thorp by Honedon, in the county of York, gentleman

Thomas Rile, late of Portington in the county of York, yeoman

Thomas Lasying, late of Newlande in the county of York, yeoman

Thomas Cecile late of Honedon, in the county of York, gentleman

William Benny, late of London, gentleman

Robert Johnson, late of Southorn in the county of York, yeoman

Robert Balby late of Wixhall in the county of York, yeoman

Richard Errald, late of Beverley in the county of York, yeoman, accessories in the death of the earl.

TNA KB 27/804, rot. 65 My thanks to David Grummitt for his assistance with completing the transcript.

# BIBLIOGRAPHY

## Archive sources.

*Archivio di Stato di Milano*
Sforza Correspondence – Foreign Powers 566 England and Scotland

*Archives Communales de Liseux*
CC25

*Archives Communal Mantes le Jolie*
BB04, BB05

*Archives de la Cote d'Or, Dijon*
B.11942, no. 258 relation Bataille de Saint Albans

*Archives Département du Nord, Lille*
B 2010
B 2026
B 2034
B2040 Recette générale des finances. Comptes et pièces comptables de
    Robert de Le Bouvcrie, receveur général de Philippe le Bon (1459-1464).
    2e compte (1460, 1er oct.-30 sept. 1461)
B 2058

*Archives Département de l'Orne*
A416

*Archives Département de la Sarthe*
H305

*Archives Département de la Seine Maritime*
Echiquier de 1448. Registres Manuel
G2133, 17 Aout 1448

*Archives Nationales de France*
Collection Dom Lenoir, 4, pièce 207
K68/19 pièces 1-2

*Bibliothèque Nationales de France*
**Manuscrits Chappée**
89, Guerre de Cent ans

**Manuscrits Dupuy**
724 Histoire du Duc Charles

**Manuscrits Français**
88 Chronique des guerres advenues en France, en Angleterre et en Bourgogne depuis l'année 1444 jusqu'en 1471
2701 Recueil d'épîtres, discours, harangues et sermons
2860 La Chronique de BERRY
2889 Chroniques Jean de Roye
3879 Histoire de Louis XI
4054 Recueil de lettres et pièces originales, et de copies de pièces indiquées comme telles dans le dépouillement qui suit. Ces pièces sont relatives aux querelles de la France et de l'Angleterre. De 1308 à 1531
4054 Domaines de France, domaines engagés, domaines aliénés, par ordre de généralités,
5051 Chronique de Charles VII, roi de France, par Jean Chartier
5084 La Chronique Enguerran de Monstrelet
15537 Recueil de pièces originales relatives principalement aux différends entre Louis XI, alors dauphin, et Charles VII. (1420-1500)
15491 Troisième et dernier volume d'une Chronique, correspondant à peu près exactement aux chapitres 1135 à 1316 de la Chronique d'Angleterre de Jehan de Wavrin, années 1451-1471.
17517 Propositions et discours relatifs à la réconciliation du roi Charles VII avec le Dauphin, plus tard Louis XI. (1458-1459)
18441 Dépositions de onze témoins dans le procès Jean II, duc d'Alençon, en 1456
18930 Chronique de Rouen, des origines à 1492
20136. Recueil de pièces relatives à l'Angleterre et à l'Écosse. (XVe-XVIIe siècle)
20354 Chroniques de Saint-Denis
20358 Chroniques d'Angleterre
20487 Papiers de Jean BOURRÉ, secrétaire et trésorier royal
24112 Grand coutumier de Normandie – Miscellanées
25775 Montres de gens de guerre.

25776 Montres des gens de guerre
26066 Notes, pièces et recueils divers (Quittances). Charles VII, roi de France.
26067 Quittances et pièces divers, Charles VII, roi de France
26068 Quittance et pièce divers, Charles VII, roi de France
26075 Charles VII, roi de France. Notes, pièces et recueils divers (Quittances).
26076 Charles VII, roi de France. Notes, pièces et recueils divers (Quittances)
26077 Charles VII, roi de France. Notes, pièces et recueils divers (Quittances)
26247 Quittances, et pièces diverses (1267-1783)

**Nouvelles acquisitions françaises**
629. Charles VII Roy de France 1443-1448
7629

*British Library*
Egerton MS 1995
Harley MS 48, folio 81
Harley MS 50 folio 49
Harley MS 116
Harley MS 326
Harley MS 4424

**Additional Manuscripts**
MS 11509 folio 37
MS 38690 item 6.
MS 46355

*Lambeth Palace Library*
MS 632

*National Archives Kew*
**Chancery**
C 1/103/41 Short title: Newbery v Bygge
C 1/27/202
C 1/27/340 Romney V Croydon
C 1/27/456 Barowe v Squyer
C 1/31/358 Redsham v Routhe. Plaintiffs
C 1/40/274
C 49/32/3 Act granting the principality of Wales to Richard, Duke of York
C49/32/7
C49/32/8
C49/63/6

C49/64/54
C 65/106 rot 13
C65/106 rot. 19
C 140/4/34
C 140/5/43
C 140/8/36

**Court of King's Bench**
KB 9/75
KB 9/928
KB 27/775 Rex
KB 27/780 Rex
KB 27/782 Rex
KB 27/784,
KB 27/803, rot. 16d
KB 27/804, rot. 65
KB 69/16
KB 149

**Court of Common Pleas**
P40/802, rot. 441
P40/ 804, rot. 237.

**Court of Chancery**
CC67/43

**Duchy of Lancaster**
DL11/97 folio 28
DL42/18 folio 135
DL29/560/8899 Ministers' Accounts Manor of Wakefield 39 Henry VI & 1
    Edward IV
DL28/33/32
DL37/26/15.
DL 39/4/15 Roll of account of the trees felled within the lordship of
    Wakefield
DL 43/11 folio 18
DL 44/98 folio 207
DL 45/K25c

**Exchequer**
E 101/71/4/930

E101/410/6

E101/410/9

E199/50/12 Accounts and particulars of account for lands in Wakefield, Flanshaw, Stanley, Newton by Wakefield and Horbury, held by John de Warenne, Earl of Surrey

E404/64/117

E404/71/5/38

**Probate**

PROB 11/18/114

**Special Collections**

SC 1/60/48

SC 8/28/1379

SC 8/29/1424 Petitioners: William Grymmesby

SC 8/29/1429

SC 8/29/1441

SC 8/29/1433

SC 8/231/11516

SC 11/991 Wakefield [Yorkshire]: Valor of the lordship, with a survey of Sandal Castle and Wakefield Park

**Privy Council**

PC 2/9 f.106

EC13/167, rot. 10

MFC 1/199

MPC 1/97

Calendar of Close Rolls, Hen IV, vol. II, 1402-1405

Calendar of Patent Rolls, 1451-1462

Calendar of patent Rolls, 1461-1467

Calendar of Patent Rolls, 1467-1477

Calendar of State Papers Relating to English Affairs in the Archives of Venice, Volume 1, 1202-1509. Originally published by Her Majesty's Stationery Office, London, 1864

*Staatsbibliothek zu Berlin*

Adolf Gottlob, 'Des Nuntius Franz Coppini Antheil an der Entthronung des Königs Heinrich VI. und seine Verurtheilung bei der Römischen Curie', in *Deutsche Zeitschrift für Geschichtswissenschaft*, 1890. pp. 75–111

Goswin Frhr von der Ropp (ed.), *Hanserecesse Zweite Abtheilung Herausgeben Vereine fur Hansiche Gedichte*, volume 3, Verlung von Duncker & Humbolt, 1881

*Surrey Record Centre*
LM/345/153

*West Yorkshire History Centre*
John Goodchild Collection: MS notes West Riding Textile Industry

## Printed Sources

Anon, *Collectanea topographica et genealogica*, London: J. B. Nicholls, 1834.

'A brief Latin chronicle', in *Three Fifteenth-Century Chronicles with Historical Memoranda by John Stowe*, ed. James Gairdner, London: 1880, pp. 164–85.

Baildon, W.P. (ed.), *Inquisitions Post Mortem relating to Yorkshire during the Reigns of Henry IV and Henry V*, Yorkshire Archaeological Society Record Series, 59, Leeds, 1918.

Barrett, Charles Raymond Booth, *Battles and Battlefields in England*, London: A D Innes & Co, 1896.

Basin, Thomas, *Histoire des règnes de Charles VII et Louis XI*, Paris: J. Renouard, 1855.

Brie, Friederich, *The Brut of England or The Chronicles of England*, London: Kegan Paul, 1906.

Boardman, Anthony W, *Towton 1461: The Anatomy of a Battle*, Gloucester: The History Press, 2022.

Bourdeaut, Arthur, 'Gilles de Bretagne entre la France et l'Angleterre' in *Mémoires de la Société d'Histoire et d'Archéologie de Bretagne* volume 1 (1920), pp. 53–145.

Buchon, Jean Alexandre, *Chroniques d'Enguerrand de Monstrelet, nouvelle édition entièrement refondue sur les manuscrits, avec notes et éclaircissements tome XIV*, Paris: Verdière & Co, 1826.

Burnett, George, *Rotuli scaccarii regum Scotorum. The Exchequer Rolls of Scotland*, Edinburgh: H.M. General Register House, 1878.

*Calendar of Close Rolls Preserved in the Public Record Office . . . Edward IV, 1461 – [1476]*. London, 1894.

Carpenter, Christine, *The Wars of the Roses: Politics and the Constitution in England, c.1437–1509*, Cambridge: Cambridge University Press, 1997.

Chrimes, B., C.D. Ross and R. A. Griffiths (eds), *Fifteenth Century England 1399-1509*, Manchester: Manchester University Press, 1972.

Coates, John, *The Hour Between Dog and Wolf*, London: Fourth Estate, 2012.

Coleman, D.C., *The Economy of England 1450-1750*, Oxford: Oxford University Press, 1977.

Contamine, Philippe, 'Chapitre VIII. Les trois temps de la reconquête finale (1449-1453)', in Philippe Contamine, Philippe (ed.), *Charles VII. Une vie, une politique*, Perrin, 2017, pp. 293–312.

Cooke, David, *Battlefield Yorkshire: From the Romans to the English Civil Wars*, Barnsley: Pen & Sword Military, 2006.

Davies, John Sylvester, *An English Chronicle*, London: Camden Society, 1856.

Davies, Norman, *Paston Letters and Papers of the Fifteenth Century*, 2 vols, Oxford: Clarendon Press, 1971.

Dawson, Jane, *Richard Duke of York and the Politics which led to the Battle of Wakefield*. (B.Ed. thesis), Bretton Hall, 1997.

Devine, M.J., *Richmondshire, 1372–1425* (PhD thesis), University of Teesside, 2006.

Dockray, Keith, 'Contemporary and Near-Contemporary Chroniclers: The North of England and the Wars of the Roses, c. 1450 – 1471', in Clark, L.; Fleming, P. (eds.), *The Fifteenth Century XVIII: Rulers, Regions and Retinues, Essays Presented to A. J. Pollard* Woodbridge: Boydell & Brewer, 2020.

Dockray, Keith, *Henry VI, Margaret of Anjou and the Wars of the Roses: From Contemporary Letters and Records*, Stroud: Fonthill Media, 2016.

Dockray, Keith, 'The Battle of Wakefield and the Wars of the Roses', *The Ricardian*, Volume IX, number 117, June 1992.

Dunphy, Graeme, and Cristian Bratu (eds), *Encyclopedie of the Medieval Chronicle*, Leiden, Netherlands: Brill, 2016.

Flenley, Ralph, *Six Town Chronicles of England*, Oxford: Clarendon Press, 1911.

Frazer, C.M., *The Court Rolls of the Manor of Wakefield from October 1433 to September 1436*, Yorkshire Archaeological Society: Leeds, 2011.

Foss, Edward, *The Lives of the Judges IV: 1377-1485*, London: Longman, Brown, Green and Longmans, 1851

Fussell, Paul, *The Great War and Modern Memory*, Oxford: Oxford University Press, 1975.

Gilson, J.P. 'A Defence of the Proscription of the Yorkists in 1459,' *The English Historical Review*, 26 (1911), pp. 512–25.

Green, Anna, and Kathleen Troup, *The Houses of History*, Manchester: Manchester University Press, 1999.

Goodman, Anthony, *The Wars of the Roses: Military Activity and English Society, 1452-97* London: Routledge, 1991.

Griffiths, Ralph Alan, 'Richard, duke of York, and the crisis of Henry VI's household in 1450-1: some further evidence', *Journal of Medieval History* volume 38, no.2 (2012): pp. 244–6.

Griffiths, Ralph, 'Local Rivalries and National Politics: the Percys, the Nevilles and the Duke of Exeter, 1452–55', in *King and Country: England and Wales in the Fifteenth Century*, London: Hambledon, 1991.

Griffiths, Ralph, 'King's council and the first protectorate', *The English Historical Review*, Volume XCIX, Issue CCCXC, January 1984, pp. 67–82.

Griffiths, Ralph, *The Reign of Henry VI*, University of California Press, 1981.

Griffiths, Ralph, 'The Winchester Session of the 1449 Parliament: A Further Comment', *Huntington Library Quarterly*, 42 (1979), pp. 189–91.

Griffiths, Ralph Alan, 'Local rivalries and national politics: the Percys, Nevilles, and the Duke of Exeter', *Speculum*, volume 43 (1968), pp. 589–632.

Grummitt, David, *A Short History of the Wars of the Roses*, London: I B Tauris, 2013.

Grummitt, David, *The Calais Garrison: War and Military Service in England, 1436-1558*, Woodbridge: The Boydell Press, 2008.

Guverich, Aron, 'The French Historical Revolution: The Annales School', in Hodder et al, *Interpreting Archaeology*, London and New York: Routledge, 1995.

Hanham, Alison, *John Benet's Chronicle, 1399-1462*, London: Palgrave Macmillan, 2016.

Hardyng, John, *Chronicle: Edited from British Library MS Lansdowne 204*, James Simpson and Sarah Peverley (eds), Vol 1, Kalamazoo: Medieval Institute Publications, 2015.

Head, Constance, 'Pope Pius II and the Wars of the Roses', *Archivum Historiae Pontificiae*, vol. 8 (1970), pp. 139–78.

Heaton, Herbert, *The Yorkshire woollen and worsted industries from the earliest times up to the Industrial Revolution*, Oxford: Clarendon Press, 1920.

Hellot, Amedée, *Les Chroniques de Normandie 1223-1453*, Rouen: Chez l'éditeur, 1881.

Hicks, Michael, *The Wars of the Roses*, London: Yale University Press, 2010.

Hicks, Michael, *Welles, Leo, sixth Baron Welles (c.1406–1461)*, Oxford Dictionary of National Biography 2004 (online ed.).

Hicks, Michael, *Warwick the Kingmaker*, Oxford: Blackwell Publishing, 2002.

Hicks, Michael, *English Political Culture in the Fifteenth Century* London: Routledge, 2002

Hicks, Michael, 'From megaphone to microscope. The correspondence of Richard, duke of York with Henry VI in 1450 revisited', *Journal of Medieval History*, volume 25 (1999), pp. 251–2.

Michael Hicks, *Bastard Feudalism: Society and Politics in the 15th Century. Richard III & his Rivals: Magnates and their Motives in the War of the Roses*, London: Hambledon, 1991.

Hicks, Michael, *Bastard Feudalism*, London: Routledge, 1995.

Hicks, Michael, *Who's who in late medieval England*, London: Shepheard-Walwyn, 1991.

Horrox, Rosemary, *Richard III*, Cambridge: Cambridge University Press, 1989.

Jalland, Patricia, 'The Influence of the Aristocracy on Shire Elections in the North of England, 1450-7', *Speculum*, vol. 47, no. 3 (1972), pp. 483–507.

Johnson, P.A., *Duke Richard of York 1411-1460*, Oxford: The Clarendon Press, 1988.

Jones, Dan, *The Hollow Crown: The Wars of the Roses and the Rise of the Tudors*, London: Faber & Faber, 2014.

Keen, M.H.. and M.J. Daniel, 'English diplomacy and the sack of Fougères in 1449', *History*, 49 (1974), pp. 375–91.

Kekewich, Margaret Lucille et al. (eds), *The Politics of Fifteenth-Century England. John Vale's Book*, Stroud: Sutton, 1995.

Kendall, Paul, *Wars of the Roses: The people, places and battlefields of the Yorkists and Lancastrians*, Barnsley: Frontline, 2023.

Kingsford, Charles Lethbridge, *Prejudice and Promise in Fifteenth Century England: The Ford Lectures 1923–4*, Oxford: Clarendon Press, 1925.

Kingsford, Charles Lethbridge, *English Historical Literature In The Fifteenth Century*, New York: Burt Franklin, 1913.

Kleineke, Hannes, 'Robert Bale's chronicle and the second battle of St. Albans', *Historical Research*, Volume 87, Issue 238 (November 2014), pp. 744–50.

Knowles, Richard, 'The Battle of Wakefield: the Topography', *The Ricardian*, Volume 9 (117), June 1992.

La Roque, Gilles-André de, *Histoire généalogique de la maison de Harcourt*, Paris: S Cramoisy, 1662.

Lander, Jack Robert, *The Wars of the Roses*, Stroud: Sutton, 1990.

Lander, Jack Robert, *Government and Community: England, 1450–1509*, Cambridge, MA.: Harvard University Press, 1980.

Laynesmith, J.L., *Cecily Duchess of York*, London: Bloomsbury Academic, 2019.

Kervyn de Lettenhove, Baron, *Œuvres de Georges Chastellain*, Brussels: F. Heussner, 1866.

Kervyn de Lettenhove, Baron, *Chroniques relatives à l'histoire de la Belgique sous la domination des ducs de Bourgogne*, Brussels: F Hayez, 1870.

Lewis, Matthew, *Richard Duke of York: King by Right*, Stroud: Amberley, 2017.

Lewis, Matthew, *The Wars of the Roses. The key players in the struggle for supremacy*, Stroud: Amberley, 2016.

Luce, Siméon, *Chronique du Mont-Saint-Michel: 1343-1468: publiée avec notes et pièces diverses relatives au mont Saint-Michel et à la défense nationale en basse Normandie pendant l'occupation anglaise*, Paris: Firmin Didot, 1878.

Maddicott, J.R., and D. M. Palliser (eds), *The Medieval State: Essays Presented to James Campbell*, London and Rio Grande, 2000.

Mayes, Phil, and Lawrance Butler, *Sandal Castle Excavations 1964-1973*, Wakefield Historical Publications, Wakefield, 1983.

Maxwell-Lyte, H.C., *A history of Dunster and of the families of Mohun & Luttrell, Part I*, St Catherine Press, 1909.

Mercer, Malcom, *The Medieval Gentry: Power, Leadership and Choice During the Wars of the Roses*, London: Continuum, 2010.

Mercer, Malcom, 'The Strength of Lancastrian Loyalism during the readption', *The Journal of Medieval Military History* Volume 5, Boydell Press, 2007, pp. 84–98.

Meserve, Margaret, and Marcello Simonette, *Pius II Commentaries*, Massachusetts: Harvard University Press, 2007.

McCulloch, D., and E. D. Jones, 'Lancastrian Politics, the French War, and the Rise of the Popular Element', *Speculum*, vol. 58, no. 1, 1983, pp. 95–138.

Minois, George, *Richard III: le roi Maudit?*, Paris: Perrin, 2022.

Pearman, A.J., 'Kentish Family of Lovelace', *Archaeologia Cantiana* Volume 10, 1876, pp. 177–84

Pearman, A.J., 'The Kentish Family of Lovelace, No. II', *Archaeologia Cantiana* Volume 20, 1893, pp. 54–63.

Petre, James, 'The Nevilles of Brancepeth and Raby 1425–1499', part 1, *The Ricardian* 5 (75) 1981, pp. 418–35.

Pinot-Duclos, Charles, *Œuvres complètes de Duclos*, Paris : Chez Belin, 1820.

Pollard, Arthur Fredrick, 'Yelverton, William (1400?-1472?)', in Sindey Lee (ed.), *Dictionary of National Biography* Vol. 63, London: Smith, Elder & Co. 1900.

Pollard, Anthony James, *Warwick the Kingmaker: Politics, Power and Fame*, London: Hambledon, 2007.

Pollard, Anthony James, *Neville, Ralph, second earl of Westmorland*, Oxford Dictionary of National Biography, 2004 (online ed.).

Pollard, Anthony James, *The North of England in the Age of Richard III*, Stroud: Alan Sutton, 1996.

Pollard, Anthony James (ed.), *Problems in Focus: The Wars of the Roses*, London: Macmillan, 1995.

Anthony James Pollard, *North-Eastern England during the Wars of the Roses: Lay Society, War, and Politics 1450-1500*, Oxford: Clarendon Press, 1990.

Pollard, Anthony James, *John and the War in France, 1427-1453*, London, Royal Historical Society, New Jersey, Humanities Press, 1983.

Pugh, T.B., *Henry V and the Southampton Plot of 1415*, Gloucester: Alan Sutton, 1989.

Richmond, Colin, 'The Nobility and the Wars of the Roses: The Parliamentary Session of January 1461', *Parliamentary History*, 18 (1999), pp. 261–9.

Riley, Henry Thomas, *Ingulph's chronicle of the abbey of Croyland with the continuations by Peter of Blois and anonymous writers*, London: G. Bell & Sons, 1908.

Riley, Henry Thomas, *Registra quorundam Abbatum Monasterii S Albani*, London: Longman and Co, 1872.

Ross, Charles, *Richard III*, London: Yale University Press, 1999.

Ross, Charles, *Edward IV*, London: Eyre Methuen, 1974.

'Rymer's Foedera with Syllabus: 1459', in *Rymer's Foedera Volume 11*, London: 1739–1745.

Sadler, John, *The Red Rose and the White: The Wars of the Roses, 1453-1487*, London: Routledge, 2013.

Sadler, John, *Towton: The Battle on Palm Sunday Field 1461*, Barnsley: Pen and Sword, 2011.

Schofield, Cora, *The Life and Reign of Edward the Fourth, King of England and France and Lord of Ireland*, 2 vols, London: Longman, Greens & Co, 1923.

Searle, William George, *Christ Church, Canterbury. I. The chronicle of John Stone, monk of Christ Church 1415-1471*, Cambridge: Deighton, Bell & co, 1902.

Seward, Desmond, *A Brief History of the Wars of the Roses.*, London: Constable and Robin, 2007.

Sharpe, Reginald, *Calendar of Letter-Books of the City of London: K, Henry VI* Volume 10, London: His Majesty's Stationery Office, 1911.

Simpkin, David, Adrian R. Bell, Anne Curry, and Andy King, *The Soldier in Later Medieval England*, Oxford: Oxford University Press, 2013.

Snow, Vernon F., *Holinshed's Chronicles England, Scotland, and Ireland*, New York: AMS, 1965

Steel, Anthony, 'The Financial Background of the Wars of the Roses', *History*, vol. 40, no. 138/139 (1955), pp. 18–30.

Stow, John, *Annales of England to 1603*.

Taylor, Thomas, *The Rectory Manor of Wakefield*, Wakefield: W H Milnes, 1886.

Tucker, Penny, 'The Earl of Warwick's use of sea-power in the late 1450s', *Southern History* Volume 42 (2020), pp. 1–20.

Visser-Fuchs, Livia, 'Warwick, by himself': Richard Neville, Earl of Warwick, 'the Kingmaker', in *Receuil des Croniques D'Engleterre of Jean de Wavrin*, Publication du Centre Européen d'études Bourguignonnes (XIVe-XVIes), 41 (2001).

Visser-Fuchs, Livia, *History as Pastime: Jean de Wavrin and His Collection of Chronicles of England*, Donnington: Shaun Tyas, 2018.

Walker, John William, *The History of the Old Parish Church of All Saints Wakefield*, Wakefield: W.H. Milnes, 1888.

Watts, John, *Henry VI and the Politics of Kingship*, Cambridge: Cambridge University Press, 1996.

Wedgwood, Josiah Clement, *The History of Parliament: Biographies of the Members of the Common House 1439–1509* London; H.M.S.O., 1936.

Wheater, William, *Knaresburgh and its Rulers*, Leeds: 1907.

# INDEX